LITURGICAL YEAR.

BY THE

VERY REV. DOM PROSPER GUERANGER,

ABBOT OF SOLESMES.

Translated from the French,
BY THE
REV. DOM LAURENCE SHEPHERD,
MONK OF THE ENGLISH-BENEDICTINE CONGREGATION

SEPTUAGESIMA.

SEPTUAGESIMA.

PREFACE.

This third section of the *Liturgical Year* is much shorter than the two preceding ones; and yet it is one of real interest. The Season of Septuagesima has only three weeks of the *Proper of the Time,* and the Feasts of the Saints are far less frequent than at other periods of the Year. The Volume we now offer to the Faithful may be called one of *transition,* inasmuch as it includes the period between two important Seasons,—Christmas and Lent. We have endeavoured to teach them how to spend these three weeks; and we flatter ourselves that our instructions will show them, that, even in this the least interesting portion of the Ecclesiastical Year, there is much to be learned. They will find the Church persevering in carrying out the

PREFACE.

one sublime idea which pervades the whole of her Liturgy; and, consequently, they must derive solid profit from imbibing the spirit peculiar to this Season.

Were we, therefore, to keep aloof from the Church during Septuagesima, we should not have a complete idea of her *Year*, of which these three weeks form an essential part. The three preliminary Chapters of this Volume will convince them of the truth of our observation; and we feel confident, that when they have once understood the ceremonies, and formulas, and instructions, offered them by the Church during this short Season, they will value it as it deserves.

CONTENTS.

PREFACE,

SEPTUAGESIMA.

		PAGE
CHAP. I.—The History of Septuagesima,		1
CHAP. II.—The Mystery of Septuagesima,		7
CHAP. III.—Practice during Septuagesima.		12
CHAP. IV.—Morning and Night Prayers for Septuagesima,		16
CHAP. V.—On hearing Mass, during the Season of Septuagesima,		31
CHAP. VI.—On Holy Communion, during Septuagesima,		67
CHAP. VII.—On the Office of Vespers for Sundays and Feasts, during Septuagesima,		74
CHAP. VIII.—On the Office of Compline, during Septuagesima,		85

PROPER OF THE TIME.

The 5th Sunday after the Epiphany,	97
The 6th Sunday after the Epiphany,	104
Saturday before Septuagesima Sunday.—Suspension of the "ALLELUIA,"	111
SEPTUAGESIMA SUNDAY,	121
Mass,	124
Vespers,	134
Monday of Septuagesima Week,	137

CONTENTS.

	PAGE
Tuesday of Septuagesima Week,	142
Wednesday of Septuagesima Week,	146
Thursday of Septuagesima Week,	149
Friday of Septuagesima Week,	151
Saturday of Septuagesima Week,	154
SEXAGESIMA SUNDAY,	158
Mass,	160
Vespers,	168
Monday of Sexagesima Week,	171
Tuesday of Sexagesima Week,	174
Wednesday of Sexagesima Week,	177
Thursday of Sexagesima Week,	180
Friday of Sexagesima Week,	183
Saturday of Sexagesima Week,	187
QUINQUAGESIMA SUNDAY,	192
Mass,	200
Vespers,	207
Monday of Quinquagesima Week,	210
Tuesday of Quinquagesima Week,	214
ASH WEDNESDAY,	218
Blessing of the Ashes,	222
Mass,	226
Thursday after Ash Wednesday,	236
Friday after Ash Wednesday,	241
Saturday after Ash Wednesday,	247
PROPER OF THE SAINTS,	252
February 3.—SAINT BLASE, Bishop and Martyr,	255
February 4.—SAINT ANDREW CORSINI, Bishop and Confessor,	258
February 5.—SAINT AGATHA, Virgin and Martyr,	262
February 6.—SAINT DOROTHY, Virgin and Martyr,	268
February 7.—SAINT ROMUALD, Abbot,	273
February 8.—SAINT JOHN OF MATHA, Confessor,	277
February 9.—SAINT APOLLONIA, Virgin and Martyr,	283

CONTENTS.

		PAGE
February 10.—Saint Scholastica, Virgin,		286
February 14.—Saint Valentine, Priest and Martyr,		298
February 15.—Saints Faustinus and Jovita, Martyrs,		300
February 18.—Saint Simeon, Bishop and Martyr,		303
February 22.—Saint Peter's Chair at Antioch,		306
February 23.—Saint Peter Damian, Cardinal and Doctor of the Church,		316
February 24.—Saint Matthias, Apostle,		323
February 26.—Saint Margarite of Cortona, Penitent,		328
March 4.—Saint Casimir, Confessor,		335
March 6.—Saints Perpetua and Felicitas, Martyrs,		339
March 7.—Saint Thomas of Aquin, Doctor of the Church,		354
March 8.—Saint John of God, Confessor,		363
March 9.—Saint Frances of Rome, Widow,		369
March 10.—The Forty Martyrs,		376
March 12.—Saint Gregory the Great, Pope and Doctor of the Church,		383
Concluding Prayer for this Season,		399
Appendix I.—The Seven Penitential Psalms,		401
Appendix II.—The Litanies for the Devotion of the Forty Hours,		413

SEPTUAGESIMA.

CHAPTER THE FIRST.

THE HISTORY OF SEPTUAGESIMA.

THE Season of Septuagesima comprises the three weeks immediately preceding Lent. It forms one of the principal divisions of the Liturgical Year, and is itself divided into three parts, each part corresponding to a week: the first is called *Septuagesima;* the second, *Sexagesima;* the third, *Quinquagesima.*

All three are named from their numerical reference to Lent, which, in the language of the Church, is called *Quadragesima,*—that is, *Forty,*—because the great Feast of Easter is prepared for by the holy exercises of *Forty Days.* The words *Quinquagesima, Sexagesima,* and *Septuagesima,* tell us of the same great Solemnity as looming in the distance, and as being the great object towards which the Church would have us now begin to turn all our thoughts, and desires, and devotion.

Now, the Feast of Easter must be prepared for by a forty-days' recollectedness and penance. Those forty-days are one of the principal Seasons of the Liturgical Year, and one of the most powerful means employed by the Church for exciting in the hearts of her children the spirit of their Christian Vocation. It is of the utmost importance, that such a Season of grace should produce its work in our souls,—the renovation of the whole spiritual life. The Church, therefore, has instituted a preparation for the holy time of Lent. She gives us the three weeks of Septuagesima, during which she withdraws us, as much as may be, from the noisy distractions of the world, in order that our hearts may be the more readily impressed by the solemn warning she is to give us, at the commencement of Lent, by marking our foreheads with ashes.

This prelude to the holy season of Lent was not known in the early ages of Christianity: its institution would seem to have originated in the Greek Church. The practice of this Church being never to fast on Saturdays, the number of fasting-days in Lent, besides the six *Sundays* of Lent, (on which, by universal custom, the Faithful never fasted,) there were also the six Saturdays, which the Greeks would never allow to be observed as days of fasting: so that their Lent was short, by twelve days, of the *Forty* spent by our Saviour in the Desert. To make up the deficiency, they were obliged to begin their Lent so many days earlier, as we will show in our next Volume.

The Church of Rome had no such motive for anticipating the season of those privations, which belong to Lent; for, from the earliest antiquity, she kept the Saturdays of Lent, (and as often, during the rest of the year, as circumstances might require,) as fasting days. At the close of the 6th century, St. Gregory the Great, alludes, in one of his Homilies, to the fast of Lent being less than Forty Days, owing to the Sundays which come during that holy season. "There are," he says, "from this Day (the "first Sunday of Lent) to the joyous Feast of Easter, "six Weeks, that is, forty-two days. As we do not "fast on the six *Sundays*, there are but thirty-six "fasting days; * * * which we offer to God as the "tithe of our year."[1]

---

[1] The sixteenth Homily on the Gospels.

It was, therefore, after the pontificate of St. Gregory, that the last four days of Quinquagesima Week, were added to Lent, in order that the number of Fasting Days might be exactly Forty. As early, however, as the 9th century, the custom of beginning Lent on *Ash Wednesday* was of obligation in the whole Latin Church. All the manuscript copies of the Gregorian Sacramentary, which bear that date, call this Wednesday the *In capite jejunii,* that is to say, *the beginning of the fast;* and Amalarius, who gives us every detail of the Liturgy of the 9th century, tells us, that it was, even then, the rule to begin the Fast four days before the first Sunday of Lent. We find the practice confirmed by two Councils, held in that century.[1] But, out of respect for the form of Divine Service drawn up by St. Gregory, the Church does not make any important change in the Office of these four days. Up to the Vespers of Saturday, when alone she begins the Lenten *rite,* she observes the rubrics prescribed for Quinquagesima Week.

Peter of Blois, who lived in the 12th century, tells us what was the practice in his days. He says: "All "Religious begin the Fast of Lent at Septuagesima; "the Greeks, at Sexagesima; the Clergy, at Quinqua-"gesima; and the rest of Christians, who form the "Church militant on earth, begin their Lent on the "Wednesday following Quinquagesima."[2] The secular Clergy, as we learn from these words, were bound to begin the Lenten Fast somewhat before the laity; though it was only by two days, that is, on Monday, as we gather from the Life of St. Ulric, Bishop of Augsburg, written in the 10th century. The Council of Clermont, in 1095, at which Pope Urban the Second presided, has a decree sanctioning the obligation of the Clergy beginning abstinence from flesh-meat at Quinquagesima. This Sunday was

---

[1] Meaux, and Soissons. [2] Sermon xiii.

called, indeed, *Dominica carnis privii*, and *Carnis privium Sacerdotum*, (that is, *Priests' Carnival Sunday*,)—but the term is to be understood in the sense of the announcement being made, on that Sunday, of the abstinence having to begin on the following day. We shall find, further on, that a like usage was observed in the Greek Church, on the three Sundays preceding Lent. This law, which obliged the Clergy to these two additional days of abstinence, was in force in the 13th century, as we learn from a Council held at Angers, which threatens with suspension all Priests who neglect to begin Lent on the Monday of Quinquagesima Week.

This usage, however, soon became obsolete; and in the 15th century, the secular Clergy, and even the Monks themselves, began the Lenten Fast, like the rest of the Faithful, on Ash Wednesday.

There can be no doubt, but that the original motive for this anticipation,—which, after several modifications, was limited to the four days immediately preceding Lent,—was to remove from the Greeks the pretext of taking scandal at the Latins, who did not fast a full Forty days. Ratramnus, in his *Controversy with the Greeks*, clearly implies it. But the Latin Church did not think it necessary to carry her condescension further, by imitating the Greek ante-lenten usages, which originated, as we have already said, in the eastern custom of not fasting on Saturdays.[1]

[1] The *Gallican Liturgy* had retained several usages of the Oriental Churches, to which it owed, in part, its origin: hence, it was not without some difficulty, that the custom of abstaining and fasting on Saturdays was introduced into Gaul. Until such time as the Churches of that country had adopted the Roman custom, in that point of discipline, they were necessitated to anticipate the Fast of Lent. The first Council of Orleans, held in the early part of the 6th century, enjoins the Faithful to observe, before Easter, *Quadragesima*, (as the Latins call *Lent*,) and not Quinquagesima, *in order*, says the Council, *that unity of custom may be maintained.* Towards the close of the same century, the fourth Council held in

Thus it was, that the Roman Church, by this anticipation of Lent by Four days, gave the exact number of *Forty Days* to the holy Season, which she had instituted in imitation of the Forty Days spent by our Saviour in the Desert. Whilst faithful to her ancient practice of looking on the Saturday as a day appropriate for penitential exercises, she gladly borrowed from the Greek Church the custom of preparing for Lent, by giving to the Liturgy of the three preceding weeks a tone of holy mournfulness. Even as early as the beginning of the 9th century, as we learn from Amalarius, the *Alleluia* and *Gloria in excelsis* were suspended in the Septuagesima Offices. The Monks conformed to the custom, although the Rule of St. Benedict prescribed otherwise. Finally, in the second half of the 11th century, Pope Alexander the Second enacted, that the total suspension of the *Alleluia* should be everywhere observed, beginning with the Vespers of the Saturday preceding Septuagesima Sunday. This Pope was but renewing a rule already sanctioned, in that same century, by Pope Leo the Ninth, and which was inserted in the body of Canon Law.[1]

---

the same City, repeals the same prohibition, and explains the intentions of the making such an enactment, by ordering that the Saturdays during Lent should be observed as days of fasting. Previously to this, that is, in the years 511 and 541, the first and second Councils of Orange had combated the same abuse, by also forbidding the imposing on the Faithful the obligation of commencing the Fast at Quinquagesima. The introduction of the Roman Liturgy into France, which was brought about by the zeal of Pepin and Charlemagne, finally established, in that country, the custom of keeping the Saturday as a day of penance; and, as we have just seen, the beginning Lent on Quinquagesima was not observed excepting by the Clergy. In the 13th century, the only Church in the Patriarchate of the West, which began Lent earlier than the Church of Rome, was that of Poland: its Lent opened on the Monday of Septuagesima, which was owing to the rites of the Greek Church being so much used in Poland. The custom was abolished, even for that country, by Pope Innocent the fourth, in the year 1248.

[1] Cap. *Hi duo.* De consec. Dist. 1.

Thus was the present important period of the Liturgical Year, after various changes, established in the Cycle of the Church. It has been there upwards of a thousand years. Its name, *Septuagesima (Seventy)*, expresses, as we have already remarked, a numerical relation to *Quadragesima (the Forty Days)*; although, in reality, there are not seventy but only sixty-three days from Septuagesima Sunday to Easter. We will speak of the mystery of the name, in the following Chapter. The first Sunday of Lent being called *Quadragesima (Forty)*, each of the three previous Sundays has a name expressive of an additional *ten*: the nearest to Lent, *Quinquagesima* (Fifty); the middle one, *Sexagesima* (Sixty); the third, *Septuagesima (*Seventy).

As the season of Septuagesima depends upon the time of the Easter celebration, it comes sooner or later, according to the changes of that great Feast. The 18th of January and the 22nd of February are called the *Septuagesima Keys*, because the Sunday, which is called *Septuagesima*, cannot be earlier in the year, than the first, nor later than the second, of these two days.

CHAPTER THE SECOND.

THE MYSTERY OF SEPTUAGESIMA.

THE Season, upon which we are now entering, is expressive of several profound mysteries. But these mysteries belong not only to the three weeks, which are preparatory to Lent; they continue throughout the whole period of time, which separates us from the great Feast of Easter.

The number *seven* is the basis of all these mysteries. We have already seen how the Holy Church came to introduce the season of Septuagesima into her Calendar. Let us now meditate on the doctrine hid under the symbols of her Liturgy. And first, let us listen to St. Augustine, who thus gives us the clue to the whole of our Season's mysteries. "There are "two times," says the Holy Doctor: "one which is "*now*, and is spent in the temptations and tribulations "of this life; the other which shall be *then*, and shall "be spent in eternal security and joy. In figure of "these, we celebrate two periods: the time '*before* "*Easter*,' and the time '*after Easter*.' That which "is '*before Easter*,' signifies the sorrow of this present "life; that which is '*after Easter*,' the blessedness "of our future state. * * Hence it is, that we "spend the first in fasting and prayer; and in the "second, we give up our fasting, and give ourselves "to praise."[1]

The Church, the interpreter of the Sacred Scriptures, often speaks to us of two *places*, which correspond with these two *times* of St. Augustine.

---

[1] Enarrations; *Psalm* clviii.

These two places are Babylon and Jerusalem. *Babylon* is the image of this world of sin, in the midst whereof the Christian has to spend his years of probation; *Jerusalem* is the heavenly country, where he is to repose after all his trials. The people of Israel, whose whole history is but one great type of the human race, was banished from Jerusalem and kept in bondage in Babylon.

Now, this captivity, which kept the Israelites exiles from Sion, lasted seventy years; and it is to express this mystery, as Alcuin, Amalarius, Ivo of Chartres, and all the great Liturgists tell us, that the Church fixed the number of *Seventy* for the days of expiation. It is true, there are but sixty-three days between Septuagesima and Easter; but the Church, according to the style so continually used in the Sacred Scriptures, uses the round number instead of the literal and precise one.

The duration of the world itself, according to the ancient Christian tradition, is divided into seven ages. The human race must pass through seven Ages before the dawning of the Day of eternal life. The first Age included the time from the creation of Adam to Noah; the second begins with Noah and the renovation of the earth by the Deluge, and ends with the vocation of Abraham; the third opens with this first formation of God's chosen people, and continues as far as Moses, through whom God gave the Law; the fourth consists of the period between Moses and David, in whom the house of Juda received the kingly power; the fifth is formed of the years, which passed between David's reign and the captivity of Babylon, inclusively; the sixth dates from the return of the Jews to Jerusalem, and takes us on as far as the Birth of our Saviour. Then, finally, comes the seventh Age; it starts with the rising of this merciful Redeemer, the Sun of Justice, and is to continue till the dread coming of the Judge of the living and the dead. These are the Seven great divisions of Time; after which, Eternity.

In order to console us in the midst of the combats, which so thickly beset our path, the Church,—like a beacon shining amidst the darkness of this our earthly abode,—shows us another *Seven*, which is to succeed the one we are now preparing to pass through. After the Septuagesima of mourning, we shall have the bright Easter with its *Seven* weeks of gladness, foreshadowing the happiness and bliss of Heaven. After having fasted with our Jesus, and suffered with him, the day will come when we shall rise together with him, and our hearts shall follow him to the highest heavens, and then after a brief interval, we shall feel descending upon us the Holy Ghost, with his *Seven* Gifts. The celebration of all these wondrous joys will take us *Seven* weeks, as the great Liturgists observe in their interpretation of the Rites of the Church:—the seven joyous weeks from Easter to Pentecost will not be too long for the future glad Mysteries, which, after all, will be but figures of a still gladder future, the future of eternity.

Having heard these sweet whisperings of hope, let us now bravely face the realities brought before us by our dear Mother the Church. We are sojourners upon this earth; we are exiles and captives in Babylon, that city which plots our ruin. If we love our country,—if we long to return to it,—we must be proof against the lying allurements of this strange land, and refuse the cup she proffers us, and with which she maddens so many of our fellow captives. She invites us to join in her feasts and her songs; but we must unstring our harps, and hang them on the willows that grow on her river's bank, till the signal be given for our return to Jerusalem.[1] She will ask us to sing to her the melodies of our dear

---

[1] Ps. cxxv.

Sion : but, how shall we, who are so far from home, have heart to *sing the Song of the Lord in a strange Land?*[1] No,—there must be no sign that we are content to be in bondage, or we shall deserve to be slaves for ever.

These are the sentiments wherewith the Church would inspire us, during the penitential Season, which we are now beginning. She wishes us to reflect on the dangers that beset us,—dangers which arise from our own selves, and from creatures. During the rest of the year, she loves to hear us chant the song of heaven, the sweet *Alleluia !*—but now, she bids us close our lips to this word of joy, because we are in Babylon. *We are pilgrims absent from our Lord;*[2]—let us keep our glad hymn for the day of his return. We are sinners, and have but too often held fellowship with the world of God's enemies ; let us become purified by repentance, for it is written, that *Praise is unseemly in the mouth of a sinner.*[3]

The leading feature, then, of *Septuagesima* is the total suspension of the *Alleluia,* which is not to be again heard upon the earth, until the arrival of that happy day, when, having suffered death with our Jesus, and having been buried together with him, we shall rise again with him to a new life.[4]

The sweet Hymn of the Angels, *Gloria in excelsis Deo,* which we have sung every Sunday since the Birth of our Saviour in Bethlehem, is also taken from us; it is only on the Feasts of the Saints, which may be kept during the week, that we shall be allowed to repeat it. The night Office of the Sunday is to lose, also, from now till Easter, its magnificent Ambrosian Hymn, the *Te Deum;* and at the end of the Holy Sacrifice, the Deacon will no longer dismiss the

---

[1] Ps. cxxxvi.
[2] II Cor. v. 6.
[3] Ecclus. xv. 9.
[4] Coloss. ii. 12.

Faithful with his solemn *Ite, Missa est*, but will simply invite them to continue their prayers in silence, and *bless the Lord*, the God of mercy, who bears with us, notwithstanding all our sins.

After the Gradual of the Mass, instead of the thrice repeated *Alleluia*, which prepared our hearts to listen to the voice of God in the Holy Gospel, we shall hear but a mournful and *protracted* chant, called, on that account, the *Tract*.

That the eye, too, may teach us, that the Season we are entering on, is one of mourning, the Church will vest her Ministers, (both on Sundays and the days during the week, which are not Feasts of Saints,) in the sombre *Purple*. Until Ash Wednesday, however, she permits the Deacon to wear his dalmatic, and the Subdeacon his tunic; but from that day forward, they must lay aside these vestments of joy, for Lent will then have begun, and our holy Mother will inspire us with the deep spirit of penance, by suppressing everything of that glad pomp, which she loves, at other seasons, to bring into the Sanctuary of her God.

CHAPTER THE THIRD.

PRACTICE DURING SEPTUAGESIMA.

THE joys of Christmastide seem to have fled far from us. The forty days of gladness brought us by the Birth of our Emmanuel are gone. The atmosphere of holy Church has grown overcast, and we are warned that the gloom is still to thicken. Have we, then, for ever lost Him, we so anxiously and longingly sighed after, during the four slow weeks of our Advent? Has our divine Sun of Justice, that rose so brightly in Bethlehem, now stopped his course, and left our guilty earth?

Not so. The Son of God, the Child of Mary, has not left us. *The Word was made Flesh* in order that he might *dwell among us*. A glory, far greater than that of his Birth, when Angels sang their hymns, awaits him, and *we* are to share it with him. Only, he must win this new and greater glory by strange countless sufferings; he must purchase it by a most cruel and ignominious death: and we, if we would have our share in the triumph of his Resurrection, must follow him in the Way of the Cross, all wet with the Tears and the Blood he shed for *us*.

The grave maternal voice of the Church will soon be heard, inviting us to the Lenten penance; but she wishes us to prepare for this *laborious baptism*, by employing these three weeks in considering the deep wounds caused in our souls by sin. True,—the beauty and loveliness of the Little Child, born to us in Bethlehem, are great beyond measure; but our souls are so needy, that they require other lessons than those He gave us of humility and simplicity.

Our Jesus is the Victim of the divine justice, and he has now attained the fulness of his age; the altar, on which he is to be slain, is ready: and since it is for us that he is to be sacrificed, we should at once set ourselves to consider, what are the debts we have contracted towards that infinite Justice, which is about to punish the Innocent One instead of us the guilty.

The mystery of a God becoming Incarnate for the love of his creature, has opened to us the path of the *Illuminative Way;* but we have not yet seen the brightest of its Light. Let not our hearts be troubled; the divine wonders we witnessed at Bethlehem are to be surpassed by those that are to grace the day of our Jesus' Triumph: but, that our eye may contemplate these future mysteries, it must be purified by courageously looking into the deep abyss of our own personal miseries. God will grant us his divine light for the discovery; and if we come to know ourselves, to understand the grievousness of original sin, to see the malice of our own sins, and to comprehend, at least in some degree, the infinite mercy of God towards us,—we shall be prepared for the holy expiations of Lent, and for the ineffable joys of Easter.

The Season, then, of Septuagesima is one of most serious thought. Perhaps we could not better show the sentiments, wherewith the Church would have her children to be filled at this period of her year, than by quoting a few words from the eloquent exhortation, given to his people, at the beginning of Septuagesima, by the celebrated Ivo of Chartres. He spoke thus to the Faithful of the 11th century:[1] "*We know,* says the Apostle, *that every creature groaneth, and travaileth in pain even till now: and not only it, but ourselves, also, who have the first-fruits of the Spirit, even we ourselves groan within ourselves, waiting for the adoption of the sons of God, the*

[1] 12th Sermon for Septuagesima.

"*redemption of our body.*¹ The *creature* here spoken
"of is the soul, that has been regenerated, from the
"corruption of sin, unto the likeness of God: she
"*groaneth* within herself, at seeing herself made sub-
"ject to vanity; she, like one that *travaileth,* is filled
"with *pain,* and is devoured by an anxious longing
"to be in that country, which is still so far off. It
"was this *travail* and *pain* that the Psalmist was
"suffering, when he exclaimed: *Wo is me, that my
"sojourning is prolonged!*² Nay, that Apostle, who
"was one of the *first* members of the Church, and had
"received the Holy *Spirit,* longed to have, in all its
"reality, that *adoption of the sons of God,* which he
"already had in hope; and he, too, thus exclaimed in
"his *pain: I desire to be dissolved, and to be with
"Christ.*³ * * * During these days, therefore, we
"must do what we do at all seasons of the Year,—only,
"we must do it more earnestly and fervently: we must
"sigh and weep after our country, from which we were
"exiled in consequence of having indulged in sinful
"pleasures; we must redouble our efforts in order to re-
"gain it by compunction and weeping of heart. * * *
"Let us now shed tears in the way, that we may
"afterwards be glad in our country. Let us now so
"run the race of this present life, that we may
"make sure of *the prize of the supernal vocation.*⁴
"Let us not be like imprudent wayfarers, for-
"getting our country, and preferring our banishment
"to our home. Let us not become like those
"senseless invalids, who feel not their ailments, and
"seek no remedy. We despair of a sick man, who
"will not be persuaded that he is in danger. No:
"let us run to our Lord, the Physician of eternal
"salvation. Let us show him our wounds, and cry
"out to him with all our earnestness: *Have mercy
"on me, O Lord, for I am weak: heal me, for my*

---

[1] Rom. viii. 22, 23.
[2] Ps. cxix. 5.
[3] Philipp. i. 23.
[4] Philipp. iii. 14.

"*bones are troubled.*[1] Then, will he forgive us our "iniquities, heal us of our infirmities, and satisfy our "desire with good things."[2]

From all this it is evident, that the Christian, who would spend Septuagesima according to the spirit of the Church, must make war upon that false security, that self-satisfaction, which are so common to effeminate and tepid souls, and produce spiritual barrenness. It is well for them, if these delusions do not insensibly lead them to the absolute loss of the true Christian spirit. He that thinks himself dispensed from that continual watchfulness, which is so strongly inculcated by our Divine Master,[3] is already in the enemy's power. He that feels no need of combat and of struggle in order to persevere and make progress in virtue, (unless he have been honoured with a privilege, which is both rare and dangerous), should fear that he is not even on the road to that Kingdom of God, which is only to be won by *violence.*[4] He that forgets the sins, which God's mercy has forgiven him, should fear his being the victim of a dangerous delusion.[5] Let us, during these days, which we are going to devote to the honest unflinching contemplation of our miseries, give glory to our God, and derive, from the knowledge of ourselves, fresh motives of confidence in Him, who, in spite of all our wretchedness and sin, humbled himself so low as to become one of us, in order that he might exalt us even to union with Himself.

[1] Ps. vi, 3.
[2] Ps. cii. 3, 5.
[3] St. Mark, xiii. 37.
[4] St. Matth. xi. 12.
[5] Ecclus. v. 5.

CHAPTER THE FOURTH.

MORNING AND NIGHT PRAYERS,

FOR SEPTUAGESIMA.

DURING the Season of Septuagesima, the Christian, on waking in the morning, should unite himself with the Church, who, at the first dawn of day, begins her Psalms of Lauds with these words of the Royal Prophet:

Miserere mei Deus, secundum magnam misericordiam tuam.	Have mercy on me, O God, according to thy great mercy.

He should, after this, profoundly adore that great God, before whom the sinner should tremble, but yet fears not to offend him, as though he deserved neither reverence nor love. It is with this deep sentiment of holy fear, that he must perform the first acts of religion, both interior and exterior, wherewith he begins each day of this present Season. The time for Morning Prayer being come, he may use the following method, which is formed upon the very prayers of the Church:—

MORNING PRAYER.

First, praise and adoration of the Most Holy Trinity:—

℣. Benedicamus Patrem et Filium, cum Sancto Spiritu:	℣. Let us bless the Father and the Son, and the Holy Ghost.
℟. Laudemus et superexaltemus eum in sæcula.	℟. Let us praise him and extol him above all, for ever.
℣. Gloria Patri et Filio, et Spiritui Sancto;	℣. Glory be to the Father, and to the Son, and to the Holy Ghost.

MORNING PRAYERS.

℟. As it was in the begining, is now, and ever shall be, world without end. Amen.

℟. Sicut erat in principio, et nunc et semper, et in sæcula sæculorum. Amen.

Then, praise to our Lord and Saviour, Jesus Christ:

℣. We adore thee, O Christ, and we bless thee.
℟. Because by thy Cross thou hast redeemed the world.

℣. Adoramus te, Christe, et benedicimus tibi.
℟. Quia per Crucem tuam redemisti mundum.

Thirdly, invocation of the Holy Ghost:

Come, O Holy Spirit, fill the hearts of thy faithful, and enkindle within them the fire of thy love.

Veni, Sancte Spiritus, reple tuorum corda fidelium, et tui amoris in eis ignem accende.

After these fundamental acts of Religion, recite the Lord's Prayer, begging your Heavenly Father to be mindful of his infinite mercy and goodness,—to *forgive* you your *trespasses*,—to come to your assistance in the *temptations* and dangers which so thickly beset the path of this life,—and finally, to *deliver* you *from evil*, by removing from you every remnant of sin, which is the great *evil*, the *evil* that offends God, and entails the sovereign *evil* of man himself.

THE LORD'S PRAYER.

Our Father, who art in heaven, hallowed be thy name: thy kingdom come: thy will be done on earth as it is in heaven. Give us this day our daily bread; and *forgive us our trespasses*, as we forgive them that trespass against us: and lead us not into temptation: but deliver us from evil. Amen.

Pater noster, qui es in cœlis, sanctificetur nomen tuum: adveniat regnum tuum: fiat voluntas tua sicut in cœlo, et in terra. Panem nostrum quotidianum da nobis hodie: et dimitte nobis debita nostra, sicut et nos dimittimus debitoribus nostris: et ne nos inducas in tentationem: sed libera nos a malo. Amen.

Then, address our Blessed Lady, using the words of the Angelical Salutation. Pray to her with confidence and love, for she is the *Refuge of Sinners*.

THE ANGELICAL SALUTATION.

Ave Maria, gratia plena, Dominus tecum; benedicta tu in mulieribus, et benedictus fructus ventris tui, Jesus.

Sancta Maria, Mater Dei, ora pro nobis peccatoribus, nunc et in hora mortis nostræ. Amen.

Hail Mary, full of grace; the Lord is with thee; blessed art thou among women, and blessed is the fruit of thy womb, Jesus.

Holy Mary, Mother of God, *pray for us sinners,* now and at the hour of our death. Amen.

After this, you should recite the *Creed,* that is, the Symbol of Faith. It contains the dogmas we are to believe; and during this season, you should dwell with loving attention on that Article, which is so full of hope,—*the Forgiveness of sins.* Let us do our utmost to merit, by our sincere conversion and amendment of our lives, that our Saviour, after the coming penitential Forty Days are over, may say to each of us those words, which are so sweet to a penitent sinner: *Go, thy sins are forgiven!*

THE APOSTLES' CREED.

Credo in Deum Patrem omnipotentem, creatorem cœli et terræ. Et in Jesum Christum Filium ejus unicum, Dominum nostrum: qui conceptus est de Spiritu Sancto, natus ex Maria Virgine, passus sub Pontio Pilato, crucifixus, mortuus, et sepultus: descendit ad inferos, tertia die resurrexit a mortuis: ascendit ad cœlos, sedet ad dexteram Dei Patris omnipotentis: inde venturus est judicare vivos et mortuos.

Credo in Spiritum Sanctum, sanctam Ecclesiam Catholicam, Sanctorum com-

I believe in God the Father Almighty, Creator of heaven and earth. And in Jesus Christ, his only Son our Lord, who was conceived by the Holy Ghost, born of the Virgin Mary; suffered under Pontius Pilate, was crucified, dead, and buried; he descended into hell, the third day he arose again from the dead; he ascended into heaven, sitteth at the right hand of God the Father Almighty; from thence he shall come to judge the living and the dead.

I believe in the Holy Ghost; the Holy Catholic Church; the communion of Saints, the *forgiveness of sins,* the resurrection of the body, and life everlasting. Amen.

munionem, remissionem peccatorum, carnis resurrectionem, vitam æternam. Amen.

After having thus made the Profession of your Faith, endeavour to excite yourself to sorrow for the sins you have committed. For this purpose, recite one of the Penitential Psalms; the first on Sunday, the second on Monday, and so on with the rest. These admirable Psalms, whereby David expressed his grief after he had fallen into sin, are most appropriate for the Season of Septuagesima. The reader will find them at the end of this volume.

Then, make an humble confession of your sins, reciting the general formula made use of by the Church.

THE CONFESSION OF SINS.

I confess to Almighty God, to blessed Mary ever Virgin, to blessed Michael the Archangel, to blessed John Baptist, to the holy Apostles Peter and Paul, and to all the saints, that I have sinned exceedingly in thought, word, and deed; through my fault, through my fault, through my most grievous fault. Therefore I beseech the blessed Mary ever Virgin, blessed Michael the Archangel, blessed John Baptist, the holy Apostles Peter and Paul, and all the saints, to pray to our Lord God for me.

May Almighty God have mercy on us, and, our sins being forgiven, bring us to life everlasting. Amen.

May the Almighty and mer-

Confiteor Deo Omnipotenti, beatæ Mariæ semper Virgini, beato Michaeli Archangelo, beato Joanni Baptistæ, sanctis Apostolis Petro et Paulo, et omnibus sanctis, quia peccavi nimis cogitatione, verbo, et opere: mea culpa, mea culpa, mea maxima culpa. Ideo precor beatam Mariam semper Virginem, beatum Michaelem Archangelum, beatum Joannem Baptistam, sanctos Apostolos Petrum et Paulum, et omnes sanctos, orare pro me ad Dominum Deum nostrum.

Misereatur nostri omnipotens Deus, et dimissis peccatis nostris, perducat nos ad vitam æternam. Amen.

Indulgentiam, absolutio-

SEPTUAGESIMA.

nem, et remissionem peccatorum nostrorum tribuat nobis omnipotens et misericors Dominus. Amen.

ciful Lord grant us pardon, absolution, and remission of our sins. Amen.

This is the proper time for making your Meditation, as no doubt you practice this holy exercise. During Septuagesima, the subject of our Meditation ought mainly to be on the evils brought on man by *Original* sin; on the necessity of an untiring resistance against our corrupt nature, whose tendencies and inclinations would lead us to destruction; on the grievousness of *Actual* sin, how it robs us of countless blessings, and exposes us to punishments both here and hereafter; on the ineffable goodness of God, who comes himself to offer reconciliation to the sinner, and who, after the salutary mournfulness and the works of penance of the weeks of Septuagesima and Lent, will give all the joy, peace, and blessing of a new life in our Risen Jesus.

The next part of your Morning Prayer must be to ask of God, by the following prayers, grace to avoid every kind of sin during the day you are just beginning. Say, then, with the Church, whose prayers must always be preferred to all others:

℣. Domine, exaudi orationem meam.

℟. Et clamor meus ad te veniat.

℣. O Lord, hear my prayer.

℟. And let my cry come unto thee.

OREMUS.

Domine, Deus omnipotens, qui ad principium hujus diei nos pervenire fecisti, tua nos hodie salva virtute, ut in hac die ad nullum declinemus peccatum, sed semper ad tuam justitiam faciendam nostra procedant eloquia, dirigantur cogitationes et

LET US PRAY.

Almighty Lord and God, who hast brought us to the beginning of this day, let thy powerful grace so conduct us through it, that we may not fall into any sin, but that all our thoughts, words, and actions may be regulated according to the rules of thy

MORNING PRAYERS.

heavenly justice, and tend to the observance of thy holy law. Through Jesus Christ our Lord. Amen.

opera. Per Dominum nostrum Jesum Christum Filium tuum, qui tecum vivit et regnat in unitate Spiritus Sancti Deus, per omnia sæcula sæculorum. Amen.

Then, beg the divine assistance for the actions of the day, that you may do them well; and say thrice:

℣. Incline unto my aid, O God.
℟. O Lord, make haste to help me.
℣. Incline unto my aid, O God.
℟. O Lord, make haste to help me.
℣. Incline unto my aid, O God.
℟. O Lord, make haste to help me.

℣. Deus, in adjutorium meum intende.
℟. Domine, ad adjuvandum me festina.
℣. Deus, in adjutorium meum intende.
℟. Domine, ad adjuvandum me festina.
℣. Deus, in adjutorium meum intende.
℟. Domine, ad adjuvandum me festina.

LET US PRAY.

Lord God, and King of heaven and earth, vouchsafe this day to rule and sanctify, to direct and govern our souls and bodies, our senses, words, and actions in conformity to thy law, and strict obedience to thy commands; that by the help of thy grace, O Saviour of the world! we may be fenced and freed from all evils. Who livest and reignest for ever and ever. Amen.

OREMUS.

Dirigere et sanctificare, regere et gubernare dignare, Domine Deus, Rex cœli et terræ, hodie corda et corpora nostra, sensus, sermones, et actus nostros in lege tua, et in operibus mandatorum tuorum, ut hic et in æternum, te auxiliante, salvi et liberi esse mereamur, Salvator mundi. Qui vivis et regnas in sæcula sæculorum. Amen.

During the day, you will do well to use the instructions and prayers which you will find in this volume, for each day of the Season, both for the Proper of the Time, and the Proper of the Saints. In the Evening, you may use the following Prayers.

NIGHT PRAYERS.

After having made the sign of the Cross, let us adore that Sovereign Lord, who has so mercifully preserved us during this day, and blessed us, every hour, with his grace and protection. For this end, let us recite the following Hymn, which the Church sings in her Vespers of Saturday:

HYMN.

Jam sol recedit igneus :
Tu lux perennis, Unitas,
Nostris, beata Trinitas,
Infunde lumen cordibus.

Te mane laudum carmine,
Te deprecamur vespere :
Digneris, ut te supplices
Laudemus inter cœlites.

Patri simulque Filio,
Tibique, Sancte Spiritus,
Sicut fuit, sit jugiter
Sæculum per omne gloria.
Amen.

℣. Vespertina oratio ascendat ad te, Domine.

℟. Et descendat super nos misericordia tua.

The radiant sun hath set : do thou, O Light unfading, O Unity and Trinity divine, pour thy rays into our hearts.

Our morning hymns give thee praise ; our even song implores thy mercy : Oh! grant us to be one day companions with the blessed in heaven, to give thee ceaseless praise.

To thee, O God, Father, Son, and Holy Ghost! may glory be, as it hath ever been, for ever and for endless ages. Amen.

℣. May our evening prayer ascend to thee, O Lord.

℟. And may thy mercy descend upon us.

After this Hymn, say the *Our Father, Hail Mary,* and the *Apostles' Creed*, as in the Morning.

Then, make the Examination of Conscience, going over in your mind all the faults you have committed during the day. Think, how great is the obstacle put by sin to the merciful designs your God would work in you; and make a firm resolution to avoid it for the time to come, to do penance for it, and to shun the occasions which might again lead you into it.

The Examination of Conscience concluded, recite the *Confiteor* (or *I confess*) with heartfelt contrition, and then give expression to your sorrow by the following Act, which we have taken from the Venerable Cardinal Bellarmine's Catechism :

ACT OF CONTRITION.

O my God, I am exceedingly grieved for having offended thee, and with my whole heart I repent for the sins I have committed : I hate and abhor them above every other evil, not only because, by so sinning, I have lost Heaven and deserve Hell, but still more because I have offended thee, O infinite Goodness, who art worthy to be loved above all things. I most firmly resolve, by the assistance of thy grace, never more to offend thee for the time to come, and to avoid those occasions which might lead me into sin.

You may then add the Acts of Faith, Hope, and Charity, to the recitation of which Pope Benedict the Fourteenth has granted an indulgence of seven years and seven quarantines for each time.

ACT OF FAITH.

O my God, I firmly believe whatsoever the Holy Catholic Apostolic Roman Church requires me to believe : I believe it, because thou hast revealed it to her, thou who art the very Truth.

ACT OF HOPE.

O my God, knowing thy almighty power, and thy infinite goodness and mercy, I hope in thee that, by the merits of the Passion and Death of our Saviour Jesus Christ, thou wilt grant me eternal life, which thou hast promised to all such as shall do the works of a good Christian ; and these I resolve to do, with the help of thy grace.

ACT OF CHARITY.

O my God, I love thee with my whole heart and above all things, because thou art the sovereign Good : I would rather lose all things than offend thee. For thy love also, I love and desire to love my neighbour as myself.

Then say to our Blessed Lady the following Anthem, which the Church uses from the Feast of the Purification to Easter:

ANTHEM TO THE BLESSED VIRGIN.

| Hail Queen of Heaven ! Hail Queen of Angels ! Hail | Ave Regina cœlorum, Ave Domina Angelorum : |

Salve radix, salve porta,
Ex qua mundo lux est orta;
Gaude, Virgo gloriosa,
Super omnes speciosa:
Vale, O valde decora,
Et pro nobis Christum exora.

℣. Dignare me laudare te, Virgo sacrata.

℟. Da mihi virtutem contra hostes tuos.

OREMUS.

Concede, misericors Deus, fragilitati nostræ præsidium: ut, qui sanctæ Dei Genitricis memoriam agimus, intercessionis ejus auxilio, a nostris iniquitatibus resurgamus. Per eumdem Christum Dominum nostrum. Amen.

blest Root and Gate, from which came Light upon the world! Rejoice, O glorious Virgin, that surpassest all in beauty! Hail, most lovely Queen! and pray to Christ for us.

℣. Vouchsafe, O Holy Virgin, that I may praise thee.

℟. Give me power against thine enemies.

LET US PRAY.

Grant, O merciful God, thy protection to us in our weakness; that we who celebrate the memory of the Holy Mother of God, may, through the aid of her intercession, rise again from our sins. Through the same Christ our Lord. Amen.

You would do well to add the Litany of our Lady. An indulgence of three hundred days, for each time it is recited, has been granted by the Church.

THE LITANY OF THE BLESSED VIRGIN.

Kyrie, eleison.
Christe, eleison.
Kyrie, eleison.
Christe, audi nos.
Christe, exaudi nos.
Pater de cœlis, Deus, miserere nobis.
Fili, Redemptor mundi, Deus, miserere nobis.
Spiritus Sancte, Deus, miserere nobis.
Sancta Trinitas, unus Deus, miserere nobis.
Sancta Maria, ora pro nobis.
Sancta Dei Genitrix, ora, *etc.*

Lord, have mercy on us.
Christ, have mercy on us.
Lord, have mercy on us.
Christ, hear us.
Christ, graciously hear us.
God the Father of heaven, have mercy on us.
God the Son, Redeemer of the world, have mercy on us.
God the Holy Ghost, have mercy on us.
Holy Trinity, one God, have mercy on us.
Holy Mary, pray for us.
Holy Mother of God, pray, *etc.*

Holy Virgin of virgins,	Sancta Virgo virginum,
Mother of Christ,	Mater Christi,
Mother of divine grace,	Mater divinæ gratiæ,
Mother most pure,	Mater purissima,
Mother most chaste,	Mater castissima,
Mother inviolate,	Mater inviolata,
Mother undefiled,	Mater intemerata,
Mother most amiable,	Mater amabilis,
Mother most admirable,	Mater admirabilis,
Mother of our Creator,	Mater Creatoris,
Mother of our Redeemer,	Mater Salvatoris,
Virgin most prudent,	Virgo prudentissima,
Virgin most venerable,	Virgo veneranda,
Virgin most renowned,	Virgo prædicanda,
Virgin most powerful,	Virgo potens,
Virgin most merciful,	Virgo clemens,
Virgin most faithful,	Virgo fidelis,
Mirror of justice,	Speculum justitiæ,
Seat of wisdom,	Sedes sapientiæ,
Cause of our joy,	Causa nostræ lætitiæ,
Spiritual vessel,	Vas spirituale,
Vessel of honour,	Vas honorabile,
Vessel of singular devotion,	Vas insigne devotionis,
Mystical Rose,	Rosa mystica,
Tower of David,	Turris Davidica,
Tower of ivory,	Turris eburnea,
House of gold,	Domus aurea,
Ark of the covenant,	Fœderis arca,
Gate of heaven,	Janua cœli,
Morning Star,	Stella matutina,
Health of the weak,	Salus infirmorum,
Refuge of sinners,	Refugium peccatorum,
Comforter of the afflicted,	Consolatrix afflictorum,
Help of Christians,	Auxilium Christianorum,
Queen of Angels,	Regina Angelorum,
Queen of Patriarchs,	Regina Patriarcharum,
Queen of Prophets,	Regina Prophetarum,
Queen of Apostles,	Regina Apostolorum,
Queen of Martyrs,	Regina Martyrum,
Queen of Confessors,	Regina Confessorum,
Queen of Virgins,	Regina Virginum,
Queen of all Saints,	Regina Sanctorum omnium,
Queen conceived without original sin.	Regina sine labe concepta.
O Lamb of God, who takest away the sins of the world, spare us, O Lord.	Agnus Dei, qui tollis peccata mundi, parce nobis, Domine.

Agnus Dei, qui tollis peccata mundi, exaudi nos, Domine.

Agnus Dei, qui tollis peccata mundi, miserere nobis.

Christe, audi nos.

Christe, exaudi nos.

℣. Ora pro nobis, sancta Dei Genitrix.

℟. Ut digni efficiamur promissionibus Christi.

O Lamb of God, who takest away the sins of the world, graciously hear us, O Lord.

O Lamb of God, who takest away the sins of the world, have mercy on us.

Christ, hear us.

Christ, graciously hear us.

℣. Pray for us, O Holy Mother of God.

℟. That we may be made worthy of the promises of Christ.

OREMUS.

Concede nos famulos tuos, quæsumus, Domine Deus, perpetua mentis et corporis sanitate gaudere: et gloriosa beatæ Mariæ, semper Virginis, intercessione, a præsenti liberari tristitia, et æterna perfrui lætitia. Per Christum Dominum nostrum. Amen.

LET US PRAY.

Grant, O Lord, we beseech thee, that we thy servants may enjoy constant health of body and mind, and by the glorious intercession of Blessed Mary, ever a Virgin, be delivered from all present affliction, and come to that joy which is eternal. Through Christ our Lord. Amen.

Here invoke the Holy Angels, whose protection is, indeed, always so much needed by us, but never so much as during the hours of night. Say with the Church:

Sancti Angeli, custodes nostri, defendite nos in prælio, ut non pereamus in tremendo judicio.

℣. Angelis suis Deus mandavit de te.

℟. Ut custodiant te in omnibus viis tuis.

Holy Angels, our loving Guardians, defend us in the hour of battle, that we may not be lost at the dreadful judgment.

℣. God hath given his Angels charge of thee.

℟. That they may guard thee in all thy ways.

OREMUS.

Deus, qui ineffabili providentia sanctos Angelos tuos ad nostram custodiam mit-

LET US PRAY.

O God, who in thy wonderful providence hast been pleased to appoint thy holy

Angels for our guardians: mercifully hear our prayers, and grant we may rest secure under their protection, and enjoy their fellowship in heaven for ever. Through Christ our Lord. Amen.

tere dignaris: largire supplicibus tuis, et eorum semper protectione defendi, et æterna societate gaudere. Per Christum Dominum nostrum. Amen.

Then beg the assistance of the Saints by the following antiphon and prayer of the Church:

ANT. All ye saints of God, vouchsafe to intercede for us and for all men, that we may be saved.

℣. Rejoice in the Lord, ye just, and be glad.

℟. And glory, all ye right of heart.

ANT. Sancti Dei omnes, intercedere dignemini pro nostra omniumque salute.

℣. Lætamini in Domino et exsultate, justi.

℟. Et gloriamini omnes recti corde.

LET US PRAY.

Protect, O Lord, thy people; and because we have confidence in the intercession of blessed Peter and Paul and thy other Apostles, ever defend and preserve us.

May all thy Saints ever help us, we beseech thee, O Lord! and grant, that, whilst we honour their merits, we may experience their intercession. Grant thy holy peace unto these our days, and drive all iniquity from thy Church. Direct and prosper unto salvation every step, and action, and desire, of us and of all thy servants. Repay our benefactors with everlasting blessings; and grant eternal rest to all the faithful departed. Through Christ our Lord. Amen.

OREMUS.

Protege, Domine, populum tuum, et Apostolorum tuorum Petri et Pauli et aliorum Apostolorum patrocinio confidentem, perpetua defensione conserva.

Omnes Sancti tui, quæsumus, Domine, nos ubique adjuvent: ut dum eorum merita recolimus, patrocinia sentiamus: et pacem tuam nostris concede temporibus, et ab Ecclesia tua cunctam repelle nequitiam: iter, actus, et voluntates nostras, et omnium famulorum tuorum, in salutis tuæ prosperitate dispone: benefactoribus nostris sempiterna bona retribue: et omnibus fidelibus defunctis requiem æternam concede. Per Christum Dominum nostrum. Amen.

And here you may add a special mention of the Saints to whom you bear a particular devotion, either as your Patrons or otherwise; as also of those whose feast is kept in the Church that day, or at least who have been commemorated in the Divine Office.

This done, remember the necessities of the Church Suffering, and beg of God that he will give to the souls in Purgatory a place of refreshment, light, and peace. For this intention recite the usual prayers.

PSALM 129.

De profundis clamavi ad te, Domine: Domine, exaudi vocem meam.

Fiant aures tuæ intendentes: in vocem deprecationis meæ.

Si iniquitates observaveris, Domine: Domine, quis sustinebit?

Quia apud te propitiatio est: et propter legem tuam sustinui te, Domine.

Sustinuit anima mea in verbo ejus: speravit anima mea in Domino.

A custodia matutina usque ad noctem: speret Israel in Domino.

Quia apud Dominum misericordia: et copiosa apud eum redemptio.

Et ipse redimet Israel; ex omnibus iniquitatibus ejus.

Requiem æternam dona eis, Domine.

Et lux perpetua luceat eis.

℣. A porta inferi.

℟. Erue, Domine, animas eorum.

℣. Requiescant in pace.

℟. Amen.

From the depths I have cried to thee, O Lord; Lord, hear my voice.

Let thine ears be attentive to the voice of my supplication.

If thou wilt observe iniquities, O Lord, Lord, who shall endure it?

For with thee there is merciful forgiveness; and by reason of thy law I have waited for thee, O Lord.

My soul hath relied on his word; my soul hath hoped in the Lord.

From the morning watch even until night, let Israel hope in the Lord.

Because with the Lord there is mercy, and with him plentiful redemption.

And he shall redeem Israel from all his iniquities.

Eternal rest give to them, O Lord.

And let perpetual light shine upon them.

℣. From the gate of hell.

℟. Deliver their souls, O Lord.

℣. May they rest in peace.

℟. Amen.

℣. O Lord, hear my prayer.

℟. And let my cry come unto thee.

℣. Domine, exaudi orationem meam.

℟. Et clamor meus ad te veniat.

LET US PRAY.

OREMUS.

O God, the Creator and Redeemer of all the faithful, give to the souls of thy servants departed the remission of their sins : that through the help of pious supplications, they may obtain the pardon they have always desired. Who livest and reignest for ever and ever. Amen.

Fidelium Deus omnium Conditor et Redemptor, animabus famulorum famularumque tuarum, remissionem cunctorum tribue peccatorum : ut indulgentiam, quam semper optaverunt, piis supplicationibus consequantur. Qui vivis et regnas in sæcula sæculorum. Amen.

Here make a special memento of such of the Faithful departed as have a particular claim upon your charity; after which, ask of God to give you his assistance, whereby you may pass the night free from danger. Say then, still keeping to the words of the Church :

Ant. Save us, O Lord, whilst awake, and watch us as we sleep; that we may watch with Christ, and rest in peace.

℣. Vouchsafe, O Lord, this night.

℟. To keep us without sin.

℣. Have mercy on us, O Lord.

℟. Have mercy on us.

℣. Let thy mercy, O Lord, be upon us.

℟. As we have hoped in thee.

℣. O Lord, hear my prayer.

℟. And let my cry come unto thee.

Ant. Salva nos, Domine, vigilantes, custodi nos dormientes : ut vigilemus cum Christo, et requiescamus in pace.

℣. Dignare, Domine, nocte ista.

℟. Sine peccato nos custodire.

℣. Miserere nostri, Domine.

℟. Miserere nostri.

℣. Fiat misericordia tua, Domine, super nos.

℟. Quemadmodum speravimus in te.

℣. Domine, exaudi orationem meam.

℟. Et clamor meus ad te veniat.

SEPTUAGESIMA.

OREMUS.
Visita, quæsumus, Domine, habitationem istam, et omnes insidias inimici ab ea longe repelle: Angeli tui sancti habitent in ea, qui nos in pace custodiant, et benedictio tua sit super nos semper. Per Dominum nostrum Jesum Christum, Filium tuum, qui tecum vivit et regnat in unitate Spiritus Sancti Deus, per omnia sæcula sæculorum. Amen.

LET US PRAY.
Visit, we beseech thee, O Lord, this house and family, and drive from it all snares of the enemy: let thy holy Angels dwell herein, who may keep us in peace, and may thy blessing be always upon us. Through Jesus Christ our Lord, thy Son, who liveth and reigneth with thee, in the unity of the Holy Ghost, God, world without end. Amen.

And that you may end the day in the same sentiments wherewith you began it, say once more to your God these words of the Royal Prophet:

Miserere mei, Deus, secundum magnam misericordiam tuam.

Have mercy on me, O God, according to thy great mercy.

CHAPTER THE FIFTH.

ON HEARING MASS, DURING THE SEASON OF SEPTUAGESIMA.

THE Christian who enters into the spirit of the Church during this Season of Septuagesima, will find an increase in his soul of that holy Fear of God, which the Psalmist tells us is *the beginning of wisdom.*[1] The consideration of what Original Sin has brought upon him, the recollection of his own sins, and the dread of God's judgments,—all combine to arouse him from the indifference which so easily fastens on the soul. He has need, therefore, of some refuge, some powerful and saving help, which may re-enkindle within his heart that christian Hope, without which he cannot be in the grace of God. Nay more,—he has need of a Victim of Propitiation, which may appease the divine anger; he has need of a Sacrifice, whereby to stay the arm of God, that he knows is raised to punish his sins.

This Victim is ready; this infinitely efficacious Sacrifice is prepared for us. *The Lamb of God, that taketh away the sins of the world,* is still on our earth. His Birth has filled us with consolation; the joy we experienced as we stood near his Crib, but which has suddenly given place for thoughts the very opposite of joy, will return to us, and be greater than when we had it at Christmas, on the Easter Day of his Resurrection: but in the interval, whilst waiting the dawn of that bright Day, which is to lead us to our Jesus purified from our sins and vigorous with our new life, we may and must trust to his

---

[1] Ps. cx. 10.

merits effecting the regeneration of our souls. When, therefore, we would offer to our God the sacrifice of *a contrite and humble heart,* let us ensure its acceptance by going to the Altar, and supplicating the Victim, who there offers himself for our sakes, that he join His infinite merits with *our* feeble works. When we leave the House of God, the weight of our sins will be lessened, our confidence in divine mercy will be increased, and our love, renewed by compunction, will be firmer and truer.

We will now endeavour to embody these sentiments in our explanation of the Mysteries of the Holy Mass, and initiate the Faithful into these divine secrets; not, indeed, by indiscreetly presuming to translate the sacred formulæ, but by suggesting such Acts, as will enable those who hear Mass, to enter into the ceremonies and spirit of the Church and the Priest.

On the three Sundays, of Septuagesima, Sexagesima, and Quinquagesima, the Mass is always celebrated according to the rite of the penitential Season we are now keeping. These Sundays are never put out by any Feast that may occur on them, unless it be that of the Patron or the Dedication of the Church. Ash-Wednesday does not admit of even that exception; the Mass of that Feria is never omitted. But, when a Saint's Feast, (and there are many such during the time of Septuagesima), falls on any other day but the four just mentioned, the Church then lays aside her purple vestments, and celebrates the Holy Sacrifice in memory of the Saint.

On the Sundays, if the Mass, at which the Faithful assist, be the *Parochial,* or, as it is often called, the Public Mass, two solemn rites precede it, and they are full of instruction and blessing;—the *Asperges,* or sprinkling of the Holy Water, and the *Procession.*

During the *Asperges,* let us ask with David, whose words are used by the Church in this ceremony, that our souls may be purified by the *hyssop* of humility, and become *whiter than snow.*

ANTIPHON OF THE ASPERGES.

Thou shalt sprinkle me with hyssop, O Lord, and I shall be cleansed; thou shalt wash me, and I shall be made whiter than snow.
Ps. Have mercy on me, O God, according to thy great mercy.
℣. Glory, &c.
Ant. Sprinkle me, &c.
℣. Show us, O Lord, thy mercy.
℟. And grant us thy salvation.
℣. O Lord, hear my prayer.

℟. And let my cry come unto thee.
℣. The Lord be with you.
℟. And with thy spirit.

Asperges me, Domine, hyssopo, et mundabor; lavabis me, et super, nivem dealbabor.
Ps. Miserere mei, Deus, secundum magnam misericordiam tuam.
℣. Gloria Patri, &c.
Ant. Asperges me, &c.
℣. Ostende nobis, Domine, misericordiam tuam.
℟. Et salutare tuum da nobis.
℣. Domine, exaudi orationem meam.
℟. Et clamor meus ad te veniat.
℣. Dominus vobiscum.
℟. Et cum spiritu tuo.

LET US PRAY.

Graciously hear us, O holy Lord, Father Almighty, Eternal God: and vouchsafe to send thy holy Angel from heaven, who may keep, cherish, protect, visit, and defend all who are assembled in this place. Through Christ our Lord.
℟. Amen.

OREMUS.

Exaudi nos, Domine sancte, Pater omnipotens, æterne Deus: et mittere digneris sanctum Angelum tuum de cœlis, qui custodiat, foveat, protegat, visitet atque defendat omnes habitantes in hoc habitaculo. Per Christum Dominum nostrum.
℟. Amen.

The *Procession*, which immediately precedes the Mass, shows us the ardour wherewith the Church advances towards her God. Let us imitate her fervour, for it is written: *The Lord is good to them that hope in him, to the soul that seeketh him.*[1]

[1] Lament. iii. 25.

But see, Christians! the Sacrifice begins! The Priest is at the foot of the altar; God is attentive, the Angels are in adoration, the whole Church is united with the Priest, whose priesthood and action are those of the great High Priest, Jesus Christ. Let us make the sign of the cross with him.

THE ORDINARY OF THE MASS.

In nomine Patris, et Filii, et Spiritus Sancti. Amen.
℣. Introibo ad altare Dei.
℟. Ad Deum qui lætificat juventutem meam.

In the name of the Father, and of the Son, and of the Holy Ghost. Amen.
I unite myself, O my God, with thy Church, whose heart is filled with the hope of soon seeing, and in all the splendour of his Resurrection, Jesus Christ thy Son, who is the true *Altar*.

Judica me, Deus, et discerne causam meam de gente non sancta : ad homine iniquo et doloso erue me.
Quia tu es, Deus, fortitudo mea : quare me repulisti? et quare tristis incedo, dum affligit me inimicus?

Like her, I beseech thee to defend me against the malice of the enemies of my salvation.
It is in thee that I have put my hope; yet do I feel sad and troubled at being in the midst of the snares which are set for me.

Emitte lucem tuam et veritatem tuam : ipsa me deduxerunt et adduxerunt in montem sanctum tuum, et in tabernacula tua.
Et introibo ad altare Dei : ad Deum qui lætificat juventutem meam.
Confitebor tibi in cithara Deus, Deus meus : quare tristis es anima mea? et quare conturbas me?
Spera in Deo, quoniam adhuc confitebor illi : Salu-

Send me, then, him who is *light* and *truth:* it is he will open to us the way to thy holy mount, to thy heavenly tabernacle.
He is the Mediator, and the living Altar; I will draw nigh to him, and be filled with joy.
When he shall have come, I will sing in my gladness. Be not sad, O my soul! Why wouldst thou be troubled?
Hope in thy Jesus, who will soon show himself to thee as

the conqueror of that Death which he will have suffered in thy stead; and *thou* wilt rise again together with him.	tare vultus mei, et Deus meus.
Glory be to the Father, and to the Son, and to the Holy Ghost.	Gloria Patri, et Filio, et Spiritui Sancto.
As it was in the beginning, is now, and ever shall be, world without end. Amen.	Sicut erat in principio, et nunc et semper, et in sæcula sæculorum. Amen.
I am to go to the altar of God, and feel the presence of him who desires to give me a new life!	℣. Introibo ad altare Dei. ℟. Ad Deum qui lætificat juventutem meam.
This my hope comes not to me as thinking that I have any merits, but from the all-powerful help of my Creator.	℣. Adjutorium nostrum in nomine Domini. ℟. Qui fecit cœlum et terram.

The thought of his being about to appear before his God, excites, in the soul of the Priest, a lively sentiment of compunction. He cannot go further in the holy Sacrifice without confessing, and publicly, that he is a sinner, and deserves not the grace he is about to receive. Listen, with respect, to this confession of God's Minister, and earnestly ask our Lord to show mercy to him; for the Priest is your Father; he is answerable for your salvation, for which he every day risks his own. When he has finished, unite with the Servers, or the Sacred Ministers, in this prayer:

May Almighty God have mercy on thee, and, forgiving thy sins, bring thee to everlasting life.	Misereatur tui omnipotens Deus, et dimissis peccatis tuis, perducat te ad vitam æternam.

The Priest having answered *Amen*, make your confession, saying with a contrite spirit:

I confess to Almighty God, to blessed Mary ever Virgin, to blessed Michael the Archangel, to blessed John Baptist,	Confiteor Deo omnipotenti, beatæ Mariæ semper Virgini, beato Michæli Archangelo, beato Joanni

Baptistæ, sanctis Apostolis Petro et Paulo, omnibus Sanctis, et tibi, Pater : quia peccavi nimis, cogitatione, verbo, et opere : mea culpa, mea culpa, mea maxima culpa. Ideo precor beatam Mariam semper Virginem, beatum Michaelem Archangelum, beatum Joannem Baptistam, sanctos Apostolos Petrum et Paulum, omnes Sanctos, et te, Pater, orare pro me ad Dominum Deum nostrum.

to the holy Apostles Peter and Paul, to all the saints, and to thee, Father, that I have sinned exceedingly in thought, word, and deed, through my fault, through my fault, through my most grievous fault. Therefore I beseech the blessed Mary ever Virgin, blessed Michael, the Archangel, blessed John Baptist, the holy Apostles Peter and Paul, and all the saints, and thee, Father, to pray to our Lord God for me.

Receive with gratitude the paternal wish of the Priest, who says to you :

Misereatur vestri omnipotens Deus, et dimissis peccatis vestris, perducat vos ad vitam æternam.
℟. Amen.
Indulgentiam, absolutionem, et remissionem peccatorum nostrorum, tribuat nobis omnipotens et misericors Dominus.
℟. Amen.

May Almighty God be merciful to you, and, forgiving your sins, bring you to everlasting life.
℟. Amen.
May the Almighty and merciful Lord grant us pardon, absolution, and remission of our sins.

℟. Amen.

Invoke the divine assistance, that you may approach to Jesus Christ.

℣. Deus, tu conversus vivificabis nos.
℟. Et plebs tua lætabitur in te.
℣. Ostende nobis, Domine, misericordiam tuam.
℟. Et Salutare tuum da nobis.

℣. Domine, exaudi orationem meam.

℣. O God, it needs but one look of thine to give us life.
℟. And thy people shall rejoice in thee.
℣. Show us, O Lord, thy mercy.
℟. And give us to know and love the Saviour whom thou hast sent unto us.
℣. O Lord, hear my prayer.

THE ORDINARY OF THE MASS.

℟. And let my cry come unto thee.

℟. Et clamor meus ad te veniat.

The Priest here leaves you to ascend to the altar; but first he salutes you:

℣. The Lord be with you.

℣. Dominus vobiscum.

Answer him with reverence:

℟. And with thy spirit.

℟. Et cum spiritu tuo.

LET US PRAY.

OREMUS.

He ascends the steps, and comes to the Holy of Holies. Ask, both for him and yourself, the deliverance from sin:

Take from our hearts, O Lord, all those sins, which make us unworthy to appear in thy presence, we ask this of thee by thy divine Son, our Lord.

Aufer a nobis quæsumus, Domine, iniquitates nostras; ut ad Sancta sanctorum puris mereamur mentibus introire. Per Christum Dominum nostrum. Amen.

When the Priest kisses the altar, out of reverence for the relics of the Martyrs which are there, say:

Generous soldiers of Jesus Christ, who have mingled your own blood with his, intercede for us that our sins may be forgiven: that so we may, like you, approach unto God.

Oramus te, Domine, per merita sanctorum tuorum, quorum reliquiæ hic sunt, et omnium sanctorum: ut indulgere digneris omnia peccata mea. Amen.

If it be a High Mass at which you are assisting, the Priest incenses the Altar in a most solemn manner; and this white cloud, which you see ascending from every part of the Altar, signifies the prayer of the Church, who addresses herself to Jesus Christ; and which this Divine Mediator then causes to ascend, united with his own, to the throne of the majesty of his Father.

The Priest then says the Introit. It is a solemn opening-anthem, in which the Church, at the very commencement of the Holy Sacrifice, gives expression to the sentiments which fill her heart.

It is followed by nine exclamations, which are even more earnest,—for they ask for mercy. In addressing them to God, the Church unites herself with the nine choirs of Angels, who are standing round the altar of Heaven, one and the same as this before which you are kneeling.

To the Father:

Kyrie eleison.	Lord, have mercy on us!
Kyrie eleison.	Lord, have mercy on us!
Kyrie eleison.	Lord, have mercy on us!

To the Son:

Christe eleison.	Christ, have mercy on us!
Christe eleison.	Christ, have mercy on us!
Christe eleison.	Christ, have mercy on us!

To the Holy Ghost:

Kyrie eleison.	Lord, have mercy on us!
Kyrie eleison.	Lord, have mercy on us!
Kyrie eleison.	Lord, have mercy on us!

As we have already mentioned, the Church abstains, during the Season of Septuagesima, from the heavenly Hymn which the Angels sang over the Crib of the Divine Babe. But, if she be keeping the Feast of a Saint, she recites this beautiful Canticle on that day. The beginning of the *Angelic Hymn* seems more suitable for heavenly than for earthly voices; but the second part is in no ways out of keeping with the sinner's wants and fears, for we there remind the Son of the Eternal Father that he is the *Lamb*, who came down from heaven that he might *take away the sins of the world*. We beseech him to *have mercy on us*, and *receive our humble prayer*. Let us foster these sentiments within us, for they are so appropriate to the present Season.

THE ANGELIC HYMN.

Glory be to God on high, and on earth peace to men of good will.

We praise thee: we bless thee: we adore thee: we glorify thee: we give thee thanks for thy great glory.

O Lord God, Heavenly King, God the Father Almighty.

O Lord Jesus Christ, the only begotten Son.

O Lord God, *Lamb of God*, Son of the Father.

Who takest away the sins of the world have mercy on us.

Who takest away the sins of the world, receive our humble prayer.

Who sittest at the right hand of the Father, have mercy on us.

For thou alone art holy, thou alone art Lord, thou alone, O Jesus Christ, together with the Holy Ghost, art most high, in the glory of God the Father. Amen.

Gloria in excelsis Deo, et in terra pax hominibus bonæ voluntatis.

Laudamus te: benedicimus te: adoramus te: glorificamus te: gratias agimus tibi propter magnam gloriam tuam.

Domine Deus Rex cœlestis, Deus Pater omnipotens.

Domine, Fili unigenite, Jesu Christe.

Domine Deus, Agnus Dei, Filius Patris.

Qui tollis peccata mundi, miserere nobis.

Qui tollis peccata mundi, suscipe deprecationem nostram.

Qui sedes ad dexteram Patris, miserere nobis.

Quoniam tu solus sanctus, tu solus Dominus, tu solus Altissimus, Jesu Christe, cum Sancto Spiritu, in gloria Dei Patris. Amen.

The Priest then turns towards the people, and again salutes them, as it were to make sure of their pious attention to the sublime act, for which all this is but the preparation.

Then follows the *Collect* or *Prayer*, in which the Church formally expresses to the divine Majesty the special intentions she has in the Mass which is being celebrated. You may unite in this prayer, by reciting with the Priest the Collects which you will find in their proper places: but on no account omit to join with the server of the Mass in answering *Amen.*

After this, comes the *Epistle,* which is, generally, a portion of one or other of the Epistles of the Apostles, or a passage from some Book of the Old Testament. Whilst it is being read, ask of God that you may profit of the instructions it conveys.

The *Gradual* is an intermediate formula of prayer between the Epistle and Gospel. It again brings to us the sentiments already expressed in the Introit. Read it with devotion, that so you may enter more and more into the spirit of the mystery proposed to you by the Church.

During every other portion of her Year, the Church here repeats her joyous *Alleluia;* but now she denies herself this demonstration of gladness, until such time as her Divine Spouse has passed through that sea of bitterness, into which our sins have plunged him. Instead of the *Alleluia,* then, she sings in a plaintive tone some verses from the Psalms, appropriate to the rest of that day's Office. This is the *Tract,* of which we have already spoken.

If it be a *High Mass,* the Deacon, meanwhile, prepares to fulfil his noble office,—that of announcing the *Good Tidings* of salvation. He prays God to cleanse his heart and lips. Then kneeling before the Priest, he asks a blessing; and, having received it, at once goes to the place where he is to sing the Gospel.

As a preparation for hearing it worthily, you may thus pray, together with both Priest and Deacon :

Munda cor meum, ac labia mea, Omnipotens Deus, qui labia Isaiæ Prophetæ calculo mundasti ignito: ita me tua grata miseratione	Alas! these ears of mine are but too often defiled with the world's vain words: cleanse them, O Lord, that so I may hear the words of eternal life,

and treasure them in my heart. Through our Lord Jesus Christ. Amen.	dignare mundare, ut sanctum Evangelium tuum digne valeam nuntiare. Per Christum Dominum nostrum. Amen.
Grant to thy ministers thy grace, that they may faithfully explain thy law; that so all, both pastors and flock, may be united to thee for ever. Amen.	Dominus sit in corde meo, et in labiis meis: ut digne et competenter annuntiem Evangelium suum: In nomine Patris, et Filii, et Spiritus Sancti. Amen.

You will stand during the Gospel, as though you were waiting the orders of your Lord; and at the commencement, make the sign of the Cross on your forehead, lips, and breast; and then listen to every word of the Priest or Deacon. Let your heart be ready and obedient. *Whilst my beloved was speaking,* says the Spouse in the Canticle, *my soul melted within me.*[1] If you have not such love as this, have at least the humble submission of Samuel, and say: *Speak, Lord! thy servant heareth.*[2]

After the Gospel, if the Priest says the Symbol of Faith, the *Credo,* you will say it with him. Faith is that gift of God, without which we cannot please him. It is Faith that makes us see *the Light which shineth in darkness,* and which *the darkness* of unbelief *did not comprehend.* It is Faith alone that teaches us what we are, whence we come, and the end for which we are made. It alone can point out to us the path whereby we may return to our God, when once we have separated ourselves from him. Let us love this admirable Faith, which, if we but make it fruitful by good works, will save us. Let us, then, say with the Catholic Church, our Mother:

THE NICENE CREED.

I believe in one God, the Father Almighty, maker of	Credo in unum Deum, Patrem omnipotentem, fac-

---

[1] Cant. v. 6.   [2] 1 Kings, iii. 10.

torem cœli et terræ, visibilium omnium et invisibilium.

Et in unum Dominum Jesum Christum, Filium Dei unigenitum. Et ex Patre natum ante omnia sæcula, Deum de Deo, lumen de lumine, Deum verum de Deo vero. Genitum non factum, consubstantialem Patri, per quem omnia facta sunt. Qui propter nos homines, et propter nostram salutem, descendit de cœlis. Et incarnatus est de Spiritu Sancto, ex Maria Virgine; ET HOMO FACTUS EST. Crucifixus etiam pro nobis sub Pontio Pilato, passus, et sepultus est. Et resurrexit tertia die, secundum Scripturas. Et ascendit in cœlum; sedet ad dexteram Patris. Et iterum venturus est cum gloria judicare vivos et mortuos; cujus regni non erit finis.

Et in Spiritum Sanctum, Dominum et vivificantem, qui ex Patre Filioque procedit. Qui cum Patre et Filio simul adoratur, et conglorificatur; qui locutus est per Prophetas. Et unam sanctam Catholicam et Apostolicam Ecclesiam. Confiteor unum Baptisma in remissionem peccatorum. Et exspecto resurrectionem mortuorum, et vitam venturi sæculi. Amen.

And in one Lord Jesus Christ, the only begotten Son of God. And born of the Father before all ages; God of God, light of light; true God of true God. Begotten, not made; consubstantial to the Father, by whom all things were made. Who for us men, and for our salvation, came down from heaven. And became incarnate by the Holy Ghost of the Virgin Mary; AND WAS MADE MAN. He was crucified also for us, under Pontius Pilate, suffered, and was buried. And the third day he rose again, according to the Scriptures. And ascended into heaven, sitteth at the right hand of the Father. And he is to come again with glory, to judge the living and the dead; of whose kingdom there shall be no end.

And in the Holy Ghost, the Lord and giver of life, who proceedeth from the Father and the Son. Who together with the Father and the Son, is adored and glorified; who spoke by the Prophets. And one holy Catholic and Apostolic Church. I confess one Baptism for the remission of sins. And I expect the resurrection of the dead, and the life of the world to come. Amen.

The Priest and the people should, by this time, have their hearts ready: it is time to prepare the offering itself. And here we come to the second part of the Holy Mass, which is called the *Oblation*, and which immediately follows that, which was called the *Mass of Catechumens*, on account of its being formerly the only part, at which the candidates for Baptism had a right to be present.

See, then, dear Christians! bread and wine are about to be offered to God, as being the noblest of inanimate creatures, since they are made for the nourishment of man; and even that is only a poor material image of what they are destined to become in our Christian Sacrifice. Their substance will soon give place to God himself, and of themselves nothing will remain but the appearances. Happy creatures, thus to yield up their own being, that God may take its place! We, too, are to undergo a like transformation, when, as the Apostle expresses it, *that which to us is mortal, shall put on immortality.*[1] Until that happy change shall be realised, let us offer ourselves to God, as often as we see the bread and wine presented to him in the Holy Sacrifice; and let us glorify Him, who, by assuming our human nature, has made us *partakers of the divine nature.*[2]

The Priest again turns to the people with the usual salutation, as though he would warn them to redouble their attention. Let us read the Offertory with him, and when he offers the Host to God, let us unite with him in saying:

All that we have, O Lord, comes from thee, and belongs to thee; it is just, therefore, that we return it unto thee. But how wonderful art thou in the inventions of thy immense love! This bread which we are offering to thee, is to give place, in a few	Suscipe, sancte Pater, omnipotens æterne Deus, hanc immaculatam hostiam, quam ego indignus famulus tuus offero tibi Deo meo vivo et vero, pro innumerabilibus peccatis et offensionibus et negligentiis meis, et pro omnibus circumstan-

[1] 1 Cor. xv. 53. [2] 2 St. Pet. i. 4.

tibus, sed et pro omnibus fidelibus christianis vivis atque defunctis; ut mihi et illis proficiat ad salutem in vitam æternan. Amen.

moments, to the sacred Body of Jesus. We beseech thee, receive, together with this oblation, our hearts which long to live by thee, and to cease to live their own life of self.

When the Priest puts the wine into the chalice, and then mingles with it a drop of water, let your thoughts turn to the divine mystery of the Incarnation, which is the source of our hope and our salvation; and say:

Deus qui humanæ substantiæ dignitatem mirabiliter condidisti, et mirabilius reformasti: da nobis per hujus aquæ et vini mysterium, ejus divinitatis esse consortes, qui humanitatis nostræ fieri dignatus est particeps, Jesus Christus Filius tuus Dominus noster: qui tecum vivit et regnat in unitate Spiritus Sancti Deus, per omnia sæcula sæculorum. Amen.

O Lord Jesus, who art *the true Vine*, and whose Blood, like a generous wine, has been poured forth under the pressure of the Cross! thou hast deigned to unite thy divine nature to our weak humanity, which is signified by this drop of water. O come and make us partakers of thy divinity, by showing thyself to us in thy sweet and wondrous visit.

The Priest then offers the mixture of wine and water, beseeching God graciously to accept this oblation, which is so soon to be changed into the reality, of which it is now but the figure. Meanwhile, say, in union with the Priest:

Offerimus tibi, Domine, calicem salutaris, tuam deprecantes clementiam: ut in conspectu divinæ Majestatis tuæ, pro nostra et totius mundi salute, cum odore suavitatis ascendat. Amen.

Graciously accept these gifts, O sovereign Creator of all things. Let them be fitted for the divine transformation, which will make them, from being mere offerings of created things, the instrument of the world's salvation.

After having thus held up the sacred gifts towards heaven, the Priest bows down: let us, also, humble ourselves, and say:

Though daring, as we do, to approach thy altar, O Lord, we cannot forget that we are sinners. Have mercy on us, and delay not to send us thy Son, who is our saving Host.	In spiritu humilitatis, et in animo contrito suscipiamur a te, Domine: et sic fiat sacrificium nostrum in conspectu tuo hodie, ut placeat tibi, Domine Deus.

Let us next invoke the Holy Ghost, whose operation is about to produce on the altar the presence of the Son of God, as it did in the womb of the Blessed Virgin Mary, in the divine mystery of the Incarnation:

Come, O Divine Spirit, make fruitful the offering which is upon the altar, and produce in our hearts Him whom they desire.	Veni, Sanctificator omnipotens æterne Deus, et benedic hoc sacrificium tuo sancto nomini præparatum.

If it be a High Mass, the Priest, before proceeding any further with the Sacrifice, takes the thurible a second time. He first incenses the bread and wine which have been just offered, and then the altar itself; hereby inviting the faithful to make their prayer, which is signified by the incense, more and more fervent, the nearer the solemn moment approaches.

But the thought of his own unworthiness becomes more intense than ever in the heart of the Priest. The public confession, which he made at the foot of the altar, is not enough; he would now, at the altar itself, express to the people, in the language of a solemn rite, how far he knows himself to be from that spotless sanctity, wherewith he should approach to God. He washes his *hands*. Our hands signify our *works*; and the Priest, though by his priesthood he bear the office of Jesus Christ, is, by his works, but man. Seeing your Father thus humble himself, do you also make an act of humility, and say with him these verses of the Psalm.

PSALM 25.

Lavabo inter innocentes manus meas: et circumdabo altare tuum, Domine.

Ut audiam vocem laudis: et enarrem universa mirabilia tua.

Domine, dilexi decorem domus tuæ, et locum habitationis gloriæ tuæ.

Ne perdas cum impiis, Deus, animam meam, et cum viris sanguinum vitam meam.

In quorum manibus iniquitates sunt: dextera eorum repleta est muneribus.

Ego autem in innocentia mea ingressus sum: redime me, et miserere mei.

Pes meus stetit in directo: in ecclesiis benedicam te, Domine.

Gloria Patri, et Filio, et Spiritui Sancto.

Sicut erat in principio, et nunc, et semper, et in sæcula sæculorum. Amen.

I, too, would wash my hands, O Lord, and become like unto those who are innocent, that so I may be worthy to come near thy altar, and hear thy sacred Canticles, and then go and proclaim to the world the wonders of thy goodness. I love the beauty of thy House, which thou art about to make the dwelling-place of thy glory. Leave me not, O God, in the midst of them that are enemies both to thee and me. Thy mercy having separated me from them, I entered on the path of innocence, and was restored to thy grace; but have pity on my weakness still; redeem me yet more, thou who hast so mercifully brought me back to the right path. In the midst of these thy faithful people, I give thee thanks. Glory be to the Father and to the Son, and to the Holy Ghost; as it was in the beginning, is now, and ever shall be, world without end. Amen.

The Priest, taking encouragement from the act of humility he has just made, returns to the middle of the altar, and bows down full of respectful awe, begging of God to receive graciously the Sacrifice which is about to be offered to him, and expresses the intentions for which it is offered. Let us do the same.

THE ORDINARY OF THE MASS.

O Holy Trinity, graciously accept the Sacrifice we have begun. We offer it in remembrance of the Passion, Resurrection, and Ascension of our Lord Jesus Christ. Permit thy Church to join with this intention that of honouring the ever glorious Virgin Mary, the Blessed Baptist John, the holy Apostles Peter and Paul, the Martyrs whose relics lie here under our altar awaiting their resurrection, and the Saints whose memory we this day celebrate. Increase the glory they are enjoying, and receive the prayers they address to thee for us.

Suscipe, sancta Trinitas, hanc oblationem, quam tibi offerimus ob memoriam Passionis, Resurrectionis, et Ascensionis Jesu Christi Domini nostri : et in honore beatæ Mariæ semper Virginis, et beati Joannis Baptistæ, et sanctorum Apostolorum Petri et Pauli, et istorum, et omnium Sanctorum : ut illis proficiat ad honorem, nobis autem ad salutem : et illi pro nobis intercedere dignentur in cœlis, quorum memoriam agimus in terris. Per eumdem Christum Dominum nostrum. Amen.

The Priest again turns to the people ; it is for the last time before the sacred Mysteries are accomplished. He feels anxious to excite the fervour of the people. Neither does the thought of his own unworthiness leave him ; and before entering the cloud with the Lord, he seeks support in the prayers of his brethren who are present. He says to them :

Brethren, pray that my Sacrifice, which is yours also, may be acceptable to God, our Almighty Father.

Orate, fratres : ut meum ac vestrum sacrificium acceptabile fiat apud Deum Patrem omnipotentem.

This request made, he turns again to the altar, and you will see his face no more, until our Lord himself shall have come down from heaven upon that same altar. Assure the Priest that he has your prayers, and say to him :

May our Lord accept this Sacrifice at thy hands, to the praise and glory of his name, and for our benefit and that of his holy Church throughout the world.

Suscipiat Dominus sacrificium de manibus tuis, ad laudem et gloriam nominis sui, ad utilitatem quoque nostram totiusque Ecclesiæ suæ sanctæ.

Here the Priest recites the prayers called *the Secrets*, in which he presents the petition of the whole Church for God's acceptance of the Sacrifice, and then immediately begins to fulfil that great duty of religion,—*Thanksgiving*. So far he has adored God, and has sued for mercy; he has still to give thanks for the blessings bestowed on us by the bounty of our heavenly Father, and expressly for that chiefest of all his gifts—the Messias. We are on the point of receiving a new visit of this Son of God; the Priest, in the name of the Church, is about to give expression to the gratitude of all mankind. In order to excite the Faithful to that intensity of gratitude which is due to God for all his gifts, he interrupts his own and their silent prayer by terminating it aloud, saying:

Per omnia sæcula sæculorum!

For ever and ever!

In the same feeling, answer your *Amen!* Then he continues:

℣. Dominus vobiscum.
℟. Et cum spiritu tuo.
℣. Sursum corda!

℣. The Lord be with you.
℟. And with thy spirit.
℣. Lift up your hearts!

Let your response be sincere:

℟. Habemus ad Dominum.

℟. We have them fixed on God.

And when he adds:

℣. Gratias agamus Domino Deo nostro.

℣. Let us give thanks to the Lord our God.

Answer him with all the earnestness of your soul:

℟. Dignum et justum est.

℟. It is meet and just.

THE ORDINARY OF THE MASS.

Then the Priest:

THE PREFACE

(For the Sundays.)

It is truly meet and just, right and available to salvation, that we should always and in all places give thanks to thee, O Holy Lord, Father Almighty, Eternal God. Who together with thy Only Begotten Son and the Holy Ghost art one God and one Lord: not in a singularity of one Person, but in a Trinity of one substance. For what we believe of thy glory, as thou hast revealed, the same we believe of thy Son and of the Holy Ghost, without any difference or distinction. So that in the confession of the true and eternal Deity, we adore a distinction in the Persons, an unity in the essence, and an equality in the Majesty. Whom the Angels and Archangels, the Cherubim also and Seraphim praise, and cease not daily to cry out with one voice, saying, Holy, &c.

Vere dignum et justum est, æquum et salutare, nos tibi semper, et ubique gratias agere, Domine sancte, Pater omnipotens, æterne Deus. Qui cum unigenito Filio tuo et Spiritu Sancto unus es Deus, unus es Dominus: non in unius singularitate Personæ, sed in unius Trinitate substantiæ. Quod enim de tuâ gloriâ, revelante te, credimus, hoc de Filio tuo, hoc de Spiritu Sancto, sine differentiâ discretionis sentimus. Ut in confessione veræ, sempiternæque Deitatis, et in Personis proprietas, et in essentiâ unitas, et in Majestate adoretur æqualitas. Quam laudant Angeli atque Archangeli, Cherubim quoque ac Seraphim; qui non cessant clamare quotidiè, unâ voce dicentes, Sanctus, &c.

THE PREFACE

(For the Week-days.)

It is truly meet and just, right and available to salvation, that we should always and in all places give thanks to thee, O Holy Lord, Father Almighty, Eternal God: through Christ our Lord; by whom the

Vere dignum et justum est, æquum et salutare, nos tibi semper et ubique gratias agere: Domine sancte, Pater omnipotens, æterne Deus, per Christum Dominum nostrum; per quem majes-

tatem tuam laudant Angeli, adorant Dominationes, tremunt Potestates, Cœli, cœlorumque Virtutes, ac beata Seraphim, socia exsultatione concelebrant. Cum quibus et nostras voces, ut admitti jubeas deprecamur, supplici confessione dicentes.	Angels praise thy majesty, the Dominations adore it, the Powers tremble before it; the Heavens and the heavenly Virtues, and the blessed Seraphim, with common jubilee, glorify it. Together with whom, we beseech thee that we may be admitted to join our humble voices, saying:

Here unite with the Priest, who, on his part, unites himself with the blessed Spirits, in giving thanks to God for the unspeakable Gift: bow down and say:

Sanctus, Sanctus, Sanctus, Dominus Deus sabaoth! Pleni sunt cœli et terræ gloria tua. Hosanna in excelsis! Benedictus qui venit in nomine Domini. Hosanna in excelsis!	Holy, Holy, Holy, Lord God of hosts! Heaven and earth are full of thy glory. Hosanna in the highest! Blessed be the Saviour who is coming to us in the name of the Lord who sends him. Hosanna be to him in the highest!

After these words commences the *Canon*, that mysterious prayer, in the midst of which heaven bows down to earth, and God descends unto us. The voice of the Priest is no longer heard; yea, even at the altar, all is silence. Let a profound respect stay all distractions, and keep our senses in submission to the soul. Let us fix our eyes on what the Priest does in the Holy Place.

THE CANON OF THE MASS.

In this mysterious colloquy with the great God of heaven and earth, the first prayer of the sacrificing Priest is for the Catholic Church, his and our Mother.

THE ORDINARY OF THE MASS. 51

O God, who manifestest thyself unto us by means of the mysteries which thou hast entrusted to thy holy Church, our Mother; we beseech thee, by the merits of this sacrifice, that thou wouldst remove all those hindrances which oppose her during her pilgrimage in this world. Give her peace and unity. Do thou thyself guide our Holy Father the Pope, thy Vicar on earth. Direct thou our Bishop, who is our sacred link of unity; and watch over all the orthodox children of the Catholic Apostolic Roman Church.	Te igitur, clementissime Pater, per Jesum Christum Filium tuum Dominum nostrum, supplices rogamus ac petimus, uti accepta habeas, et benedicas hæc dona, hæc munera, hæc sancta sacrificia illibata, in primis quæ tibi offerimus pro Ecclesia tua sancta Catholica: quam pacificare, custodire, adunare, et regere digneris toto orbe terrarum, una cum famulo tuo Papa nostro N., et Antistite nostro N., et omnibus orthodoxis, atque catholicæ et apostolicæ fidei cultoribus.

Here pray, together with the Priest, for those whose interests should be dearest to you.

Permit me, O God, to intercede with thee in more earnest prayer for those, for whom thou knowest that I have a special obligation to pray: * * * Pour down thy blessings upon them. Let them partake of the fruits of this divine Sacrifice, which is offered unto thee in the name of all mankind. Visit them by thy grace, pardon them their sins, grant them the blessings of this present life and of that which is eternal.	Memento, Domine, famulorum famularumque tuarum N. et N., et omnium circumstantium, quorum tibi fides cognita est, et nota devotio : pro quibus tibi offerimus, vel qui tibi offerunt hoc sacrificium laudis, pro se, suisque omnibus, pro redemptione animarum suarum, pro spe salutis et incolumitatis suæ ; tibique reddunt vota sua æterno Deo, vivo et vero.

Here let us commemorate the Saints: they are that portion of the Body of Jesus Christ, which is called the *Church Triumphant*.

But the offering of this Sacrifice, O my God, does not unite us with those only of our	Communicantes, et memoriam venerantes, in primis gloriosæ semper Virgi-

nis Mariæ, Genitricis Dei et Domini nostri Jesu Christi: sed et beatorum Apostolorum ac Martyrum tuorum, Petri et Pauli, Andreæ, Jacobi, Joannis, Thomæ, Jacobi, Philippi, Bartholomæi, Matthæi, Simonis, et Thaddæi: Lini, Cleti, Clementis, Xysti, Cornelii, Cypriani, Laurentii, Chrysogoni, Joannis et Pauli, Cosmæ et Damiani, et omnium sanctorum tuorum, quorum meritis precibusque concedas, ut in omnibus protectionis tuæ muniamur auxilio. Per eumdem Christum Dominum nostrum. Amen.

brethren who are still in this transient life of trial: it brings us closer to those also, who are already in possession of heaven. Therefore it is, that we wish to honour by it the memory of the glorious and ever Virgin Mary, of whom Jesus was born to us; of the Apostles, Confessors, Virgins, and of all the Saints; that so they may assist us, by their powerful intercession, to become worthy to contemplate thee, as they now do, in the mansion of thy glory.

The priest, who, up to this time, had been praying with his hands extended, now joins them, and holds them over the bread and wine, as the High Priest of the Old Law did over the figurative victim: he thus expresses his intention of bringing these gifts more closely under the notice of the Divine Majesty, and of marking them as the material offering whereby we profess our *dependence,* and which is, in a few instants, to yield its place to the living Host, upon whom all our iniquities are to be laid.

Hanc igitur oblationem servitutis nostræ, sed et cunctæ familiæ tuæ, quæsumus Domine, ut placatus accipias: diesque nostros in tua pace disponas, atque ab æterna damnatione nos eripi, et in electorum tuorum jubeas grege numerari. Per Christum Dominum nostrum. Amen.
Quam oblationem tu Deus in omnibus quæsumus, be-

Vouchsafe, O God, to accept this offering which this thy assembled family presents to thee as the homage of its most happy servitude. In return, give us peace, save us from thy wrath, and number us among thy elect, through Him who is coming to us—thy Son our Saviour.

Yea, Lord, this is the moment when this bread is to

THE ORDINARY OF THE MASS. 53

become his sacred Body, which is our food; and this wine is to be changed into his Blood, which is our drink. Ah! delay no longer, but send to us this divine Son our Saviour!	nedictam, adscriptam, ratam, rationabilem, acceptabilemque facere digneris; ut nobis Corpus et Sanguis fiat dilectissimi Filii tui Domini nostri Jesu Christi.

And here the Priest ceases to act as man; he now becomes more than a mere minister of the Church. His word becomes that of Jesus Christ, with all its power and efficacy. Prostrate yourself in profound adoration; for God himself is about to descend upon our Altar, coming down from heaven.

What, O God of heaven and earth, my Jesus, the long expected Messias, what else can I do at this solemn moment but adore thee, in silence, as my sovereign Master, and open my whole heart to thee, as to its dearest King! Come, then, Lord Jesus, come!	Qui pridie quam pateretur, accepit panem in sanctas ac venerabiles manus suas: et elevatis oculis in cœlum, ad te Deum Patrem suum omnipotentem, tibi gratias agens, benedixit, fregit, deditque discipulis suis, dicens: Accipite, et manducate ex hoc omnes. Hoc EST ENIM CORPUS MEUM.

The Divine Lamb is now lying on our Altar! Glory and love be to him for ever! But he is come, that he may be immolated. Hence, the Priest, who is the minister of the will of the Most High, immediately pronounces over the Chalice those sacred words, which will produce the great mystical immolation, by the separation of the Victim's Body and Blood. The substances of bread and wine have ceased to exist: the species alone are left, veiling, as it were, the Body and Blood, lest fear should keep us from a mystery, which God gives us in order to give us confidence. Let us associate ourselves to the Angels, who tremblingly look upon this deepest wonder.

Simili modo postquam cœnatum est, accipiens et hunc præclarum Calicem in sanctas ac venerabiles manus suas: item tibi gratias agens, benedixit, deditque discipulis suis, dicens: Accipite et bibite ex eo omnes. HIC EST ENIM CALIX SANGUINIS MEI, NOVI ET ÆTERNI TESTAMENTI: MYSTERIUM FIDEI: QUI PRO VOBIS ET PRO MULTIS EFFUNDETUR IN REMISSIONEM PECCATORUM. Hæc quotiescumque feceritis, in mei memoriam facietis.

O Precious Blood! thou price of my salvation! I adore thee! Wash away my sins, and give me a purity above the whiteness of snow. Lamb ever slain, yet ever living, thou comest to take away the sins of the world! Come also and reign in me by thy power and by thy love.

The Priest is now face to face with God. He again raises his hands towards heaven, and tells our heavenly Father, that the oblation, now on the altar, is no longer an earthly offering, but the Body and Blood, the whole Person, of his divine Son.

Unde et memores, Domine, nos servi tui, sed et plebs tua sancta, ejusdem Christi Filii tui Domini nostri tam beatæ Passionis, necnon et ab inferis Resurrectionis, sed et in cœlos gloriosæ Ascensionis: offerimus præclaræ majestati tuæ de tuis donis ac datis Hostiam puram, Hostiam sanctiam, Hostiam immaculatam: Panem sanctum vitæ æternæ, et Calicem salutis perpetuæ.

Supra quæ propitio ac sereno vultu respicere digneris: et accepta habere, sicuti accepta habere dignatus es munera pueri tui justi Abel, et sacrificium Patri-

Father of infinite holiness, the Host so long expected is here before thee! Behold this thy eternal Son, who suffered a bitter passion, rose again with glory from the grave, and ascended triumphantly into heaven. He is thy Son; but he is also our Host, Host pure and spotless, —our Meat and Drink of everlasting life.

Heretofore thou didst accept the sacrifice of the innocent lambs offered to thee by Abel; and the sacrifice which Abraham made thee of his son Isaac, who, though immolated,

THE ORDINARY OF THE MASS. 55

yet lived; and, lastly, the sacrifice, which Melchisedech presented thee, of bread and wine. Receive our Sacrifice, which is above all those others. It is the Lamb, of whom all others could be but figures: it is the undying Victim: it is the Body of thy Son, who is the Bread of Life, and his Blood, which, whilst a Drink of immortality for us, is a tribute adequate to thy glory.

archæ nostri Abrahæ, et quod tibi obtulit summus Sacerdos tuus Melchisedech, sanctum sacrificium, immaculatam hostiam.

The Priest bows down to the altar, and kisses it as the throne of love on which is seated the Saviour of men.

But, O God of infinite power, these sacred gifts are not only on this altar here below; they are also on that sublime Altar of heaven, which is before the throne of thy divine Majesty. These two altars are but one and the same, on which is accomplished the great mystery of thy glory and our salvation. Vouchsafe to make us partakers of the Body and Blood of the august Victim, from whom flow every grace and blessing.

Supplices te rogamus, omnipotens Deus: jube hæc perferri per manus sancti Angeli tui in sublime Altare tuum, in conspectu divinæ Majestatis tuæ: ut quotquot ex hac altaris participatione, sacrosanctum Filii tui Corpus et Sanguinem sumpserimus, omni benedictione cœlesti et gratia repleamur. Per eumdem Christum Dominum nostrum. Amen.

Nor is the moment less favourable for making supplication for the Church Suffering. Let us, therefore, ask the divine Liberator, who has come down among us, that he mercifully visit, by a ray of his consoling light, the dark abode of Purgatory, and permit his Blood to flow, as a stream of mercy's dew, from this our altar, and refresh the panting captives there. Let us pray expressly for those among them, who have a claim on our suffrages.

Memento etiam, Domine, famulorum famularumque tuarum N. et N., qui nos præcesserunt cum signo fidei, et dormiunt in somno pacis. Ipsis Domine, et omnibus in Christo quiescentibus, locum refrigerii, lucis et pacis, ut indulgeas, deprecamur. Per eumdem Christum Dominum nostrum. Amen.

Dear Jesus! let the happiness of this thy visit extend to every portion of thy Church. Thy face gladdens the elect in the holy City; even our mortal eyes can see beneath the veil of our delighted faith; ah! hide not thyself from those brethren of ours, who are imprisoned in the place of expiation. Be thou refreshment to them in their flames, light in their darkness, and peace in their agonies of torment.

This duty of charity fulfilled, let us pray for ourselves, sinners, alas! and who profit so little by the visit, which our Saviour pays us. Let us, together with the Priest, strike our breast, saying:

Nobis quoque peccatoribus famulis tuis, de multitudine miserationum tuarum sperantibus, partem aliquam et societatem donare digneris cum tuis sanctis Apostolis et Martyribus: cum Joanne, Stephano, Mathia, Barnaba, Ignatio, Alexandro, Marcellino, Petro, Felicitate, Perpetua, Agatha, Lucia, Agnete, Cæcilia, Anastasia, et omnibus Sanctis tuis; intra quorum nos consortium, non æstimator meriti, sed veniæ, quæsumus, largitor admitte. Per Christum Dominum nostrum. Per quem hæc omnia, Domine, semper bona creas, sanctificas, vivificas, benedicis, et præstas nobis: per ipsum, et cum ipso et in ipso, est tibi Deo Patri omnipotenti, in unitate Spiritus Sancti, omnis honor et gloria.

Alas! we are poor sinners, O God of all sanctity! yet do we hope that thy infinite mercy will grant us to share in thy kingdom, not, indeed, by reason of our works, which deserve little more than punishment, but because of the merits of this Sacrifice, which we are offering to thee. Remember, too, the merits of thy holy Apostles, of thy holy Martyrs, of thy holy Virgins, and of all thy Saints. Grant us, by their intercession, grace in this world, and glory eternal in the next: which we ask of thee, in the name of our Lord Jesus Christ, thy Son. It is by him thou bestowest upon us thy blessings of life and sanctification; and by him also, with him, and in him, in the unity of the Holy Ghost, may honour and glory be to thee!

THE ORDINARY OF THE MASS. 57

Whilst saying these last few words, the Priest has taken up the sacred Host, which was on the altar; he has held it over the chalice, thus re-uniting the Body and Blood of the divine Victim, in order to show that He is now immortal. Then raising up both Chalice and Host, he offers to God the most noble and perfect homage which the divine Majesty could receive.

This solemn and mysterious rite ends the Canon. The silence of the Mysteries is broken. The Priest concludes his long prayers, by saying aloud, and so giving the faithful the opportunity of expressing their desire that his supplications be granted:

For ever and ever.	Per omnia sæcula sæculorum.

Answer him with faith, and in a sentiment of union with your holy Mother the Church:

Amen! I believe the mystery which has just been accomplished. I unite myself to the offering which has been made, and to the petitions of the Church.	Amen.

It is time to recite the Prayer, which our Saviour himself has taught us. Let it ascend up to heaven together with the sacrifice of the Body and Blood of Jesus Christ. How could it be otherwise than heard, when he himself who made it for us, is in our very hands now whilst we say it? As this prayer belongs in common to all God's children, the Priest recites it aloud, and begins by inviting us all to join in it.

LET US PRAY.	OREMUS.
Having been taught by a saving precept, and following the form given us by a divine instruction, we thus presume to speak:	Præceptis salutaribus moniti, et divina institutione formati, audemus dicere:

THE LORD'S PRAYER.

Pater noster, qui es in cœlis : Sanctificetur nomen tuum : Adveniat regnum tuum : Fiat voluntas tua, sicut in cœlo, et in terra : Panem nostrum quotidianum da nobis hodie : Et dimitte nobis debita nostra, sicut et nos dimittimus debitoribus nostris. Et ne nos inducas in tentationem.	Our Father, who art in heaven, hallowed be thy name ; thy kingdom come ; thy will be done on earth as it is in heaven. Give us this day our daily Bread ; *and forgive us our trespasses*, as we forgive them that trespass against us ; and lead us not into temptation.

Let us answer, with deep feeling of our misery :

Sed libera nos a malo.	But deliver us from evil.

The Priest falls once more into the silence of the holy Mysteries. His first word is an affectionate *Amen* to your last petition—*deliver us from evil*—on which he forms his own next prayer : and could he pray for anything more needed ? *Evil* surrounds us everywhere, and the Lamb on our altar has been sent to expiate it and deliver us from it.

Libera nos, quæsumus, Domine, ab omnibus malis, præteritis, præsentibus et futuris : et, intercedente beata et gloriosa semper Virgine Dei Genitrice Maria, cum beatis Apostolis tuis Petro et Paulo, atque Andrea, et omnibus Sanctis, da propitius pacem in diebus nostris : ut ope misericordiæ tuæ adjuti, et a peccato simus semper liberi, et ab omni perturbatione securi. Per eumdem Dominum nostrum Jesum Christum Filium tuum, qui tecum vivit	How many, O Lord, are the evils which beset us ! Evils *past*, which are the wounds left on the soul by our sins, and strengthen her wicked propensities. Evils *present*, that is, the sins now at this very time upon our soul ; the weakness of this poor soul ; and the temptations which molest her. There are, also, *future* evils, that is the chastisement which our sins deserve from the hand of thy justice. In presence of this Host of our Salvation, we beseech thee O Lord, to deliver

THE ORDINARY OF THE MASS. 59

us from all these evils, and to accept in our favour the intercession of Mary the Mother of Jesus, of thy holy Apostles Peter and Paul and Andrew. Liberate us, break our chains, give us peace: through Jesus Christ, thy Son, who with thee liveth and reigneth God.

et regnat in unitate Spiritus Sancti Deus.

The Priest is anxious to announce the Peace, which he has asked and obtained; he therefore finishes his prayer aloud, saying:

World without end.

℞. Amen.

Per omnia sæcula sæculorum.

℞. Amen.

Then he says:

May the Peace of our Lord be ever with you.

Pax Domini sit semper vobiscum.

To this paternal wish, reply:

℞. And with thy spirit.

℞. Et cum spiritu tuo.

The Mystery is drawing to a close: God is about to be united with man, and man with God, by means of Communion. But first, an imposing and sublime rite takes place at the altar. So far the Priest has announced the Death of Jesus; it is time to proclaim his Resurrection. To this end, he reverently breaks the sacred Host; and having divided it into three parts, he puts one into the Chalice, thus reuniting the Body and Blood of the immortal Victim. Do you adore and say:

Glory be to thee, O Saviour of the world, who didst, in thy Passion, permit thy precious Blood to be separated from thy sacred Body, afterwards uniting them again together by thy divine power.

Hæc commixtio et consecratio Corporis et Sanguinis Domini nostri Jesu Christi, fiat accipientibus nobis in vitam æternam. Amen.

Offer now your prayer to the ever-living Lamb, whom St. John saw on the Altar of Heaven *standing, though slain:* say to this your Lord and King, who has taken upon himself all our iniquities, in order to wash them away by his Blood:

Agnus Dei, qui tollis peccata mundi, miserere nobis.	Lamb of God, who takest away the sins of the world, have mercy on us.
Agnus Dei, qui tollis peccata mundi, miserere nobis.	Lamb of God, who takest away the sins of the world, have mercy on us.
Agnus Dei, qui tollis peccata mundi, dona nobis pacem.	Lamb of God, who takest away the sins of the world, give us *Peace.*

Peace is the grand object of our Saviour's coming into the world: he is the *Prince of Peace.* The divine Sacrament of the Eucharist ought therefore to be the Mystery of Peace, and the bond of Catholic Unity; for, as the Apostle says, *all we who partake of one Bread, are all one Bread and one Body.*[2] It is on this account that the Priest, now that he is on the point of receiving, in Communion, the Sacred Host, prays that fraternal Peace may be preserved in the Church, and more especially in this portion of it, which is assembled round the altar. Pray with him, and for the same blessing:

Domine Jesu Christe, qui dixisti Apostolis tuis: Pacem relinquo vobis, pacem meam do vobis: ne respicias peccata mea, sed fidem Ecclesiæ tuæ: eamque secundum voluntatem tuam pacificare, et coadunare digneris. Qui vivis et regnas Deus, per omnia sæcula sæculorum. Amen.	Lord Jesus Christ, who saidst to thy Apostles, "my peace I leave with you, my peace I give unto you:" regard not my sins, but the faith of thy Church, and grant her that peace and unity which is according to thy will. Who livest and reignest God for ever and ever. Amen.

[1] Apoc. v. 6.   [2] 1 Cor. x. 17.

THE ORDINARY OF THE MASS. 61

If it be a High Mass, the Priest here gives the kiss of peace to the Deacon, who gives it to the Sub-Deacon, and he to the Choir. During this ceremony, you should excite within yourself feelings of Christian charity, and pardon your enemies, if you have any. Then continue to pray with the Priest:

Lord Jesus Christ, Son of the living God, who, according to the will of thy Father, through the co-operation of the Holy Ghost, hast by thy death given life to the world; deliver me by this thy most sacred Body and Blood from all my iniquities, and from all evils; and make me always adhere to thy commandments, and never suffer me to be separated from thee, who with the same God the Father and the Holy Ghost, livest and reignest God for ever and ever. Amen.	Domine Jesu Christe, Fili Dei vivi, qui ex voluntate Patris, cooperante Spiritu Sancto, per mortem tuam mundum vivificasti: libera me per hoc sacrosanctum Corpus, et Sanguinem tuum, ab omnibus iniquitatibus meis, et universis malis, et fac me tuis semper inhærere mandatis, et a te nunquam separari permittas. Qui cum eodem Deo Patre et Spiritu Sancto vivis et regnas Deus in sæcula sæculorum. Amen.

If you are going to Communion at this Mass, say the following Prayer; otherwise prepare yourself to make a Spiritual Communion:

Let not the participation of thy Body, O Lord Jesus Christ, which I, though unworthy, presume to receive, turn to my judgment and condemnation; but through thy mercy may it be a safeguard and remedy both to my soul and body. Who with God the Father, in the unity of the Holy Ghost, livest and reignest God for ever and ever. Amen.	Perceptio Corporis tui Domine Jesu Christe, quod ego indignus sumere præsumo, non mihi proveniat in judicium et condemnationem: sed pro tua pietate prosit mihi ad tutamentum mentis et corporis, et ad medelam percipiendam. Qui vivis et regnas cum Deo Patre in unitate Spiritus Sancti Deus, per omnia sæcula sæculorum. Amen.

When the Priest takes the Host into his hands, in order to his receiving it in Communion, say:

Panem cœlestem accipiam, et nomen Domini invocabo.	Come, my dear Jesus, come!

When he strikes his breast, confessing his unworthiness, say thrice with him these words, and in the same disposition as the Centurion of the Gospel, who first used them:

Domine, non sum dignus, ut intres sub tectum meum: sed tantum dic verbo, et sanabitur anima mea.	Lord, I am not worthy thou shouldst enter under my roof; say it only with one word of thine, and my soul will be healed.

Whilst the Priest receives the sacred Host, if you also are to communicate, adore profoundly your God, who is ready to take up his abode within you, and again say to him with the spouse: *Come, Lord Jesus, come!*

But should you not be going to receive sacramentally, make a Spiritual Communion. Adore Jesus Christ who thus visits your soul by his grace, and say to him:

Corpus Domini nostri Jesu Christi, custodiat animam meam in vitam æternam. Amen.	I give thee, O Jesus, this heart of mine, that thou mayest dwell in it, and do with me what thou wilt.

Then the Priest takes the Chalice, in thanksgiving, and says:

Quid retribuam Domino pro omnibus, quæ retribuit mihi? Calicem salutaris accipiam, et nomen Domini invocabo. Laudans invocabo Dominum, et ab inimicis meis salvus ero.	What return shall I make to the Lord for all he hath given to me? I will take the Chalice of salvation, and will call upon the name of the Lord. Praising I will call upon the Lord, and I shall be saved from mine enemies.

THE ORDINARY OF THE MASS.

But if you are to make a Sacramental Communion, you should, at this moment of the Priest's receiving the precious Blood, again adore the God who is coming to you, and keep to your prayer: *Come, Lord Jesus, come!*

If, on the contrary, you are going to communicate only spiritually, again adore your divine Master, and say to him:

| I unite myself to thee, my beloved Jesus! do thou unite thyself to me! and never let us be separated. | Sanguis Domini nostri Jesu Christi custodiat animam meam in vitam æternam. Amen. |

It is here that you must approach to the altar, if you are going to Communion. The dispositions suitable for Holy Communion, during this season of Septuagesima, are given in the next Chapter.

The Communion being finished, and whilst the Priest is purifying the Chalice the first time, say:

| Thou hast visited me, O God, in these days of my pilgrimage; give me grace to treasure up the fruits of this visit for my future eternity. | Quod ore sumpsimus, Domine, pura mente capiamus: et de munere temporali fiat nobis remedium sempiternum. |

Whilst the Priest is purifying the Chalice the second time, say:

| Be thou for ever blessed, O my Saviour, for having admitted me to the sacred mystery of thy Body and Blood. May my heart and senses preserve, by thy grace, the purity which thou hast imparted to them; and I thus be rendered less unworthy of thy divine visit. | Corpus tuum, Domine, quod sumpsi, et Sanguis quem potavi, adhæreat visceribus meis: et præsta ut in me non remaneat scelerum macula, quem pura et sancta refecerunt Sacramenta. Qui vivis et regnas in sæcula sæculorum. Amen. |

The Priest having read the Antiphon called the *Communion*, which is the first part of his Thanksgiving for the favour just received from God, whereby he has renewed his divine presence among us,—turns to the people with the usual salutation; after which he recites the Prayers, called the *Postcommunion*, which are the completion of the Thanksgiving. You will join him here also, thanking God for the unspeakable gift he has just lavished on you, and asking him, with most earnest entreaty, that he will bestow upon you a lasting spirit of compunction.

These Prayers having been recited, the Priest again turns to the people, and full of joy for the immense favour he and they have been receiving, he says:

| Dominus vobiscum. | The Lord be with you. |

Answer him:

Et cum spiritu tuo.	And with thy spirit.
Ite, Missa est.	Go, the Mass is finished.
℟. Deo gratias.	℟. Thanks be to God.

The Priest makes a last Prayer, before giving you his blessing; pray with him:

| Placeat tibi, sancta Trinitas, obsequium servitutis meæ, quod oculis tuæ majestatis indignus obtuli, tibi sit acceptabile, mihique, et omnibus, pro quibus illud obtuli, sit, te miserante, propitiabile. Per Christum Dominum nostrum. Amen. | Eternal thanks be to thee, O adorable Trinity, for the mercy thou hast showed to me, in permitting me to assist at this divine Sacrifice. Pardon me the negligence and coldness wherewith I have received so great a favour, and deign to confirm the Blessing, which thy Minister is about to give me in thy Name. |

The Priest raises his hand, and thus blesses you:

| Benedicat vos omnipotens Deus, Pater, et Filius, et Spiritus Sanctus. | May the Almighty God, Father, Son, and Holy Ghost, bless you! |
| ℟. Amen. | ℟. Amen. |

THE ORDINARY OF THE MASS. 65

He then concludes the Mass, by reading the first fourteen verses of the Gospel according to St. John, which tell us of the eternity of the Word, and of the mercy which led him to take upon himself our *flesh*, and to *dwell among us*. Pray that you may be of the number of those, who, now that he has come *unto his own, receive him*, and are made *the sons of God*.

℣. The Lord be with you.
℟. And with thy spirit.

℣. Dominus vobiscum.
℟. Et cum spiritu tuo.

THE LAST GOSPEL.

The beginning of the Holy Gospel according to John.

Initium sancti Evangelii secundum Joannem.

Ch. 1.

Cap. 1.

In the beginning was the Word, and the Word was with God, and the Word was God. The same was in the beginning with God. All things were made by him, and without him was made nothing that was made. In him was life, and the life was the light of men; and the light shineth in the darkness, and the darkness did not comprehend it. There was a man sent from God, whose name was John. This man came for a witness, to give testimony of the light, that all men might believe through him. He was not the light, but was to give testimony of the light. That was the true light which enlighteneth every man that cometh into this world. He was in the world, and the world was made by him, and the world knew him not. He came unto his own, and his own received

In principio erat Verbum, et Verbum erat apud Deum, et Deus erat Verbum. Hoc erat in principio apud Deum. Omnia per ipsum facta sunt; et sine ipso factum est nihil. Quod factum est, in ipso vita erat, et vita erat lux hominum: et lux in tenebris lucet, et tenebræ eam non comprehenderunt. Fuit homo missus a Deo, cui nomen erat Joannes. Hic venit in testimonium, ut testimonium perhiberet de lumine, ut omnes crederent per illum. Non erat ille lux, sed ut testimonium perhiberet de lumine. Erat lux vera, quæ illuminat omnem hominem venientem in hunc mundum. In mundo erat, et mundus per ipsum factus est, et mundus eum non cognovit. In propria venit, et sui eum non receperunt. Quotquot autem receperunt eum, dedit eis potestatem filios Dei fieri, his, qui credunt in nomine ejus : qui non ex sanguinibus, neque ex voluntate carnis, neque ex voluntate viri, sed ex Deo nati sunt. ET VERBUM CARO FACTUM EST, et habitavit in nobis : et vidimus gloriam ejus, gloriam quasi Unigeniti a Patre, plenum gratiæ et veritatis.

℞. Deo gratias.

him not. But as many as received him, to them he gave power to be made the sons of God; to them that believe in his name, who are born, not of blood, nor of the will of the flesh, nor of the will of man, but of God. AND THE WORD WAS MADE FLESH, and dwelt among us; and we saw his glory, as it were the glory of the Only-Begotten of the Father, full of grace and truth.

℞. Thanks be to God.

CHAPTER THE SIXTH.

ON HOLY COMMUNION, DURING SEPTUAGESIMA.

We have already said, that the Christian, who, by the meditations suitable to the spirit of Septuagesima, has come to a clearer knowledge, not only of the sad consequences of original sin, but also of the malice of his own personal faults,—should be all the more eager to assist at the Holy Sacrifice, wherein is offered the Victim of man's salvation. But, now that his own unworthiness is more than ever evident to him, ought he to abstain from partaking, by Holy Communion, of this life-giving and purifying Host? Such is not our Saviour's will. He came down from heaven, *not to judge, but to save us.*[1] He knows how long and rugged is the road we have to traverse, before we reach that happy day, on which we shall rest with him, in the joy of his Resurrection. *He has compassion on us;* he fears lest we *faint in the way;*[2] and he, therefore, offers us the divine Food, which gives light and strength to our souls, and refreshes them in their toil. We feel that our hearts are not yet pure enough; let us, then, with an humble and contrite heart, go to him, who is come that he may restore to our souls their original beauty. Let us, at all times, remember the solemn injunction, which this Saviour so graciously deigned to give us: *Except ye eat the Flesh of the Son of Man, ye shall not have life in you.*[3]

If, therefore, sin has no longer dominion over us; if we have destroyed it by true sorrow and sincere

---

[1] St. John, iii. 17.
[2] St. Matth. xv. 32.
[3] St. John, vi. 54.

confession, made efficacious by the absolution of God's Priest;—let us not deprive ourselves of *the Bread of Life*,[1] no matter how great soever our infirmities may seem; for it is for us that our Jesus has prepared the Feast. If we feel that the chains of sin are still upon us; if by self-examination, made with the light of the Truth that is now granted to us, we discover in our souls certain stains, which the false principles of the world and too easy a conscience had hitherto made us wink at;—let us lose no time, let us make a good Confession: and when we have made our peace with the God of mercy, let us approach the Holy Table, and receive the pledge of our reconciliation.

Yes, let us go to Holy Communion, during this season of Septuagesima, with a most heart-felt conviction of our unworthiness. It may be, that hitherto we have sometimes gone with too much familiarity, on account of our not sufficiently understanding our nothingness, our misery, and the infinite holiness of the God, who thus unites himself with his sinful creatures. Henceforth, our heart shall be more truthful; blending together the two sentiments of humility and confidence, we will say, with an honest conviction, those words of the Centurion of the Gospel, which the Church puts upon our lips, when she is distributing to us the Bread of Life: *Lord, I am not worthy that thou shouldst enter under my roof; say but the word, and my soul shall be healed.*[2]

We will here give, as in the two preceding Seasons, Acts which may serve as a preparation for Holy Communion during these weeks of Septuagesima. There are souls that feel the want of some such assistance as this; and, for the same reason, we will add a form of Thanksgiving for after Communion.

---

[1] St. John, vi. 35. [2] St. Matth. viii. 8.

BEFORE COMMUNION.

ACT OF FAITH.

The signal grace which thou, O my God, hast granted to me, that I should know the wounds of my soul, has revealed to me the greatness of my misery. I have been taught how deep was the darkness that covered me, and how much I needed thy Divine Light. But, whilst the torch of Faith has thus shown me the abyss of my own poor nature, it has also taught me how wonderful are the works, which thy love of thy ungrateful creature has made thee undertake, in order that thou mightest raise him up and save him. It was for me thou didst assume my human nature, and wast born at Bethlehem; it is for me that thou art soon to shed thy Blood on the Cross. Thou commandest me to believe these miracles of thy love. I do believe them, O my God, humbly and gratefully. I also believe, and with an equally lively Faith, that in a few moments, thou art to give thyself to me in this ineffable Mystery of Holy Communion. Thou sayest to me: *This is my Body—this is my Blood:*—thy word is enough; in spite of my unworthiness seeming to forbid the possibility of such Communion, I believe, I consent, I bow me down before thine infinite Truth. Oh! can there be Communion between the God of all holiness and a Sinner such as I?— And yet, thou assurest me, that thou art verily coming to me! I tremble, O Eternal Truth—but I believe. I confess that thy love of me is infinite, and that having resolved to give thyself to thy poor and sinful creature, thou wilt suffer no obstacle to stand in thy way!

ACT OF HUMILITY.

During the season just past, I have often contemplated, O my Jesus, thy coming from thy high throne into the bosom of Mary, thy uniting thy divine person to our weak mortal nature, and thy being born in the crib of a poor stable: and when I thought on these humiliations of my God, they taught me not only to love *thee* tenderly, but to know also my own nothingness, for I saw more clearly what an infinite distance there is between the Creature and his Creator; and, seeing these prodigies of thy immense love, I gladly confessed my own vileness. But now, dearest Saviour, I am led to consider something far more humiliating than the lowliness of my nature. That *Nothingness* should be but nothingness; is not a sin. No,—it is my sins that appal me. Sin has so long tyrannised over me; its consequences are still upon me; it has given me such dangerous tendencies; and I am so weak in resisting its bidding. When my first Parent sinned, he hid himself, lest he should meet thee; and thou biddest *me come* unto thee, not to sentence me to the punishment I deserve but to give me, oh! such a mark of love,—union with thyself! Can this be? Art thou not the infinitely holy God?—I must needs yield, and come, for thou art my sovereign Master; and who is there that dares resist thy will? I come, then, humbling myself, even to my very nothingness, before thee, and beseeching thee to pardon my coming, for I come because thou wilt have it so.

ACT OF CONTRITION.

And shall I, O my Jesus, confess thus the grievousness and multitude of my sins, without promising thee to sin no more? Thou wishest this sinner to be reconciled with thee, thou desirest to press him to thy Sacred Heart:—and could *he*, whilst thanking thee for this thy wonderful condescension, still love the accursed cause which made him thine enemy?—No, my infinitely merciful God, no! I will not, like my first Parent, seek to escape thy justice, but, like the Prodigal Son, I will arise and go to my Father; like Magdalene, I will take courage and enter the banquet-hall; and, though trembling at the sight of my sins, I will comply with thy loving invitation. My heart has no further attachment to sin, which I hate and detest as the enemy of thy honour and my own happiness. I am resolved to shun it from this time forward, and to spare no pains to free myself from its tyranny. There shall be no more of that easy life which chilled my love, nor of that studied indifference which dulled my conscience, nor of those dangerous habits which led me to stray from my loyalty to thee. Despise not, O God, this my humble and contrite heart.

ACT OF LOVE.

Such is thy love for us in this world, O my Jesus, that, as thyself sayest, thou art *come not to judge, but to save.* I should not satisfy thee, in this happy Communion hour, were I to offer thee but this salutary fear, which has led me to thy sacred feet, and this shame-stricken conscience, which makes me tremble in thy holy presence. The visit thou art about to pay me, is a visit of Love. The Sacrament, which is going to unite me to thee, is the Sacrament of thy Love. Thou, my Good Shepherd, hast said, that he *loves* most, who has been *forgiven* most. *My* heart then must dare to love thee; it must love thee with all its warmth; the very recollection of its past disloyalty must make its loving thee doubly needed and doubly fervent. Ah! sweet Lord!—see this poor heart of mine; strengthen it, console it, drive away its fears, make it feel that thou art its Jesus! It has come back to thee, because it *feared* thee; if it *love* thee, it will never again leave thee.

And thou, O Mary, *Refuge of Sinners*, help me to love Him, who is thy Son, and our Brother.—Holy Angels!—ye who live eternally on that love, which has never ceased to glow in your mighty spirits,—remember, I reverently pray you, that this God created me, as he did you, that I might love him.—All ye holy Saints of God! I beseech you, by the love wherewith ye are inebriated in heaven, graciously give me a thought, and prepare now my heart to be united with him. Amen.

AFTER COMMUNION.

ACT OF ADORATION.

Thou art here within me, great God of heaven! Thou art, at this moment, residing in a sinner's heart! I, yea, I, am thy temple, thy throne, thy resting-place!—How shall I worthily adore thee, thee that hast deigned to come down into this abyss of my lowliness and misery? The angels veil their faces in thy presence; thy Saints lay their crowns at thy feet; and I, that am but a sinful mortal, how shall I sufficiently honour thee, O Infinite Power, Infinite Wisdom, Infinite Goodness?—This soul, wherein thou art now dwelling, has presumed so many times to set thee at defiance, and boldly disobey and break thy commands. And thou canst come to me after all this, and bring all thy beauty and greatness with thee!—What else can I do, but give thee the homage of a heart, that knows not how to bear the immensity of the honour thou art now lavishing on me? Yes, my own wonderful and loving God, I adore thee; I acknowledge thee to be the Sovereign Being, the Creator and preserver of all creatures, and the undisputed Master of everything that belongs to me. I delightedly confess my dependence on thee, and offer thee, with all my heart, my humble service.

ACT OF THANKSGIVING.

Thy greatness, O my God, is infinite; but thy goodness to me is incomprehensible. Thy being now, present within this breast of mine is, I know, a proof of that immense power, which shows itself where and when it wills; but it is also a mark of thy love for me. Thou art come to my soul, that thou mayest be closely united with her, comfort her, give her a new life, and bring her all good things. Oh! who will teach me how to value this grace, and thank thee for it in a becoming way? But, how shall I hope to value it as I ought, when I am not able to understand either the love, that brings thee thus within me, nor my own need of having thee? And when I think of my inability to make thee a suitable return of thanks, I feel as though I can give thee nothing but my speechless gratitude. Yet thou willest that this my heart, poor as it is, should give thee its thanks; thou takest delight in receiving its worthless homage. Take it, then, my loving Jesus! I give it thee with all possible joy, and beseech thee to reveal unto me the immensity of thy gift, and to *enrich* me more that I may *give* thee more.

ACT OF LOVE.

But nothing will satisfy thee, O my Infinite Treasure unless I give thee my *love*. Thou hast ever loved *me*, and thou art still loving me; I must love thee in return! Thou hast borne with me, thou hast forgiven me, thou art, at this moment, overpowering me with honour and riches; and all this out of love for me! The return thou askest of me, is my *love*. Gratitude will not content thee—thou wilt have my *love!*—But, Jesus, my dear Jesus!—my past life—the long years I have spent in offending thee—rise up before me, and tell me to hide myself from thee! And yet, whither could I go without carrying thee within me, for thou hast taken up thine abode in my inmost soul? No,— I will not run from thee! I will summon all the energies of my heart, to tell thee, that I love thee; that thy love for me has emboldened me; that I belong to thee; that I love thee above all else that I love; and that henceforth, all my joy and happiness shall be in pleasing thee, and doing whatsoever thou askest of me.

ACT OF OBLATION.

I know, dear Jesus, that what thou askest of me is not the passing sentiment of a heart excited by the thought of thy goodness towards it. Thou hast loved me from eternity; thou lovedst me, even when I was doing nothing for thee; thou hast given me light to know my miseries; thou hast shielded me against thine own angry justice; thou hast mercifully pardoned me a countless number of times; thou art even now embracing me with tenderest love;—and all these works of thy almighty hand have been but for one end,—to make me give myself to thee, and live, at last, for thee. It is this thou wouldst obtain of me, by granting me this precious earnest of thy love, which I have just received. Thou hast said, speaking of this ineffable gift: *As I live by the Father; so he that eateth me, the same also shall live by me.*[1] Henceforth, O *Bread, which came down from heaven!*[2] thou art the source of my life. Now, more than ever, my life belongs to thee. I give it unto thee. I dedicate unto thee my soul, my body, my faculties, my whole being. Do thou direct and govern me. I resign myself entirely into thy hands. I am blind, but thy light will guide me; I am weak, but thy power will uphold me; I am inconstant, but thy unchangeableness will give me stability. I trust unreservedly in thy mercy, which never abandons them that hope in thee.

O Mary! pray for me, that I lose not the fruit of this Visit.—Holy Angels! watch over this dwelling-place of your Lord, which he has so mercifully chosen: let nothing defile it.—Oh! all ye Saints of God! pray for the sinner, unto whom he has given this pledge of his Divine pardon.

---

[1] St. John, vi. 58.   [2] *Ibid.* 51.

CHAPTER THE SEVENTH.

OF THE OFFICE OF VESPERS FOR SUNDAYS AND FEASTS,

DURING SEPTUAGESIMA.

The Office of *Vespers*, or *Even-Song*, consists firstly of the Five following Psalms, and Antiphons. According to our custom, we preface each Psalm with a short explanation, in order to draw the attention to what is most in harmony with the spirit of Septuagesima.

After the *Pater* and *Ave* have been said in secret, the Church commences this Hour with her favourite supplication:

℣. Deus' in adjutorium meum intende.
℟. Domine, ad adjuvandum me festina.
Gloria Patri, et Filio, et Spiritui Sancto:

Sicut erat in principio et nunc et semper, et in sæcula sæculorum. Amen.
Laus tibi, Domine, Rex æternæ gloriæ.
ANT. Dixit Dominus.

℣. Incline unto my aid, O God.
℟. O Lord, make haste to help me.
Glory be to the Father, and to the Son, and to the Holy Ghost.

As it was in the beginning, is now, and ever shall be, world without end. Amen.
Praise be to thee, O Lord, King of eternal glory.
ANT. The Lord said.

The first Psalm is a prophecy of the future glory of the Messias. It shows us his triumph; after his humiliations and his Cross, the Man-God shall sit on the *right hand* of his Father. Moreover, he is to come again into this world,—to *judge* it, and *crush*

SUNDAY'S VESPERS.

the proud *heads* of sinners. While thus celebrating his Glory, let us not forget his Justice.

PSALM 109.

The Lord said to my Lord, *his Son:* Sit thou at my right hand, *and reign with me.*

Until, *on the day of thy last coming,* I make thy enemies thy footstool.

O Christ! the Lord thy *Father*, will send forth the sceptre of thy power out of Sion: *from thence* rule thou in the midst of thy enemies.

With thee is the principality in the day of thy strength, in the brightness of the saints: *For the Father hath said to thee:* From the womb before the day-star I begot thee.

The Lord hath sworn, and he will not repent: *he hath said, speaking of thee, the God-Man:* Thou art a Priest for ever, according to the order of Melchisedech.

Therefore, O Father, the Lord *thy Son* is at thy right hand: he hath broken kings in the day of his wrath.

He shall *also* judge among nations: *in that terrible coming,* he shall fill the ruins *of the world:* he shall crush the heads in the land of many.

He cometh now in humility; he shall drink, in the way, of the torrent *of sufferings:* therefore, shall he lift up the head.

ANT. The Lord said to my Lord, sit thou at my right hand.

ANT. Faithful.

Dixit Dominus Domino meo: * Sede a dextris meis.

Donec ponam inimicos tuos: * scabellum pedum tuorum.

Virgam virtutis tuæ emittet Dominus ex Sion: * dominare in medio inimicorum tuorum.

Tecum principium in die virtutis tuæ in splendoribus sanctorum: * ex utero ante luciferum genui te.

Juravit Dominus, et non pœnitebit eum: * Tu es Sacerdos in æternum secundum ordinem Melchisedech.

Dominus a dextris tuis:* confregit in die iræ suæ reges.

Judicabit in nationibus, implebit ruinas: * conquassabit capita in terra multorum.

De torrente in via bibet: * propterea exaltabit caput.

ANT. Dixit Dominus Domino meo sede a dextris meis.

ANT. Fidelia.

The following Psalm commemorates the mercies of God to his *people*—the promised *Covenant*—the *Redemption*—his *Fidelity* to his word. But it also tells us that the *Name* of the Lord is *terrible* because it is *holy;* and concludes by telling us, that *the fear of the Lord is the beginning of wisdom.*

PSALM 110.

Confitebor tibi, Domine, in toto corde meo : * in concilio justorum et congregatione.

I will praise thee, O Lord, with my whole heart : in the counsel of the just, and in the congregation.

Magna opera Domini : * exquisita in omnes voluntates ejus.

Great are the works of the Lord : sought out according to all his wills.

Confessio et magnificentia opus ejus : * et justitia ejus manet in sæculum sæculi.

His work is praise and magnificence : and his justice continueth for ever and ever.

Memoriam fecit mirabilium suorum, misericors et miserator Dominus : * escam dedit timentibus se.

He hath made a remembrance of his wonderful works, being a merciful and gracious Lord : he hath given food to them that fear him.

Memor erit in sæculum testamenti sui : * virtutem operum suorum annuntiabit populo suo.

He will be mindful for ever of his covenant *with men:* he will show forth to his people the power of his works.

Ut det illis hereditatem Gentium : * opera manuum ejus veritas et judicium.

That he may give them, *his Church,* the inheritance of the Gentiles : the works of his hand are truth and judgment.

Fidelia omnia mandata ejus, confirmata in sæculum sæculi : * facta in veritate et æquitate.

All his commandments are faithful, confirmed for ever and ever : made in truth and equity.

Redemptionem misit populo suo : * mandavit in æternum testamentum suum.

He hath sent redemption to his people ; he hath *thereby* commanded his covenant for ever.

Sanctum et terrible nomen ejus : * initium sapientiæ timor Domini.

Holy and terrible is his name: the fear of the Lord is the beginning of wisdom.

Intellectus bonus omnibus

A good understanding to all

that do it: his praise continueth for ever and ever.

Ant. Faithful are all his commandments; confirmed for ever and ever.

Ant. In his commandments.

facientibus eum : * laudatio ejus manet in sæculum sæculi.

Ant. Fidelia omnia mandata ejus; confirmata in sæculum sæculi.

Ant. In mandatis.

The next Psalm sings the happiness of the *just man*, and his hopes on the day of his Lord's coming. It tells us, likewise, of the confusion and despair which will torment the *sinner*, who, during life, was insensible to his own interests, and deaf to the invitations made him by the Church.

PSALM 111.

Blessed is the man that feareth the Lord: he shall delight exceedingly in his commandments.

His seed shall be mighty upon earth: the generation of the righteous shall be blessed.

Glory and wealth shall be in his house: and his justice remaineth for ever and ever.

To the righteous a light is risen up in darkness: he is merciful, and compassionate, and just.

Acceptable is the man that showeth mercy and lendeth; he shall order his words with judgment: because he shall not be moved for ever.

The just shall be in everlasting remembrance: he shall not fear the evil hearing.

His heart is ready to hope in the Lord; his heart is strengthened: he shall not

Beatus vir, qui timet Dominum : * in mandatis ejus volet nimis.

Potens in terra erit semen ejus : * generatio rectorum benedicetur.

Gloria, et divitiæ in domo ejus : * et justitia ejus manet in sæculum sæculi.

Exortum est in tenebris lumen rectis : * misericors, et miserator, et justus.

Jucundus homo, qui miseretur et commodat, disponet sermones suos in judicio : * quia in æternum non commovebitur.

In memoria æterna erit justus : * ab auditione mala non timebit.

Paratum cor ejus sperare in Domino, confirmatum est cor ejus : * non commovebitur donec despiciat inimicos suos.

Dispersit, dedit pauperibus, justitia ejus manet in sæculum sæculi : * cornu ejus exaltabitur in gloria.

Peccator videbit, et irascetur, dentibus suis fremet et tabescet : * desiderium peccatorum peribit.

ANT. In mandatis ejus cupit nimis.

ANT. Sit nomen Domini.

be moved until he look over his enemies.

He hath distributed, he hath given to the poor ; his justice remaineth for ever and ever : his horn shall be exalted in glory.

The wicked shall see, and shall be angry ; he shall gnash with his teeth, and pine away; the desire of the wicked shall perish.

ANT. In his commandments he delighteth exceedingly.

ANT. May the name of the Lord.

The Psalm, *Laudate pueri*, is a Canticle of praise to the Lord, who, from his high heaven, has taken pity on the fallen human race, and facilitated its return to its Maker.

PSALM 112.

Laudate, pueri, Dominum : * laudate nomen Domini.

Sit nomen Domini benedictum * ex hoc nunc et usque in sæculum.

A solis ortu usque ad occasum : * laudabile nomen Domini.

Excelsus super omnes Gentes Dominus : * et super cœlos gloria ejus.

Quis sicut Dominus Deus noster qui in altis habitat : * et humilia respicit in cœlo et in terra ?

Suscitans a terra inopem :* et de stercore erigens pauperem.

Praise the Lord, ye children ; praise ye the name of the Lord.

Blessed be the name of the Lord : from henceforth now and for ever.

From the rising of the sun unto the going down of the same, the name of the Lord is worthy of praise.

The Lord is high above all nations : and his glory above the heavens.

Who is as the Lord our God, who dwelleth on high : and looketh down on the low things in heaven and in earth ?

Raising up the needy from the earth : and lifting up the poor out of the dunghill.

That he may place him with princes: with the princes of his people.	Ut collocet eum cum principibus: *cum principibus populi sui.
Who maketh a barren woman to dwell in a house, the joyful mother of children.	Qui habitare facit sterilem in domo: *matrem filiorum lætantem.
ANT. May the name of the Lord be for ever blessed.	ANT. Sit nomen Domini benedictum in sæcula.
ANT. We that live.	ANT. Nos qui vivimus.

The fifth Psalm, *In exitu*, recounts the prodigies witnessed under the ancient Covenant: they were *figures*, whose realities are to be accomplished in us, if we will but return to the Lord our God. He will deliver *Israel* from Egypt, emancipate the *Gentiles* from their idolatry, and pour out a *blessing* on every man who will consent to fear and love the Lord.

PSALM 113.

When Israel went out of Egypt, the house of Jacob from a barbarous people.	In exitu Israel de Ægypto: *domus Jacob de populo barbaro.
Judea was made his sanctuary, Israel his dominion.	Facta est Judæa sanctificatio ejus: *Israel potestas ejus.
The sea saw and fled; Jordan was turned back.	Mare vidit, et fugit: *Jordanis conversus est retrorsum.
The mountains skipped like rams: and the hills like the lambs of the flock.	Montes exsultaverunt ut arietes: *et colles sicut agni ovium.
What ailed thee, O thou sea, that thou didst flee: and thou, O Jordan, that thou wast turned back?	Quid est tibi, mare, quod fugisti: *et tu, Jordanis, quia conversus es retrorsum?
Ye mountains that ye skipped like rams: and ye hills like lambs of the flock?	Montes exsultastis sicut arietes: *et colles sicut agni ovium?
At the presence of the Lord the earth was moved, at the presence of the God of Jacob.	A facie Domini mota est terra a facie Dei Jacob.
Who turned the rock into pools of water, and the stony hills into fountains of waters.	Qui convertit petram in stagna aquarum: *et rupem in fontes aquarum.

SEPTUAGESIMA.

Non nobis, Domine, non nobis: * sed nomini tuo da gloriam.

Super misericordia tua, et veritate tua : * nequando dicant Gentes: Ubi est Deus eorum ?

Deus autem noster in cœlo : * omnia quæcumque voluit, fecit.

Simulacra Gentium argentum et aurum : * opera manuum hominum.

Os habent, et non loquentur : * oculos habent, et non videbunt.

Aures habent, et non audient :* nares habent et non odorabunt.

Manus habent, et non palpabunt, pedes habent et non ambulabunt : * non clamabunt in gutture suo.

Similes illis fiant qui faciunt ea : * et omnes qui confidunt in eis.

Domus Israël speravit in Domino : * adjutor eorum, et protector eorum est.

Domus Aaron speravit in Domino : * adjutor eorum, et protector eorum est.

Qui timent Dominum, speraverunt in Domino : * adjutor eorum, et protector eorum est.

Dominus memor fuit nostri : * et benedixit nobis.

Benedixit domui Israel : * benedixit domui Aaron.

Benedixit omnibus qui timent Dominum : * pusillis cum majoribus.

Adjiciat Dominus super vos : * super vos, et super filios vestros.

Not to us, O Lord, not to us : but to thy name give glory.

For thy mercy, and for thy truth's sake : lest the Gentiles should say : Where is their God ?

But our God is in heaven : he hath done all things whatsoever he would.

The idols of the Gentiles are silver and gold : the works of the hands of men.

They have mouths, and speak not : they have eyes, and see not.

They have ears, and hear not : they have noses, and smell not.

They have hands, and feel not : they have feet, and walk not : neither shall they cry out through their throat.

Let them that make them become like unto them : and all such as trust in them.

The house of Israel hath hoped in the Lord : he is their helper and their protector.

The house of Aaron hath hoped in the Lord : he is their helper and their protector.

They that feared the Lord have hoped in the Lord : he is their helper and their protector.

The Lord hath been mindful of us, and hath blessed us.

He hath blessed the house of Israel : he hath blessed the house of Aaron.

He hath blessed all that fear the Lord, both little and great.

May the Lord add blessings upon you: upon you, and upon your children.

Blessed be you of the Lord, who made heaven and earth.	Benedicti vos a Domino: * qui fecit cœlum et terram.
The heaven of heaven is the Lord's: but the earth he has given to the children of men.	Cœlum cœli Domino : * terram autem dedit filiis hominum.
The dead shall not praise thee, O Lord: nor any of them that go down to hell.	Non mortui laudabunt te, Domine : *neque omnes qui descendunt in infernum.
But we that live bless the Lord: from this time now and for ever.	Sed nos qui vivimus, benedicimus Domino : * ex hoc nunc et usque in sæculum.
ANT. We that live bless the Lord.	ANT. Nos qui vivimus, bendedicimus Domino.

After these five Psalms, a short Lesson from the holy Scriptures is then read. It is called *Capitulum*, because it is always very short. The ones for these Sundays are given in the *Proper* of each.

After the Capitulum, follows the Hymn, *Lucis Creator*. It was written by St. Gregory the Great. It sings of Creation, and celebrates the praises of that portion of it, which was called forth on this first day,—the *Light*. The Saint teaches us to ask that our soul may be roused,—be loosed from the spells of this life,—and turn all her energies to eternal things.

HYMN.*

O infinitely good Creator of the Light! by thee was produced the Light of day, providing thus the world's begin-	Lucis Creator optime, Lucem dierum proferens ; Primordiis lucis novæ, Mundi parans originem.

---

* According to the Monastic Rite, it is as follows :—

℟. *breve.* Quam magnificata sunt, *Opera tua Domine. Quam. ℣. Omnia in Sapientia fecisti. * Opera. Gloria Patri, &c. Quam.

Lucis Creator Optime,
Lucem dierum proferens ;
Primordiis lucis novæ,
Mundi parans originem.

Qui mane junctum vesperi
Diem vocari præcipis,
Tetrum chaos illabitur,
Audi preces cum fletibus.

Ne mens gravata crimine,
Vitæ sit exul munere,
Dum nil perenne cogitat,
Seseque culpis illigat.

Cœlorum pulset intimum,
Vitale tollat præmium :
Vitemus omne noxium,
Purgemus omne pessimum.

Præsta, Pater piissime,
Patrique compar Unice,
Cum Spiritu Paraclito
Regnans per omne sæculum.
Amen.

SEPTUAGESIMA.

Qui mane junctum vesperi
Diem vocari præcipis,
Illabitur tetrum chaos,
Audi preces cum fletibus.

Ne mens gravata crimine,
Vitæ sit exsul munere,
Dum nil perenne cogitat,
Seseque culpis illigat.

Cœleste pulset intimum,
Vitale tollat præmium :
Vitemus omne noxium,
Purgemus omne pessimum.

Præsta, Pater piissime,
Patrique compar Unice,
Cum Spiritu Paraclito
Regnans per omne sæculum.
Amen.

℣. Dirigatur, Domine, oratio mea,

℞. Sicut incensum in conspectu tuo.

ning with the beginning of the new made Light.

Thou biddest us call the time from morn till eve, *Day;* this *day* is over ; dark Night comes on,—oh ! hear our tearful prayers.

Let not our soul, weighed down by crime, mis-spend thy gift of life, and, forgetting what is eternal, be earth-tied by her sins.

Oh ! may we strive to enter our heavenly home, and bear away the prize of life : may we shun what would injure us, and cleanse our soul from her defilements.

Most merciful Father ! and thou, his Only Begotten Son, co-equal with him, reigning for ever with the Holy Paraclete! grant this our prayer. Amen.

℣. May my prayer, O Lord, ascend,

℞. Like incense in thy sight.

Then is said the *Magnificat* Antiphon, which is to be found in the *Proper.* After this, the Church sings the Canticle of Mary, the *Magnificat,* in which are celebrated the Divine Maternity and all its consequent blessings. This exquisite Canticle is an essential part of the Vespers throughout the year. Let us unite with *all generations,* and *call* her "*Blessed ;*" but let us, also, enter into those sentiments of *Humility,* which she recommends to us both by her words and her example. Her inspired lips speak to us this promise: If the Great God, whose triumph is to gladden us on the glorious Day of Easter, find us humble and submissive,—he will *exalt* us, yea, raise us up even to himself ; if we confess our misery and *poverty* to him, he will *enrich* us, even to the *full,* with every blessing.

OUR LADY'S CANTICLE.

(St. Luke, i.)

My soul doth magnify the Lord;	Magnificat : * anima mea Dominum :
And my spirit hath rejoiced in God my Saviour.	Et exsultavit spiritus meus : * in Deo salutari meo.
Because he hath regarded the humility of his handmaid : for, behold from henceforth all generations shall call me Blessed.	Quia respexit humilitatem ancillæ suæ : * ecce enim ex hoc Beatam me dicent omnes generationes.
Because he that is mighty hath done great things to me : and holy is his name.	Quia fecit mihi magna qui potens est : * et sanctum nomen ejus.
And his mercy is from generation unto generation, to them that fear him.	Et misericordia ejus a progenie in progenies : * timentibus eum.
He hath showed might in his arm : he hath scattered the proud in the conceit of their heart.	Fecit potentiam in brachio suo : * dispersit superbos mente cordis sui.
He hath put down the mighty from their seat : and hath exalted the humble.	Deposuit potentes de sede : * et exaltavit humiles.
He hath filled the hungry with good things : and the rich he hath sent empty away.	Esurientes implevit bonis : * et divites dimisit inanes.
He hath received Israel his servant, being mindful of his mercy.	Suscepit Israël puerum suum : * recordatus misericordiæ suæ.
As he spake to our fathers, to Abraham and to his seed for ever.	Sicut locutus est ad patres nostros : * Abraham et semini ejus in sæcula.

The *Magnificat* Antiphon is then repeated. The Prayer, or Collect, will be found in the Proper of each Sunday.

The Vespers end with the following Versicles :

℣. Let us bless the Lord.	℣. Benedicamus Domino.
℟. Thanks be to God.	℟. Deo gratias.
℣. May the souls of the Faithful departed, through the mercy of God, rest in peace.	℣. Fidelium animæ per misericordiam Dei requiescant in pace.
℟. Amen.	℟. Amen.

CHAPTER THE EIGHTH.

ON THE OFFICE OF COMPLINE,

DURING SEPTUAGESIMA.

This Office, which concludes the day, commences by a warning of the dangers of the night: then immediately follows the public Confession of our sins, as a powerful means of propitiating the divine justice, and obtaining God's help, now that we are going to spend so many hours in the unconscious and therefore dangerous state of sleep, which is also such an image of death.

The Lector, addressing the Priest, says to him:

℣. Jube, Domine, benedicere. | Pray, Father, give thy blessing.

The Priest answers:

Noctem quietam, et finem perfectum concedat nobis Dominus omnipotens.
℞. Amen.

May the Almighty Lord grant us a quiet night and a perfect end.
℞. Amen.

The Lector then reads these words, from the first Epistle of St. Peter:

Fratres: Sobrii estote, et vigilate: quia adversarius vester diabolus, tamquam leo rugiens circuit quærens quem devoret: cui resistite fortes in fide. Tu autem, Domine, miserere nobis.

Brethren, be sober and watch: for your adversary the devil goes about like a roaring lion, seeking whom he may devour: resist him, being strong in faith. But thou, O Lord, have mercy on us.

COMPLINE.   85

The Choir answers:

℟. Thanks be to God.   ℟. Deo gratias.

Then, the Priest:

℣. Our help is in the name of the Lord.   ℣. Adjutorium nostrum in nomine Domine.

The Choir:

℟. Who hath made heaven and earth.   ℟. Qui fecit cœlum et terram.

Then the Lord's Prayer is recited in secret; after which the Priest says the *Confiteor;* and, when he has finished, the Choir says:

May Almighty God be merciful to thee, and, forgiving thy sins, bring thee to everlasting life.   Misereatur tui omnipotens Deus, et dimissis peccatis tuis, perducat te ad vitam æternam.

The Priest having answered *Amen,* the Choir repeats the *Confiteor,* thus:

I confess to Almighty God, to Blessed Mary ever Virgin, to blessed Michael the Archangel, to blessed John Baptist, to the holy Apostles Peter and Paul, to all the saints, and to thee, Father, that I have sinned exceedingly in thought, word, and deed, through my fault, through my fault, through my most grievous fault. Therefore I beseech the Blessed Mary ever Virgin, blessed Michael the Archangel, blessed John Baptist, the holy Apostles Peter and Paul, and all the saints, and thee, Father, to pray to our Lord God for me.   Confiteor Deo Omnipotenti, beatæ Mariæ semper Virgini, beato Michaeli Archangelo, beato Joanni Baptistæ, sanctis Apostolis Petro et Paulo, omnibus sanctis, et tibi Pater: quia peccavi nimis, cogitatione, verbo, et opere: mea culpa, mea culpa, mea maxima culpa. Ideo precor beatam Mariam semper Virginem, beatum Michaelem Archangelum, beatum Joannem Baptistam, sanctos Apostolos Petrum et Paulum, omnes sanctos, et te, Pater, orare pro me ad Dominum Deum nostrum.

The Priest then says:

Misereatur vestri omnipotens Deus, et dimissis peccatis vestris, perducat vos ad vitam æternam.

℟. Amen.

Indulgentiam, absolutionem, et remissionem peccatorum nostrorum, tribuat nobis omnipotens et misericors Dominus.

℟. Amen.

℣. Converte nos, Deus, Salutaris noster.

℟. Et averte iram tuam a nobis.

℣. Deus, in adjutorium meum intende.

℟. Domine, ad adjuvandum me festina.

Gloria Patri, &c.

Laus tibi, Domine, Rex æternæ gloriæ.

ANT. Miserere.

May Almighty God be merciful to you, and, forgiving your sins, bring you to everlasting life.

℟. Amen.

May the Almighty and merciful Lord grant us pardon, absolution, and remission of our sins.

℟. Amen.

℣. Convert us, O God, our Saviour.

℟. And turn away thy anger from us.

℣. Incline unto my aid, O God.

℟. O Lord make haste to help me.

Glory, &c.

Praise be to thee, O Lord, King of eternal glory.

ANT. Have mercy.

The *first* Psalm expresses the confidence with which the just man *sleeps in peace;* but it, also, rebukes those tepid Christians, whose *dull hearts* are but too often enslaved to *vanity* and *lies,* and exhorts them to examine, at the close of the day, the thoughts of their *hearts,* and be *sorry for them* at that time of stillness and repose.

PSALM 4.

Cum invocarem exaudivit me Deus justitiæ meæ : * in tribulatione dilatasti mihi.

Miserere mei : * et exaudi orationem meam.

Filii hominum, usquequo

When I called upon him, the God of my justice heard me : when I was in distress, thou hast enlarged me.

Have mercy on me : and hear my prayer.

O ye sons of men, how long

will you be dull of heart? why do you love vanity, and seek after lying?	gravi corde : * ut quid diligitis vanitatem, et quæritis mendacium?
Knew ye also that the Lord hath made his Holy One wonderful : the Lord will hear me, when I shall cry unto him.	Et scitote quoniam mirificavit Dominus sanctum suum : * Dominus exaudiet me, cum clamavero ad eum.
Be ye angry, and sin not : the things you say in your hearts, be sorry for them upon your beds.	Irascimini, et nolite peccare : * quæ dicitis in cordibus vestris, in cubilibus vestris compungimini.
Offer up the sacrifice of justice, and trust in the Lord : many say, who showeth us good things?	Sacrificate sacrificium justitiæ, et sperate in Domino : * multi dicunt : Quis ostendit nobis bona?
The Light of thy countenance, O Lord, is signed upon us : thou hast given gladness in my heart.	Signatum est super nos lumen vultus tui Domine : * dedisti lætitiam in corde meo.
By the fruit of their corn, their wine, and oil, they are multiplied.	A fructu frumenti, vini et olei sui : * multiplicati sunt.
In peace, in the self same, I will sleep, and I will rest.	In pace in idipsum : * dormiam et requiescam.
For thou, O Lord, singularly hast settled me in hope.	Quoniam tu, Domine, singulariter in spe : * constituisti me.

The Church has introduced here the first six Verses of the thirtieth Psalm, because they contain the prayer which our Saviour made when dying: *Into thy hands, O Lord, I commend my spirit!*—words so beautifully appropriate in this Office of the close of day.

PSALM 30.

In thee, O Lord, have I hoped, let me never be confounded : deliver me in thy justice.	In te, Domine, speravi, non confundar in æternum: * in justitia tua libera me.
Bow down thy ear to me : make haste to deliver me.	Inclina ad me aurem tuam : * accelera ut eruas me.

Esto mihi in Deum protectorum, et in domum refugii : * ut salvum me facias.	Be thou unto me a God, a protector and a house of refuge, to save me.
Quoniam fortitudo mea, et refugium meum es tu : * et propter nomen tuum deduces me, et enutries me.	For thou art my strength, and my refuge : and for thy name's sake thou wilt lead me, and nourish me.
Educes me de laqueo hoc, quem absconderunt mihi : * quoniam tu es protector meus.	Thou wilt bring me out of this snare, which they have hidden for me : for thou art my protector.
In manus tuas commendo spiritum meum : * redemisti me, Domine, Deus veritatis.	Into thy hands I commend my spirit: thou hast redeemed me, O Lord, the God of truth.

The *third* Psalm gives the motives of the Just man's confidence, even during the dangers of the night. The description here given of Peace of mind, should make the sinner long for a reconciliation with his God, that so he, too, may enjoy that divine protection, without which there can be no security or happiness in this life of peril and misery.

PSALM 90.

Qui habitat in adjutorio Altissimi : * in protectione Dei cœli commorabitur.	He that dwelleth in the aid of the Most High, shall abide under the protection of the God of heaven.
Dicet Domino : Susceptor meus es tu, et refugium meum : * Deus meus, sperabo in eum.	He shall say to the Lord : Thou art my protector, and my refuge : my God, in him will I trust.
Quoniam ipse liberavit me de laqueo venantium : * et a verbo aspero.	For he hath delivered me from the snare of the hunters: and from the sharp word.
Scapulis suis obumbrabit tibi : * et sub pennis ejus sperabis.	He will overshadow thee with his shoulders: and under his wings thou shalt trust.
Scuto circumdabit te veritas ejus : * non timebis a timore nocturno.	His truth shall compass thee with a shield : thou shalt not be afraid of the terror of the night.

COMPLINE. 89

Of the arrow that flieth in the day: of the business that walketh about in the dark: of invasion, or of the noonday devil.

A thousand shall fall at thy side, and ten thousand at thy right hand: but it shall not come nigh thee.

But thou shalt consider with thy eyes: and shalt see the reward of the wicked.

Because *thou hast said:* Thou, O Lord, art my hope: thou hast made the Most High thy refuge.

There shall no evil come to thee, nor shall the scourge come near thy dwelling.

For he hath given his Angels charge over thee: to keep thee in all thy ways.

In their hands they shall bear thee up: lest thou dash thy foot against a stone.

Thou shalt walk upon the asp and basilisk: and thou shalt trample under foot the lion and the dragon.

God will say of thee: Because he hoped in me, I will deliver him: I will protect him, because he hath known my Name.

He will cry to me, and I will hear him: I am with him in tribulation, I will deliver him, and I will glorify him.

I will fill him with length of days: and I will show him my Salvation.

A sagitta volante in die, a negotio perambulante in tenebris: * ab incursu, et dæmonio meridiano.

Cadent a latere tuo mille, et decem millia a dextris tuis: * ad te autem non appropinquabit.

Verumtamen oculis tuis considerabis: * et retributionem peccatorum videbis.

Quoniam tu es, Domine, spes mea: Altissimum posuisti refugium tuum.

Non accedet ad te malum: * et flagellum non appropinquabit tabernaculo tuo.

Quoniam Angelis suis mandavit de te: * ut custodiant te in omnibus viis tuis.

In manibus portabunt te: * ne forte offendas ad lapidem pedem tuum.

Super aspidem et basiliscum ambulabis: * et conculcabis leonem et draconem.

Quoniam in me speravit, liberabo eum: * protegam eum, quoniam cognovit nomen meum.

Clamabit ad me, et ego exaudiam eum: * cum ipso sum in tribulatione, eripiam eum, et glorificabo eum.

Longitudine dierum replebo eum: * et ostendam illi Salutare meum.

The *fourth* Psalm invites the *Servants* of God to persevere, with fervour, in the prayers they offer during the *Night.* The Faithful should say this Psalm in a spirit of gratitude to God, for his raising up, in the Church, adorers of his holy name, whose grand vocation is to *lift up their hands*, day and night, for the safety of Israel. On such prayers depend the happiness and destinies of the world.

PSALM 133.

Ecce nunc benedicite Dominum : * omnes servi Domini.

Qui statis in domo Domini : * in atriis domus Dei nostri.

In noctibus extollite manus vestras in sancta : * et benedicite Dominum.

Benedicat te Dominus ex Sion : * qui fecit cœlum et terram.

ANT. Miserere mei, Domine, et exaudi orationem meam.

Behold now bless ye the Lord, all ye servants of the Lord.

Who stand in the house of the Lord, in the courts of the house of our God.

In the nights lift up your hands to the holy places, and bless ye the Lord.

Say to Israel: May the Lord out of Sion bless thee, he that made heaven and earth.

ANT. Have mercy on me, O Lord, and hear my prayer.

HYMN.*

Te lucis ante terminum,
Rerum Creator, poscimus,
Ut pro tua clementia
Sis præsul et custodia.

Procul recedant somnia,
Et noctium phantasmata ;
Hostemque nostrum comprime,
Ne polluantur corpora.

Præsta, Pater piissime,
Patrique compar Unice,

Before the closing of the light, we beseech thee, Creator of all things ! that in thy clemency, thou be our protector and our guard.

May the dreams and phantoms of night depart far from us ; and do thou repress our enemy, lest our bodies be profaned.

Most merciful Father ! and thou, his Only Begotten Son,

---

* According to the Monastic Rite, as follows :—

Te lucis ante terminum,
Rerum Creator, poscimus,
Ut solita clementia
Sis præsul ad custodiam.
Procul recedant somnia
Et noctium phantasmata

Hostemque nostrum comprime
Ne polluantur corpora.
Præsta Pater omnipotens,
Per Jesum Christum Dominum,
Qui tecum in perpetuum
Regnat cum Sancto Spiritu.

co-equal with him! reigning for ever with the Holy Paraclete! grant this our prayer. Amen.

Cum Spiritu Paraclito Regnans per omne sæculum. Amen.

CAPITULUM.

(Jeremias, xiv.)

But thou art in us, O Lord, and thy holy name has been invoked upon us: forsake us not, O Lord our God.

Tu autem in nobis es, Domine, et nomen sanctum tuum invocatum est super nos; ne derelinquas nos, Domine Deus noster.

℟. Into thy hands, O Lord: * I commend my spirit. Into thy hands.

℣. Thou hast redeemed us, O Lord God of truth. * I commend.

Glory. Into thy hands.

℣. Preserve us, O Lord, as the apple of thine eye.

℞. Protect us under the shadow of thy wings.

ANT. Save us.

℟. In manus tuas, Domine: * Commendo spiritum meum. In manus tuas.

℣. Redemisti nos, Domine Deus veritatis. * Commendo.

Gloria. In manus tuas.

℣. Custodi nos, Domine, ut pupillam oculi.

℞. Sub umbra alarum tuarum protege nos.

ANT. Salva nos.

The Canticle of the venerable Simeon—who, whilst holding the divine Infant in his arms, proclaimed him to be the *Light of the Gentiles,* and then slept the sleep of the just,—admirably expresses the repose of heart which the soul, that is in the Grace of God, will experience in her Jesus; for, as the Apostle says, *we may live together with Jesus, whether we are awake or asleep.*[1]

CANTICLE OF SIMEON.

(St. Luke, ii.)

Now dost thou dismiss thy servant, O Lord, according to thy word, in peace.

Nunc dimittis servum tuum Domine: * secundum verbum tuum in pace.

---

[1] 1 Thess. v. 10.

SEPTUAGESIMA.

Quia viderunt oculi mei : * salutare tuum.
Quod parasti : * ante faciem omnium populorum.
Lumen ad revelationem Gentium : * et gloriam plebis tuæ Israel.
Gloria Patri, et Filio, &c.
ANT. Salva nos, Domine, vigilantes : custodi nos dormientes, ut vigilemus cum Christo, et requiescamus in pace.

Because my eyes have seen thy Salvation.
Which thou hast prepared before the face of all peoples.
The light to the revelation of the Gentiles, and the glory of thy people Israel.
Glory, &c.
ANT. Save us, O Lord, whilst awake, and watch us as we sleep; that we may watch with Christ, and rest in peace.

PRAYERS.

Kyrie eleison.
Christe eleison.
Kyrie eleison.
Pater noster.
℣. Et ne nos inducas in tentationem.
℟. Sed libera nos a malo.
Credo in Deum, &c.
℣. Carnis resurrectionem.

℟. Vitam æternam. Amen.

℣. Benedictus es, Domine Deus patrum nostrorum.
℟. Et laudabilis et gloriosus in sæcula.
℣. Benedicamus Patrem et Filium cum Sancto Spiritu.
℟. Laudemus, et superexaltemus eum in sæcula.
℣. Benedictus es, Domine, in firmamento cœli.

℟. Et laudabilis, et gloriosus et superexaltatus in sæcula.
℣. Benedicat et custodiat nos omnipotens et misericors Dominus. ℟. Amen.

Lord have mercy on us.
Christ have mercy on us. Lord have mercy on us.
Our Father.
℣. And lead us not into temptation.
℟. But deliver us from evil.
I believe in God, &c.
℣. The resurrection of the body.
℟. And life everlasting. Amen.

℣. Blessed art thou, O Lord God of our fathers.
℟. And praiseworthy and glorious for ever.
℣. Let us bless the Father and the Son, with the Holy Ghost.
℟. Let us praise, and magnify him for ever.
℣. Thou art blessed O Lord, in the firmament of heaven.
℟. And praiseworthy, and glorious, and magnified for ever.
℣. May the Almighty and merciful Lord bless us and keep us. ℟. Amen.

COMPLINE. 93

℣. Vouchsafe, O Lord, this night.
℟. To keep us without sin.

℣. Have mercy on us, O Lord.
℟. Have mercy on us.
℣. Let thy mercy be upon us, O Lord.
℟. As we have hoped in thee.
℣. O Lord, hear my prayer.

℟. And let my cry come unto thee.

℣. Dignare, Domine, nocte ista.
℟. Sine peccato nos custodire.

℣. Miserere nostri, Domine.
℟. Miserere nostri.
℣. Fiat misericordia tua, Domine, super nos.
℟. Quemadmodum speravimus in te.
℣. Domine, exaudi orationem meam.
℟. Et clamor meus ad te veniat.

After these *Prayers*, (which are omitted if the Office be of a *double* rite,) the Priest says:

℣. The Lord be with you.
℟. And with thy spirit.

℣. Dominus vobiscum.
℟. Et cum spiritu tuo.

LET US PRAY.

Visit, we beseech thee, O Lord, this house and family, and drive from it all snares of the enemy: let thy holy Angels dwell herein, who may keep us in peace, and may thy blessing be always upon us. Through Jesus Christ our Lord, thy Son, who liveth and reigneth with thee, in the unity of the Holy Ghost, God, world without end. Amen.

℣. The Lord be with you.
℟. And with thy spirit.
℣. Let us bless the Lord.
℟. Thanks be to God.
May the Almighty and merciful Lord, Father, Son, and Holy Ghost, bless and preserve us.
℟. Amen.

OREMUS.

Visita, quæsumus Domine, habitationem istam, et omnes insidias inimici ab ea longe repelle: Angeli tui sancti habitent in ea, qui nos in pace custodiant: et benedictio tua sit super nos semper. Per Dominum nostrum Jesum Christum Filium tuum, qui tecum vivit et regnat in unitate Spiritus Sancti Deus, per omnia sæcula sæculorum. Amen.
℣. Dominus vobiscum.
℟. Et cum spiritu tuo.
℣. Benedicamus Domino.
℟. Deo gratias.
Benedicat et custodiat nos omnipotens et misericors Dominus, Pater, et Filius, et Spiritus Sanctus.
℟. Amen.

SEPTUAGESIMA.

ANTHEM TO THE BLESSED VIRGIN.

Ave Regina cœlorum,
Ave Domina Angelorum :
Salve Radi, salve Porta,
Ex qua mundo lux est orta ;
Gaude, Virgo gloriosa,
Super omnes speciosa :
Vale, o valde decora,
Et pro nobis Christum exora.
℣. Dignare me laudare te, Virgo sacrata.
℟. Da mihi virtutem contra hostes tuos.

Hail Queen of Heaven! Hail Queen of Angels! Hail blest Root and Gate, from which came Light upon the world! Rejoice, O glorious Virgin, that surpassest all in beauty! Hail most lovely Queen! and pray to Christ for us.
℣. Vouchsafe, O Holy Virgin, that I may praise thee.
℟. Give me power against thine enemies.

OREMUS.

Concede, misericors Deus, fragilitati nostræ præsidium : ut, qui sanctæ Dei Genitricis memoriam agimus, intercessionis ejus auxilio, a nostris iniquitatibus resurgamus. Per eumdem Christum Dominum nostrum.
℟. Amen.
℣. Divinum auxilium maneat semper nobiscum.
℟. Amen.*

LET US PRAY.

Grant, O merciful God, thy protection to us in our weakness ; that we who celebrate the memory of the Holy Mother of God, may, through the aid of her intercession, rise again from our sins. Through the same Christ our Lord.
℟. Amen.
℣. May the divine assistance remain always with us.
℟. Amen.*

Then, in secret, *Pater, Ave,* and *Credo;* page 17.

---

* In the Monastic Rite, this *Response* is as follows :

℟. Et cum fratribus nostris absentibus. Amen.

℟. And with our absent Brethren. Amen.

SEPTUAGESIMA.

PROPER OF THE TIME.

SOME of the *Sundays after the Epiphany* have to be omitted, when Easter comes early in the year. But when that great Solemnity comes late, the Sundays before Septuagesima may be as many as six. We have given the first four in our Second *Christmas* Volume; we now give the remaining two.

During this brief period, the Church no longer dwells on the mysteries of our Lord's Infancy. She listens to his teachings and admires his miracles, but she selects no special circumstances of his Life. The colour of the Vestments she uses on these Sundays, is *Green;* we have elsewhere explained its symbolism. Frequently a Saint's Feast, of a *Double* rite, falls on these same days; the Sunday's Office is then omitted, and a mere *commemoration* is made of it.

We give the Mass and Vespers of these two Sundays without anything further than our usual commentary, inasmuch as they very rarely have to be said. We omit the week-days altogether, since they offer no particular Mystery for meditation; and their omission may be supplied, by perusing the instructions, &c., given for the Saint's Feasts, which have to be celebrated on those days.

THE FIFTH SUNDAY

AFTER THE EPIPHANY.

MASS.

INTROIT.

Adore God, all ye his Angels: Sion heard and was glad, and the daughters of Juda rejoiced.
Ps. The Lord hath reigned; let the earth rejoice, let many islands be glad. ℣. Glory, &c. Adore.

Adorate Deum omnes Angeli ejus : audivit et lætata est Sion: et exsultaverunt filiæ Judæ.
Ps. Dominus regnavit: exsultet terra, lætentur insulæ multæ. ℣. Gloria Patri. Adorate.

COLLECT.

Preserve, we beseech thee, O Lord, thy family by thy constant mercy, that we, who confide solely in the support of thy heavenly grace, may be always defended by thy protection. Through, &c.

Familiam tuam, quæsumus Domine, continua pietate custodi : ut quæ in sola spe gratiæ cœlestis innititur, tua semper protectione muniatur. Per Dominum.

SECOND COLLECT.

Preserve us, O Lord, we beseech thee, from all dangers of soul and body : and by the intercession of the glorious and blessed Mary, the ever Virgin-Mother of God, of thy blessed Apostles, Peter and

A cunctis nos, quæsumus Domine, mentis et corporis defende periculis : et intercedente beata et gloriosa semper Virgine Dei Genitrice Maria, cum beatis Apostolis tuis Petro et Paulo atque beato N. et omnibus Sanctis, salutem nobis tribue benignus et pacem ; ut destructis adversitatibus et erroribus universis, Ecclesia tua secura tibi serviat libertate.

Paul, of blessed N., (*here is mentioned the Titular Saint of the Church,*) and of all the Saints, grant us in thy mercy, health and peace ; that all adversities and errors being removed, thy Church may serve thee with undisturbed liberty.

A third Collect is added, at the choice of the Priest.

EPISTLE.

Lectio Epistolæ beati Pauli Apostoli ad Colossenses.

Lesson of the Epistle of St. Paul the Apostle to the Collossians.

Cap. iii.

Ch. iii.

Fratres, induite vos, sicut electi Dei, sancti, et dilecti, viscera misericordiæ, benignitatem, humilitatem, modestiam, patientiam, supportantes invicem, et donantes vobismetipsis, si quis adversus aliquem habet querelam : sicut et Dominus donavit vobis, ita et vos. Super omnia autem hæc, charitatem habete, quod est vinculum perfectionis : et pax Christi exsultet in cordibus vestris, in qua et vocati estis in uno corpore ; et grati estote. Verbum Christi habitet in vobis abundanter, in omnis sapientia, docentes, et commonentes vosmetipsos, psalmis, hymnis, et canticis spiritualibus, in gratia cantantes in cordibus vestris Deo. Omne quodcumque facitis, in verbo aut in opere, omnia in nomine Domini nostri Jesu Christi, gratias agentes Deo et Patri per Jesum Christum Dominum nostrum.

Brethren, put ye on therefore as the elect of God, holy, and beloved, the bowels of mercy, benignity, humility, modesty, patience ; bearing with one another, and forgiving one another, if any have a complaint against another ; even as the Lord hath forgiven you, so you also. But above all these things have charity, which is the bond of perfection ; and let the peace of Christ rejoice in your hearts, wherein also you are called in one body ; and be ye thankful. Let the word of Christ dwell in you abundantly in all wisdom, teaching and admonishing one another in psalms, hymns, and spiritual canticles, singing in grace in your hearts to God. All whatsoever you do in word, or in work, all things do ye in the name of the Lord Jesus Christ, giving thanks to God and the Father, through Jesus Christ our Lord.

The Christian,—trained as he has been in the school of the Man-God, who deigned to dwell upon this earth,—should ever show mercy towards his fellow-men. This world, which has been purified by the presence of the Incarnate Word, would become an abode of *Peace,* if we were but to live in such manner as to merit the titles, given us by the Apostle, of *elect of God, holy, and beloved.* The *Peace* here spoken of should, first of all, fill the heart of every Christian, and give it an uninterrupted joy, which would be ever pouring itself forth in *singing* the praises of God. But it is mainly on the Sundays, that the Faithful, by taking part with the Church in her *psalms, hymns, and spiritual canticles,* fulfil this duty so dear to their hearts. Let us, moreover, in our every day life, practise the advice given us by the Apostle,—of doing all things in the name of our Lord Jesus Christ, in order that we may, in all things, find favour with our Heavenly Father.

GRADUAL.

The Gentiles shall fear thy Name, O Lord, and all the kings of the earth thy glory.

℣. For the Lord hath built up Sion, and he shall be seen in his glory.

Alleluia, alleluia.

℣. The Lord hath reigned, let the earth rejoice; let many islands be glad. Alleluia.

Timebunt gentes Nomen tuum, Domine, et omnes reges terræ gloriam tuam.

℣. Quoniam ædificavit Dominus Sion, et videbitur in majestate sua.

Alleluia, alleluia.

℣. Dominus regnavit: exsultet terra, lætentur insulæ multæ. Alleluia.

GOSPEL.

Sequel of the Holy Gospel according to Matthew.

Ch. xiii.

At that time: Jesus spoke this parable to the multitude, saying: The kingdom of hea-

Sequentia sancti Evangelii secundum Matthæum.

Cap. xiii.

In illo tempore: Dixit Jesus turbis parabolam hanc: Simile factum est regnum cœlorum homini, qui seminavit bonum semen in agro suo. Cum autem dormirent homines, venit inimicus ejus, et superseminavit zizania in medio tritici, et abiit. Cum autem crevisset herba, et fructum fecisset, tunc apparuerunt et zizania. Accedentes autem servi patrisfamilias, dixerunt ei: Domine, nonne bonum semen seminasti in agro tuo? Unde ergo habet zizania? Et ait illis: Inimicus homo hoc fecit. Servi autem dixerunt ei: Vis, imus, et colligimus ea? Et ait: Non: ne forte colligentes zizania, eradicetis simul et triticum. Sinite utraque crescere usque ad messem, et in tempore messis dicam messoribus: Colligite primum zizania, et alligate ea in fasiculos ad comburendum, triticum autem congregate in horreum meum.

ven is likened to a man that sowed good seed in his field. But while men were asleep, his enemy came and oversowed cockle among the wheat and went his way. And when the blade was sprung up, and brought forth fruit, then appeared also the cockle. Then the servants of the good man of the house, coming said to him: Sir, didst thou not sow good seed in thy field? whence then hath it cockle? And he said to them: An enemy hath done this. And the servants said to him: Wilt thou that we go and gather it up? And he said: No, lest perhaps gathering up the cockle, you root up the wheat also together with it. Let both grow until the harvest, and in the time of harvest I will say to the reapers: Gather up first the cockle, and bind it in bundles to burn, but the wheat gather ye into my barn.

The *Kingdom of Heaven*, here spoken of by our Lord, is the Church Militant,—the society of them that believe in him. And yet, the *field* he has tilled with so much care is *oversowed* with *cockle;* heresies have crept in, scandals have abounded; are we, on that account, to have misgivings about the foresight of the Master, who knows all things, and without whose permission nothing happens? Far from us be such a thought! He himself tells us that these things must needs be. Man has been gifted with free-will; it is for him to choose between good and evil; but, God will turn all to his own greater glory. Heresies, then, like weeds in a field, may spring up in the Church; but the day must come when they will be uprooted; some of them will wither on the parent-stems, but the whole *cockle* shall *be gathered into bundles to burn.* Where are now the heresies that sprang up in the first ages of the Church ? And in another hundred years, what will have become of the heresy, which, under the pretentious name of *The Reformation,* has caused incalculable evil ? It is the same with the scandals which rise up within the pale of the Church ;—they are a hard trial ; but trials must come. The Divine Husbandman wills not that this *cockle* be torn up, lest the *wheat* should suffer injury. First of all, the mixture of good and bad is an advantage ; it teaches the good not to put their hopes in man, but in God. Then too, the mercy of our Lord is so great, that at times the very *cockle* is converted, by Divine grace, into *wheat.* We must, therefore, have patience. But, whereas it is *while the men are asleep that the enemy oversows* the field with *cockle,* it behoves us to pray for Pastors, and ask their Divine Master to bless them with that Vigilance, which is the primary condition of the flock being safe, and is so essential a quality in every Bishop, that his very name is,—*one who watches.*

OFFERTORY.

The right hand of the Lord hath wrought strength, the right hand of the Lord hath exalted me : I shall not die, but live, and shall declare the works of the Lord.	Dextera Domini fecit virtutem, dextera Domine exaltavit me : non moriar, sed vivam, et narrabo opera Domini.

SECRET.

We offer thee, O Lord, this sacrifice of propitiation, that thou wouldst mercifully forgive us our sins, and guide our faltering hearts. Through, &c.	Hostias tibi, Domine, placationis offerimus, ut et delicta nostra miseratus absolvas, et nutantia corda tu dirigas. Per Dominum.

SECOND SECRET.

Graciously grant us, O God our Saviour, that by virtue of this Sacrament, thou mayest	Exaudi nos, Deus Salutaris noster, ut per hujus Sacramenti virtutem, a cunc-

tis nos mentis et corporis hostibus tuearis, gratiam tribuens in præsenti, et gloriam in futuro.

defend us from all enemies, both of soul and body; giving us grace in this life, and glory in the next.

A third Secret, at the choice of the Priest, is added.

COMMUNION.

Mirabantur omnes de his, quæ procedebant de ore Dei.

All wondered at the words that came from the mouth of God.

POSTCOMMUNION.

Quæsumus, omnipotens Deus, ut illius salutaris capiamus effectum, cujus per hæc mysteria pignus accepimus. Per Dominum.

We beseech thee, O Almighty God, that we may one day receive the effects of that salvation, of which we have received the pledge in these mysteries. Through, &c.

SECOND POSTCOMMUNION.

Mundet et muniat nos, quæsumus, Domine, divini Sacramenti munus oblatum : et, intercedente beata Virgine Dei genitrice Maria, cum beatis Apostolis tuis Petro et Paulo, atque beato N. et omnibus Sanctis, a cunctis nos reddat et perversitatibus expiatos, et adversitatibus expeditos.

May the oblation of this divine Sacrament, we beseech thee, O Lord, both cleanse and defend us; and, by the intercession of Blessed Mary, the Virgin-Mother of God, together with that of thy blessed Apostles, Peter and Paul, as likewise of blessed N., and of all the Saints, free us from all sin, and deliver us from all adversity.

The third Postcommunion is at the choice of the Priest.

VESPERS.

The Psalms, and Antiphons, as in *page* 74.

CAPITULUM.
(II. *Cor.* 1.)

Benedictus Deus et Pater Domini nostri Jesu Christi,

Blessed be the God and Father of our Lord Jesus

FIFTH SUNDAY AFTER EPIPHANY.

Christ, the Father of mercies, and the God of all consolation, who comforteth us in all our tribulations.	Pater misericordiarum et Deus totius consolationis, qui consolatur nos in omni tribulatione nostra.

The Hymn and Versicle, *page* 81.

ANTIPHON OF THE *Magnificat*.

Gather up first the cockle, and bind it in bundles to burn : but gather the wheat into my barn, saith the Lord.	Colligite primum zizania, et alligate ea in fasciculos ad comburendum : triticum autem congregate in horreum meum, dicit Dominus.

LET US PRAY.   OREMUS.

Preserve, we beseech thee, O Lord, thy family by thy constant mercy : that we, who confide solely in the support of thy heavenly grace, may be always defended by thy protection. Through, &c.	Familiam tuam, quæsumus Domine, continua pietate custodi : ut quæ in sola spe gratiæ cœlestis innititur, tua semper protectione muniatur. Per Dominum.

THE SIXTH SUNDAY

AFTER THE EPIPHANY.

MASS.

INTROIT.

Adorate Deum omnes Angeli ejus: audivit et lætata est Sion: et exsultaverunt filiæ Judæ.
Ps. Dominus regnavit; exsultet terra, lætentur insulæ multæ. ℣. Gloria Patri. Adorate.

Adore God, all ye his Angels: Sion heard and was glad, and the daughters of Juda rejoiced.
Ps. The Lord hath reigned; let the earth rejoice, let many islands be glad. ℣. Glory, &c. Adore.

COLLECT.

Præsta quæsumus omnipotens Deus: ut semper rationabilia meditantes, quæ tibi sunt placita et dictis exsequamur et factis. Per Dominum.

Grant, we beseech thee, O Almighty God, that being always intent upon what is reasonable and just, we may, both in word and deed, perform what is acceptable to thee. Through, &c.

For the other Collects, see *page* 97.

EPISTLE.

Lectio Epistolæ beati Pauli Apostoli ad Thessalonicenses.
I. *Cap.* 1.
Fratres, gratias agimus Deo semper pro omnibus vobis, memoriam vestri facientes in orationibus nos-

Lesson of the Epistle of Saint Paul the Apostle to the Thessalonians.
I. *Ch.* i.
Brethren, we give thanks to God always for you all: making a remembrance of you in our prayers without ceasing:

being mindful of you in the work of your faith, and labour, and charity, and of the enduring of the hope of our Lord Jesus Christ, before God and our Father; knowing, brethren beloved of God, your election. For our Gospel hath not been to you in word only, but in power also, and in the Holy Ghost, and in much fulness, as you know what manner of men we have been among you for your sakes. And you became followers of us, and of the Lord, receiving the word in much tribulation, with joy of the Holy Ghost; so that you were made a pattern to all that believe, in Macedonia and in Achaia. For from you was spread abroad the word of the Lord, not only in Macedonia and in Achaia, but also in every place your faith, which is towards God, is gone forth, so that we need not speak any thing. For they themselves relate of us, what manner of entering in we had unto you; and how you turned to God from idols, to serve the living and true God, and to wait for his Son from heaven (whom he raised up from the dead) Jesus, who hath delivered us from the wrath to come.

tris sine intermissione, memores operis fidei vestræ, et laboris, et charitatis, et sustinentiæ spei Domini nostri Jesu Christi, ante Deum et Patrem nostrum: scientes, fratres dilecti a Deo, electionem vestram: quia Evangelium nostrum non fuit ad vos in sermone tantum, sed et in virtute, et in Spiritu Sancto, et in plenitudine multa, sicut scitis quales fuerimus in vobis propter vos. Et vos imitatores nostri facti estis et Domini, excipientes verbum in tribulatione multa, cum gaudio Spiritus Sancti: ita ut facti sitis forma omnibus credentibus in Macedonia, et in Achaïa. A vobis enim diffamatus est sermo Domini, non solum in Macedonia, et in Achaïa, sed et in omni loco fides vestra, quæ est ad Deum, profecta est, ita ut non sit nobis necesse quidquam loqui. Ipsi enim de nobis annuntiant qualem introitum habuerimus ad vos: et quomoda conversi estis ad Deum a simulacris, servire Deo vivo, et vero, et exspectare Filium ejus de cœlis (quem suscitavit ex mortuis) Jesum, qui eripuit nos ab ira ventura.

The praise which the Apostle here gives to the Thessalonians for their fervour in the faith they had embraced, conveys a reproach to the Christians of our own times. These neophytes of Thessalonica, who, a short time before, were worshippers of idols, had become so earnest in the practice of the Christian religion, that even the Apostle is filled with admiration. *We* are the descendants of countless Christian ancestors; we received our regeneration by Baptism at our first coming into the world; we were taught the doctrine of Jesus Christ from our earliest childhood;—and yet, our faith is not as strong, or our lives as holy, as were those of the early Christians. Their main occupation was the *serving the living and true God*, and the *waiting* for the coming of their Saviour; *our* Hope is precisely the same as that which made *their* hearts so fervent; how comes it that our Faith is not like theirs in its generosity? We love this present life, as though we had not the firm conviction that it is to pass away.

As far as depends upon *us*, we are handing down to future generations a Christianity very different from that which our Saviour established, which the Apostles preached, and which the pagans of the first ages thought they were bound to purchase at any price or sacrifice.

GRADUAL.

Timebunt gentes Nomen tuum, Domine, et omnes reges terræ gloriam tuam.

℣. Quoniam ædificavit Dominus Sion, et videbitur in majestate sua.

Alleluia, alleluia.

℣. Dominus regnavit: exsultet terra, lætentur insulæ multæ. Alleluia.

The Gentiles shall fear thy Name, O Lord, and all the kings of the earth thy glory.

℣. For the Lord hath built up Sion, and he shall be seen in his glory.

Alleluia, alleluia.

℣. The Lord hath reigned: let the earth rejoice: let many islands be glad. Alleluia.

GOSPEL.

Sequentia sancti Evangelii secundum Matthæum.

Cap. xiii.

In illo tempore: Dixit Jesus turbis parabolam hanc: Simile est regnum cœlorum grano sinapis, quod acci-

Sequel of the holy Gospel according to Matthew.

Ch. xiii.

At that time: Jesus spoke to the multitude this parable: The kingdom of heaven is like to a grain of mustard-seed, which a man took and sowed in his field. Which indeed is the least of all seeds; but when it is grown up, it is greater than all herbs, and becometh a tree, so that the birds of the air come and dwell in the branches thereof. Another parable he spoke to them: The kingdom of heaven is like to leaven, which a woman took and hid in three measures of meal, until the whole was leavened. All these things Jesus spoke in parables to the multitudes, and without parables he did not speak to them; that the word might be fulfilled which was spoken by the Prophet, saying: I will open my mouth in parables, I will utter things hidden from the foundation of the world.

piens homo seminavit in agro suo, quod minimum quidem est omnibus seminibus: cum autem creverit, majus est omnibus oleribus, et fit arbor, ita ut volucres cœli veniant, et habitent in ramis ejus. Aliam parabolam locutus est eis. Simile est regnum cœlorum fermento, quod acceptum mulier abscondit in farinæ satis tribus, donec fermentatum est totum. Hæc omnia locutus est Jesus in parabolis ad turbas: et sine parabolis non loquebatur eis: ut impleretur quod dictum erat per Prophetam dicentem Aperiam in parabolis os meum, eructabo abscondita a constitutione mundi.

Our Lord here teaches us, under the symbolism of two parables, what we are to believe concerning his Church, which is his *Kingdom*,—a Kingdom that rises indeed here on the earth, but is to be perfected in *Heaven*. What is this *grain of mustard-seed*, which is hid under ground, is unseen by man's eye, then appears as the *least* of herbs, but, finally, becomes a *tree?* It is the Word of God, at first hidden in Judea, trampled on by man's malice even so as to be buried in a tomb, but, at length, rising triumphantly and reaching rapidly to every part of the world. Scarcely had a hundred years elapsed since Jesus was put to death, and his Church was vigorous even far beyond the limits of the Roman Empire. During the past nineteen centuries, every possible effort has been made to up-root the *Tree* of God; persecution, diplomacy, human wisdom,—all have tried, and all have but wasted their time. True,—they succeeded, from time to time, in severing a branch; but another grew in its place, for the sap of the *Tree* is vigorous beyond measure. The *birds* that *come and dwell* upon it, are, as the Holy Fathers interpret it, the souls of men aspiring to the eternal goods of the better world. If we are worthy of our name of "Christians," we shall love this *Tree*, and find our rest and safety no where but beneath its shade.— The *Woman*, of whom the second parable speaks, is the Church, our Mother. It was she that, from the commencement of Christianity, took the teaching of her Divine Master, and *hid* it in the very heart of men, making it the *leaven* of their salvation. The *three measures of meal* which she *leavened* into bread, are the three great families of mankind, the three that came from the children of Noah, who are the three fathers of the whole human race. Let us love this Mother of ours; and let us bless that heavenly *leaven*, which made us become children of God, by making us children of the Church.

OFFERTORY.

Dextera Domini fecit virtutem, dextera Domini exaltavit me: non moriar, sed vivam, et narrabo opera Domini.	The right hand of the Lord hath wrought strength, the right hand of the Lord hath exalted me: I shall not die, but live, and shall declare the works of the Lord.

SECRET.

Hæc nos oblatio, Deus, mundet, quæsumus, et renovet, gubernet, et protegat. Per Dominum.	May this oblation, O God, we beseech thee, cleanse, renew, govern, and protect us. Through. *&c.*

The other secrets are given in *page* 101.

COMMUNION.

All wondered at the words that came from the mouth of God.	Mirabantur omnes de his, quæ procedebant de ore Dei.

POSTCOMMUNION.

Being fed, O Lord, with heavenly dainties, we beseech thee, that we may always hunger after them, for by them we have true life. Through, &c.	Cœlestibus, Domine, pasti deliciis, quæsumus, ut semper eadem, per quæ veraciter vivimus, appetamus. Per Dominum.

The other Postcommunions are given in *page* 102.

VESPERS.

The Psalms and Antiphons, as in *page* 74.

CAPITULUM.

(II. *Cor.* 1.)

Blessed be the God and Father of our Lord Jesus Christ, the Father of mercies, and the God of all consolation, who comforteth us in all our tribulations.	Benedictus Deus et Pater Domini nostri Jesu Christi, Pater misericordiarum et Deus totius consolationis, qui consolatur nos in omni tribulatione nostra.

The Hymn and Versicle, *page* 81.

ANTIPHON OF THE *Magnificat.*

The kingdom of heaven is like to leaven, which a woman took and hid in three measures of meal, until the whole was leavened.	Simile est regnum cœlorum fermento, quod acceptum mulier abscondit in farinæ satis tribus, donec fermentatum est totum.

SEPTUAGESIMA.

OREMUS.

Præsta, quæsumus omnipotens Deus: ut semper rationabilia meditantes, quæ tibi sunt placita, et dictis exsequamur et factis. Per Dominum.

LET US PRAY.

Grant, we beseech thee, O Almighty God, that being always intent upon what is reasonable and just, we may, both in word and deed, perform what is acceptable to thee. Through, &c.

SATURDAY BEFORE SEPTUAGESIMA SUNDAY.

SUSPENSION OF THE "ALLELUIA."

THE Calendar of the Liturgical Year will soon bring us to the commemoration of the Passion and Resurrection of our Redeemer; we are but nine weeks from these great Solemnities. It is time for the Christian to be preparing his soul for a fresh visit from his Saviour; a visit even more sacred and more important than that he so mercifully paid us at his Birth.

Our holy Mother the Church knows how necessary it is for her to rouse our hearts from their lethargy, and give them an active tendency towards the things of God. On this day, the eve of Septuagesima, she uses a powerful means for the infusing her own spirit into the minds of her children. She takes the song of heaven away from us:—she forbids our further uttering that *Alleluia*, which is so dear to us, as giving us a fellowship with the Choirs of Angels, who are for ever repeating it. How is it, that we poor mortals, sinners, and exiles on earth, have dared to become so familiar with this hymn of a better land? It is true, our Emmanuel, who established peace between God and men, brought it us from Heaven, on the glad Night of his Birth; and *we* have had the courage to repeat it after the Angels, and shall chant it with renewed enthusiasm, when we reach our Easter. But to sing the *Alleluia* worthily, we must have our hearts set on the country whence it came. It is not a mere word, nor a profane unmeaning melody; it is the song that recals the land we are banished from, it is the sweet sigh of the soul longing to be at Home.

The word *Alleluia* signifies *Praise God:* but it says much more than this, and says it as no other word or words could. The Church is not going to interrupt her giving *Praise* to God during these nine weeks. She will replace this heaven-lent word by a formula also expressive of *Praise: Laus tibi, Domine, Rex æternæ gloriæ! Praise be to thee, O Lord, King of eternal glory!* But this is the language of earth; whereas *Alleluia* was sent us from heaven. "*Alleluia,*" says the devout Abbot Rupert, "is like a stranger amidst our other words. Its "mysterious beauty is as though a drop of heaven's "overflowing joy had fallen down on our earth. The "Patriarchs and Prophets relished it, and then the "Holy Ghost put it on the lips of the Apostles, from "whom it flowed even to us. It signifies the eternal "Feast of the Angels and Saints, which consists in "their endless praise of God, and in their ceaseless "singing their ever new admiration of the beauty of the "God, on whose Face they are to gaze for everlasting "ages. This mortal life of ours can in no wise attain "such bliss as this. But, to know where it is to be "found, and have a foretaste of it by the happiness "of hope, and to hunger and thirst for what we thus "taste,—this, this is the perfection of saints here "below. For this reason, the word *Alleluia* has not "been translated; it has been left in its original "Hebrew, as a stranger to tell us that there is a joy "in *his* native land, which could not dwell in *ours:* "he has come among us to signify, rather than to "express, that joy."[1]

During this season of Septuagesima, we have to

---

[1] De divinis Officiis. Lib. 1, cap. 35.

gain a clear knowledge of the miseries of our banishment, under pain of being left for ever in this tyrant Babylon. It was, therefore, necessary that we should be put on our guard against the allurements of our place of exile. It is with this view, that the Church, taking pity on our blindness and our dangers, gives us this solemn warning. By taking from us our *Alleluia*, she virtually tells us, that our lips must first be cleansed, before they again be permitted to utter this word of Angels and Saints; and that our hearts, defiled as they are by sin and attachment to earthly things, must be purified by repentance. She is going to put before our eyes the sad spectacle of the fall of our first Parents, that dire event whence came all our woes, and our need of Redemption. This tender Mother weeps over us, and would have us weep with her.

Let us, then, comply with the law she thus imposes upon us. If spiritual joy is thus taken away from us, what are we to think of the frivolous amusements of the world? And if vanities and follies are insults to the spirit of Septuagesima, would not *sin* be an intolerable outrage on that same spirit? We have been too long the slaves of this tyrant. Our Saviour is soon to appear, bearing his Cross; and his Sacrifice is to restore fallen man to all his rights. Surely, we can never allow that precious Blood to fall uselessly on our souls, as the morning dew that rains on the parched sands of a desert! Let us, with humble hearts, confess that we are sinners, and,—like the Publican of the Gospel, who dared not so much as to raise up his eyes,—let us acknowledge, that it is only right that we should be forbidden, at least for a few weeks, those divine songs of joy, with which our guilty lips had become too familiar; and that we should interrupt those sentiments of presumptuous confidence, which prevented our hearts from having the holy fear of God.

That indifference for the Liturgy of the Church, which is the strongest indication of a weak faith, and which now reigns so universally in the world, is the reason why so many, even *practical*, Catholics can witness this yearly suspension of the *Alleluia*, without profiting by the lesson it conveys. A passing remark, or a chance thought, is the most they give to it, for they care for no other devotions but such as are private; the spirit of the Church, in her various Seasons, is quite beneath their notice. If these lines should meet their eye, we would beg of them to reflect for a moment that the Church is their Mother; that her authority is the highest on earth; that her wisdom enables her to know what is *best* for her children. Why, then, keep aloof from her spirit, as though there were some other to be found, that could better lead them to their God? why be indifferent in this present instance? why deem of no interest to piety this suspension of the *Alleluia*, which she, the Church, considers as one of the principal and most solemn incidents in her Liturgical Year? Perhaps we shall be doing them a service, by showing them how keenly this interruption of the word of heavenly joy was felt by the Christians of those ages, when Faith was the grand ruling principle, not only with society at large, but with each individual.

The farewell to *Alleluia*, in the Middle Ages, varied in the different Churches. Here, it was an affectionate enthusiasm, speaking the beauty of the celestial word; there, it was a heart-felt regret at the departure of the much loved companion of all their prayers.

We begin with two Antiphons, which would seem to be of *Roman* origin. We find them in the *Antiphonarium* of Saint Cornelius of Compiégne, published by Dom Denys de Sainte Marthe. They are a farewell to "*Alleluia*" made by our Catholic fore-

EVE OF SEPTUAGESIMA.

fathers in the 9th century; they express, too, the hope of its coming back, as soon as the Resurrection of Jesus shall have brightened up the firmament of the Church.

ANT. May the good Angel of the Lord accompany thee, Alleluia, and give thee a good journey, that thou mayst come back to us in joy, Alleluia, Alleluia.

ANT. Alleluia, abide with us to-day, and to-morrow thou shalt set forth, Alleluia; and when the day shall have risen, thou shalt proceed on thy way, Alleluia, Alleluia, Alleluia.

ANT. Angelus Domini bonus comitetur tecum, Alleluia, et bene disponat itineri tuo, ut iterum cum gaudio revertaris ad nos, Alleluia, Alleluia.

ANT. Alleluia, mane apud nos hodie, et crastina proficisceris, Alleluia; et dum ortus fuerit dies, ambulabis via tua, Alleluia, Alleluia, Alleluia.

The Gothic Church of Spain thus saluted the "*Alleluia,*" on the eve of its interruption. We merely make a selection from what is almost a complete Office.

HYMN.

Citizens of heaven! give forth Alleluia in your holy canticles; sing with one voice your eternal Alleluia.

Inhabitants of light everlasting! make heaven resound, as ye sing to the great God, in your hymning choirs, the eternal Alleluia.

The glorious city of God will receive you,—the city which echoes with songs of joy, and awakens the eternal Alleluia.

Ye have conquered; go, take the fair beauty of the starry land, wherein ye may chant the eternal Alleluia.

Alleluia piis edite laudibus,
Cives ætherei, psallite unanimiter
Alleluia perenne.

Hinc vos perpetui luminis accolæ,
Ad summum resonate hymniferis choris
Alleluia perenne.

Vos urbs eximia suscipiet Dei,
Quæ lætis resonans cantibus, excitat
Alleluia perenne.

Almum sidereæ jam patriæ decus
Victores capite, quo canere possitis
Alleluia perenne.

Illic Regis honor vocibus inclytis
Jocundum reboat carmine perpetim
Alleluia perenne.
Hoc fessis requies, hoc cibus, hoc potus
Oblectans reduces, haustibus affluens
Alleluia perenne.

Te suavisonis conditor affatim
Rerum carminibus, laudeque pangimus
Alleluia perenne.
Te Christe celebrat gloria vocibus
Nostris, omnipotens, ac tibi dicimus
Alleluia perenne :
Alleluia perenne. Amen.
Felici reditu gaudia sumite,
Reddentes Domino glorificum melos,
Alleluia perenne.

'Tis there the glory of the King is proclaimed with sweetest voices, singing ever their joyous, their eternal Alleluia.

This is the rest to the wearied ; this is the food and drink giving delight to exiles reaching home ; and this is their cup of overflowing nectar ;—the eternal Alleluia.

We, too, O God, Creator of all things ! in sweetest hymns we praise thee, singing our eternal Alleluia.

To thee, Jesus Almighty ! our voices give glory : to thee we say : Eternal Alleluia ! Eternal Alleluia ! Amen.

Be glad on the day of its happy return ; and return to your Lord with your melody of glory,—the eternal Alleluia.

CAPITULUM.

Alleluia in cœlo, et in terra : in cœlo perpetuatur, et in terra cantatur. Ibi sonat jugiter : hic fideliter. Illic perenniter, hic suaviter. Illic feliciter, hic concorditer : illic ineffabiliter, hic instanter. Illic sine syllabis : hic modulis. Illic ab Angelis, hic a populis, quam Christo Domino nascente in laude et confessione nimis ejus, non solum in cœlo, sed et in terra cœlicolæ cecinerunt : dum gloriam in excelsis Deo, et

Alleluia is in heaven and on earth : it is eternal in heaven, and is even sung on earth. There, unceasingly ; here, faithfully. There, everlastingly ; here, sweetly. There, happily ; here, concordantly. There, ineffably ; here, heartily. There, it needs no syllables ; here, it needs our melodies. There, it has Angels for its chanters ; here, it has men. When Christ our Lord was born, the heavenly host gave him exceeding praise and honour, singing Alleluia both in heaven and on earth, and proclaiming glory to God in the highest, and peace on earth to men of good will. Therefore do we beseech thee, O Lord, that, as we strive to imitate the Angels in their ministry of praise, we may live in such manner as to deserve to be their companions in eternal life.

pacem in terra bonæ voluntatis hominibus nuntiaverunt. Quæsumus ergo, Domine, ut quorum ministeria nitimur imitari laudando, eorum mereamur consortium beatæ vitæ vivendo.

ANTHEM.

Thou shalt go, Alleluia; thy journey shall be prosperous, Alleluia; and again come back to us with joy, Alleluia. For they shall bear thee up in their hands, lest at any time thou dash thy foot against a stone. And again come back to us with joy, Alleluia.

Ibis, Alleluia. Prosperum iter habebis, Alleluia; et iterum cum gaudio revertaris ad nos, Alleluia. In manibus enim suis portabunt te: ne unquam offendas ad lapidem pedem tuum. Et iterum cum gaudio revertaris ad nos, Alleluia.

BENEDICTION.

May Alleluia, that sacred and joyful word, resound to God's praise from the lips of all people.
℟. Amen.
May this word, which expresses glory as chanted by the choirs of Angels, be sweet as sung by the voices of believers.
℟. Amen.
And may that which noiselessly gleams in the citizens of heaven, yield fruit in your hearts by ever growing love.
℟. Amen.
May the Lord's good Angel go with thee, Alleluia; and prepare all good things

Alleluia, nomen pium, atque jocundum, dilatetur ad laudem Dei in ora omnium populorum.
℟. Amen.
Sit in vocibus credentium clara quæ in Angelorum ostenditur concentibus gloriosa.

℟. Amen.
Et, quæ in æternis civibus sine sonorum strepitu enitet, in vestris cordibus effectu planiore fructificet.
℟. Amen.
Angelus Domini bonus comitetur tecum, Alleluia; et omnia bona præparet iti-

neri tuo. Et iterum cum gaudio revertaris ad nos, Alleluia.

for thy journey. And again come back to us with joy, Alleluia.

The Churches of Germany, in the Middle Ages, expressed their farewell to the "*Alleluia*" in the following fine Sequence, which is to be found in all their Missals up to the 15th century.

SEQUENCE.

Cantemus cuncta melodum nunc Alleluia.

In laudibus æterni regis, hæc plebs resultet Alleluia.

Hoc denique cœlestes chori cantent in altum Alleluia.

Hoc beatorum per prata Paradisiaca psallant concentus Alleluia.

Quin et astrorum micantia luminaria jubilent altum Alleluia.

Nubium cursus, ventorum volatus, fulgurum coruscatio et tonitruum sonitus, dulce consonent simul Alleluia.

Fluctus et undæ, imber et procellæ, tempestas et serenitas, cauma, gelu, nix, pruinæ, saltus, nemora pangant Alleluia.

Hinc variæ volucres Creatorem laudibus concinite cum Alleluia.

Ast illic respondeant voces altæ diversarum bestiarum Alleluia.

Istinc montium celsi vertices sonent Alleluia.

Hinc vallium profunditates saltent Alleluia.

Let us all now sing the melodious Alleluia.

In praise of the Eternal King, let this assembly give forth Alleluia.

And let the heavenly choirs loudly chant Alleluia.

Let the choir of the Blessed sing in the land of Paradise, Alleluia.

Nay, let the bright stars hymn one loud Alleluia.

Fleet clouds, swift winds, flashing lightning, and pealing thunder,—let all unite in a sweet Alleluia.

Waves and billows, showers and storms, tempest and calm, heat, cold, snow, frost, woods and groves, let them tell their Alleluia.

And ye countless birds, sing the praises of your Maker with an Alleluia.

To which let the loud-voiced beasts respond another Alleluia.

Let the high mountain-tops ring with Alleluia,

And the deep valleys echo— Alleluia.

Thou, too, deep jubilant sea, say Alleluia;
And thou, boundless earth, Alleluia!
Now let the whole race of men say its praiseful Alleluia,

And oft to its Creator give this canticle of thanks,—Alleluia!
He loves to hear this word eternally repeated,—Alleluia;

And Jesus, too, applauds the song, the heavenly Alleluia.

Do you, then, Brethren, be glad, and sing: Alleluia!
And you, Little Children, never fail to respond: Alleluia!
Let all, then, sing together: Alleluia to the Lord; Alleluia to Christ; and to the Holy Ghost, Alleluia!
Praise be to the Eternal Trinity, whose glory was declared at the baptism of our Lord! Sing we, then,—Alleluia!

Tu quoque maris jubilans abysse, dic Alleluia.
Necnon terrarum molis immensitates: Alleluia.
Nunc omne genus humanum laudans exsultet Alleluia.

Et Creatori grates frequentans consonet Alleluia.

Hoc denique nomen audire jugiter delectatur Alleluia.

Hoc etiam carmen cœleste comprobat ipse Christus Alleluia.

Nunc vos socii cantate lætantes: Alleluia.
Et vos pueruli respondete semper: Alleluia.
Nunc omnes canite simul, Alleluia Domino, Alleluia Christo, Pneumatique Alleluia.
Laus Trinitati æternæ in baptismo Domini quæ clarificatur: hinc canamus Alleluia.

The Churches of France, in the 13th century, and long even after that, used to sing at Vespers of the Saturday before Septuagesima, the following beautiful Hymn:

HYMN.

The sweet Alleluia-song, the word of endless joy, is the melody of heaven's choir, chanted by them that dwell for ever in the house of God.

O joyful mother, O Jerusalem our City, Alleluia is the

Alleluia dulce carmen,
  Vox perennis gaudii,
Alleluia laus suavis
  Est choris cælestibus,
Quam canunt Dei manentes
  In domo per secula.
Alleluia læta mater
  Concivis Jerusalem;

Alleluia vox tuorum
  Civium gaudentium :
Exsules nos flere cogunt
Babylonis flumina.
Alleluia non meremur
  In perenne psallere ;
Alleluia vox reatus
  Cogit intermittere ;
Tempus instat quo peracta
  Lugeamus crimina.
Unde laudando precamur
  Te beata Trinitas,
Ut tuum nobis videre
  Pascha des in æthere,
Quo tibi læti canamus
  Alleluia perpetim.
    Amen.
	language of thy happy citizens. The rivers of Babylon, where we poor exiles live, force *us* to weep. We are unworthy to sing a ceaseless Alleluia. Our sins bid us interrupt our Alleluia. The time is at hand when it behoves us to bewail our crimes. We, therefore, beseech thee whilst we praise thee, O Blessed Trinity! that thou grant us to come to that Easter of heaven, where we shall sing to thee our joyful everlasting Alleluia. Amen.

In the present form of the Liturgy, the farewell to *Alleluia* is more simple. The Church, at the conclusion of to-day's Vespers, repeats the mysterious words four times:

Benedicamus Domino, Alleluia, Alleluia. Deo gratias, Alleluia, Alleluia.	Let us bless the Lord, Alleluia, Alleluia. Thanks be to God, Alleluia, Alleluia.

This song of heaven, then, is taken from us. It will return, when the triumph of Jesus' Resurrection is proclaimed upon our earth.

SEPTUAGESIMA SUNDAY.

The holy Church calls us together to-day, in order that we may hear from her lips the sad history of the fall of our First Parents. This awful event implies the Passion and cruel Death of the Son of God made Man, who has mercifully taken upon himself to expiate this and every subsequent sin committed by Adam and us his children. It is of the utmost importance that we should understand the greatness of the remedy; we must, therefore, consider the grievousness of the wound inflicted. For this purpose, we will spend the present week in meditating on the nature and consequences of the sin of our First Parents.

Formerly, the Church used to read in her Matins of to-day that passage of the Book of Genesis, where Moses relates to all future generations, but in words of most impressive and sublime simplicity, how the first sin was brought into the world. In the present form of the Liturgy, the reading of this history of the Fall is deferred till Wednesday, and the preceding days give us the account of the six days of Creation. We will anticipate the great instruction, and begin it at once, inasmuch as it forms the basis of the whole week's teaching.

From the Book of Genesis.	De Libro Genesis.
Ch. III.	*Cap. III.*
Now the serpent was more subtle than any of the beasts of the earth, which the Lord God had made. And he said to the woman: Why hath God commanded you, that you	Sed et serpens erat callidior cunctis animantibus terræ, quæ fecerat Dominus Deus. Qui dixit ad mulierem : Cur præcepit vobis Deus ut non comederetis de

omni ligno paradisi? Cui respondit mulier: De fructu lignorum quæ sunt in paradiso vescimur: de fructu vero ligni, quod est in medio paradisi, præcepit nobis Deus ne comederemus, et ne tangeremus illud, ne forte moriamur. Dixit autem serpens ad mulierem: Nequaquam morte moriemini; scit enim Deus quod in quocumque die comederitis ex eo, aperientur oculi vestri, et eritis sicut dii, scientes bonum et malum. Vidit igitur mulier, quod bonum esset lignum ad vescendum, et pulchrum oculis, aspectuque delectabile: et tulit de fructu illius, et comedit: deditque viro suo, qui comedit. Et aperti sunt oculi amborum.

Cumque cognovissent se esse nudos, consuerunt folia ficus, et fecerunt sibi perizomata. Et cum audissent vocem Domini Dei deambulantis in paradiso, ad auram post meridiem, abscondit se Adam et uxor ejus a facie Domini Dei, in medio ligni paradisi. Vocavitque Dominus Deus Adam, et dixit ei: Ubi es? Qui ait: Vocem tuam audivi in paradiso, et timui, eo quod nudus essem et abscondi me. Qui dixit: Quis enim indicavit tibi quod nudus esses, nisi quod ex ligno de quo præceperam tibi, ne comederes, comedisti? Dixitque Adam: Mulier, quam de-

should not eat of every tree of paradise? And the woman answered him, saying: Of the fruit of the trees that are in paradise we do eat; but of the fruit of the tree which is in the midst of paradise, God hath commanded us that we should not eat, and that we should not touch it, lest perhaps we die. And the serpent said to the woman: No, you shall not die the death; for God doth know, that in what day soever you shall eat thereof, your eyes shall be opened, and you shall be as gods, knowing good and evil. And the woman saw that the tree was good to eat, and fair to the eyes, and delightful to behold: and she took of the fruit thereof, and did eat: and gave to her husband, who did eat. And the eyes of them both were opened.

And when they perceived themselves to be naked, they sewed together fig-leaves, and made themselves aprons. And when they heard the voice of the Lord God walking in paradise, at the afternoon air, Adam and his wife hid themselves from the face of the Lord God, amidst the trees of paradise. And the Lord God called Adam, and said to him: Where art thou? And he said: I heard thy voice in paradise, and I was afraid, because I was naked, and I hid myself. And he said to him: And who hath told thee that thou wast naked, but that thou hast eaten of the tree whereof I commanded thee that thou

SEPTUAGESIMA SUNDAY. 123

shouldst not eat? And Adam said: The woman, whom thou gavest me, to be my companion, gave me of the tree, and I did eat. And the Lord God said to the woman: Why hast thou done this? And she answered: The serpent deceived me, and I did eat.

And the Lord God said to the serpent: Because thou hast done this thing, thou art cursed among all cattle, and beasts of the earth: upon thy breast shalt thou go, and earth shalt thou eat all the days of thy life. I will put enmities between thee and the woman, and thy seed and her seed; she shall crush thy head, and thou shalt lie in wait for her heel. To the woman, also, he said: I will multiply thy sorrows, and thy conceptions: in sorrow shalt thou bring forth children, and thou shalt be under thy husband's power, and he shall have dominion over thee. And to Adam he said: Because thou hast hearkened to the voice of thy wife, and hast eaten of the tree, whereof I commanded thee that thou shouldst not eat, cursed is the earth in thy work: with labour and toil shalt thou eat thereof all the days of thy life. Thorns and thistles shall it bring forth to thee, and thou shalt eat the herbs of the earth. In the sweat of thy face shalt thou eat bread, till thou return to the earth, out of which thou wast taken: for dust thou art, and into dust thou shalt return.

disti mihi sociam, dedit mihi de ligno, et comedi. Et dixit Dominus Deus ad mulierem: Quare hoc fecisti? Quæ respondit: Serpens decepit me, et comedi.

Et ait Dominus Deus ad serpentem: Quia fecisti hoc, maledictus es inter omnia animantia, et bestias terræ: super pectus tuum gradieris, et terram comedes cunctis diebus vitæ tuæ. Inimicitias ponam inter te et mulierem, et semen tuum et semen illius; ipsa conteret caput tuum, et tu insidiaberis calcaneo ejus. Mulieri quoque dixit: Multiplicabo ærumnas tuas, et conceptus tuos: in dolore paries filios, et sub viri potestate eris, et ipse dominabitur tibi. Adæ vero dixit: Quia audisti vocem uxoris tuæ, et comedisti de ligno, ex quo præceperam tibi ne comederes, maledicta terra in opere tuo: in laboribus comedes ex ea cunctis diebus vitæ tuæ. Spinas et tribulos germinabit tibi, et comedes herbam terræ. In sudore vultus tui vesceris pane, donec revertaris in terram, de qua sumptus es quia pulvis es, et in pulverem reverteris.

Oh! terrible page of man's history! It alone explains to us our present position on the earth. It tells us what we are in the eyes of God, and how humbly we should comport ourselves before his divine Majesty. We will make it the subject of this week's meditation. And now, let us prepare to profit by the Liturgy of this Sunday, which we call *Septuagesima.*

In the Greek Church, it is called *Prophōné,* (*Proclamation,*) because on this day they announce to the people the coming Fast of Lent, and the precise day of Easter. It is also called the *Sunday of the Prodigal Son,* because that Parable is read in their Liturgy for this Sunday, as an invitation to sinners to draw nigh to the God of Mercy. But it is the last day of the week, *Prophōné,* which, by a strange custom, begins with the preceding Monday, as do also the two following weeks.

MASS.

The Station, at Rome, is in the Church of Saint Laurence *outside the walls.* The ancient Liturgists observe how there is the relation of martyrdom between the just Abel, (whose being murdered by Cain is the subject of one of the Responsories of to-day's Matins,) and the courageous Martyr, over whose tomb the Church of Rome commences her Septuagesima.

The Introit describes the fears of *death,* wherewith Adam and his whole posterity are tormented, in consequence of sin. But, in the midst of all this misery, there is heard a cry of hope, for man is still permitted to ask mercy from his God. God gave man a promise, on the very day of his condemnation:

SEPTUAGESIMA SUNDAY. 125

—the sinner needs but to confess his miseries, and the very Lord, against whom he sinned, will become his *Deliverer*.

INTROIT.

The groans of death surrounded me, and the sorrows of hell encompassed me; and in my affliction I called upon the Lord, and he heard my voice from his holy temple.

Ps. I will love thee, O Lord, my strength: the Lord is my firmament, my refuge, and my deliverer. ℣. Glory. The groans.

Circumdederunt me gemitus mortis, dolores inferni circumdederunt me: et in tribulatione mea invocavi Dominum, et exaudivit de templo sancto suo vocem meam.

Ps. Diligam te, Domine, fortitudo mea: Dominus firmamentum meum, et refugium meum, et liberator meus. ℣. Gloria Patri, Circumdederunt.

In the Collect, the Church acknowledges that her children justly suffer the chastisements, which are the consequences of sin; but she beseeches her divine Lord to send them that Mercy, which delivers from misery.

COLLECT.

Mercifully hear, we beseech thee, O Lord, the prayers of thy people; that we who are justly afflicted for our sins, may be mercifully delivered for the glory of thy name. Through, &c.

Preces populi tui, quæsumus, Domine, clementer exaudi: ut qui juste pro pecatis nostris affligimur, pro tui nominis gloria misericorditer liberemur. Per Dominum.

SECOND COLLECT.

Preserve us, O Lord, we beseech thee, from all dangers of soul and body: and by the intercession of the glorious and blessed Mary, the ever Virgin-Mother of God, of the blessed

A cunctis nos, quæsumus, Domine, mentis et corporis defende periculis: et intercedente beata et gloriosa semperque Virgine Dei Genitrice Maria, cum beatis

Apostolis tuis Petro et Paulo, atque beato N., et omnibus Sanctis, salutem nobis tribue benignus et pacem : ut destructis adversitatibus et erroribus universis, Ecclesia tua secura tibi serviat libertate.

Apostles, Peter and Paul, of Blessed N., (*here is mentioned the Titular Saint of the Church,*) and of all the Saints, grant us, in thy mercy, health and peace ; that all adversities and errors being removed, thy Church may serve thee with undisturbed liberty.

The Priest adds a third Collect, which is left to his own choice.

EPISTLE.

Lectio Epistolæ beati Pauli Apostoli ad Corinthios.

Lesson of the Epistle of Saint Paul the Apostle to the Corinthians.

I. *Cap. IX.*

I. *Ch. IX.*

Fratres, nescitis quod ii qui in stadio currunt, omnes quidem currunt, sed unus accipit bravium ? Sic currite, ut comprehendatis. Omnis autem, qui in agone contendit, ab omnibus se abstinet : et illi quidem ut corruptibilem coronam accipiant, nos autem incorruptam. Ego igitur sic curro, non quasi in incertum : sic pugno, non quasi aerem verberans : sed castigo corpus meum et in servitutem redigo : ne forte cum aliis prædicaverim, ipse reprobus efficiar. Nolo enim vos ignorare, fratres, quoniam patres nostri omnes sub nube fuerunt, et omnes mare transierunt, et omnes in Moyse, baptizati sunt, in nube et in mari : et omnes eamdem escam spiritalem manducaverunt et omnes

Brethren, know you not that they that run in the race, all run indeed, but one receiveth the prize ? So run that you may obtain. And every one that striveth for the mastery, refraineth himself from all things ; and they indeed that they may receive a corruptible crown, but we an incorruptible one. I therefore so run, not as at an uncertainty : I so fight, not as one beating the air : but I chastise my body and bring it into subjection : lest, perhaps, when I have preached to others, I myself should become a castaway. For I would not have you ignorant, brethren, that our fathers were all under the cloud, and all passed through the sea, and all in Moses were baptised in the cloud, and in the sea : and did all eat the same spiritual food ; and all

drank the same spiritual drink: (and they drank of the spiritual rock that followed them, and the rock was Christ.) But with the most of them God was not well pleased.	eumdem potum spiritalem biberunt (bibebant autem de spiritali, consequente eos petra; petra autem erat Christus): Sed non in pluribus eorum beneplacitum est Deo.

These stirring words of the Apostle deepen the sentiments already produced in us by the sad recollections of which we are this day reminded. He tells us, that this world is *a race*, wherein all must run; but that they alone win *the prize*, who run well. Let us, therefore, rid ourselves of everything that could impede us, and make us lose our crown. Let us not deceive ourselves: we are never sure, until we reach the goal. Is our conversion more solid than was St. Paul's? Are our good works better done, or more meritorious, than were his? Yet, he assures us, that he was not without the fear that he might perhaps be lost; for which cause, he chastises his body, and keeps it in subjection to the spirit. Man, in his present state, has not the same will for all that is right and just, which Adam had before he sinned, and which, notwithstanding, he abused to his own ruin. We have a bias which inclines us to evil; so that our only means of keeping our ground is by sacrificing the flesh to the spirit. To many this is very harsh doctrine; hence, they are sure to fail,—they never can win the *prize*. Like the Israelites spoken of by our Apostle, they will be left behind to die in the desert, and so lose the Promised Land. Yet, they saw the same miracles that Josue and Caleb saw! So true is it that nothing can make a salutary impression on a heart, which is obstinately bent on fixing all its happiness in the things of this present life; and though it is forced, each day, to own that they are vain, yet each day it returns to them, vainly but determinedly loving them.

The heart, on the contrary, that puts its trust in God, and mans itself to energy by the thought of the divine assistance being abundantly given to him that asks it,—will not flag or faint in the *race*, and will win the heavenly *prize*. God's eye is unceasingly on all them that toil and suffer. These are the truths expressed in the Gradual.

GRADUAL.

Adjutor in opportunitatibus, in tribulatione sperent in te qui noverunt te, quoniam non derelinquis quærentes te, Domine.

Quoniam non in finem oblivio erit pauperis; patientia pauperum non peribit in æternum: exsurge, Domine, non prævaleat homo.

A helper in due time, in tribulation: let them trust in thee, who know thee, for thou hast not forsaken them that seek thee, O Lord.

For the poor man shall not be forgotten to the end; the patience of the poor man shall not perish for ever: arise, O Lord, let not man prevail.

The Tract sends forth our *cry* to God, and the *cry* is from the very *depths* of our misery. Man is humbled exceedingly by the Fall; but he knows, that God is full of *mercy*, and that, in his goodness, he punishes our *iniquities* less than they deserve: were it not so, none of us could hope for pardon.

TRACT.

De profundis clamavi ad te, Domine: Domine, exaudi vocem meam.

℣. Fiant aures tuæ intendentes in orationem servi tui.

℣. Si iniquitates observaveris, Domine: Domine, quis sustinebit?

℣. Quia apud te propitiatio est, et propter legem tuam sustinui te, Domine.

Out of the depths I have cried to thee, O Lord: Lord, hear my voice.

℣. Let thine ears be attentive to the voice of my supplication.

℣. If thou, O Lord, wilt mark iniquities, Lord, who shall stand it?

℣. For with thee there is merciful forgiveness, and by reason of thy law, I have waited for thee, O Lord.

SEPTUAGESIMA SUNDAY. 129

GOSPEL.

Sequel of the holy Gospel according to Matthew.

Ch. XX.

At that time, Jesus spoke to his disciples this parable: The kingdom of heaven is like to a householder who went out early in the morning to hire labourers into his vineyard. And having agreed with the labourers for a penny a day, he sent them into his vineyard. And going out about the third hour, he saw others standing in the market-place idle. And he said to them: Go you also into my vineyard, and I will give you what shall be just. And they went their way. And again he went out about the sixth and the ninth hour, and did in like manner. But about the eleventh hour he went out and found others standing, and he saith to them: Why stand you here all the day idle? They say to him: Because no man hath hired us. He saith to them: Go you also into my vineyard. And when evening was come, the lord of the vineyard saith to his steward: Call the labourers and pay them their hire, beginning from the last even to the first. When, therefore, they were come that came about the eleventh hour, they received every man a penny. But when the first also came, they thought that they should receive more: and they also received every man a penny. And receiving it they mur-

Sequentia sancti Evangelii secundum Matthæum.

Cap. XX.

In illo tempore, dixit Jesus discipulis suis parabolam hanc: Simile est regnum cœlorum homini patrifamilias, qui exiit primo mane conducere operarios in vineam suam. Conventione autem facta cum operariis ex denario diurno, misit eos in vineam suam. Et egressus circa horam tertiam, vidit alios stantes in foro otiosos, et dixit illis: Ite et vos in vineam meam, et quod justum fuerit, dabo vobis. Illi autem abierunt. Iterum autem exiit circa sextam et nonam horam, et fecit similiter. Circa undecimam vero exiit; et invenit alios stantes, et dicit illis: Quid hic statis tota die otiosi? Dicunt ei: Quia nemo nos conduxit. Dixit illis: Ite et vos in vineam meam. Cum sero autem factum esset, dicit Dominus vineæ procuratori suo: Voca operarios, et redde illis mercedem, incipiens a novissimis usque ad primos. Cum venissent ergo qui circa undecimam horam venerant, acceperunt singulos denarios. Venientes autem et primi, arbitrati sunt quod plus essent accepturi: acceperunt autem et ipsi singulos denarios. Et accipientes murmurabant adversus patremfamilias, dicentes: Hi novissimi una hora fecerunt, et pares illos nobis fecisti qui portavimus pondus diei et æstus? At ille respondens uni eorum, dixit: Amice, non facio tibi injuriam; nonne ex denario convenisti mecum? Tolle quod tuum est, et vade: volo autem et huic novissimo dare sicut et tibi. Aut non licet mihi quod volo facere? An oculus tuus nequam est, quia ego bonus sum? Sic erunt novissimi primi, et primi novissimi. Multi enim sunt vocati, pauci vero electi.

mured against the master of the house, saying: These last have worked but one hour, and thou hast made them equal to us that have borne the burden of the day, and the heats. But he answering said to one of them: Friend, I do thee no wrong: didst thou not agree with me for a penny? Take what is thine, and go thy way: I will also give to this last even as to thee. Or, is it not lawful for me to do what I will? Is thy eye evil, because I am good? So shall the last be first, and the first last. For many are called, but few chosen.

It is of importance, that we should well understand this Parable of the Gospel, and why the Church inserts it in to-day's Liturgy. Firstly, then, let us recall to mind on what occasion our Saviour spoke this Parable, and what instruction he intended to convey by it to the Jews. He wishes to warn them of the fast approach of the day when their Law is to give way to the Christian Law; and he would prepare their minds against the jealousy and prejudice which might arise in them, at the thought that God was about to form a Covenant with the Gentiles. The *Vineyard* is the Church in its several periods, from the beginning of the world to the time of God himself coming to dwell among men, and form all true believers into one visible and permanent society. The *Morning* is the time, from Adam to Noah; the *Third Hour* begins with Noah and ends with Abraham; the *Sixth Hour* includes the period which elapsed between Abraham and Moses; and lastly, the *Ninth Hour* opens with the age of the Prophets, and closes with the Birth of the Saviour. The Messias came at the *Eleventh*

SEPTUAGESIMA SUNDAY. 131

Hour, when the world seemed to be at the decline of its day. Mercies unprecedented were reserved for this last period, during which, Salvation was to be given to the Gentiles by the preaching of the Apostles. It is by this mystery of Mercy that our Saviour rebukes the Jewish pride. By the selfish murmurings made against the *Master of the House* by the early *Labourers*, our Lord signifies the indignation which the Scribes and Pharisees would show at the Gentiles being adopted as God's children. Then, he shows them how their jealousy would be chastised : Israel, that had laboured before us, shall be rejected for their obduracy of heart, and we Gentiles, the *last* comers, shall be made *first*, for we shall be made members of that Catholic Church, which is the Spouse of the Son of God.

This is the interpretation of our Parable given by St. Augustine and St. Gregory the Great, and by the generality of the Holy Fathers. But it conveys a second instruction, as we are assured by the two Holy Doctors just named. It signifies the calling given by God to each of us individually, pressing us to labour, during this life, for the *Kingdom* prepared for us. The *Morning* is our childhood. The *Third Hour*, according to the division used by the ancients in counting their day, is sun-rise ; it is our youth. The *Sixth Hour*, by which name they called our mid-day, is manhood. The *Eleventh Hour*, which immediately preceded sun-set, is old age. The *Master of the House* calls his *Labourers* at all these various *Hours*. They must go that very hour. They that are called in the Morning may not put off their starting for the Vineyard, under pretext of going afterwards, when the Master shall call them later on. Who has told them that they shall live to the Eleventh Hour ? They are called at the Third Hour ; they may be dead at the Sixth. God will call to the labours of the last hour such as shall be living when that hour comes; but, if we should die at midday, that last call will not avail *us*. Besides, God has not promised us a second call, if we excuse ourselves from the first.

At the Offertory, the Church invites us to celebrate the praises of God. God has mercifully granted us, that the hymns we sing to the glory of his name, should be our consolation in this vale of tears.

OFFERTORY.

Bonum est confiteri Domino, et psallere nomini tuo, Altissime.	It is good to give praise to the Lord, and to sing to thy name, O Most High.

SECRET.

Muneribus nostris, quæsumus, Domine, precibusque susceptis: et cœlestibus nos munda mysteriis, et clementer exaudi. Per Dominum.	Having received, O Lord, our offerings and prayers, cleanse us, we beseech thee by these heavenly mysteries, and mercifully hear us. Through, *&c.*

SECOND SECRET.

Exaudi nos, Deus Salutaris noster: ut per hujus Sacramenti virtutem, a cunctis nos mentis et corporis hostibus tuearis, gratiam tribuens in præsenti, et gloriam in futuro.	Graciously grant us, O God our Saviour, that by virtue of this Sacrament, thou mayest defend us from all enemies, both of soul and body; giving us grace in this life, and glory in the next.

The third Secret is left to the Priest's own choice.

In the Communion-Antiphon, the Church prays that man, having now been regenerated by the Bread of heaven, may regain that likeness to his God which Adam received at his creation. The greater our misery, the stronger should be our hope in Him, who descended to us that we might ascend to him.

COMMUNION.

Make thy face to shine upon thy servant; save me in thy mercy. Let me not be confounded, O Lord, for I have called upon thee.

Illumina faciem tuam super servum tuum, et salvum me fac in tua misericordia: Domine, non confundar, quoniam invocavi te.

POSTCOMMUNION.

May thy Faithful, O God, be strengthened by thy gifts; that by receiving them, they may ever hunger after them, and hungering after them, they may have their desires satisfied in the everlasting possession of them. Through, &c.

Fideles tui, Deus, per tua dona firmentur: ut eadem et percipiendo requirant, et quærendo sine fine percipiant. Per Dominum.

SECOND POSTCOMMUNION.

May the oblation of this divine Sacrament, we beseech thee, O Lord, both cleanse and defend us; and by the intercession of Blessed Mary, the Virgin-Mother of God, together with that of thy blessed Apostles, Peter and Paul, as likewise of blessed N., and of all the Saints, free us from all sin, and deliver us from all adversity.

Mundet et muniat nos, quæsumus Domine, divini Sacramenti munus oblatum, et intercedente beata Virgine Dei Genitrice Maria, cum beatis Apostolis Petro et Paulo, atque beato N. et omnibus Sanctis, a cunctis nos reddat et perversitatibus expiatos, et adversitatibus expeditos.

The third Postcommunion is left to the Priest's own choice.

VESPERS.

The Psalms and Antiphons, are given in *page* 74.

CAPITULUM.

(I. *Cor. IX.*)

Fratres, nescitis quod ii, qui in stadio currunt, omnes quidem currunt, sed unus accipit bravium? Sic currite, ut comprehendatis.

Brethren, know you not, that they that run in the race, all run indeed, but one receiveth the prize? So run, that you may obtain.

For the Hymn and Versicle, see *page* 81.

ANTIPHON OF THE *Magnificat*.

ANT. Dixit paterfamilias operariis suis: Quid hic statis tota die otiosi? At illi respondentes, dixerunt: Quia nemo nos conduxit. Ite et vos in vineam meam: et quod justum fuerit, dabo vobis.

ANT. The householder said to the labourers: Why stand you here all the day idle? But they answering, said to him: Because no man hath hired us. Go ye, also, into my vineyard, and I will give you what is just.

OREMUS.

Preces populi tui, quæsumus Domine, clementer exaudi, ut qui juste pro peccatis nostris affligimur, pro tui Nominis gloria misericorditer liberemur. Per Dominum.

LET US PRAY.

Mercifully hear, we beseech thee, O Lord, the prayers of thy people; that we who are justly afflicted for our sins, may be mercifully delivered for the glory of thy name. Through, &c.

For each day of this Week we select a few stanzas from the Hymn, which the Greek Liturgy uses in her Office for the Sunday preceding the Fast of Lent. It is a lamentation over Adam's Fall.

IN DOMINICA TYROPHAGI.

Excidit e paradiso voluptatis Adamus, Domini præ-

Because he broke the commandment of his Lord, and

SEPTUAGESIMA SUNDAY.

was led by intemperance to taste a food which was to be one of bitterness to him, Adam was banished from the paradise of delight, and condemned to till the earth whence himself was taken, and to eat his bread in the sweat of his brow. Let us, therefore, covet temperance, lest, like him, we may have to weep out of paradise; let us be temperate and enter heaven.

God, my Creator, took dust from the earth, quickened me with a living soul, graciously made me the king of all visible things on earth, and gave me fellowship with the Angels; but crafty Satan, making the serpent his instrument, allured me with food, banished me far from the glory of God, and made me a slave to death in the bowels of the earth: but thou O God, art my Lord, and full of mercy,—recal me from exile.

Being deceived by the craft of the enemy, I, miserable man, violated thy commandment, O Lord, and being stripped of the garment which thy divine hand had woven for me, I am now clad with leaves of the fig-tree, and with a skin garment; I am condemned to eat a bread for which I must toil with the sweat of my brow, and the earth is cursed, so that it may yield me thorns and thistles: but do thou, that in after times tookest flesh from the Virgin, recal and restore me to Paradise.

ceptum, amaro cibo intemperanter degustato, transgressus, damnatusque fuit terræ unde desumptus fuerat colendæ, suoque pani per sudorem multum comedendo; nos igitur temperantiam appetamus, ne velut ille extra paradisum ploremus, sed intus admittamur.

Conditor meus Dominus, pulvere e terra accepto, me vivifico spiritu animavit, atque visibilium omnium super terram dominatione, Angelorumque consortio dignatus est; dolosus autem Satan, serpentis instrumento usus, esca decepit, et a Dei gloria procul amandavit, mortique in infimis terræ addixit: tu vero, utpote Dominus, atque benignus, ab exilio me revoca.

Stola divinitus texta spoliatus fui miser ego, divino præcepto tuo, Domine, ex inimici fraude violato, foliisque ficulneis et pelliceis tunicis modo circumdor; panem laboris in sudore manducandi sententiam excepi, utque spinas et tribulos tellus mihi ferat, diris devota est; sed qui postremis temporibus e Virgine incarnatus es, revocatu me in paradisum restitue.

Paradise, omni honore dignissime, pulcherrima species, tabernaculum divinitus structum, perenne gaudium et oblectamentum, gloria justorum, Prophetarum lætitia, Sanctorumque domicilium, foliorum tuorum sonitu Conditorem universorum deprecare, ut fores, quas prævaricatione clausi, mihi adaperiat, utque dignus efficiar ligni vitæ participatione, eoque gaudio quod dulcissime prius in temetipso degustavi.

O Paradise!—most worthy of all our reverence, beautiful beyond measure, tabernacle built by God, joy and delight without end, glory of the just, joy of the Prophets, and dwelling of the Saints,—may thy prayers, the sound of thy leaves, obtain for me from the Creator of all things, that thy gates, which my sin hath shut against me, may be thrown open to me, and that I may be made worthy to partake of the tree of life, and of that joy, which I once so sweetly tasted in thy bosom.

MONDAY

OF SEPTUAGESIMA WEEK.

THE serpent said to the Woman: *Why hath God commanded you, that ye should not eat of every tree of paradise?*[1] Thus opened the conversation, which our mother Eve so rashly consents to hold with God's enemy. She ought to have refused all intercourse with Satan; she did not; and thereby she imperils the salvation of the whole human race.

Let us recal to mind the events that have happened up to this fatal hour. God, in his omnipotence and love, has created two beings, upon whom he has lavished all the riches of his goodness. He has destined them for immortality; and this undying life is to have everything that can make it perfectly happy. The whole of nature is made subject to them. A countless posterity is to come from them, and love them with all the tenderness of grateful children. Nay, this God of goodness, who has created them, deigns to be on terms of intimacy with them; and such is their simple innocence, that this adorable condescension does not seem strange to them. But, there is something far beyond all this. He, whom they have hitherto known by favours of an inferior order, prepares for them a happiness which surpasses all they could picture with every effort of thought. They must first go through a trial; and if faithful,

---

[1] Gen. iii. 1.

God will bestow the great gift as a recompense they have merited; and this is the gift:—he will give them to know him *in himself,* make them partakers of his own glory, and make their happiness infinite and eternal. Yes, this is what God has done, and is preparing to do for these two beings, who, but a while ago, were nothing.

In return for all these gratuitous and magnificent gifts, God asks of them but one thing; and it is, that they acknowledge his dominion over them. Nothing, surely, can be sweeter to them than to make such a return; nothing could be more just. All they are, and all they have, and all the lovely creation around them, has been produced out of nothing by the lavish munificence of this God; they must, then, live for him, faithful, loving, and grateful. He asks them to give him one only proof of this fidelity, love, and gratitude: he bids them not to eat of the fruit of one single tree. The only return he asks for all the favours he has bestowed upon them, is the observance of this easy commandment. His sovereign justice will be satisfied by this act of obedience. They ought to accept such terms with hearty readiness, and comply with them with a holy pride, as being not only the tie which will unite them with their God, but as the only means in their power of paying him what he asks of them.

But, there comes another voice, the voice of a creature, and it speaks to the woman:—*Why hath God commanded you, that ye should not eat of every tree?* And Eve dares, and has the heart, to listen to him that asks why her divine Benefactor has put a command upon her! She can bear to hear the justice of God's will called in question! Instead of protesting against the sacrilegious words, she tamely answers them! Her God is blasphemed, and she is not indignant!—How dearly we shall have to pay for this ungrateful indifference, this indiscretion!

And the woman answered him, saying: Of the fruit of the trees that are in Paradise we do eat; but of the fruit of the tree which is in the midst of paradise, God hath commanded us that we should not eat, and that we should not touch it, lest perhaps we die.[1] Thus, Eve not only listens to the serpent's question; she answers him; she converses with the wicked spirit that tempts her. She exposes herself to danger; her fidelity to her Maker is compromised. True, the words she uses show that she has not forgotten his command; but they imply a certain hesitation, which savours of pride and ingratitude.

The Spirit of Evil finds that he has excited, in this heart, a love of independence; and, that if he can but persuade her that she will not suffer from her disobedience, she is his victim. He, therefore, further addresses her with these blasphemous and lying words: *No, ye shall not die the death; for God knoweth, that in what day soever ye shall eat thereof, your eyes shall be opened, and ye shall be as gods, knowing good and evil.*[2] What he proposes to Eve is open rebellion. He has enkindled within her that perfidious love of self, which is man's worst evil, and which, if it be indulged, breaks the tie between him and his Creator. Thus, the blessings God has bestowed, the obligation of gratitude, personal interest,—all are to be disregarded and forgotten. Ungrateful man would become god; he would imitate the rebel Angels; he shall *fall* as they did.

---

[1] Gen. iii. 2, 3.   [2] *Ibid*, 4, 5.

IN DOMINICA TYROPHAGI.

Adesdum anima mea infelix, actus tuos hodie defle, memoria recolens priorem in Eden nuditatem, propter quam deliciis et perenni gaudio excidisti.

Pro multa pietate atque miserationibus, Conditor creaturæ et factor universorum, me pulvere prius animatum una cum Angelis tuis te collaudare præcepisti.

Propter bonitatis divitias, plantas tu, Conditor et Domine, Paradisi delicias in Eden, jubens me speciosis jucundisque minimeque caducis fructibus oblectari.

Hei mihi! anima mea misera, fruendarum Eden voluptatum facultatem a Deo acceperas, vetitumque tibi ne scientiæ lignum manducares: qua de causa Dei legem violasti?

(Virgo Dei Genitrix, utpote Adami ex genere filia, per gratiam vero Christi Dei Mater, nunc me revoca ex Eden ejectum.)

Serpens dolosus honorem meum quondam mihi invidens, in Evæ auribus dolum insusurravit, unde ego deceptus, hei mihi! e vitæ sede exsulavi.

Manu temere extensa, scientiæ lignum degustavi, quod ne contingerem mihi Deus omnino præscripserat, et cum acerbo doloris sensu divinam gloriam exsul amisi.

Come, my poor soul! bewail this day thy deeds. Think within thyself of that sin which made thee naked in Eden, and robbed thee of delight and joy eternal.

Creator of me and of all things; in thy great goodness and mercy, thou, having made me out of dust, and given me a soul, didst command me to unite with the Angels in praising thee.

My Maker and Lord! in the riches of thy goodness, thou plantest a Paradise of delights in Eden, and biddest me feast on its lovely, sweet, and incorruptible fruits.

Woe is me, O my wretched soul! Thy God permitted thee that thou shouldst enjoy the Eden of delights, if thou wouldst obey him and not eat of the tree of knowledge. Wherefore didst thou violate his law?

(O Virgin-Mother of God! Daughter of Adam by nature, but Mother of Christ by grace! recal me now the exile from Eden.)

The crafty serpent envying me such honour, whispered his guile into Eve's ear; and I, alas! deceived by her, was banished from the land of life.

Rashly stretching forth my hand, I tasted of the tree of knowledge, which God forbad me even to touch; and then, with keen sense of grief, I, an exile, lost the glory of God.

Alas, miserable me! How came I not to know the snare? How was it that I suspected not the enemy's craft and envy? My soul was darkened, and I set at naught my Creator's command.

(O most venerable one! my hope and refuge! who by giving birth to thy Jesus, didst cover the nakedness of fallen Adam, clothe me too, O Virgin, with this incorruptible garb!)

Hei mihi! misera anima mea, quomodo dolum non nosti? Quomodo fraudem et inimici invidiam minime sensisti? Sed mente obtenebrata Conditoris tui mandatum neglexisti.

(Spes et protectio mea, O veneranda, quæ sola olim lapsi Adami nuditatem cooperuisti puerperio tuo, rursus, O pura, me incorruptionis veste circumda.)

TUESDAY

OF SEPTUAGESIMA WEEK.

The serpent's promises had stifled, in Eve's heart, every sentiment of Love for the God that had created her and loaded her with blessings: she ambitions to be god like Him! Her Faith, too, is wavering; she is not sure but what God may have deceived her, by threatening her with death should she disobey his command. Flushed by pride, she looks up to the Forbidden Fruit; it seems *good to eat,* and it is *fair to her eyes.*[1] So that her senses too conspire against God, and against her own happiness. The sin is already committed in her heart; it needs but a formal act to make it complete. She cares for nothing but self; God is no more heeded than if he did not exist;—she stretches forth her daring hand; she plucks the Fruit; she puts it to her mouth, and eats!

God had said, that if she broke his commandment, she should die; she has eaten, she has sinned, and yet she lives as before! Her pride exults at this triumph, and, convinced that she is too strong for God's anger to reach her, she resolves on making Adam a partner in her victory. Boldly she hands him the Fruit, which she herself has eaten without any evil coming to her. Whether it were, that he was emboldened by the impunity of his wife's sin, or that, from a feeling of blind affection, he wished to

---

[1] Gen. iii. 6.

share the lot of her, who was the *flesh of his flesh and the bone of his bones*,—our First Father, also, forgets all he owes to his Creator, and, as though there had never been aught of love between him and his God, he basely does as Eve suggests;—he eats of the Fruit, and by that act ruins himself and all his posterity.

No sooner have they broken the tie which united them with God, than they sink into themselves. As long as God dwells in the creature, whom he has raised to the supernatural state, his *being* is complete; but, let that creature drive his God away from himself by sin, and he finds himself in a state worse than nothing,—the state of *evil*. That soul, which, a moment before, was so beautiful and pure, is a hideous wreck. Thus was it with our First Parents: they stand alone; creatures without God; and an intolerable shame seizes them. They thought to become gods, they aspired at Infinite Being; see them now:—sinners, the prey of concupiscence. Hitherto, their innocence was their all-sufficient garb; the world was obedient to them; they knew not how to blush, and there was nothing to make them fear; but now, they tremble at their nakedness, and must needs seek a place wherein to hide!

The same self-love that had worked their ruin, had made them forget the greatness and goodness of God, and despise his commandment. Now that they have committed the great sin, the same blindness prevents them from even thinking of confessing it, or asking the forgiveness of the Master they have offended. A sullen fear possesses them. They can think of nothing but how and where to hide!

IN DOMINICA TYROPHAGI.

Unhappy me! Thou hadst laden me, O Lord, with	Miser ego, honore a te, Domine, in Eden affectus

fui: hei mihi! quomodo in errorem inductus, et diabolica invidia appetitus, depulsus sum e facie tua.

Angelorum ordines, Paradisi ornamenta, et plantarum quæ illic sunt decus, me fraude misera abductum et a Deo longius digressum lugete.

Pratum beatum, plantatæ a Deo arbores, Paradisi deliciæ, e foliis velut ex oculis lacrymas nunc effundite super me, nudum et a Dei gloria abdicatum.

(Domina sancta, quæ fidelibus omnibus Paradisi januas ab Adam per inobedientiam quondam clausas aperuisti, misericordiæ mihi fores expande.)

Invidens mihi olim inimicus, hominum osor, beatum Paradisi domicilium, me specie serpentis supplantavit, atque ab æterna gloria submovit.

Lugeo et animo discrucior, oculisque lacrymarum multitudinem adjungere exopto, respiciens et intelligens partam mihi ex transgressione nuditatem.

Dei manus me e terra plasmavit; at in terram rursus revertendi miser legem accepi; quisnam me ejectum a Deo, et inferos pro Eden assecutum non defleat?

(Te, labis omnis expers honours in Eden. But, alas! I was led into sin; I became a victim to the envy of the devil; I have been driven from thy face.

O ye choirs of Angels! ye that give Paradise such beauty, and to its flowers their loveliness! weep over me the dupe of wretched craft, now far from your God.

O fair garden Land! O ye trees, charm of Paradise, planted by God's own hand, let your leaves be turned into eyes, and shed your tears over me, for I am a naked king, dethroned of God's glory.

(O holy Mother! thou that didst throw open to the Faithful those gates of heaven that had been shut by Adam's disobedience, open now to me the gates of God's mercy.)

The enemy, the hater of mankind, envied me my blissful home in Eden; under the form of a serpent he supplanted me, and robbed me of eternal glory.

My soul weeps and is racked, and I fain would give floods of tears to mine eyes, when I see and understand the nakedness that has come to me by my transgression.

The hand of God formed me out of the earth; but I have miserably brought on myself the sentence,—I must return into the earth. Who is there that will not weep over me, that have lost my God, and have given up Eden for hell?

Sinless Mother of God!

the Faithful throughout the world proclaim thee to be the mystic throne of glory. I, then, that am fallen, beseech thee, Spotless Virgin!—prepare me for a throne in heaven!)

Dei Genitrix, fideles universi mysticum gloriæ thalamum annunciamus, unde lapsum me, precor, o pura, aptum fac Paradisi thalamum.)

WEDNESDAY

OF SEPTUAGESIMA WEEK.

The guilty pair appear before the great God, whom they have offended; and instead of acknowledging their guilt, they would palliate and excuse it. But Divine Justice pronounces their condemnation, and the sentence shall be felt by their posterity, even to the last generation. The two beings, that had committed the heinous crime, had been enriched with every gift of nature and grace. It was not with them, as it is with us. Concupiscence which gives us an inclination for what is wrong; ignorance and forgetfulness which cloud the intellect of fallen man, —these miseries had nothing whatever to do with the fall of our First Parents. They sinned through sheer ingratitude. They began by weighing the proposal of revolt, when they ought to have spurned it with indignation and conquered by flight. Then, by degrees, the proposed crime seemed no great harm, because, though God would lose their obedience, *they* would gain by the disobedience! And at length, the love of God was made to give place to the love of self, and they declared their independence! Yet, God had mercy on them, because of their posterity.

The Angels were all created at one and the same instant, and each of them was subjected to the trial, which was to decide his eternal future. Each Angel depended on his own act,—on his own choice between fidelity to his Creator or rebellion against him; so that, they who rebelled, drew on themselves the eternity of God's chastisement. The human race, on the contrary, existed not save as represented in its two First Parents, and was plunged by and with them into the abyss of God's reprobation : therefore, God, who spared not the Angels, mercifully spared the human race.

But, let us listen to the three sentences pronounced by God after the fall of Man. The first is against the serpent, and is the severest. The curse, which is already upon him, is deepened, and the pardon, which is about to be promised to the human race, is to be given in the form of an anathema against that wicked spirit, that has dared to war with God in the work of his hands.

I will put enmities between thee and the woman: she shall crush thy head.[1] Thus does God avenge himself of his enemy. The victory won over the woman is made to turn against the proud conqueror, and become his humiliation and his defeat. In his fiendish craft, he had directed his first attack, not against the man, but against the woman. She, by nature, was weaker and more credulous; and if he conquered *her*, he hoped,—too well, alas!—that *Adam* would be led to turn against his Creator, in order not to displease the creature. All happened as he willed it:—but now, see how God uses the *woman*, to foil and punish him. He enkindles in her heart an implacable hatred against his and our enemy. This cruel serpent may raise his proud head, and, here and there, find men that will adore him : the day will come, when a Woman's foot *shall crush* this *head*, which refused to bend before God. This daughter of Eve, whom all generations are to call *Blessed*,[2] shall be prefigured by other women,—

---

[1] Gen. iii. 15.   [2] St. Luke, i. 48.

by Debora, Judith, Esther, and others, all celebrated for their victories over the Serpent—: she shall be followed, until the end of time, by an uninterrupted succession of Christian Virgins and Matrons, who, with all their weakness, shall be powerful in co-operating with God's designs, and, as the Apostle says, *the unbelieving husband shall be sanctified by the believing wife.*[1]

Thus will God punish the serpent's pride. Before pronouncing upon our First Parents the sentence they have deserved, he promises to bless their posterity, and pours into their own hearts a ray of hope.

IN DOMINICA TYROPHAGI.

Tunc sedit Adamus, ploravitque contra Paradisi delicias, oculos manibus feriens, atque dicebat: Misericors, miserere mei lapsi.

Intuitus Adamus Angelum impellentem claudentemque divini horti fores, ingemuit vehementer, dicebatque: Misericors, miserere mei lapsi.

Doleas vices, Paradise, domini tui ad mendicitatem detrusi, foliorumque tuorum sonitu Conditorem deprecare ne te claudat. Misericors, miserere mei lapsi.

Then did Adam look back on the Eden of delights, and sitting wept; he hid his face in his hands, and said: O merciful God! have mercy on me the fallen one!

He saw the Angel that drove him from the Garden of God; and as he beheld him shutting its gates against him, he heaved a deep sigh, and said: O merciful God! have mercy on me the fallen one!

Weep, Eden, over thy master thus made poor! Let the rustling of thy leaves become a prayer, asking our Creator that he close thee not. O merciful God! have mercy on me the fallen one!

---

[1] I. Cor vii. 14.

THURSDAY

OF SEPTUAGESIMA WEEK.

FORGIVENESS is promised; but atonement must be made. Divine Justice must be satisfied, and future generations be taught that sin can never pass unpunished. Eve is the guiltier of the two, and her sentence follows that of the serpent. Destined by God to aid man in peopling the earth with happy and faithful children; formed by this God out of man's own substance, *flesh of his flesh, and bone of his bones*;—woman was to be on an equality with man; but sin has subverted this order, and God's sentence is this: Conjugal union, notwithstanding the humiliation of concupiscence now brought upon it, is to be, as before, holy and sacred; but it is to be inferior in dignity, both before God and man, to the state of Virginity, which disdains the ambitions of flesh.

Secondly, woman shall be mother still, as she would have been in the state of innocence; but her honour shall be a burden. Moreover, she shall give birth to her children amidst cruel pains, and sometimes even death must be the consequence of her infant's coming into the world. The sin of Eve shall thus be memorialised at every birth, and nature shall violently resist the first claims of him, whom sin has made her unwelcome lord.

Lastly, she who was at first created to enjoy equality of honour with man, is now to forfeit her independence. Man is to be her superior, and she must obey him. For long ages, this obedience will be no better than slavery; and this degradation shall continue till that Virgin comes, whom the world shall have expected for four thousand years, and whose humility shall crush the serpent's head. *She* shall restore her sex to its rightful position, and give to Christian woman that influence of gentle persuasiveness, which is compatible with the duty imposed upon her by Divine justice, and which can never be remitted:—the duty of submission.

IN DOMINICA TYROPHAGI.

Dominator sæculorum omnium Domine, qui me voluntate tua procreasti, dolosi draconis invidia quondam afflictum, teque, Salvator, ad iracundiam concitantem, ne despicias, Deus, sed revoca me.

Hei mihi! pro stola splendida, turpitudinis indumentis obvolutus, lugeo, Salvator, exitium meum, et fide ad te clamo; ne despicias me, bone Deus, sed revoca.

Serpentium, ferarumque dominus effectus, quo pacto serpenti animabus exitiali familiariter congressus es, inimico veluti bono consiliario usus? O errorem tuum, miserrima anima mea!

(Canimus te, Maria, Dei gratia plena, lucidum divinæ incarnationis tabernaculum; quare me cupiditatibus fœde obtenebratum illumina, fons misericordiæ, spes eorum quos omnis spes dereliquit.)

O Lord! King of all ages! who didst create me by thy love; I have been injured by the envy of the crafty serpent, and have provoked thee, my Saviour, to anger: but despise me not, O God! Call me back to thee.

Alas! my bright robe has been changed into this garb of shame. I bewail my ruin, O Saviour, and to thee do I cry with confidence: My good God! Despise me not, but call me back to thee.

How, my soul, couldst thou, that wast made the lord of serpents and beasts, treat the soul-slaying serpent with familiarity, and use thine enemy as a trusty counsellor? Bewail, my wretched soul, thy fatal error!

(To thee do we sing, O Mary, full of divine grace! Hail bright tabernacle of the Incarnation! O fount of mercy, hope of them that are in despair, enlighten me that am dishonoured by the dark clouds of my passions.)

FRIDAY

OF SEPTUAGESIMA WEEK.

THE curse, which is henceforth to lie so heavily on every human being, has been expressed in the sentence pronounced against Eve; the curse, to which the earth itself is to be subjected, is Adam's sentence. *Because thou hast hearkened to the voice of thy wife, and hast eaten of the tree, whereof I commanded thee, that thou shouldst not eat, cursed is the Earth in thy work* (that is, *on account of what thou hast done*).[1] Adam had excused his sin. God does not admit his excuse; yet he mercifully makes allowance for him, seeing that he sinned, not so much to gratify himself, as to please the frail creature, that had been formed out of his own substance. He is not the originator of the disobedient act. God, therefore, sentences him to the personal humiliation of *labour and toil*, and of *eating his bread in the sweat of his brow.*[2] Outside the Garden of Eden, there lies the immense desert of the Earth. It is to be the valley of tears; and there must Adam dwell in exile for upwards of nine hundred years, with the sad recollection in his heart of the few happy days spent in Paradise! This desert is barren: Adam must give it fruitfulness by his toil, and draw from it, by the sweat of his brow, his own and his children's nourishment. If, in after ages, some men shall live *without*

---

[1] Gen. iii. 17.   [2] *Ibid.*, 17, 19.

toil, they are the exception confirming the general law and chastisement. *They* rest, because others have laboured long and hard for them; neither will God ratify their exceptional dispensation from *labour*, except on the condition that they give encouragement, by their charity and other virtues, to their fellow-men, in whom Adam's sentence is literally carried out. Such is the necessity of *toil*, that if it be refused, the earth will yield but *thorns and thistles*;[1] such, too, the importance of this law imposed on fallen Man, that idleness shall not only corrupt his heart, it shall also enervate his bodily strength.

Before his Sin, the trees of Paradise bent down their branches, and man fed on their delicious fruits; but now, he must till the earth and draw from it, with anxiety and fatigue, the seed which is to give him bread. Nothing could better express the penal relation, between him and the earth, from which he was originally formed, and which is henceforth to be his tomb, than this law to which God sentences him,—of being indebted to the earth for the nourishment which is to keep him in life. And yet, here also Divine Mercy shall show itself; for, when God shall have been appeased, it shall be granted to man to unite himself to his Creator by eating the *Bread of Life*, which is to come down from heaven, and whose efficacy for the nourishing of our souls, shall be greater than ever the fruit of the Tree of Life could have been, for the immortalising our bodily existence.

IN DOMINICA TYROPHAGI.

Dulcis ad vescendum fructus scientiæ in Eden visus est mihi, amore capto;	My desire blinded me; and the fruit that grew on Eden's tree of knowledge seemed to

[1] Gen. iii. 18.

FRIDAY OF SEPTUAGESIMA WEEK.

me to be sweet to eat; but it has been turned into bitterness. Unhappy me, who have been driven from my home of Paradise by intemperance!

O God of the universe! O merciful Lord! look with pity upon my lowliness, and suffer me to dwell near thy divine Eden, that so my eyes may turn towards the fair land I have lost, and I, by my tears, regain it.

I weep, and sigh, and am afflicted, as I behold the Cherubim guarding, with a flaming sword, the gate of Paradise, which is shut against all sinners. Alas! how can I enter, unless thou, my Saviour, grant me admission?

O Christ, my Saviour, my hope is in thy great mercy, and in the Blood which flowed from thy sacred Side, whereby thou didst sanctify mankind, and open, O good Jesus, to them that serve thee, the gate of Paradise, which heretofore was shut against Adam.

(O gate of life! Spiritual Gate, which God has kept for himself! O Virgin-Mother of God, espoused to none but him!—open to me, by thy prayers, the once closed gate of heaven; that so I may glorify thee, who after God, art my helper and sure refuge!)

at demum in bilem conversus est. Hei mihi! misera anima, quomodo intemperantia te e Paradisi laribus exturbavit?

Deus universorum, misericordiæ Domine, ad humilitatem meam benigne respice, nec a divino Eden longe me ejicias, quo venustates unde excidi aspiciens, fletibus rursus amissa bona recipiam.

Fleo, ingemo, atque lamentor Cherubim ad Paradisi ingressum custodiendum igneo ense locata conspiciens, transgressoribus omnibus, hei mihi! inaccessum, nisi tu, Salvator, aditum mihi facilem præstes.

Confido in multitudine misericordiæ tuæ, Christe salvator, ac divini lateris tui sanguine, unde hominum naturam sanctificasti, et colentibus te aperuisti, o bone, Paradisi portas antea Adamo præclusas.

(Vitæ porta, impervia, spiritualis, virgo Deipara, innupta, pande mihi precibus tuis Paradisi clausas olim fores, quo te meam post Deum auxiliatricem firmumque refugium glorificem.)

SATURDAY

OF SEPTUAGESIMA WEEK.

THE sentence pronounced by the Almighty upon our First Parents was to fall upon their children, to the end of time. We have been considering, during this Week of Septuagesima, the penalties of the great Sin; but the severest and most humiliating of them all remains to be told. It is the transmission, to the whole human race, of *Original Sin*. It is true, that the merits of the promised Redeemer will be applied to each individual man in the manner established by God at various periods of time: still, this spiritual *Regeneration*,—whilst cleansing us from the leprosy which covered us, and restoring us to the dignity of children of God,—will not remove every scar of the old wound. It will save us from eternal death, and restore us to life; but, as long as our pilgrimage lasts, we shall be weak and sickly. Thus it is, that *Ignorance* makes us to be shortsighted in those great truths, which should engross all our thoughts; and this fills us with illusions, which, by an unhappy inclination of our will, we cling to and love. *Concupiscence* is ever striving to make our soul a slave to the body; and in order to escape this tyranny, our life has to be one continual struggle. An unruly love for Independence is unceasingly making us desire to be our own masters, and forget that we were born to obey. We find pleasure in Sin, whereas Virtue rewards us with nothing, in this life, save with the consciousness of our having done our duty.

Knowing all this, we are filled with admiration and love when we think of thee, O Mary! thou purest of God's creatures. Thou art our Sister in nature; thou art a Daughter of Eve; but thou wast conceived without sin, and art therefore the honour of the human race. Thou art of the same flesh and blood as ourselves; and yet thou art Immaculate. The divine decree, which condemned us to inherit the disgrace of Original Sin, could not include thy most pure Conception; and the serpent felt, as thy foot crushed his haughty head, that thou hadst never been under his power. In thee, O Mary! we find our nature such as it was when our God first created it. Hail, then, spotless *Mirror of Justice!*

O Mary! beautiful in thine unsullied holiness, pray for us who are weighed down by the consequences of that sin of our First Parents, which God would not suffer to approach thee. Thou art the implacable enemy of the Serpent; watch over us, lest his sting inflict death on our souls. We were conceived in sin, and born in sorrow; pray for us that we may so live as to merit blessing. We are condemned to toil, to suffering, and to death; intercede for us, that our atonement may find acceptance with our Lord. We are exposed to the treachery of our evil inclinations; we are in love with this present life; we forget eternity; we are ever striving to deceive our own hearts;—how could we escape hell, were the grace of thy Divine Son not unceasingly offered to us, enabling us to triumph over all our enemies? Thou, O Immaculate Mother of Jesus, art the *Mother of Divine Grace!* Pray for us, that we, who glory in being thy kindred by nature, may be daily more and more enriched with this priceless gift.

Let us salute the Blessed Mother of God in the words of the following Sequence, taken from the ancient Missal of Cluny. Catholic piety has consecrated to Mary the Saturday of each week.

SEQUENCE.

Ad laudem Matris Dei
Modulemur licet rei,
   Poscentes remedia.

Hæc nostræ forma spei,
Spes mirandæ speciei,
   Quæ vernat in gloria.

Hæc virtutis nutrime tum,
Spes solaris, sola laris
   Terreni fiducia.

Stella maris quæ vocaris,
Passus rectos et directos,
   Da pacis suffragia.
Sicut sidus naufrago,
Fulgens dux in pelago,
   Tu præclara.

Mundi lux in tenebris,
Stella nitens celebris,
   Deo chara.

In sede cœlica
Residens, hæc mellica
Admitte cantica,
   Virgo pia.
Paventi psallere,
Trementi pro scelere
   Des ausus,
   Tu plausus,
   Veri vena.
Tu cœli regina,
Mundi medicina,
Munda scelus nostrum,
   Piissima.

In mortis ruina,
Nos ad vitam mina,
   Placans Deum,
   Tu benignissima.

Let us, though sinners, sing a hymn in praise of the Mother of God ; let us sing our prayer for help.

Oh ! how well may we hope in Her, that beautiful Mother, whose glory is bright as Spring !

It is she that trains us to virtue, and warms our earthly home with the sunny beam of hope.

Thou that art called *Star of the Sea*, direct us, steer us, get us the calm of peace.

Thou brightly shinest on life's sea, guiding us, as does the friendly Star which leads the shipwrecked into port.

Thou art a light to worldlings in their darkness, thou art the shining well-known Star, so dear to God.

Seated on thy heavenly throne, receive, O Virgin-Mother, these our sweet canticles.

To the sinner who fears to sing, do thou, Fount of Truth, give courage and applause.

Thou art the Queen of heaven, thou art the solace of the world ; may thy loving prayers cleanse us from our guilt.

We have merited death; but intercede for us to God, most merciful Queen ! and so lead us unto life.

SATURDAY OF SEPTUAGESIMA WEEK.

O Mary, dear Mother! Mother of thy Creator! Virgin ever Merciful! enlighten us that are sitting in the shades of death.

That guided by thee our Star, and protected by the Cross of thy Son, we may, through thy intercession, be brought to the enjoyment of light eternal. Amen.

Chara parens, O Maria,
Patris parens, Virgo pia,
Nos in umbræ mortis via
　　Sedentes illumina!

Ut te nobis stella duce,
Tui Nati tuti Cruce,
Mereamur cœli luce
　　Per te frui, Domina.
　　Amen.

SEXAGESIMA SUNDAY.

The Church offers to our consideration, during this week of Sexagesima, the history of Noah and the deluge. Man has not profited by the warnings already given him. God is obliged to punish him once more, and by a terrible chastisement. There is found out of the whole human race one just man; God makes a covenant with him, and with us through him. But, before he draws up this new alliance, he would show that he is the Sovereign Master, and that man, and the earth whereon he lives, subsist solely by his power and permission.

As the ground-work of this week's instructions, we give a short passage from the Book of Genesis: it is read in the Office of this Sunday's Matins.

De Libro Genesis.	From the Book of Genesis.
Cap. VI.	*Ch. VI.*
Videns autem Deus quod multa malitia hominum esset in terra, et cuncta cogitatio cordis intenta esset ad malum omni tempore, pœnituit eum quod hominem fecisset in terra. Et tactus dolore cordis intrinsecus : Delebo, inquit, hominem quem creavi, a facie terræ, ab homine usque ad animantia, a reptili usque	And God seeing that the wickedness of men was great on the earth, and that all the thought of their heart was bent upon evil at all times, it repented him that he had made man on the earth. And being touched inwardly with sorrow of heart, he said : I will destroy man, whom I have created, from the face of the earth, from man even to

beasts, from the creeping thing even to the fowls of the air. For it repenteth me that I have made them. But Noah found grace before the Lord.	ad volucres cœli. Pœnitet enim me fecisse eos. Noë vero invenit gratiam coram Domino.
These are the generations of Noah: Noah was a just and perfect man in his generations: he walked with God. And he begot three sons: Sem, Cham, and Japheth. And the earth was corrupted before God, and was filled with iniquity. And when God had seen that the earth was corrupted, (for all flesh had corrupted its way upon the earth,) he said to Noah: The end of all flesh is come before me: the earth is filled with iniquity through them, and I will destroy them with the earth.	Hæ sunt generationes Noë: Noë vir justus atque perfectus fuit in generationibus suis, cum Deo ambulavit. Et genuit tres filios, Sem, Cham, et Japhet. Corrupta est autem terra coram Deo, et repleta est iniquitate. Cumque vidisset Deus terram esse corruptam (omnis quippe caro corruperat viam suam super terram) dixit ad Noë: Finis universæ carnis venit coram me: repleta est terra iniquitate a facie eorum, et ego disperdam eos cum terra.

This awful chastisement of the human race by the Deluge was a fresh consequence of sin. This time, however, there was found one just man; and it was through him and his family that the world was restored. Having once more mercifully renewed his covenant with his creatures, God allows the earth to be re-peopled, and makes the three sons of Noah become the Fathers of the three great families of the human race.

This is the Mystery of the Divine Office during the week of Sexagesima. The Mystery expressed in to-day's Mass is of still greater importance, and the first is but a figure of the second. The earth is deluged by sin and heresy. But *the Word of God*, the *Seed* of life, is ever producing a new generation,— a race of men, who, like Noah, fear God. It is the Word of God that produces those happy children, of whom the Beloved Disciple speaks, saying: *they are born not of blood, nor of the will of the flesh, nor of* *the will of man, but of God.*¹ Let us endeavour to be of this family; or, if we already be numbered among its members, let us zealously maintain our glorious position. What we have to do, during these days of Septuagesima, is to escape from the Deluge of worldliness, and take shelter in the Ark of salvation; we have to become that *good soil,* which yields a hundred-fold from the heavenly *Seed.* Let us flee from the wrath to come, lest we perish with the enemies of God: let us hunger after that *Word of God,* which *converteth and giveth life to souls.*²

With the Greeks, this is the seventh day of their week *Apocreōs*, which begins on the Monday after our Septuagesima Sunday. They call this week *Apocreōs*, because they then begin to abstain from flesh-meat, which abstinence is observed till Easter Sunday.

MASS.

At Rome, the *Station* is in the Basilica of *Saint Paul outside the walls.* It is around the tomb of the Doctor of the Gentiles,—the zealous sower of the divine Seed,—the Father by his preaching, of so many nations,—that the Roman Church assembles her children on this Sunday, whereon she is about to announce to them, how God spared the earth on the condition that it should be peopled with true believers and with faithful adorers of his Name.

The Introit, which is taken from the Psalms, cries out to our Lord for help. The human race is all but extinct after the Deluge, and is here represented as beseeching its Creator to bless and increase it. The Church adopts the same prayer, and asks her Saviour to multiply the children of the Word, as he did in former days.

SEXAGESIMA SUNDAY.

INTROIT.

Arise, why sleepest thou, O Lord? Arise, and cast us not off to the end. Why turnest thou thy face away? and forgettest our tribulation? Our belly cleaveth to the earth. Arise, O Lord, help us, and deliver us.

Ps. We have heard, O God, with our ears: our fathers have declared to us thy wonders. ℣. Glory. Arise.

Exsurge, quare obdormis, Domine? Exsurge, et ne repellas in finem; quare faciem tuam avertis, oblivisceris tribulationem nostram? Adhæsit in terra venter noster : exsurge, Domine, adjuva nos, et libera nos.

Ps. Deus, auribus nostris audivimus : patres nostri annuntiaverunt nobis. ℣. Gloria Patri. Exsurge.

In the Collect, the Church expresses the confidence she puts in the prayers of the great Apostle St. Paul, that zealous sower of the divine Seed, who laboured more than the other Apostles in preaching the Word to the Gentiles.

COLLECT.

O God, who seest that we place no confidence in anything we do : mercifully grant that, by the protection of the Doctor of the Gentiles, we may be defended against all adversity. Through, &c.

Deus, qui conspicis quia ex nulla nostra actione confidimus : concede propitius, ut contra adversa omnia, Doctoris gentium protectione, muniamur. Per Dominum.

Then are added two other Collects, as in the Mass of Septuagesima Sunday, *page* 125.

The Epistle is that admirable passage from one of St. Paul's Epistles, in which the great Apostle, for the honour and interest of his sacred ministry, is necessitated to write his defence against the calumnies of his enemies. We learn from this his apology, what labours the Apostles had to go through, in order to sow the Word of God in the barren soil of the Gentile world, and make it Christian.

EPISTLE.

Lectio Epistolæ beati Pauli Apostoli ad Corinthios.

II. *Cap. XI.*

Fratres, libenter suffertis insipientes, cum sitis ipsi sapientes. Sustinetis enim si quis vos in servitutem redigit, si quis devorat, si quis accipit, si quis extollitur, si quis in faciem vos cædit. Secundum ignobilitatem dico, quasi nos infirmi fuerimus in hac parte. In quo quis audet (in insipientia dico), audeo et ego. Hebræi sunt? et ego. Israelitæ sunt? et ego. Semen Abrahæ sunt? et ego. Ministri Christi sunt? (ut minus sapiens dico,) plus ego: in laboribus plurimis, in carceribus abundantius, in plagis supra modum, in mortibus frequenter. A Judæis quinquies quadragenas, una minus, accepi. Ter virgis cæsus sum, semel lapidatus sum, ter naufragium feci, nocte et die in profundo maris fui; in itineribus sæpe, periculis fluminum, periculis latronum, periculis ex genere, periculis ex gentibus, periculis in civitate, periculis in solitudine, periculis in mari, periculis in falsis fratribus; in labore et ærumma, in vigiliis multis, in fame et siti, in jejuniis multis, in frigore et nuditate; præter illa, quæ extrinsecus sunt, instantia

Lesson of the Epistle of Saint Paul the Apostle to the Corinthians.

II. *Ch. XI.*

Brethren, you gladly suffer the foolish, whereas yourselves are wise. For you suffer if a man bring you into bondage, if a man devour you, if a man take from you, if a man be lifted up, if a man strike you on the face. I speak according to dishonour, as if we had been weak in this part. Wherein if any man dare (I speak foolishly) I dare also. They are Hebrews: so am I. They are Israelites: so am I. They are the seed of Abraham: so am I. They are the ministers of Christ: (I speak as one less wise), I am more: in many more labours, in prisons more frequently, in stripes above measure, in deaths often. Of the Jews five times did I receive forty stripes, save one. Thrice was I beaten with rods, once I was stoned, thrice I suffered shipwreck; a night and a day I was in the depth of the sea. In journeying often, in perils of waters, in perils of robbers, in perils from my own nation, in perils from the Gentiles, in perils in the city, in perils in the wilderness, in perils in the sea, in perils from false brethren. In labour and painfulness, in much watchings, in hunger and thirst, in fastings often, in cold and nakedness. Besides these things which are

SEXAGESIMA SUNDAY. 163

without; my daily instance, the solicitude for all the churches. Who is weak, and I am not weak? Who is scandalised, and I am not on fire? If I must needs glory, I will glory of the things that concern my infirmity. The God and Father of our Lord Jesus Christ, who is blessed for ever, knoweth that I lie not. At Damascus the governor of the nation under Aretas the king, guarded the city of the Damascenes, to apprehend me; and through a window in a basket was I let down by the wall, and so escaped his hands. If I must glory, (it is not exepdient indeed,) but I will come to the visions and revelations of the Lord. I know a man in Christ about fourteen years ago, (whether in the body, I know not, or out of the body, I know not, God knoweth,) such a one rapt even to the third heaven. And I know such a man, (whether in the body, or out of the body I cannot tell, God knoweth,)how he was caught up into paradise, and heard secret words, which it is not granted to man to utter. For such a one I will glory; but for myself I will glory nothing, but in my infirmities. For though I should have a mind to glory, I shall not be foolish : for I will say the truth. But I forbear, lest any man should think of me above that which he seeth in me, or anything he heareth from me. And lest the greatness of the revelations should

mea quotidiana, sollicitudo omnium Ecclesiarum. Quis infirmatur, et ego non infirmor ? Quis scandalizatur, et ego non uror ? Si gloriari oportet, quæ infirmitatis meæ sunt, gloriabor. Deus et Pater Domini nostri Jesu Christi, qui est benedictus in secula, scit quod non mentior. Damasci præpositus gentis, Aretæ regis, custodiebat civitatem Damascenorum, ut me comprehenderet; et per fenestram in sporta dimissus sum per murum, et sic effugi manus ejus. Si gloriari oportet,(non expedit quidem,) veniam autem ad visiones et revelationes Domini. Scio hominem in Christo ante annos quatuordecim, (sive in corpore nescio, sive extra corpus nescio,Deus scit,)raptum hujusmodi usque ad tertium cœlum. Et scio hujusmodi hominem, (sive in corpore nescio, sive extra corpus nescio, Deus scit,) quoniam raptus est in paradisum, et audivit arcana verba quæ non licet homini loqui. Pro hujusmodi gloriabor : pro me autem nihil gloriabor, nisi in infirmitatibus meis. Nam, etsi voluero gloriari, non ero insipiens ; veritatem enim dicam : parco autem, ne quis me existimet supra id quod videt in me, aut aliquid audit ex me. Et ne magnitudo revelationum extollat me, datus est mihi stimulus carnis meæ, angelus Satanæ, qui me colaphizet. Propter quod ter Dominum rogavi ut discederet a me : et dixit mihi Sufficit tibi gratia mea ; nam virtus in infirmitate perficitur. Libenter igitur gloriabor in infirmitatibus meis, ut inhabitet in me virtus Christi.

lift me up, there was given me a sting of my flesh, an angel of Satan to buffet me. For which thing I thrice besought the Lord that it might depart from me : and he said to me : My grace is sufficient for thee : for power is made perfect in infirmity. Gladly, therefore, will I glory in my infirmities, that the power of Christ may dwell in me.

In the Gradual, the Church beseeches her Lord to give her strength against those who oppose the mission he has entrusted to her, of gaining for him a new people, adorers of his sovereign Majesty.

GRADUAL.

Sciant gentes, quoniam nomen tibi Deus : tu solus Altissimus super omnem terram.
℣. Deus meus, pone illos ut rotam, et sicut stipulam ante faciem venti.

Let the Gentiles know that God is thy name : thou alone art the Most High over all the earth.
℣. O my God, make them like a wheel, and as stubble before the wind.

Whilst the earth is being *moved*, and is suffering those terrible revolutions, which, deluge-like, come first on one nation and then on another,—the Church prays for her Faithful Children, in order that they may be spared, for they are the *elect*, and the hope of the world. It is thus she prays in the following Tract, which precedes the Gospel of the *Word*.

TRACT.

Commovisti, Domine, terram, et conturbasti eam.
℣. Sana contritiones ejus, quia mota est.

Thou hast moved the earth, O Lord, and hast troubled it.
℣. Heal the breaches thereof, for it is moved.

SEXAGESIMA SUNDAY.

℣. That they may flee from before the bow : that thy elect may be delivered.

℣. Ut fugiant a facie arcus : ut liberentur electi tui.

GOSPEL.

Sequel of the holy Gospel according to Luke.

Ch. VIII.

At that time, when a very great multitude was gathered together, and hastened out of the cities to meet Jesus, he spoke by a similitude. A sower went out to sow his seed ; and as he sowed, some fell by the way-side, and it was trodden down, and the fowls of the air devoured it. And other some fell upon a rock and as soon as it was sprung up, it withered away, because it had no moisture. And other some fell among thorns ; and the thorns growing up with it, choked it. And other some fell upon good ground, and sprung up, and yielded fruit a hundredfold. Saying these things he cried out : He that hath ears to hear, let him hear. And his disciples asked him what this parable might be. To whom he said : To you it is given to know the mystery of the kingdom of God ; but to the rest in parables : that seeing they may not see, and hearing they may not understand. Now the parable is this : The seed is the word of God. And, they by the way-side, are they that hear ; then the devil cometh, and taketh

Sequentia sancti Evangelii secundum Lucam.

Cap. VIII.

In illo tempore, cum turba plurima convenirent, et de civitatibus properarent ad Jesum, dixit per similitudinem. Exiit, qui seminat, seminare semen suum : et, dum seminat, aliud cecidit secus viam, et conculcatum est, et volucres cœli comederunt illud. Et aliud cecidit supra petram : et natum, aruit ; quia non habebat humorem. Et aliud cecidit inter spinas, et simul exortæ spinæ suffocaverunt illud. Et aliud cecidit in terram bonam : et ortum fecit fructum centuplum. Hæc dicens clamabat : Qui habet aures audiendi, audiat. Interrogabant autem eum discipuli ejus, quæ esset hæc parabola. Quibus ipse dixit : Vobis datum est nosse mysterium regni Dei, cæteris autem in parabolis ; ut videntes non videant, et audientes non intelligant. Est autem hæc parabola. Semen est verbum Dei. Qui autem secus viam, hi sunt qui audiunt : deinde venit diabolus, et tollit verbum de corde eorum, ne credentes salvi fiant. Nam qui supra petram : qui cum audierint, cum gaudio suscipiunt verbum : et hi radices non habent : qui ad tempus credunt, et in tempore tentationis recedunt. Quod autem in spinas cecidit ; hi sunt, qui audierunt, et a solicitudinibus, et divitiis, et voluptatibus vitæ, euntes, suffocantur, et non referunt fructum. Quod autem in bonam terram : hi sunt, qui in corde bono et optimo audientes verbum retinet, et fructum afferunt in patientia.

the word out of their hearts, lest believing they should be saved. Now they upon the rock, are they who when they hear, receive the word with joy : and these have no roots ; for they believe for a while, and in time of temptation fall away. And that which fell among thorns, are they who have heard, and going their way, are choked with the cares and the riches and pleasures of this life, and yield no fruit. But that on the good ground, are they, who, in a good and perfect heart hearing the word, keep it, and bring forth fruit in patience.

St. Gregory the Great justly remarks, that this Parable needs no explanation, since Eternal Wisdom himself has told us its meaning. All that we have to do, is to profit by this divine teaching, and become the good soil, wherein the heavenly Seed may yield a rich harvest. How often have we not, hitherto, allowed it to be trampled on by them that passed by, or to be torn up by the birds of the air? How often has it not found our heart like a stone, that could give no moisture, or like a thorn plot, that could but choke? We listened to the *Word* of God; we took pleasure in hearing it; and from this we argued well for ourselves. Nay, we have often received this *Word* with joy and eagerness. Sometimes, even, it took root within us. But, alas! something always came to stop its growth.—Henceforth, it must both grow and yield fruit. The *Seed* given to us is of such quality, that the Divine Sower has a right to expect a *hundred-fold*. If the soil, that is, if our *heart*, be *good ;*—if we take the trouble to prepare it, by profiting of the means afforded us by the Church ;—we shall have an abundant harvest to show our Lord on that grand Day, when, rising triumphant from his Tomb, he shall come to share with his faithful people the glory of his Resurrection.

Inspirited by this hope, and full of confidence in Him, who has once more thrown his Seed in this long ungrateful soil, let us sing with the Church, in her Offertory, these beautiful words of the Royal Psalmist:—they are a prayer for holy resolution and perseverance.

OFFERTORY.

Perfect thou my goings in thy paths; that my footsteps be not moved. O incline thy ear unto me and hear my words. Show forth thy wonderful mercies; who saveth them that hope in thee, O Lord.	Perfice gressus meos in semitis tuis, ut non moveantur vestigia mea: inclina aurem tuam et exaudi verba mea: mirifica misericordias tuas, qui salvos facis sperantes in te, Domine.

SECRET.

May the sacrifice we have offered to thee, O Lord, always enliven us and defend us. Through, &c.	Oblatum tibi, Domine, sacrificium vivificet nos semper, et muniat. Per Dominum.

To this are added the other Secrets, as on Septuagesima Sunday, *page* 132.

The visit, which our Lord makes to us in the Sacrament of his Love, is the grand means whereby he gives fertility to our souls. Hence it is, that the Church invites us, in the Communion-Antiphon, to draw nigh to the Altar of our God; there, our heart shall regain all the youthful fervour of its best days.

COMMUNION.

I will go up to the altar of God; to God, who rejoiceth my youth.	Introibo ad altare Dei, ad Deum qui lætificat juventutem meam.

POSTCOMMUNION.

Supplices te rogamus, omnipotens Deus; ut quos tuis reficis sacramentis, tibi etiam placitis moribus dignanter deservire concedas. Per Dominum.	Grant, we humbly beseech thee, O Almighty God, that those whom thou refreshest with thy sacraments, may, by a life well pleasing to thee, worthily serve thee. Through &c.

Two other Postcommunions are said after this, as on Septuagesima Sunday, *page* 133.

VESPERS.

The Psalms and Antiphons are given in *page* 74.

CAPITULUM.

(II. *Cor. XI.*)

Fratres, libenter suffertis insipientes, cum sitis ipsi sapientes: sustinetis enim si quis vos in servitutem redigit, si quis devorat, si quis accipit, si quis extollitur, si quis in faciem vos cædit.	Brethren, you gladly suffer the foolish, whereas yourselves are wise: for you suffer if a man bring you into bondage, if a man devour you, if a man take from you, if a man be lifted up, if a man strike you on the face.

For the Hymn and Versicle, see *page* 81.

ANTIPHON OF THE *Magnificat*.

ANT. Vobis datum est nosse mysterium Dei, cæteris autem in parabolis, dixit Jesus discipulis suis.	ANT. To you it is given to know the mystery of the kingdom of God, but to the others in parables, said Jesus to his disciples.

SEXAGESIMA SUNDAY. 169

LET US PRAY.

O God, who seest that we place no confidence in anything we do: mercifully grant that, by the protection of the Doctor of the Gentiles, we may be defended against all adversity. Through, &c.

OREMUS.

Deus qui conspicis quia ex nulla nostra actione confidimus : concede propitius, ut contra adversa omnia Doctoris Gentium protectione muniamur. Per Dominum.

We will end our Sunday by a Hymn taken from the ancient Breviaries of the Churches of France : it will help us to keep up in our souls the sentiments proper to the Season of Septuagesima.

HYMN.

The days of ease are about to close ; the days of holy observance are returning ; the time of temperance is at hand; let us seek our Lord in purity of heart.

Our Sovereign Judge will be appeased by our hymns and praise. He who would have us sue for grace, will not refuse us pardon.

The slavish yoke of Pharaoh, and the fetters of cruel Babylon, have been borne too long: let man now claim his freedom, and seek his heavenly country, Jerusalem.

Let us quit this place of exile ; let us dwell with the Son of God. Is it not the servant's glory, to be made co-heir with his Lord ?

O Jesus ! be thou our guide through life. Remember, that we are thy sheep, for whom

Dies absoluti prætereunt:
Dies observabiles redeunt.
Tempus adest sobrium :
Quæramus puro corde Dominum.

Hymnis et in confessionibus
Judex complacabitur Dominus.
Non negabit hic veniam,
Qui vult ut homo quærat gratiam.

Post jugum servile Pharaonis,
Post catenas diræ Babylonis:
Liber homo patriam
Quærat cœlestem Hierosolymam.

Fugiamus de hoc exilio :
Habitemus cum Dei Filio :
Hoc decus est famuli
Si sit cohæres sui Domini.

Sis Christe nobis dux hujus vitæ :
Memento quod sumus oves tuæ,

Pro quibus ipse tuam Pastor ponebas morte animam.
Gloria sit Patri et Filio : Sancto simul honor Paracleto :
Sicut erat pariter In principio et nunc et semper. Amen.

thou, the Shepherd, didst lay down thine own life.

Glory be to the Father, and to the Son ; honour too be to the Holy Paraclete : as it was in the beginning, now is, and shall ever be. Amen.

MONDAY

OF SEXAGESIMA WEEK.

All flesh had corrupted its way upon the earth.[1] The terrible lesson, then, which men had received, by being driven out of Paradise, in the person of our First Parents, had been without effect. Neither the certainty of death, when they would have to stand before the Divine Judge,—nor the humiliations which attend man's first coming into this world,— nor the pains and fatigues and trials which beset the whole path of life,—had subdued men's hearts, or brought them into submission to that Sovereign Master whose hand lay thus heavy upon them. They had the divine promise that a Saviour should be given to them, and that this Redeemer, (who was to be the Son of Her that was *to crush the Serpent's head,*) would not only bring them Salvation, but would moreover re-instate them in all the happiness and honours they had lost:—but even this was not enough to make them rise above the base passions of corrupt nature. The example of Adam's nine hundred years' penance, and the admonitions *he* could so feelingly give that had received such proofs of God's love and anger, began to lose their influence upon his children; and when he at last descended into the grave, his posterity grew more and more heedless of what they owed to their Creator. The

[1] Gen. vi. 12.

long life, which had been granted to man in this the first Age of the World, was made but a fresh means of offending Him who gave it. When, finally, the sons of Seth took to themselves wives of the family of Cain, the human race reached the height of wickedness, rebelled against the Lord, and made their own passions be their god.

Yet, all this while, they had had granted to them the power of resisting the evil propensities of their hearts. God had offered them his Grace, whereby they were enabled to conquer pride and concupiscence. The merits of the Redeemer to come were even then present to Divine Justice, and the Blood of the Lamb, *slain,* as St. John tells us, *from the beginning of the world,*[1] was applied, in its merits, to this, as to every generation, which existed before the Great Sacrifice was really immolated. Each individual of the human family might have been *just,* as Noah was, and, like him, have *found favour* with the Most High; but, *the thought of their heart was bent upon evil,* and not upon good, and the earth grew covered with enemies of God. Then it was, that *it repented God that he made man,*[2] as the Sacred Scripture forcibly expresses it. He decreed that man's life on earth should be shortened, in order that the thought of death might be ever before us. He, moreover, resolves to destroy, by a universal Deluge, the whole of this perverse generation, saving only one family. The world would thus be renewed, and man would learn from this awful chastisement to serve and love this his Sovereign Lord and God.

We find the following liturgical formula in the Mozarabic Missal. Nothing could be more appropriate to the Season of Septuagesima.

---

[1] Apoc. xiii. 8. [2] Gen. vi. 6.

MISSA.

(Dominica ante carnes tollendas.)

Behold, now are close at hand those days of salvation, which the cycle of the year brings round to us, and in which we desire, by the exercise of salutary abstinence, to apply a remedy to our evil doings. For, as the Apostle says: *This is the acceptable time*, and, *these are the days of salvation*, wherein a spiritual cure is given to the soul that seeks it, and the evil delights of sin are rooted from the mind. Hereby, we, whose evil habits are ever forcing us to a downward tendency, are, by the uplifting mercy of God, encouraged to rise above this earth ; that thus, by the devout observance of what these days require, we may not only be delivered from the guilt of our sins, but may moreover deserve to be companions with the elect in eternal bliss. Amen.

Ecce jam in proximo sunt dies illi salutis, in quibus revoluto anni circulo, per salutaris abstinentiæ opus, remedia cupimus suscipere pravorum actuum nostrorum. Etenim sicut ait Apostolus : Hoc est acceptabile tempus, et hi sunt dies salutis, in quibus spiritualis medela exquirenti adveniat animæ, et mala dulcia scrabra peccaminum evellantur a mente ; ut qui consuetudine noxia semper cogimur deorsum fluere, tandem divina nos erigente clementia, conemur sursum surgere, ut horum dierum votiva exhibentes susceptione, et malorum nostrorum levemur a crimine, et beatitudinis electorum mereamur compotes esse. Amen.

TUESDAY

OF SEXAGESIMA WEEK.

When we reflect upon the terrible events, which happened in the First Age of the world, we are lost in astonishment at the wickedness of man, and at the effrontery wherewith he sins against his God. How was it, that the dread words of that God which were spoken against our First Parents in Eden, could be so soon forgotten? How could the children of Adam see their father suffering and doing such endless penance, without humbling themselves and imitating this model of repentance? How was it, that the promise of a Mediator, who was to re-open the gate of heaven for them, could be believed, and yet not awaken in their souls the desire of making themselves worthy to be His ancestors, and partakers of that grand regeneration, which he was to bring to mankind? And yet, the years which followed the death of Adam, were years of crime and scandal; nay, he himself lived to see one of his own children become the murderer of a brother.—But, why be thus surprised at the wickedness of these our first brethren? The earth is now six thousand years old in the continued reception of divine blessings and chastisements;—and are men less dull of heart, less ungrateful, less rebellious towards their Maker? For the generality of men, we mean, of those who deign to believe in the Fall and Chastisement of our First Parents, and in the destruction of the world by the Deluge,—what are these great Truths? Mere historical facts, which have never once inspired them with a fear of God's justice. More favoured than these early generations of the human race, they know that the Messias has been sent, that God has come down upon the earth, that he has been made Man, that he has broken Satan's rule, that the way to heaven has been made easy by the graces embodied, by the Redeemer, in the Sacraments;—and yet, sin reigns and triumphs in the midst of Christianity. Undoubtedly, the *just* are more numerous than they were in the days of Noah: but then, what riches of grace has not our Redeemer poured out on our degenerate race, by the ministry of his Spouse the Church? Yes, there are Faithful Christians to be found upon the earth, and the number of the Elect is every day being added to: but the multitude is living at enmity with God, and their actions are in contradiction with their Faith.

When, therefore, the Holy Church reminds us of those times, wherein *all flesh had corrupted its way*, she is urging us to think about our own conversion. Her motive in relating to us the history of the sins committed at the beginning of the world, is to induce us to examine our own consciences. Why, too, does she read to us those pages of Sacred Writ, which so vividly describe the flood-gates of heaven opening and deluging the guilty earth,—if not that she would warn us against mocking that great God, who thus chastised the sins of his rebellious creatures? Last week, we were called upon to consider the sad consequences of Adam's sin,—a sin which we ourselves did not commit, but the effects of which lie so heavy upon us. This week, we must reflect upon the sins we ourselves have committed. Though God had loaded us with favours, guided us by his light, redeemed us with his Blood, and strengthened us against all our enemies by his grace,—yet have we *corrupted our way,* and caused our God to *repent* his having created us. Let us confess our wickedness, and humbly acknowledge that we owe it to *the mercies of the Lord, that we have not been consumed.*[1]

The Ambrosian Missal contains the following exhortation for this Season of the Year.

TRANSITORIUM.

(Dominica in Septuagesima.)

Convertimini omnes simul ad Deum mundo corde et animo, in oratione, jejuniis, et vigiliis multis. Fundite preces vestras cum lacrymis; ut deleatis chirographa peccatorum vestrorum, priusquam vobis repentinus superveniat interitus; antequam vos profundum mortis absorbeat; et cum Creator noster advenerit, paratos nos inveniat.

Be converted to God, all ye people, in purity of heart and soul, in prayer, fasting, and much watching. Pour out your prayers with tears; that the hand-writing of your sins may be blotted out, before sudden destruction come upon you, and before the deep flood of death engulph you. When our Creator comes, let him find us ready.

---

[1] Lament. iii. 22.

WEDNESDAY

OF SEXAGESIMA WEEK.

O GOD of Infinite Justice! we have sinned; we have abused the life thou hast given us: and when we read, in thy Scriptures, how thine anger chastised the sinners of former days, we are forced to acknowledge, that we have deserved to be treated in like manner. We have the happiness to be Christians, and Children of thy Church; the light of Faith, and the power of thy Grace, have brought us once more into thy friendship;—but, how can we forget that we were once thy enemies? And are we so deeply rooted in virtue, that we can promise ourselves perseverance in it to the end? *Pierce, O Lord! pierce my flesh with thy Fear.*[1] Man's heart is hard, and unless it fear thy Sovereign Majesty, it may again offend thee.

We are penetrated with fear, when we remember that thou didst bury the world and destroy mankind by the waters of the Deluge; for we learn by this, how thy patience and long-suffering may be changed into inexorable anger. Thou art just, O Lord! and who shall presume to take scandal, or to murmur, when thy wrath is enkindled against sinners?

We have defied thy justice, we have braved thine anger; for, though thou hast told us that thou wilt

[1] Ps. cxviii. 120.

never more destroy sinners by a Deluge of water,—yet do we know that thou hast created, in thy hatred for sin, a Fire, which shall eternally prey on them that depart this life, without being first reconciled with thy offended Majesty.

O wonderful dignity of our human nature! We cannot be indifferent towards that Infinite Being that created us:—we must be his friends or his enemies! It could not have been otherwise. He gave us understanding and free-will: we know what is good and what is evil, and we must choose the one or the other: we cannot remain neutral. If we choose *good*, God turns towards us and loves us; if *evil*, we separate from Him, who is our Sovereign Good. But, whereas he bears most tender mercy towards this frail creature, whom he created out of pure love; and because he wills that all men should be saved;—he waits with patience for the sinner to return to him, and, in countless ways, draws his heart to repentance.

But, wo to him that obeys not the divine call, when that call is the last! Then justice takes place of mercy, and revelation tells us how *fearful a thing it is to fall into the hands of the living God!*[1] Let us, then, *flee from the wrath to come*,[2] by making our peace with the God we have offended. If we be already restored to grace, let us walk in his fear, until love shall have grown strong enough in our hearts to make us *run the way of the commandments*.[3]

The following Prayer is from the Mozarabic Breviary of the Gothic Church of Spain.

---

[1] Heb. x. 31.   [2] St. Matth. iii. 7.   [3] Ps. cxviii. 32.

ORATIO.

(In capite jejunii.)

Turn away thy face from our sins, O Lord, and blot out all our iniquities. Take from thine eyes the guilt of our sinful pleasures, and mercifully incline thine ear to our confession. Have mercy, we beseech thee, upon us thy suppliants, O thou that lookest with pity on them that are in affliction, and givest to the disconsolate a penitent heart, that so they may praise thy name. The publican who stood afar off and struck his breast, found forgiveness by this alone, that he confessed his sin; do thou, in like manner, mercifully hear us sinners: and as thou didst give to him the fruit his prayer deserved, so also vouchsafe to grant unto us, thy suppliant unworthy servants, the pardon of our sins. Amen.

Averte faciem tuam a peccatis nostris, Domine, et omnes iniquitates nostras dele; remove ab oculis tuis malarum nostrarum facinus voluptatum, nostræque confessioni clementer tuum appone auditum. Miserere, quæsumus, rogantibus nobis, qui propitius respicis in adversis, et qui desperatis cor pœnitens tribuis ad confessionem gloriæ tuæ. Sed quia publicanus a longe stans et percutiens pectus suum, sola confessione purgatus est similiter et nos peccatores exaudi; ut sicut illi meritos petitionis suæ fructus donasti, ita et nobis supplicantibus indignis servis tuis veniam digneris impendere peccatis. Amen.

THURSDAY

IN SEXAGESIMA WEEK.

God promised Noah that he would never more punish the earth with a Deluge. But, in his justice, he has many times visited the sins of men with a scourge, which, in more senses than one, bears a resemblance to a Deluge:—the Invasion of Enemies. We meet with these Invasions in every age; and each time, we see the hand of God. We can trace the crimes that each of them was sent to punish, and in each we find a manifest proof of the infinite justice wherewith God governs the world.

It is not requisite that we should here mention the long list of these revolutions, which we might almost say make up the history of mankind, for in its every page we read of conquests, extinction of races, destruction of nations, and violent amalgamations, which effaced the traditions and character of the several peoples that were thus forced into union. We will confine our considerations to the two great Invasions, which the just anger of God has permitted to come upon the world, since the commencement of the Christian era.

The Roman Empire had made itself as pre-eminent in crime as it was in power. It conquered the world, and then corrupted it. Idolatry and immorality were the civilization it gave to the nations which had come under its sway. Christianity could save *individuals* in the great Empire, but the *Empire* itself could not be made Christian. God let loose upon it the deluge of Barbarians. The stream of the wild Invasion rose to the very dome of the Capitol; the Empire was engulfed. The ruthless ministers of Divine Justice were conscious of their being chosen for this mission of vengeance, and they gave themselves the name of *God's Scourge.*

When, later on, the Christian Nations of the East had lost the Faith, which they themselves had transmitted to the *Western* World;—when they had disfigured the sacred Symbol of Faith by their blasphemous heresies;—the anger of God sent upon them, from Arabia, the deluge of Mahometanism. It swept away the Christian Churches, that had existed from the very times of the Apostles. Jerusalem,—the favoured Jerusalem, on which Jesus had lavished his tenderest love,—even she became a victim to the infidel hordes. Antioch and Alexandria, with their Patriarchates, were plunged into the vilest slavery; and, at length, Constantinople, that had so obstinately provoked the divine indignation, was made the very Capital of the Turkish Empire.

And we, the Western Nations, if we return not to the Lord our God, shall *we* be spared? Shall the flood-gates of Heaven's vengeance,—shall the torrent of fresh Vandals,—ever be menacing to burst upon us, yet never come? Where is the country of our own Europe, that has not *corrupted its way,* as in the days of Noah? that has not made *conventions against the Lord and against his Christ?*[1] that has not clamoured out that old cry of revolt: *Let us break their bonds asunder, let us cast away their yoke from us?*[2]—Well may we fear, lest the time is at hand, when, despite our haughty confidence in our means of defence, Christ our Lord, to whom all nations have been given by the Father, *shall rule us with a*

---

[1] Ps. ii. 2.   [2] *Ibid.,* 3.

rod of iron, and break us in pieces like a potter's vessel.[1] Let us propitiate the anger of our offended God, and follow the inspired counsel of the Royal Prophet: *Serve ye the Lord with fear; embrace the discipline of his Law; lest, at any time, the Lord be angry, and ye perish from the just way.*[2]

We find the following beautiful words in the Ambrosian Liturgy for Septuagesima. They occur in the Missal.

TRANSITORIUM.

(Dominica in Septuagesima.)

Venite, convertimini ad me, dicit Dominus. Venite flentes, fundamus lacrymas ad Deum : quia nos negleximus, et propter nos terra patitur. Nos iniquitatem fecimus, et propter nos fundamenta commota sunt. Festinemus iram Dei antevertere, flentes, et dicentes : Qui tollis peccata mundi, miserere nobis.	Come, be converted unto me, saith the Lord. Let us come weeping, and pour out our tears before God, for we have been negligent, and because of us is the earth suffering. We have committed iniquity, and because of us are the foundations of the world moved. Let us hasten to avert the wrath of God ; let us weep, and say : O thou, that takest away the sins of the world, have mercy upon us !

---

[1] Ps. ii. 9.   [2] *Ibid.* 13.

FRIDAY

OF SEXAGESIMA WEEK.

God chastises the world by the Deluge; but he is faithful to the promise made to our First Parents, that the head of the Serpent should be crushed. The human race has to be preserved, therefore, until the time shall come for the fulfilment of this promise. The Ark gives shelter to the *just* Noah, and to his family. The angry waters reach even to the tops of the highest mountains; but the frail yet safe vessel rides peacefully on the waves. When the day fixed by God shall come, they that dwell in this Ark shall once more tread the earth, purified as it then will be; and God will say to them, as heretofore to our First Parents: *Increase, and multiply, and fill the* earth.[1]

Mankind, then, owes its safety to the Ark! O saving Ark! that wast planned by God himself, and didst sail unhurt amidst the universal wreck!—But, if we can thus bless this *contemptible wood*,[2]—how fervently should we not love that other *Ark*, of which Noah's was but the figure, and which, for now eighteen-hundred years, has been saving and bringing men to their God? How fervently should we not bless that *Church*, the Spouse of our Jesus, out of which there is no salvation, and in which we find that *Truth* which *delivers us* from error and doubt,[3] that Grace which purifies the heart, and that Food

---

[1] Gen. ix. 1.   [2] Wisd. x. 4.   [3] St. John, viii. 32.

which nourishes the soul and fits her for immortality!

O sacred Ark! thou art inhabited, not by one family alone, but by people of every nation under the sun. Ever since that glorious day, when our Lord launched thee in the sea of this world, thou hast been tossed by tempests, yet never wrecked. Thou wilt reach the eternal shore, witnessing, by thy unworn vigour and beauty, to the divine guidance of the Pilot, who loves thee, both for thine own sake, and for the work thou art doing for his glory. It is by thee that he peoples the world with his elect, and it is for them that he created the world.[1] *When he is angry, he remembers mercy*,[2] because of thee, for it is through thee that he has made his covenant with mankind.

O venerable Ark! be thou our Refuge in the deluge. When Rome's great Empire, that was *drunk with the blood of the Martyrs*,[3] sank beneath the invasion of the Barbarians, the Christians were safe, because sheltered by thee; the waters slowly subsided, and the race of men, that had fled to thee for protection, though conquered according to the flesh, was victorious by the spirit. Kings, who till then had been haughty despots and barbarians, kissed reverently the hand of the slave, who now was his Pastor and baptised him. New people sprang up, and, with the Gospel as their Law, began their glorious career in those very countries which the Cæsars had degraded and forfeited.

When the Saracen invasion came, sweeping into ruin the Eastern world, and menacing the whole of Europe, which would have been lost, had not the energy of thy sons repelled the infidel horde,—was it not within thee, O Ark of salvation! that the few Christians took refuge, who had resisted schism and

---

[1] St. Matth. xxiv. 22.   [2] Hab. iii. 2.   [3] Apoc. xvii. 6.

heresy, and who, whilst the rest of their brethren apostatised from the faith, still kept alive the holy flame? Under thy protection, they are even now perpetuating, in their unfortunate countries, the traditions of Faith, until the divine Mercy shall bring happier times, and themselves be permitted to multiply, as did of old the sons of Sem, in that land once so glorious and holy.

Oh! happy we, dear Church of God! that are sheltered within thee, and protected by thee against that wild sea of anarchy, which the sins of men have let loose on our earth! We beseech our Lord, that he check the tempest with that word of his omnipotence: *Thus far thou shalt come, and no further, and here shalt thou break thy swelling waves.*[1] But if it be decreed by his Divine Justice, that it prevail for a time, we know that it cannot reach such as dwell in thee. Of this happy number are we. In thy peaceful bosom, dear Mother, we find those true riches, the riches of the soul, of which no violence can deprive us.[2] The Life thou givest us, is the only real life. Our true Fatherland, is the kingdom formed by thee. Keep us, O thou Ark of our God! Keep us, and all that are dear to us, and shelter us beneath thy roof, until the deluge of *iniquity be passed away.*[3] When the earth, purified by its chastisements, shall once more receive the Seed of the Divine Word, which produces the Children of God,—those among us, whom thou shalt not have led to our eternal home, will then venture forth, and preach to the world the principles of authority and law, of family and social rights:—those sacred principles, which came from Heaven, and which thou, O Holy Church, art commissioned to maintain and teach, even to the end of time.

---

[1] Job, xxxviii. 11.   [2] St. Matth. vi. 19.   [3] Ps. lvi. 2.

We borrow from the Mozarabic Missal, the following eloquent appeal to Divine Mercy.

PRAYER.

(In Dominica V. post Epiphaniam:)

Exaudi nos Domine Deus noster, et humanæ iniquitatis oblitus, divinæ solius misericordiæ recordare. Exaudi, quæsumus, dum peccare non pateris, dum emendare nos præcipis, dum rogare permittis : dum patientia redditum quærendæ correctionis exspectat : dum justitia metum futuræ discussionis insinuat : dum misericordia locum evadendæ mortis ostentat. Inveniant ante oculos tuos sacrificia nostra gratiam : peccata veniam : vulnera medicinam : suspiria pietatem : flagella consolationem : lamenta temperiem : tempora quietam : officia dignitatem : vota mercedem. Mereatur petitio effectum, contritio solatium, consecratio Sacramentum. Oblatio sanctificatione pinguescat, trepidatio securitate proficiat, ut in omnibus multiplici pietatis tuæ gratia redundante, erigas plebem, dum lætificas sacerdotem. Amen.

Graciously hear, O Lord our God, and forgetting man's iniquity, remember only thine own mercy. Graciously hear us, we beseech thee, O thou that forbiddest us to sin, that commandest us to repent, that permittest us to pray! Thy patience awaits our return to the needed repentance ; thy justice inspires us with a fear of the future judgment ; thy mercy shows us how we may avoid death. May our sacrifices find favour in thine eyes; our sins, pardon ; our wounds, cure ; our sighs, pity ; our chastisements, consolation ; our tears, joy ; our days, peace; our duties, honour ; our prayers, reward. May our petition produce its effect ; our contrition, forgiveness ; our consecration, the Sacred Mystery. May our oblation be rich unto sanctification, and our fear be productive of security ; that thus in all things, by the manifold and overflowing grace of thy mercy, thou mayest bless the people, whilst thou givest joy to the priest. Amen.

SATURDAY

OF SEXAGESIMA WEEK.

ON the Saturday of the preceding Week,—which was devoted to the consideration of the Fall of our First Parents, both in its own malice and in its sad consequences upon us,—we turned our thoughts towards our Blessed Lady, who, though a Daughter of Eve, was, by the special mercy of God, preserved from the stain of Original Sin. Let us end *this* week with a like act of veneration and love towards this Immaculate Queen of Heaven. We, even the most saintly among us, have not only been stained with Original Sin;—we have our Actual sins to grieve over and do penance for. This should give us a higher appreciation of Her, the one single member of the human family who never committed the slightest sin. Let us turn towards her, and give expression to our feelings.

We, O Mary! have *corrupted our way;* we have disobeyed our Lord; we have broken his Law; we have preferred our own selfish gratifications to the service we owed him: but thou wast ever filled with his holy Love, and there passed not even a shadow of sin upon thy soul, O spotless *Mirror of Justice* and holiness! *Virgin most Faithful!* the grace of thy Son ever triumphed in thy Heart. *Mystical Rose!* the fragrance of thy virtues unceasingly ascended to his Throne, changing only in its daily increase of sweetness. *Tower of Ivory!* fair beyond measure, without one spot to mar thy purity! *House of Gold!* thou didst ever reflect the precious Gifts of the Holy Ghost. Have pity, then, upon us, for we are Sinners.

We have obliged our God to *repent that he made us*: but in thee, dear Mother, he has ever been well pleased. Thou art the *good land*, wherein his Divine Seed yielded its thousand-fold of fruit: pray for us, that he give fresh fertility to our hearts, and root up from them the *thorns*, which *choke* the heavenly plant. We are defiled by sin; may he, through the merit of the tears thou didst shed at the foot of the Cross, mercifully cleanse us. If thy divine Son have already pardoned us, there are the consequences of our sins, which still weaken and humble us, like the sores of wounds that have been cured: take us, sweet Mother of our Jesus, under the mantle of thy tender care. We have too little dread of sin; we are so often on the verge of offending our God;—oh! get courage for these poor children of thine, and firmness of resolution, and ambition for holiness of life. Thy intercession must win for us that precious devotedness to God's honour, which kills the root of sin,—love of our own selves. Oh! accursed self-love, which may lead *us* to hell, who are now perhaps in the grace of thy Divine Son!

The deluge, brought on by our sins, is hurrying its vengeance against mankind; and we, O Mary! are resolved to seek our refuge in the Ark of the Church, the safe shelter created for us by thy Jesus. But, we presume to pray to thee for our brethren throughout the world. Our God has given thee a power to stay his anger, and to win for guilty mortals an extension of mercy: show this power now, for our world is provoking its Maker to destroy it. If the flood-gate of his just indignation burst upon the face of our earth, millions of souls, that have been redeemed by the

Blood of thy Divine Son, would be lost eternally. If the sweet Dove of Peace bring her olive-branch, only when that terrible Justice is appeased,—it would be too late for thy loving Heart. Come before the Deluge, O beautiful Rainbow of our Father's Reconciliation! A Mother's love,—a Mother, who is the very Queen of Mercy,—emboldens us to sue for universal mercy. Can the prayer of Her, in whose purity and innocence the very God of Holiness finds no blemish, be denied? Pray him, then, to pardon *us*, and all sinners!

We select a few stanzas from the celebrated Complaint to Mary, composed by the Monk Euthymius. The Greek Church has inserted it in her Liturgy.

CANON.

O Blessed Lady! how shall I worthily lament over my impure life, and the multitude of my grievous sins? I know not how to address thee, most chaste Virgin! I tremble with fear; but do thou help me.	Quomodo, O Domina, vitam meam impuram et immensorum peccatorum meorum multitudinem lamentabor? Nescio quid dicam tibi, castissima, et male metuo; sed adjuva me.
I will speak of my wickedness and my hateful sins; but where shall I begin? Alas! what will become of me, a wretched sinner?—Do thou, O Blessed Lady, have compassion on me before my departure from this life.	Unde exordiar dicere ego miser de improbitate mea, et delictis nefandis? Ha! quid de me fiet? Verum age, Domina, et mei ante exitum ex hac luce miserere.
I, having gone in every path that sinner ever trod, how shall I find now the way of salvation, O Immaculate Virgin? Yet have I recourse to thy goodness; despise me not, for I repent from my heart.	Omnem viam peccatorum cum ambulassem, immaculata Virgo, salutis semitam haudquaquam inveni. Sed ad bonitatem tuam confugio; ne me ex animo pœnitentem aspernare.

Mortis horam, o purissima, terribileque tribunal assidue cogito; sed peccandi consuetudine vehementer ad peccatum illicior. Fer mihi opem.

Bonorum exitiabilis inimicus cernens me nunc nudum, et patrono ac tutore destitutum, et a divinis virtutibus alienissimum, ad devorandum me irruit. Præveni, et averte illum, o Domina.

Proh dolor, imaginem Dei in me ego miser mentis arrogantia contaminavi. Quo in posterum me vertam? Festina, Virgo, ad auxilium.

Angelorum ordines et exercitus, Virtutes cœlorum, potentiam Filii tui contremiscunt, o castissima. Ego vero desperatus omni timore vaco.

In fovea delictorum meorum suffocatum non me derelinquas, Domina. Improbissimus enim hostis me desperatione conflictantem videns, ridet; sed tu potenti manu tua me erige.

Formidabile est judicium, o misera et stolida anima mea, et pœna horribilis atque sempiterna. Nihilominus vel nunc ante Matrem judicis, ac Dei tui supplex procumbe. Cur enim te ipsam desperas?

O intaminata Virgo, ego ob multitudinem immensorum peccatorum meorum

My thoughts are ever on the hour of death, and on the dread tribunal; and yet an evil habit violently tempts me to sin. O most pure Virgin, do thou help me!

The deadly enemy of all that is good,—seeing me poor and naked, without patron or protector, and most destitute of heavenly virtue,—rushes forward that he may devour me. O Blessed Lady! forbid him, and drive him far from me.

Alas, unhappy me! in the arrogance of my soul, I have defiled the image of God that was in me. Whither shall I now turn? Hasten to my assistance, O Virgin ever Holy!

The Choirs and Hosts of Angels, the heavenly Powers, tremble in the presence of thy all-powerful Son, O Immaculate Mother! and I, who have nothing wherein to hope, am so devoid of fear!

Suffer me not, O Blessed Lady! to perish in the pit, I have fallen into, of my sins. The cruel enemy sees me struggling in despair, and mocks me. Do thou stretch forth thy hand, that can so well deliver me.

Awful is the judgment of God, unhappy senseless soul! and everlasting is the punishment. But turn thee, whilst yet there is time, and prostrate in prayer before the Mother of thy Judge and Lord. Why wouldst thou despair?

O Immaculate Virgin! the multitude of my grievous sins has set a thick darkness around me ; the eyes of my soul, and my understanding, are blinded. Wherefore, I beseech thee, quickly lead me, by the brightness of thy light, to sweet freedom from my passions.

Grant me an unceasing sorrow, O Blessed Lady, and a fount of tears, that I may wash away my countless sins and wounds, and gain eternal life.

Lo! I thy servant, most sinless Virgin! approach thee in deep reverence and love, for I know the power of thy prayer. Great, indeed, with her Son, is the power of the Mother's prayer, and his heart is moved when she asks,—O most Blessed Mother!

O Mother worthy of the whole world's praise! thy Son will be to me a merciful and compassionate Judge. Despise me not, but let me find favour in his sight, that he may set me on the right hand of his most just tribunal ; for in thee have I put my trust.

repletus sum tenebris, oculique animæ meæ et mens mea immutata sunt. Quare tu luminis tui splendoribus ad dulcedinem in vacuitate passionum sitam celeriter me revoca.

Gemitus perennes mihi largire, Domina, fontemque lacrymarum, ut tam multa flagitia mea vulneraque inexplicabilia eluam, quo vitam æternam adipiscar.

En ego servus tuus, incorruptissima Virgo, multo cum timore et desiderio ad te accedo ; gnarus quantum sæpenumero tua valuerit deprecatio. Valet sane plurimum, o benedictissima, apud Filium Matris supplicatio, et ejus viscera commovet.

Judicem misericordem et benignum exspecto Filium tuum, o linguis omnium prædicanda ; ne me despicias, sed eum mihi redde propitium, ut me tunc ad dexteram tribunalis sui incorrupti statuat: in te enim speravi.

QUINQUAGESIMA SUNDAY.

The Church gives us to-day another subject for our meditation: it is the Vocation of Abraham. When the waters of the Deluge had subsided, and mankind had once more peopled the earth, the immorality, which had previously excited God's anger, again grew rife among men. Idolatry, too, into which the ante-diluvian race had not fallen, now showed itself, and human wickedness seemed thus to have reached the height of its malice. Foreseeing that the nations of the earth would fall into rebellion against him, God resolved to select one people that should be peculiarly his, and among whom should be preserved those sacred truths, which the Gentiles were to lose sight of. This new people was to originate from one man, who would be the father and model of all future believers. This was Abraham. His faith and devotedness merited for him that he should be chosen to be the Father of the children of God, and the head of that spiritual family, to which belong all the elect, both of the old and new Testament.

It is necessary, therefore, that we should know Abraham, our father and our model. This is his grand characteristic:—fidelity to God, submissiveness to his commands, abandonment and sacrifice of everything in order to obey his holy will. Such ought to be the prominent virtues of every Christian. Let us, then, study the life of our great Patriarch, and learn the lessons it teaches.

The following passage from the Book of Genesis, which the Church gives us in her Matins of to-day, will serve as the text of our considerations.

From the Book of Genesis.	De libro Genesis.
Ch. XII.	*Cap. XII.*
And the Lord said to Abram : Go forth out of thy country, and from thy kindred, and out of thy father's house, and come into the land which I shall show thee. And I will make of thee a great nation, and I will bless thee, and magnify thy name, and thou shalt be blessed. I will bless them that bless thee, and curse them that curse thee ; and in thee shall all the kindred of the earth be blessed. So Abram went out as the Lord had commanded him, and Lot went with him. Abram was seventy-five years old when he went forth from Haran. And he took Saraï his wife, and Lot, his brother's son, and all the substance which they had gathered, and the souls which they had gotten in Haran: and they went out to go into the land of Chanaan. And when they were come into it, Abram passed through the country into the place of Sichem, as far as the noble vale : now the Chanaanite was at that time in the land. And the Lord appeared to Abram, and said to him : To thy seed will I give this land. And he built there an altar to the Lord, who had appeared to him. And passing on from thence to a mountain, that was on	Dixit autem Dominus ad Abram : Egredere de terra tua, et de cognatione tua, et de domo patris tui, et veni in terram quam monstrabo tibi. Faciamque te in gentem magnam, et benedicam tibi, et magnificabo nomen tuum, erisque benedictus. Benedicam benedicentibus tibi, et maledicam maledicentibus tibi ; atque in te benedicentur universæ cognationes terræ. Egressus est itaque Abram sicut præceperat ei Deus, et ivit cum eo Lot. Septuaginta quinque annorum erat Abram, cum egrederetur de Haran. Tulitque Saraï uxorem suam, et Lot filium fratris sui, universamque substantiam quam possederant, et animas quas fecerant in Haran : et egressi sunt ut irent in terram Chanaan. Cumque venissent in eam, pertransivit Abram terram usque ad locum Sichem, usque ad convallem illustrem: Chananæus autem tunc erat in terra. Apparuit autem Dominus Abram, et dixit ei: Semini tuo dabo terram hanc. Qui ædificavit ibi altare Domino, qui apparuerat ei. Et inde transgrediens ad montem, qui erat contra orientem Bethel

tetendit ibi tabernaculum suum, ab occidente habens Bethel, et ab oriente Haï. Ædificavit quoque ibi altare Domino, et invocavit Nomen ejus.	the east side of Bethel, he there pitched his tent, having Bethel on the west, and Haï on the east. He built there, also, an altar to the Lord, and called upon his Name.

Could the Christian have a finer model than this holy Patriarch, whose docility and devotedness in following the call of his God are so perfect? We are forced to exclaim, with the Holy Fathers: " O true " Christian, even before Christ had come on the " earth! He had the spirit of the Gospel, before the " Gospel was preached! He was an Apostolic man, " before the Apostles existed!" God calls him: he leaves all things,—his country, his kindred, his father's house,—and he goes into an unknown land. God leads him,—he is satisfied; he fears no difficulties; he never once looks back. Did the Apostles themselves more? But, see how grand is his reward. God says to him: *In thee shall all the kindred of the earth be blessed.* This Chaldean is to give to the world Him that shall bless and save it. Death will, it is true, close his eyes ages before the dawning of that day, when one of his race, who is to be born of a Virgin and be united personally with the Divine Word, shall redeem all generations, past, present, and to come. But, meanwhile, till Heaven shall be thrown open to receive this Redeemer and the countless just, who have won the crown, Abraham shall be honoured, in the Limbo of expectation, in a manner becoming his great virtue and merit. It is *in his Bosom,*[1] that is, around him, that our First Parents, (having atoned for their sin by penance,) Noah, Moses, David, and all the just, including poor Lazarus, received that rest and happiness, which were a foretaste and a preparation for eternal bliss in Heaven.

---

[1] St. Luke, xvi. 22.

Thus is Abraham honoured; thus does God requite the love and fidelity of them that serve him.

When the fulness of time came, the Son of God, who was also Son of Abraham, declared his Eternal Father's power, by saying, that he was about to *raise up* a new progeny of Abraham's children from the very *stones*, that is, from the Gentiles.[1] We Christians are this new generation. But, are we worthy children of our Father?—Let us listen to the Apostle of the Gentiles: *By faith, Abraham, when called (by God), obeyed to go out into a place, which he was to receive for an inheritance: and he went out not knowing whither he went. By faith, he abode in the land, dwelling in tents, with Isaac and Jacob, the co-heirs of the same promise; for he looked for a City that hath foundations, whose builder and maker is God.*[2]

If, therefore, we be children of Abraham, we must, as the Church tells us, during Septuagesima, look upon ourselves as exiles on the earth, and dwell, by hope and desire, in that true country of ours, from which we are now banished, but towards which we are each day drawing nigher, if, like Abraham, we are faithful in those various stations allotted us by our Lord. We are commanded to *use this world as though we used it not;*[3] to have an abiding conviction of our *not having here a lasting City,*[4] and of the misery and danger we incur, when we forget that Death is one day to separate us from every thing we possess in this life.

How far from being true children of Abraham are those Christians who spend this and the two following days in intemperance and dissipation, because Lent is so soon to be upon us! We can easily understand how the simple manners of our Catholic

---

[1] St. Matth. iii. 9.   [2] Heb. xi. 8, 9, 10.
[3] I. Cor. vii. 31.   [4] Heb. xiii. 14.

forefathers could keep a *leave-taking* of the ordinary way of living, which Lent was to put a stop to, and reconcile their innocent *Carnival* with Christian gravity; just as we can understand how their rigorous observance of the laws of the Church for Lent would inspire certain festive customs at Easter. Even in our own times, a joyous Shrovetide is not to be altogether reprobated, provided the Christian sentiment of the approaching holy Season of Lent be strong enough to check the evil tendency of corrupt nature: otherwise the original intention of an innocent custom would be perverted, and the forethought of Penance could in no sense be considered as the prompter of our joyous farewell to ease and comforts. While admitting all this, we would ask, what right or title have *they* to share in these Shrovetide rejoicings, whose Lent will pass and find them out of the Church, because they will not have complied with the precept of Easter Communion? And they, too, who claim dispensations from abstinence and fasting during Lent, and, from one reason or another, evade every penitential exercise during the solemn Forty Days of Penance, and will find themselves at Easter as weighed down by the guilt and debt of their sins as they were on Ash Wednesday,—what meaning, we would ask, can there possibly be in *their* feast-making at Shrovetide?

Oh! that Christians would stand on their guard against such delusions as these, and gain that holy *liberty of Children of God*,[1] which consists in not being slaves to flesh and blood, and preserves man from moral degradation! Let them remember, that we are now in that holy Season, when the Church denies herself her songs of holy joy, in order the more forcibly to remind us that we are living in a Babylon of spiritual danger, and to excite us to regain that

---

[1] Rom. viii. 21.

genuine Christian spirit, which everything in the world around us is quietly undermining. If the disciples of Christ are necessitated, by the position they hold in society, to take part in the profane amusements of these few days before Lent, let it be with a heart deeply imbued with the maxims of the Gospel. If, for example, they are obliged to listen to the music of theatres and concerts, let them imitate Saint Cecily, who thus sang, in her heart, in the midst of the excitement of worldly harmonies: *May my heart, O God, be pure, and let me not be confounded!* Above all, let them not countenance certain dances, which the world is so eloquent in defending, because so evidently according to its own spirit; and therefore they who encourage them, will be severely judged by Him, who has already pronounced *wo* upon the world. Lastly, let those who must go, on these days, and mingle in the company of worldlings, be guided by St. Francis of Sales, who advises them to think, from time to time, on such considerations as these:—that while all these frivolous, and often dangerous, amusements are going on, there are countless souls being tormented in the fire of hell, on account of the sins they committed on similar occasions; that, at that very hour of the night, there are many holy Religious depriving themselves of sleep in order to sing the divine praises and implore God's mercy upon the world, and upon them that are wasting their time in its vanities; that there are thousands in the agonies of death, whilst all that gaiety is going on; that God and his Angels are attentively looking upon this thoughtless group; and finally, that life is passing away, and death so much nearer each moment.[1]

We grant, that, on these three days immediately preceding the penitential Season of Lent, some pro-

---

[1] Introduction to a Devout Life, *Part* III., *Chapter* 33.

vision was necessary to be made for those countless souls, who seem scarce able to live without some excitement. The Church supplies this want. She gives a substitute for frivolous amusements and dangerous pleasures; and those of her children upon whom Faith has not lost its influence, will find, in what she offers them, a feast surpassing all earthly enjoyments, and a means whereby to make amends to God, for the insults offered to his Divine Majesty during these days of Carnival. The Lamb, that taketh away the sins of the world, is exposed upon our Altars. Here, on this his throne of mercy, he receives the homage of them who come to adore him, and acknowledge him for their King; he accepts the repentance of those who come to tell him how grieved they are at having ever followed any other Master than Him; he offers himself to his Eternal Father for poor sinners, who not only treat his favours with indifference, but seem to have made a resolution to offend him during these days more than at any other period of the year.

It was the pious Cardinal Gabriel Paleotti, Archbishop of Bologna, who first originated the admirable devotion of the *Forty Hours*. He was a cotemporary of St. Charles Borromeo, and, like him, was eminent for his pastoral zeal. His object in this solemn *Exposition* of the Most Blessed Sacrament, was to offer to the Divine Majesty some compensation for the sins of men, and, at the very time when the world was busiest in deserving his anger, to appease it by the sight of his own Son, the Mediator between heaven and earth. St. Charles immediately introduced the Devotion into his own diocese and province. This was in the 16th Century. Later on, that is, in the 18th Century, Prosper Lambertini was Archbishop of Bologna; he zealously continued the pious design of his ancient predecessor, Paleotti, by encouraging his flock to devotion towards the

Blessed Sacrament during the three days of Carnival; and when he was made Pope, under the name of Benedict the Fourteenth, he granted many Indulgences to all who, during these days, should visit our Lord in this Mystery of his Love, and should pray for the pardon of sinners. This favour was, at first, restricted to the Faithful of the Papal States; but in the year 1765 it was extended, by Pope Clement the Thirteenth, to the universal Church. Thus, the *Forty Hours' Devotion* has spread throughout the whole world, and become one of the most solemn expressions of Catholic Piety. Let us, then, who have the opportunity, profit by it during these three last days of our preparation for Lent. Let us, like Abraham, retire from the distracting dangers of the world, and seek the Lord our God. Let us go apart, for at least one short hour, from the dissipation of earthly enjoyments; and, kneeling in the Presence of our Jesus, merit the grace to keep our hearts innocent and detached, whilst sharing in those we cannot avoid.[1]

We will now resume our considerations upon the Liturgy of Quinquagesima Sunday. The passage of the Gospel selected by the Church, is that wherein our Saviour foretells to his Apostles the Sufferings he was to undergo in Jerusalem. This solemn announcement prepares us for Passiontide. We ought to receive it with feeling and grateful hearts, and make it an additional motive for imitating the devoted Abraham, and giving our whole selves to our God. The ancient Liturgists tell us, that the blind man of Jericho, (spoken of, in this same Gospel,) is a figure of those poor sinners, who, during these days, are blind to their Christian character, and rush into excesses, which even Paganism would have

---

[1] The *Litanies* for the *Forty Hours* are given at the end of this Volume.

coveted. The blind man recovered his sight, because he was aware of his wretched state, and desired to be cured and to see. The Church wishes us to have a like desire, and she promises us that it shall be granted.

In the Greek Church, this Sunday is called *Tyrophagos,* because it is the last day on which is allowed the use of *white meats,* or, as we call them, *milk-meats.* Beginning with to-morrow, it is forbidden to eat them, for Lent then begins, and with all the severity wherewith the Oriental Churches observe it.

MASS.

The *Station* is in the Church of *St. Peter,* on the Vatican. The choice was suggested, as we learn from the Abbot Rupert's *Treatise on the Divine Offices,* by the Lesson of the Law given to Moses, which used then to be read in this Sunday's Office. Moses was looked upon, by the early Christians of Rome, as a type of St. Peter. The Church having, since that time, substituted the Vocation of Abraham for the passage from Exodus, (which is now deferred till Lent),—the Station for this Sunday is still in the Basilica of the Prince of the Apostles, who was prefigured also by Abraham, *the Father of believers.*

The Introit is the prayer of mankind, blind and wretched as the poor man of Jericho; it asks for pity from its Redeemer, and beseeches him to *guide* and *feed* it.

INTROIT.

Esto mihi in Deum protectorem, et in locum refugii, ut salvum me facias:	Be thou unto me a God, a protector, and a house of refuge, to save me; for thou art

my strength, and my refuge; and for thy name's sake thou wilt lead me, and nourish me.

Ps. In thee, O Lord, have I hoped, let me never be confounded; deliver me in thy justice, and rescue me. ℣. Glory. Be thou.

quoniam firmamentum meum, et refugium meum es tu: et propter Nomen tuum dux mihi eris et enutries me.

Ps. In te, Domine, speravi, non confundar in æternum: in justitia tua libera me, et eripe me. ℣. Gloria Patri. Esto.

COLLECT.

Mercifully hear our prayers, we beseech thee, O Lord, and being freed from the chains of our sins, preserve us from all adversity. Through, &c.

Preces nostras, quæsumus, Domine, clementer exaudi: atque a peccatorum vinculis absolutos, ab omni nos adversitate custodi. Per Dominum.

Then are added two other Collects, as in the Mass for Septuagesima Sunday, *page* 125.

EPISTLE.

Lesson of Saint Paul the Apostle to the Corinthians.

Lectio Epistolæ beati Pauli Apostoli ad Corinthios.

I. *Ch. XIII.*

I. *Cap. XIII.*

Brethren, if I speak with the tongues of men and of angels, and have not charity, I am become as sounding brass, or a tinkling cymbal. And if I should have prophecy, and should know all mysteries, and all knowledge, and if I should have all faith, so that I could remove mountains, and have not charity, I am nothing. And if I should distribute all my goods to feed the poor, and if I should deliver my body to be burned, and have not charity, it profiteth me

Fratres, si linguis hominum loquar, et Angelorum, charitatem autem non habeam, factus sum velut æs sonans, aut cymbalum tinniens. Et si habuero prophetiam, et noverim mysteria omnia, et omnem scientiam: et si habuero omnem fidem, ita ut montes transferam, charitatem autem non habuero, nihil sum. Et si distribuero in cibos pauperum omnes facultates meas; et si tradidero corpus meum ita ut ardeam, charitatem autem non habuero, nihil mihi prodest. Charitas patiens est, benigna est: charitas non æmulatur, non agit perperam, non inflatur, non est ambitiosa, non quærit quæ sua sunt, non irritatur, non cogitat malum, non gaudet super iniquitate, congaudet autem veritati: omnia suffert, omnia credit, omnia sperat, omnia sustinet. Charitas nunquam excidit: sive prophetiæ evacuabuntur, sive linguæ cessabunt, sive scientia destruetur. Ex parte enim cognoscimus, et ex parte prophetamus. Cum autem venerit quod perfectum est, evacuabitur quod ex parte est. Cum essem parvulus, loquebar ut parvulus, sapiebam ut parvulus, cogitabam ut parvulus. Quando autem factus sum vir, evacuavi quæ erant parvuli. Videmus nunc per speculum in ænigmate: tunc autem facie ad faciem. Nunc cognosco ex parte: tunc autem cognoscam sicut et cognitus sum. Nunc autem manent fides, spes, charitas, tria hæc: major autem horum est charitas.

nothing. Charity is patient, is kind, charity envieth not, dealeth not perversely; it is not puffed up, it is not ambitious, seeketh not her own, is not provoked to anger, thinketh no evil, rejoiceth not in iniquity, but rejoiceth with the truth; beareth all things, believeth all things, hopeth all things, endureth all things. Charity never fadeth away; whether prophecies shall be made void, or tongues shall cease, or knowledge shall be destroyed. For we know in part, and we prophesy in part; but when that which is perfect is come, that which is in part shall be done away. When I was a child, I spoke as a child, I understood as a child, I thought as a child; but when I became a man, I put away the things of a child. We now see through a glass in a dark manner; but then, face to face. Now I know in part; but then I shall know, even as I am known. And now there remain faith, hope, charity, these three; but the greatest of these is charity.

How appropriate for this Sunday is the magnificent eulogy of *Charity*, here given by our Apostle! This virtue, which comprises the love both of God and our Neighbour, is the *light* of our souls. Without Charity, we are in darkness, and all our works are profitless. The very power of working miracles cannot give hope of salvation, unless he who does them have Charity. Unless we are in Charity, the most heroic acts of other virtues are but one snare more for our souls. Let us beseech our Lord to give us this *light*. But, let us not forget, that however richly he may bless us with it here below, the fulness of its brightness is reserved for when we are in heaven; and that the sunniest day we can have in this world, is but darkness when compared with the splendour of our eternal charity. *Faith* will then give place, for we shall be face-to-face with all Truth; *Hope* will have no object, for we shall possess all Good; *Charity* alone will continue, and, for this reason, is greater than Faith and Hope, which must needs accompany her in this present life. This being the glorious destiny reserved for man, when redeemed and *enlightened* by Jesus,—is it to be wondered at, that we should leave all things, in order to follow such a Master? What should surprise us, and what proves how degraded is our nature by sin, is to see Christians, who have been baptised in this Faith and this Hope, and have received the first-fruits of this Love, indulging, during these days, in every sort of worldliness, which is only the more dangerous because it is fashionable. It would seem as though they were making it their occupation to extinguish within their souls the last ray of heavenly light, like men that had made a covenant with darkness. If there be Charity within our souls, it will make us feel these offences that are committed against our God, and inspire us to pray to him to have mercy on these poor *blind* sinners, for they are our brethren.

In the Gradual and Tract, the Church sings the praises of God's goodness towards his elect. He has set them free from the slavish yoke of the world, by *enlightening* them with his grace; they are his own children, the favoured *sheep of his pasture*.

GRADUAL.

Tu es Deus qui facis mirabilia solus : notam fecisti in gentibus virtutem tuam.

℣. Liberasti in brachio tuo populum tuum, filios Israel et Joseph.

Thou art God, thou alone dost wonders : thou hast made thy power known among the nations.

℣. Thou hast delivered thy people, the children of Israel and Joseph, by the strength of thine arm.

TRACT.

Jubilate Deo omnis terra: servite Domino in lætitia.

℣. Intrate in conspectu ejus, in exsultatione ; scitote quoniam Dominus ipse est Deus.

℣. Ipse fecit nos, et non ipsi nos: nos autem populus ejus et oves pascuæ ejus.

Sing joyfully to God, all the earth : serve ye the Lord with gladness.

℣. Come in before his presence with joy : know ye that the Lord he is God.

℣. He made us, and not we ourselves : and we are his people and the sheep of his pasture.

GOSPEL.

Sequentia sancti Evangelii secundum Lucam.

Cap. XVIII.

In illo tempore, assumpsit Jesus duodecim, et ait illis: Ecce ascendimus Jerosolymam, et consummabuntur omnia quæ scripta sunt per Prophetas de Filio hominis. Tradetur enim gentibus, et illudetur, et flagellabitur, et conspuetur, et postquam flagellaverint, occident eum, et tertia die resurget. Et ipsi nihil horum intellexerunt, et erat verbum istud absconditum ab eis, et non intelligebant quæ dicebantur. Factum est autem, cum appropinquaret Jericho, cæ-

Sequel of the holy Gospel according to Luke.

Ch. XVIII.

At that time, Jesus took unto him the twelve, and said to them : Behold we go up to Jerusalem, and all things shall be accomplished which were written by the prophets concerning the Son of Man. For he shall be delivered to the Gentiles, and shall be mocked, and scourged, and spit upon ; and after they have scourged him, they will put him to death, and the third day he shall rise again. And they understood none of these things. And this word was hid from them, and they understood not the things that were said. Now it came to pass, that when he drew nigh to Jericho, a certain blind man sat by the way-side, begging. And when he heard the multitude passing by, he asked what this meant. And they told him that Jesus of Nazareth was passing by. And he cried out: Jesus, Son of David, have mercy on me. And they that went before, rebuked him, that he should hold his peace. But he cried out much more: Son of David, have mercy on me. And Jesus standing, commanded him to be brought unto him. And when he was come near, he asked him, saying: What wilt thou that I do to thee? But he said: Lord, that I may see. And Jesus said to him: Receive thy sight; thy faith hath made thee whole. And immediately he saw, and followed him, glorifying God. And all the people when they saw it, gave praise to God.

cus quidam sedebat secus viam, mendicans. Et cum audisset turbam prætereuntem, interrogabat quid hoc esset. Dixerunt autem ei, quod Jesus Nazarenus transiret. Et clamavit dicens: Jesu, fili David, miserere mei. Et qui præibant, increpabant eum ut taceret. Ipse vero magis clamabat: Fili David, miserere mei. Stans autem Jesus, jussit illum adduci ad se. Et cum appropinquasset, interrogavit illum dicens: Quid tibi vis faciam? At ille dixit: Domine, ut videam. Et Jesus dixit illi: Respice, fides tua te salvum fecit. Et confestim vidit, et sequebatur illum, magnificans Deum. Et omnis plebs ut vidit, dedit laudem Deo.

Jesus tells his Apostles, that his bitter Passion is at hand; it is a mark of his confidence in them; but, they understand not what he says. They are as yet too carnal-minded to appreciate our Saviour's mission; still, they do not abandon him; they love him too much to think of separating from him. Greater by far than this, is the *blindness* of those false Christians, who, during these three days, not only do not think of the God, who shed his Blood and died for them, but are striving to efface from their souls every trace of the divine image! Let us adore that sweet Mercy, which has drawn us, as it did Abraham, from the midst of a sinful people; and let us, like the blind man of our Gospel, cry out to our

Lord, beseeching him to grant us an increase of his holy *light*. This was his prayer: *Lord! that I may see.* God has given us his light; but he gave it us, in order to excite within us the desire of *seeing* more and more clearly. He promised Abraham, that he would show him the place he had destined for him; may he grant us, also, *to see* the land of the living! But our first prayer must be, that he show us himself, as St. Augustin has so beautifully expressed it, that we may love him, and show us our own selves, that we may cease to love ourselves.

In the Offertory, the Church prays that her children may have the *light* of life, which consists in knowing the Law of God. She would have our lips *pronounce* his doctrine and the divine commandments, which he has brought us from heaven.

OFFERTORY.

| Benedictus es, Domine, doce me justificationes tuas: in labiis meis pronuntiavi omnia judicia oris tui. | Blessed art thou, O Lord, teach me thy justifications: with my lips I have pronounced all the judgments of thy mouth. |

SECRET.

| Hæc hostia, Domine, quæsumus, emundet nostra delicta; et ad sacrificium celebrandum, subditorum tibi corpora, mentesque sanctificet. Per Dominum. | May this offering, we beseech thee, O Lord, cleanse away our sins; and sanctify the bodies and souls of thy servants, to prepare them for worthily celebrating this sacrifice. Through, &c. |

Then are added two other Secrets, as given in the Mass of Septuagesima Sunday, *page* 132.

The Communion-Antiphon commemorates the miracle of the Manna, which fed, in the desert, the descendants of Abraham; and yet, this food, though it came from heaven, did not preserve them from death. The *living* Bread, which *we* have had given to us from heaven, gives eternal *light* to the soul: and he who eats it worthily, shall never die.

COMMUNION.

They did eat and were filled exceedingly, and the Lord gave them their desire: they were not defrauded of that which they craved.	Munducaverunt et saturati sunt nimis, et desiderium eorum attulit eis Dominus: non sunt fraudati a desiderio suo.

POSTCOMMUNION.

We beseech thee, O Almighty God, that we who have taken this heavenly food, may be defended by it from all adversity. Through, &c.	Quæsumus, omnipotens Deus; ut qui cœlestia alimenta percepimus, per hæc contra omnia adversa muniamur. Per Dominum.

Then are added two other Postcommunions, as on Septuagesima Sunday, *page* 133.

VESPERS.

The Psalms and Antiphons are given in *page* 74.

CAPITULUM.
(I. *Cor. XIII.*)

Brethren, if I speak with the tongues of men and of Angels, and have not charity, I am become as sounding brass, or as a tinkling cymbal.	Fratres, si linguis hominum loquar et Angelorum, charitatem autem non habeam, factus sum velut æs sonans, aut cymbalum tinniens.

For the Hymn and Versicle, see *page* 84.

ANTIPHON OF THE *Magnificat.*

ANT. But Jesus standing, ordered the blind man to be brought, and saith to him: What wilt thou, that I do for thee?	ANT. Stans autem Jesus jussit cæcum adduci ad se, et ait illi: Quid vis ut faciam tibi? Domine, ut vi-

deam. Et Jesus ait illi: Respice, fides tua te salvum fecit. Et confestim vidit, et sequebatur illum, magnificans Deum.

Lord, that I may see. And Jesus saith to him: See: thy faith hath made thee whole. And he immediately saw, and followed him, praising God.

OREMUS.

Preces nostras, quæsumus, Domine, clementer exaudi: atque a peccatorum vinculis absolutos, ab omni nos adversitate custodi. Per Dominum.

LET US PRAY.

Mercifully hear our prayers, we beseech thee, O Lord, and deliver us from the chains of our sins, and preserve us from all adversity. Through, &c.

Before the day is over, we may recite the following stanzas of the Hymn, in which the Greek Church proclaims the annual Fast of Lent.

HYMN.

(Feria II. Tyrophagi.)

Advenit nunc, ver designans præpurgatrix hebdomas hæc sacrorum jejuniorum, omnino veneranda, corporibus et animabus omnium lucem ministrans.

En reserata est pænitentiæ janua, Dei amatores; adeste igitur, alacriter ipsam ingrediamur, priusquam a Christo nobis velut indignis claudatur.

Puritatem, abstinentiam, et modestiam et fortitudinem, ac prudentiam, orationes et lacrymas comparemus, fratres, per quæ patet nobis justitiæ semita.

Ne corpori saginando, neque ciborum deliciis incumbamus, mortales, imo vero parcimonia ipsum pinguefaciamus, quo semper in pugnis cum adversario, animæ junctum prævaleat.

The week, the harbinger of Spring, is come; the week that cleanses away sin by the sacred and ever venerable Fast, which enlightens the body and soul of every man.

Lo! the gate of penance is thrown open, O ye that love God! Come, then, let us joyously go in, before Christ shut it against us as being unworthy to enter.

Brethren, let us prepare, and bring with us purity, abstinence, and modesty, and fortitude, and prudence, and prayers, and tears; for it is by these we enter on the path of justice.

Be not solicitous, O mortals! about the body how you may pamper it, nor seek delicacies in what you give it to eat; give it, rather, fulness of vigour by abstinence; that so, it may aid the soul to conquer in the battle with the enemy.

This day, O ye that love God! begins the Fast, which is to prepare our souls and bodies by expiation, and infuse into our hearts the generous light of the sacred and venerable Passion of Christ.

Let us, O ye people! enter on our Fast with a glad heart; for lo! the spiritual combat begins. Let us throw off the effeminacy of the flesh, redouble the gifts of the spirit, and suffer with Christ, as it behoves them that are his servants; that thus, we may rejoice together with him, and our souls be enlightened by the in-dwelling of the Holy Ghost within us.

Let us, O ye Faithful! cheerfully receive the divinely inspired messenger of our Fast, as did the Ninivites; and as the harlots and the publicans did, of old, receive John, when he preached penance unto them. Let us prepare, by abstinence, for a participation in the Sacrifice of our Lord on Sion. Let his divine laver be preceded by that of our tears. Let us beseech him to show unto us, when the time is come, the consummation of both Paschs, —the figurative, and the true. Let us put ourselves in readiness to adore the Cross and Resurrection of Christ; saying unto him: Let me not be confounded in my expectation, O thou the Lover of mankind.

Primum jejunium præviæ expiationis animarum, et corporum nostrorum ortum est hodie, spargens in cordibus nostris, Dei amatores, sacræ et venerandæ Christi Passionis, luminis instar, largum splendorem.

Læto animo amplectamur jejunium, o populi: advenit siquidem spiritualium certaminum exordium: abjiciamus carnis mollitudinem, animæ charismata augeamus, compatiamur, ut servi Christi, quo tanquam filii Dei, conglorificemur, animasque nostras Spiritus Sanctus in nobis inhabitans illuminabit.

Alacriter excipiamus, fideles, divinitus inspiratum jejunii nuntium, ut olim Ninivitæ, itemque meretrices, et publicani ab Joanne pœnitentiæ prædicationem acceperunt. Præparemur per abstinentiam ad participationem Dominici in Sion sacrificii; prius lacrymis quam divina ejus lotione purgemur, petamus typici ibi Paschatis consummationem, et veri demonstrationem intueri; parati simus ad Crucis et Resurrectionis Christi Dei adorationem, clamantes ad ipsum: Ne confundas nos ab exspectatione nostra, o philanthrope.

MONDAY

OF QUINQUAGESIMA WEEK.

The life of a faithful Christian, like that of the Patriarch Abraham, is neither more nor less than a courageous journeying onwards to the place destined for him by his Creator. He must put aside everything that could impede his progress, nor must he look back. This is, undoubtedly, hard doctrine; but if we reflect, for a moment, on the dangers which surround *fallen* man during his earthly pilgrimage, and on what our own sad experience has taught us,—we shall not think it hard or strange, that our Saviour has made the renouncing and *denying* ourselves, an essential condition of our salvation. But, independently of this, is it not far better to put our life under God's guidance, than to keep it in our own? Are we so wise or so strong, as to be able to guide ourselves? We may resist as we please,—but God is our Sovereign Lord and Master; and by giving us free-will, whereby we may either resist his will or follow it, he has not abdicated his own infinite rights to his creatures' obedience. Our refusal to obey would not make him the less our Master.

Had Abraham, after receiving the divine call, chosen to remain in Chaldea, and refused to break up the home which God bade him leave,—God would then have selected some other man to be the Patriarch of his chosen people, and Father of that very family, which was to have the Messias as one of its children. This substituting one for another in the order of grace, is frequently forced upon Divine Justice: but what a terrible punishment it is for him that caused the substitution! When a soul refuses salvation, heaven does not therefore lose one of its elect: God, finding that he is despised by the one he called, offers the grace to another, until his call is followed.

The Christian Life consists in this untiring unreserved obedience to God. The first effect of this spirit of submission, is, that it takes the soul from the region of sin and death, wherein she was wasting away her existence; it takes her from the dark Chaldea, and places her in the promised land of light. Lest she should faint on her way along the narrow path, and fall a victim to the dangers which never leave her, because they are in her own self,— God asks her for sacrifices, and these brace her. Here, again, we have Abraham for our model. God loves him, and promises him the richest of blessings; he gives him a son, as pledge of the promise; and then, shortly after, tests the holy Patriarch's devotedness, by commanding him to slay with his own hand this dear child, on whom he has been told to build his hopes!

Man's path on earth is Sacrifice. We cannot *go out* from evil except by the way of self-resistance, nor keep our footing on good ground but by constant combating. Let us imitate Abraham:—fix our eye stedfastly on *the eternal hills,* and consider this world as a mere passing dwelling, a *tent,* put up for a few days. Our Jesus has said to us: *I came, not to send peace, but the sword; for I came to separate.*[1] Separation, then, and trials are sure to be sent us; but we are equally sure that they are for

---

[1] St. Matth. x. 34, 35.

our good, since they are sent us by Him who so loved us, that he became one of ourselves. But this same Jesus has also said: *Where thy treasure is, there too is thy heart.*[1] Christians! can our treasure be in this wretched world? No,—it must be in that fair Land above. There, then, must we be, in desire and affection.

These are the thoughts the Church would have us meditate upon during these days, which immediately precede the Forty of Lent. They will help to purify our hearts and make them long to be with their God. The noise of the world's sins and scandals reaches our ears: let us pray, that the *Kingdom* of God may *come* to us and to those poor sinners; for God's infinite mercy can *change them*, if he will, into *children of Abraham*. Not a day passes but he so *changes* many a sinner. He has, perhaps, shown that miracle of his mercy to *us*, and those words of the Apostle may be applied to us: *You, who some time were afar off, are now made nigh* (to God) *by the blood of Christ.*[2]

Let us pray for ourselves and for all sinners, in these beautiful words of the Mozarabic Breviary.

PRAYER.

Dum te, omnipotens Deus, nostræ delinquentiæ reddunt adversum, tua inspiratione, quæsumus, nostra te invocatio propitium et confessio faciat esse placatum: ut, te miserante, nec tribulatio se-	We beseech thee, O Almighty God! that whereas our sins have angered thee against us, our prayers and praise, which thou inspirest, may propitiate and please thee: that thus, by thy mercy, the vexations of this world

---

[1] St. Matth. vi. 21.   [2] Eph. ii. 13.

may not cast down our soul, nor hurtful delusion possess her, nor the darkness of unbelief surround her; but may we gleam with the light of thy countenance, wherewith thou hast signed us, and ever, by firmness in the true faith, walk in the brightness of the same. Amen.

cularis nostram mentem dejiciat, nec persuasio nociva possideat, nec infidelitas tenebrosa concludat; sed vultus tui super nos signato lumine fulgeamus, semperque in eodem splendore stabilitate veræ fidei gradiamur. Amen.

TUESDAY

OF QUINQUAGESIMA WEEK.

The fundamental rule of Christian life, is, as almost every page of the Gospel tells us, that we should live out of the world,—separate ourselves from the world,—hate the world. The *World* is that ungodly land which Abraham, our sublime model, is commanded by God to quit. It is that Babylon of our exile and captivity, where we are beset with dangers. The beloved Disciple cries out to us: *Love not the World, nor the things which are in the World. If any man love the World, the charity of the Father is not in him.*[1] Our most merciful Jesus, at the very time that he was about to offer himself as a sacrifice for all men, spoke these awful words: *I pray not for the World.*[2] When we were baptised, and were signed with the glorious and indelible character of *Christians,* the condition required of us, and accepted, was that we should renounce the Works and Pomps of the World,—(which we expressed under the name of *Satan,*)—and this solemn Baptismal Vow we have often renewed.

But, what is the meaning of our promise to *renounce the World?* Is it, that we cannot be Christians, unless we flee into the desert, and separate ourselves from our fellow-creatures? Such cannot be God's will for *all*, since, in that same Scripture,

---

[1] I. St. John, ii. 15. [2] St. John, xvii. 9.

wherein he commands us to flee from the World, he also tells us what are our duties to each other, and sanctions and blesses those ties which he himself has willed should exist among us. His Apostle, also, tells us *to use this World as though we did not use it.*[1] It is not, therefore, forbidden us to live in, and use, the World. Then, what means this renouncing the World? Can there be contradiction in God's commandments? Is it possible that we are condemned to wander blindly on the brink of a precipice, into which we must at last inevitably fall?

There is neither contradiction nor snare. If by the *World*, we mean these visible things around us which God created in his power and goodness; if we mean this outward world, which he made for his own glory and our benefit;—it is worthy of its divine Author, and to us, if we but use it aright, is a ladder whereby our souls may ascend to their God. Let us gratefully use this world; go through it, without making it the object of our hope; not waste upon it that love, which God alone deserves; and ever be mindful, that we are not made for this, but for another and a happier, World.

But the majority of men are not thus prudent in their use of the World. Their hearts are fixed upon *it*, and not upon heaven. Hence it was, that when the Creator deigned to come into this World, in order that he might save it, *the World knew him not.*[2] Men were called after the name of the object of their love. They shut their eyes to the *light;* they became *darkness;*—God calls *them "the World."*

In this sense, then, the *World* is everything that is opposed to our Lord Jesus Christ, that refuses to recognise him, and that resists his divine guidance. Those false maxims which tend to weaken the love of God in our souls; which recommend the vanities

---

[1] I. Cor. vii. 31.   [2] St. John, i. 10.

that fasten our hearts to this present life; which cry down everything that can raise us above our weaknesses or vices; which decoy and gratify our corrupt nature by dangerous pleasures, which, far from helping us to the attainment of our last end, only mislead us;—all these are "*the World.*"

And this *World* is everywhere, and holds a secret league within our very hearts. Sin has brought it, and given it prominence, into this exterior world, which God himself created. Now, we must conquer it, and trample upon it, or we shall perish with it. There is no being neutral; we must be its enemies, or its slaves. During these three days, its triumphs are fearful; and thousands of those who, at their Baptism, swore eternal enmity to it, are enrolling themselves its votaries. Let us pray for them; but let us also tremble for ourselves; and that our courage may not fail us, let us ponder those consoling words, which our Saviour, at his Last Supper, addressed to his Eternal Father. He is speaking of his Disciples, and he says: *Father! I have given them thy word, and the world hath hated them, because they are not of the world, as I also am not of the World. I pray not, that thou shouldst take them out of the World, but that thou shouldst keep them from Evil.*[1]

As an appropriate conclusion of this day, we may use this formula of the Ambrosian Liturgy. It puts two truths in contrast: the spiritual indifference of worldlings, and the dread severity of God's future judgment.

INGRESSA.
(Dominica in Quinquagesima.)

Jucunda est præsens vita et transit : terribile est, Christe, judicium tuum, et	Sweet is this present life, but it passes away; terrible, O Christ, is thy Judgment,

[1] St. John, xvii. 14, 15.

and it endures for ever. Let us, therefore, cease to love what is unstable, and fix our thoughts on the fear of what is eternal; saying: Christ, have mercy upon us!

permanet. Quapropter incertum amorem relinquamus, et de infinito timore cogitemus, clamantes: Christe, miserere nobis.

ASH WEDNESDAY.

Yesterday, the World was busy in its pleasures, and the very Children of God were taking a joyous farewell to mirth: but this morning, all is changed. The solemn announcement, spoken of by the Prophet, has been proclaimed in Sion:[1]—the solemn Fast of Lent, the Season of expiation, the approach of the great Anniversaries of our Redemption. Let us, then, rouse ourselves, and prepare for the spiritual combat.

But, in this battling of the spirit against the flesh, we need good armour. Our holy Mother the Church knows how much we need it; and therefore does she summon us to enter into the House of God, that she may arm us for the holy contest. What this armour is we know from St. Paul, who thus describes it: *Have your loins girt about with Truth, and having on the Breast-plate of Justice. And your feet shod with the preparation of the Gospel of peace. In all things, taking the Shield of Faith. Take unto you the Helmet of Salvation, and the Sword of the spirit, which is the word of God.*[2] The very Prince of the Apostles, too, addresses these solemn words to us: *Christ having suffered in the flesh, be ye also armed with the same thought.*[3] We are entering, to-day, upon a long campaign of the warfare spoken of by

---

[1] See the Epistle of to-day's Mass.   [2] Eph. vi. 14-17.
[3] I. St. Peter, iv. 1.

the Apostles:—forty days of battle,—forty days of penance. We shall not turn cowards, if our souls can but be impressed with the conviction, that the battle and the penance must be gone through. Let us listen to the eloquence of the solemn Rite which opens our Lent. Let us go whither our Mother leads us,—that is, to the scene of *The Fall*.

The enemies we have to fight with, are of two kinds:—*internal*, and *external*:—the first are our *Passions*; the second are the *Devils*. Both were brought on us by Pride, and man's Pride began when he refused to obey his God. God forgave him his sin, but he punished him. The punishment was Death, and this was the form of the Divine Sentence: *Thou art dust, and into dust thou shalt return.*[1] O that we had remembered this! The recollection of what we are and what we are to be, would have checked that haughty rebellion, which has so often led us to break the law of God. And if, for the time to come, we would persevere in loyalty to him,—we must humble ourselves, accept the Sentence, and look on this present life as a path to the grave. The path may be long, or short:—but to the Tomb it must lead us. Remembering this, we shall see all things in their true light. We shall love that God, who has deigned to set his heart on us, notwithstanding our being creatures of death : we shall hate, with deepest contrition, the insolence and ingratitude, wherewith we have spent so many of our few days of life, that is, in sinning against our Heavenly Father: and we shall be not only willing, but eager, to go through these days of penance, which he so mercifully gives us for making reparation to his offended Justice.

This was the motive the Church had in enriching her Liturgy with the solemn Rite, at which we are to

[1] Gen. iii. 19.

assist this morning. When, upwards of a thousand years ago, she decreed the anticipation of the Lenten Fast by the last four days of Quinquagesima Week,— she instituted this impressive ceremony of signing the forehead of her Children with Ashes, whilst saying to them those awful words, wherewith God sentenced us to death: *Remember, O Man, that thou art dust, and into dust thou shalt return!* But the making use of Ashes as a symbol of humiliation and penance, is of a much earlier date than the institution we allude to. We find frequent mention of it in the Old Testament. Job, though a Gentile, sprinkled his flesh with Ashes, that, thus humbled, he might propitiate the divine mercy:[1] and this was two thousand years before the coming of our Saviour. The Royal Prophet tells us of himself, that he mingled Ashes with his bread, because of the divine *anger and indignation*.[2] Many such examples are to be met with in the Sacred Scriptures; but so obvious is the analogy between the *sinner*, who thus signifies his grief, and the *object*, whereby he signifies it, that we read such instances without the attention of surprise. When *fallen* man would humble himself before the Divine Justice, which has sentenced his body to turn again into Dust,—how could he more aptly express his contrite acceptance of the sentence, than by sprinkling himself, or his food, with Ashes, which is the dust of wood consumed by fire? This earnest acknowledgment of his being himself but Dust and Ashes, is an act of humility, and humility ever gives him confidence in that God, who resists the proud and pardons the humble.

It is probable, that, when this ceremony of the Wednesday in Quinquagesima Week was first instituted, it was not intended for all the Faithful, but only for such as had committed any of those crimes, for which

---

[1] Job. xvi. 16. [2] Ps. ci. 10.

the Church inflicted a public penance; and these alone received the Ashes. Before the Mass of the day began, they presented themselves at the Church, where the people were all assembled. The Priests received the confession of their sins, and then clothed them in sackcloth, and sprinkled Ashes on their heads. After this ceremony, the Clergy and the Faithful prostrated, and recited aloud the Seven Penitential Psalms. A Procession, in which the Penitents walked bare-footed, then followed; and on its return, the Bishop addressed these words to the Penitents: "Behold, we drive you from the doors of "the Church, by reason of your sins and crimes, as "Adam, the first man, was driven out of Paradise, "because of his transgression." The Clergy then sang several Responsories, taken from the Book of Genesis, and in which mention was made of the sentence pronounced by God when he condemned man to eat his bread in the sweat of his brow, for that the earth was cursed on account of sin. The doors were then shut, and the Penitents were not to pass the threshold until Maundy Thursday, when they were to come and receive Absolution.

Dating from the 11th Century, the discipline of Public Penance began to fall into disuse, and the holy rite of putting Ashes on the heads of all the Faithful indiscriminately, became so general, that, at length, it was considered as forming an essential part of the Roman Liturgy. Formerly, it was the practice to approach bare-footed to receive this solemn *Memento* of our nothingness; and we find, that even so early as the 12th century, the Pope himself, when passing from the Church of Saint Anastasia to that of Saint Sabina, at which the Station was held, went the whole distance bare-footed, as also did the Cardinals, who accompanied him. The Church no longer requires this exterior penance; but she is as anxious as ever, that the holy ceremony, at which we are about to assist, should produce in us the sentiments she intended to convey by it, when she first instituted it.

As we have just mentioned, the Station, in Rome, is at Saint Sabina, on the Aventine Hill. It is under the patronage of this holy Martyr that she opens the penitential Season of Lent.

THE BLESSING OF THE ASHES.

The Function begins with the Blessing of the Ashes, which are to be put on our foreheads. These Ashes are made from the Palms, which were blessed the previous Palm Sunday. The Blessing they are now to receive in this their new form, is given in order that they may be made more worthy of that mystery of contrition and humility, which they are intended to symbolise.

The Choir begins by chanting this Antiphon, which is a prayer for Mercy.

ANTIPHON.

Exaudi nos, Domine, quoniam benigna est misericordia tua : secundum multitudinem miserationum tuarum, respice nos Domine.

Ps. Salvum me fac Deus : quoniam intraverunt aquæ usque ad animam meam. ℣. Gloria Patri. Exaudi nos.

Hear us, O Lord, for thy mercy is kind : look on us, O Lord, according to the multitude of thy mercies.

Ps. Save me, O God : for the waters have reached my soul. ℣. Glory, &c. Hear us, &c.

The Priest, standing at the Altar, and having the *Ashes* near him, begs of God, by the following Prayers, that he would make them an instrument of our sanctification.

℣. Dominus vobiscum.
℟. Et cum spiritu tuo.

℣. The Lord be with you.
℟. And with thy spirit.

LET US PRAY.

O Almighty and eternal God, spare those that repent, show mercy to those that humbly entreat thee; and vouchsafe to send from heaven thy holy Angel, to bless, and sanctify these ashes, that they may be a wholesome remedy to all who humbly call upon thy holy name, and conscious of their sins, accuse themselves, and deplore their crimes in sight of thy divine Majesty, or humbly and earnestly have recourse to thy sovereign bounty; and grant, by our calling on thy most holy Name, that whoever shall be touched by these ashes for the remission of their sins, may receive health of body and defence of soul. Through Christ our Lord. ℟. Amen.

OREMUS.

Omnipotens sempiterne Deus, parce pœnitentibus; propitiare supplicantibus: et mittere digneris sanctum Angelum tuum de cœlis, qui benedicat, et sanctificet hos cineres, ut sint remedium salubre omnibus Nomen sanctum tuum humiliter implorantibus, ac semetipsos pro conscientia delictorum suorum accusantibus, ante conspectum divinæ clementiæ tuæ facinora sua deplorantibus, vel serenissimam pietatem tuam suppliciter obnixeque flagitantibus: et præsta per invocationem sanctissimi Nominis tui: ut quicumque per eos aspersi fuerint, pro redemptione peccatorum suorum, corporis sanitatem et animæ tutelam percipiant. Per Christum Dominum nostrum. ℟. Amen.

LET US PRAY.

O God, who desirest the conversion, and not the death of sinners, graciously consider the weakness of human nature, and mercifully vouchsafe to bless these ashes, which we design to receive on our heads, in token of our humiliation, and to obtain forgiveness; that we, who know that we are but ashes, and must return to dust because of our wickedness, may obtain, through thy mercy, pardon of all our sins, and the recom-

OREMUS.

Deus, qui non mortem sed pœnitentiam desideras peccatorum: fragilitatem conditionis humanæ benignissime respice: et hos cineres, quos causa proferendæ humilitatis, atque promerendæ veniæ, capitibus nostris imponi decernimus, benedicere pro tua pietate dignare: ut, qui nos cinerem esse, et ob pravitatis nostræ demeritum in pulverem reversuros cognoscimus, peccatorum omnium veniam, et præmia pœnitentibus promissa, misericorditer consequi mereamur. Per Christum Dominum nostrum. ℞. Amen.

pense promised to penitents. Through Christ our Lord. ℞. Amen.

OREMUS.

Deus qui humiliatione flecteris et satisfactione placaris : aurem tuæ pietatis inclina precibus nostris : et capitibus servorum tuorum, horum cinerum aspersione contactis, effunde propitius gratiam tuæ benedictionis : ut eos et spiritu compunctionis repleas, et quæ juste postulaverint efficaciter tribuas ; et concessa perpetuo stabilita et intacta manere decernas. Per Christum Dominum nostrum. ℞. Amen.

LET US PRAY.

O God, who art appeased by humiliation, and pacified by satisfaction, incline to our prayers the ears of thy mercy ; and pour upon the heads of thy servants, covered with these ashes, the grace of thy blessing, so as both to fill them with the spirit of compunction, and to grant them the effects of their just desires ; and, when granted, to remain stable and untouched for ever. Through Christ our Lord. ℞. Amen.

OREMUS.

Omnipotens sempiterne Deus, qui Ninivitis in cinere et cilicio pœnitentibus indulgentiæ tua remedia præstitisti : concede propitius, ut sic eos imitemur habitu, quatenus veniæ prosequamur obtentu. Per Dominum. ℞. Amen.

LET US PRAY.

O Almighty and eternal God, who forgavest the Ninivites, when they did penance in sackcloth and ashes ; mercifully grant us so to imitate their penance, that we may obtain pardon of our sins. Through, &c. ℞. Amen.

Having said the last of these prayers, the Priest sprinkles the *Ashes* with Holy Water, and censes them. The first in order of the Priests who are present, marks the Celebrant's forehead with them. Then the ministers on the Altar and the Clergy receive them from the Celebrant, who, finally, gives them to the Faithful.

When the Priest puts the holy emblem of penance

upon *you,* accept, in a spirit of submission, the sentence of Death, which God himself pronounces against you : *Remember, O man, that thou art dust, and into dust thou shalt return !* Humble yourself, and remember what it was that brought the punishment of Death upon us :—man wished to be *as a god,* and preferred his own will to that of his Sovereign Master. Reflect, too, on that long list of sins, which you have added to the sin of your First Parents, and adore the mercy of your God, who asks only one death for all these your transgressions.

During the time of the Priest's giving the Ashes, the Choir is singing the following Antiphons and Responsory.

ANTHEM.

Let us change our dress for ashes and sackcloth ; let us fast and weep in the presence of the Lord ; for our God is very merciful to forgive us our sins.

Immutemur habitu, in cinere et cilicio : jejunemus et ploremus ante Dominum, quia multum misericors est dimittere peccata nostra Deus noster.

ANTHEM.

The priests, the ministers of the Lord, shall weep between the porch and the altar, and say : Spare, O Lord, O spare thy people, and shut not the mouths of those who praise thee, O Lord.

Inter vestibulum et altare plorabunt sacerdotes ministri Domini, et dicent : Parce, Domine ; parce populo tuo : et ne claudas ora canentium te, Domine.

RESPONSORY.

Let us amend of the sins we have committed through ignorance ; lest suddenly overtaken by the day of our death, we seek for time to do penance, and be not able to find

Emendemus in melius quæ ignoranter peccavimus: ne subito præoccupati die mortis, quæramus spatium pœnitentiæ, et invenire non possimus. * Attende, Domine, et miserere, quia peccavimus tibi.

Ps. Adjuva nos Deus salutaris noster: et propter honorem Nominis tui Domine, libera nos. * Attende.
℣. Gloria Patri. * Attende.

it.* Look down on us, O Lord, and take pity; for we have sinned against thee.

Ps. Help us, O God our Saviour: and deliver us for the glory of thy name, O Lord. * Look down, &c. ℣. Glory, &c. Look down, &c.

As soon as all the Faithful have received the Ashes, the Priest sings the following Prayer:

℣. Dominus vobiscum.
℟. Et cum spiritu tuo.

℣. The Lord be with you.
℟. And with thy spirit.

OREMUS.

Concede nobis, Domine, præsidia militiæ christianæ sanctis inchoare jejuniis: ut contra spirituales nequitias pugnaturi, continentiæ muniamur auxiliis. Per Christum Dominum nostrum.
℟. Amen.

LET US PRAY.

Grant us, O Lord, to begin with holy fasting our christian warfare; that being to fight against spiritual wickedness, we may be aided therein by temperance. Through Christ our Lord.
℟. Amen.

MASS.

The soul has regained her confidence by the act of humility she has performed. She approaches the God of Mercy, and reminds him of the tender love he bears to his creature Man, and of the patience wherewith he waits for his repentance. These are the sentiments expressed in the Introit, which is taken from the Book of Wisdom.

INTROIT.

Misereris omnium, Domine, et nihil odisti eorum

Thou, O Lord, hast mercy on all, and hatest none of

ASH WEDNESDAY. 227

those things which thou hast created; thou winkest at the sins of men, to draw them to repentance, and thou pardonest them; because thou art the Lord our God.

Ps. Have mercy on me, O God, have mercy on me; for my soul trusteth in thee. ℣. Glory, &c. Thou, O Lord, &c.

quæ fecisti, dissimulans peccata hominum propter pœnitentiam, et parcens illis: quia tu es Dominus Deus noster.

Ps. Miserere mei Deus, miserere mei; quoniam in te confidit anima mea. ℣. Gloria Patri. Misereris.

In the Collect, the Church prays that her Children may have the two-fold grace, of a fervent commencement, and steady perseverance, in the salutary Fast of Lent.

COLLECT.

Grant, O Lord, that thy Faithful may enter on this solemn and venerable fast with suitable piety, and go through it with unmolested devotion. Through, &c.

Præsta, Domine, fidelibus tuis, ut jejuniorum veneranda solemnia, et congrua pietate suscipiant, et secura devotione percurrant. Per Dominum.

SECOND COLLECT.

Preserve us, O Lord, we beseech thee, from all dangers of soul and body: and by the intercession of the glorious and Blessed Mary, the ever Virgin-Mother of God, of thy blessed Apostles, Peter and Paul of blessed N. (*here is mentioned the Titular Saint of the Church*), and of all the Saints, grant us, in thy mercy, health and peace; that all adversities and errors being removed, thy Church may serve thee with undisturbed liberty.

A cunctis nos, quæsumus Domine, mentis et corporis defende periculis: et intercedente beata et gloriosa semperque Virgine Dei Genitrice Maria, cum beatis Apostolis tuis Petro et Paulo, atque beato N. et omnibus Sanctis, salutem nobis tribue benignus et pacem: ut, destructis adversitatibus et erroribus universis, Ecclesia tua secura tibi serviat libertate.

THIRD COLLECT.

Omnipotens sempiterne Deus, qui vivorum dominaris simul et mortuorum, omniumque misereris, quos tuos fide et opere futuros esse prænoscis : te supplices exoramus ; ut pro quibus effundere preces decrevimus, quosque vel præsens seculum adhuc in carne retinet, vel futurum jam exutos corpore suscepit, intercedentibus omnibus Sanctis tuis, pietatis tuæ clementia, omnium delictorum suorum veniam consequantur. Per Dominum.

O Almighty and Eternal God, who hast dominion over the living and the dead, and art merciful to all whom thou knowest will be thine by faith and good works : we humbly beseech thee, that they, for whom we have proposed to offer our prayers, whether this world still retains them in the flesh, or the next world hath already received them divested of their bodies, may, by the clemency of thine own goodness, and the intercession of thy saints, obtain pardon and full remission of their sins. Through, &c.

EPISTLE.

Lectio Joelis Prophetæ.

Lesson from the Prophet Joel.

Cap. II.

Ch. II.

Hæc dicit Dominus : Convertimini ad me in toto corde vestro, in jejunio, et in fletu, et in planctu. Et scindite corda vestra, et non vestimenta vestra, et convertimini ad Dominum Deum vestrum : quia benignus et misericors est, patiens et multæ misericordiæ, et præstabilis super malitia. Quis scit si convertatur et ignoscat, et relinquat post se benedictionem, sacrificium et libamen Domino Deo vestro? Canite tuba in Sion, sanctificate jejunium, vocate cœtum, congregate populum, sanctifi-

Thus saith the Lord : Be converted to me with all your heart, in fasting, in weeping, and in mourning. And rend your hearts, and not your garments, and turn to the Lord your God : for he is gracious and merciful, patient and rich in mercy, and ready to repent of the evil. Who knoweth but he will return, and forgive, and leave a blessing behind him ; sacrifice and libation to the Lord your God ? Blow the trumpet in Sion, sanctify a fast, call a solemn assembly, gather together the people, sanctify the Church, assemble the ancients, gather together the little ones, and them that suck at the breasts: let the bridegroom go forth from his bed, and the bride out of the bride-chamber. Between the porch and the altar the priests, the Lord's ministers, shall weep, and shall say: Spare, O Lord, spare thy people; and give not thine inheritance to reproach, that the heathens should rule over them. Why should they say among the nations: Where is their God? The Lord hath been zealous for his land, and hath spared his people. And the Lord answered, and said to his people: Behold I will send you corn, and wine, and oil; you shall be filled with them, and I will no more make you a reproach among the nations, saith the Lord Almighty.

cate Ecclesiam, coadunate senes, congregate parvulos et sugentes ubera : egrediatur sponsus de cubili suo, et sponsa de thalamo suo. Inter vestibulum et altare plorabunt sacerdotes ministri Domini, et dicent: Parce, Domine, parce populo tuo: et ne des hæreditatem tuam in opprobrium, ut dominentur eis nationes. Quare dicunt in populis: Ubi est Deus eorum? Zelatus est Dominus terram suam, et pepercit populo suo. Et respondit Dominus, et dixit populo suo: Ecce ego mittam vobis frumentum, et vinum, et oleum, et replebimini eis: et non dabo vos ultra opprobrium in gentibus: dicit Dominus omnipotens.

We learn from this magnificent passage of the Prophet Joel how acceptable to God is the expiation of Fasting. When the penitent sinner inflicts corporal penance upon himself, God's justice is appeased. We have a proof of it in the Ninivites. If the Almighty pardoned an infidel city, as Ninive was, solely because its inhabitants sought for mercy under the garb of penance; what will he not do in favour of his own people, who offer him the twofold sacrifice, exterior works of mortification, and true contrition of heart? Let us, then, courageously enter on the path of penance. We are living in an age, when, through want of faith and of fear of God, those practices which are as ancient as Christianity itself, and on which we might almost say it was founded, are falling into disuse: it behoves us to be on our guard, lest we, too, should imbibe the false principles, which have so fearfully weakened the Christian spirit. Let us never forget our own personal debt to the divine Justice, which will remit neither our sins nor the punishment due to them, except inasmuch as we are ready to make satisfaction. We have just been told, that these bodies, which we are so inclined to pamper, are but dust; and as to our souls, which we are so often tempted to sacrifice by indulging the flesh, they have claims upon the body, claims of both restitution and obedience.

In the Gradual, the Church again pours forth the expressions of her confidence in the God of all goodness, for she counts upon her Children being faithful to the means she gives them of propitiating his Justice.

The Tract is that beautiful prayer of the Psalmist, which she repeats thrice during each week of Lent, and which she always uses in times of public calamity, in order to appease the anger of God.

GRADUAL.

Miserere mei Deus, miserere mei : quoniam in te confidit anima mea.

℣. Misit de cœlo, et liberavit me : dedit in opprobrium conculcantes me.

Have mercy on me O God, have mercy on me; for my soul hath trusted in thee.

℣. He hath sent from heaven, and delivered me; he hath made them a reproach that trod upon me.

TRACT.

℣. Domine non secundum peccata nostra, quæ fecimus nos, neque secundum iniquitates nostras retribuas nobis.

℣. Domine, ne memineris iniquitatum nostrarum antiquarum : cito anticipent nos misericordiæ tuæ, quia pauperes facti sumus nimis.

℣. Deal not with us, O Lord, according to our sins, which we have committed, nor punish us according to our iniquities.

℣. Remember not, O Lord, our former iniquities; let thy mercies speedily prevent us, for we are become exceeding poor.

ASH WEDNESDAY.

At this next Verse, the Priest kneels down.

℣. Help us, O God, our Saviour, and for the glory of thy name, O Lord, deliver us, and forgive us our sins for thy Name's sake.

℣. Adjuva nos, Deus Salutaris noster : et propter gloriam Nominis tui, Domine, libera nos: et propitius esto peccatis nostris, propter Nomen tuum.

GOSPEL.

Sequel of the holy Gospel according to Matthew.

Sequentia sancti Evangelii secundum Matthæum.

Ch. VI.

Cap. VI.

At that time, Jesus said to his disciples : When you fast, be not as the hypocrites, sad. For they disfigure their faces, that they may appear to men to fast. Amen, I say to you, they have received their reward. But thou, when thou fastest, anoint thy head, and wash thy face, that thou appear not to men to fast, but to thy Father, who is in secret : and thy Father, who seeth in secret, will reward thee. Lay not up for yourselves treasures on earth, where the rust and moth consume, and where thieves break through and steal. But lay up for yourselves treasures in heaven, where neither rust nor moth doth consume, and where thieves do not break through, nor steal. For where thy treasure is, there is thy heart also.

In illo tempore : Dixit Jesus discipulis suis : Cum jejunatis, nolite fieri sicut hypocritæ tristes. Exterminant enim facies suas, ut appareant hominibus jejunantes. Amen dico vobis, quia receperunt mercedem suam. Tu autem cum jejunas, unge caput tuum, et faciem tuam lava, ne videaris hominibus jejunans, sed Patri tuo, qui est in abscondito : et Pater tuus qui videt in abscondito, reddet tibi. Nolite thesaurizare vobis thesauros in terra, ubi ærugo, et tinea demolitur : et ubi fures effodiunt, et furantur. Thesaurizate autem vobis thesauros in cœlo : ubi neque ærugo, neque tinea demolitur ; et ubi fures non effodiunt, nec furantur. Ubi enim est thesaurus tuus, ibi est et cor tuum.

Our Redeemer would not have us receive the announcement of the great Fast as one of sadness and melancholy. The Christian who understands what a dangerous thing it is to be behindhand with divine Justice, welcomes the Season of Lent with joy; it consoles him. He knows, that if he be faithful in observing what the Church prescribes, his debt will be less heavy upon him. These penances, these *satisfactions*, (which the indulgence of the Church has rendered so easy,) being offered to God unitedly with those of our Saviour himself, and being rendered fruitful by that holy fellowship which blends into one common propitiatory sacrifice the good works of all the members of the Church Militant,—will purify our souls, and make them worthy to partake in the grand Easter joy. Let us not, then, be *sad* because we are to *fast;* let us be *sad* only because we have sinned and made fasting a necessity. In this same Gospel, our Redeemer gives us a second counsel, which the Church will often bring before us during the whole course of Lent: it is that of joining Almsdeeds with our Fasting. He bids us to *lay up treasures in heaven.* For this, we need intercessors; let us seek them amidst the Poor.

In the Offertory, the Church rejoices in her Children's being set free; she foresees that the wounds of our souls will be healed, for she has confidence in us that we shall persevere, and this fills her with gladness.

OFFERTORY.

Exaltabo te, Domine, quoniam suscepisti me, nec delectasti inimicos meos super me: Domine, clamavi ad te, et sanasti me.	I will extol thee, O Lord, for thou hast upholden me, and hast not made my enemies to rejoice over me. O Lord, I have cried to thee, and thou hast healed me.

SECRET.

Fac nos, quæsumus, Domine, his muneribus offerendis convenienter ap-	Grant, O Lord, that we may be duly prepared to present these our offerings, by which

ASH WEDNESDAY. 233

we celebrate the institution of this venerable mystery. Through, &c.

tari: quibus ipsius venerabilis sacramenti celebramus exordium. Per Dominum.

SECOND SECRET.

Graciously grant us, O God our Saviour, that by virtue of this Sacrament, thou mayest defend us from all enemies, both of soul and body; giving us grace in this life, and glory in the next.

Exaudi nos, Deus Salutaris noster: ut per hujus Sacramenti virtutem, a cunctis nos mentis et corporis hostibus tuearis, gratiam tribuens in præsenti, et gloriam in futuro.

THIRD SECRET.

O God, to whom alone is known the number of thine elect to be placed in eternal bliss; grant, we beseech thee, by the intercession of all thy saints, that the book of predestination may contain the names of all those whom we have undertaken to pray for, as well as those of all the Faithful. Through, &c.

Deus, cui soli cognitus est numerus electorum in superna felicitate locandus; tribue quæsumus, ut intercedentibus omnibus Sanctis tuis, universorum, quos in oratione commendatos suscepimus, et omnium fidelium nomina, beatæ prædestinationis liber adscripta retineat. Per Dominum.

The words of the Church in the Communion-Antiphon contain an instruction of great importance to us. During this long career of penance, we shall stand in need of something to keep up our courage: let us *meditate on the law* and the mysteries of our Lord. If we relish the Word of God as it is offered us by the Church on each day of this holy Season, our hearts will receive an increase of light and love, and when our Lord shall rise from his tomb, the brightness of his Resurrection will shine upon us.

COMMUNION.

He that meditateth night and day on the law of the

Qui meditabitur in lege Domini die ac nocte, dabit

fructum suum in tempore suo.

Lord, shall yield his fruit in due season.

POSTCOMMUNION.

Percepta nobis, Domine, præbeant Sacramenta subsidium: ut tibi grata sint nostra jejunia, et nobis proficiant ad medelam. Per Dominum.

May the mysteries we have received, O Lord, afford us help, that our fasting may be acceptable to thee, and become a remedy to us. Through, &c.

SECOND POSTCOMMUNION.

Mundet et muniat nos, quæsumus, Domine, divini Sacramenti munus oblatum: et intercedente beata Virgine Dei Genitrice Maria, cum beatis Apostolis Petro et Paulo, atque beato N. et omnibus Sanctis, a cunctis nos reddat et perversitatibus expiatos, et adversitatibus expeditos.

May the oblation of this divine Sacrament, we beseech thee, O Lord, both cleanse and defend us; and by the intercession of Blessed Mary, the Virgin-Mother of God, together with that of thy blessed Apostles, Peter and Paul, as likewise of blessed N., and of all the Saints, free us from all sin, and deliver us from all adversity.

THIRD POSTCOMMUNION.

Purificent nos, quæsumus, omnipotens et misericors Deus, Sacramenta quæ sumpsimus: et intercedentibus omnibus Sanctis tuis, præsta ut hoc tuum Sacramentum non sit nobis reatus ad pœnam, sed intercessio salutaris ad veniam: sit ablutio scelerum, sit fortitudo fragilium, sit contra omnia mundi pericula firmamentum: sit vivorum atque mortuorum fidelium remissio omnium delictorum. Per Dominum.

May the Mysteries we have received, purify us, we beseech thee, O Almighty and merciful God; and grant, by the intercession of all thy saints, that this thy Sacrament may not increase our guilt to punishment, but be a means of obtaining pardon in order to salvation. May it wash away sin, strengthen our frailty, secure us against the dangers of the world; and procure forgiveness for all the faithful, both living and dead. Through, &c.

ASH WEDNESDAY.

Every day during Lent, Sundays excepted, the Priest, before dismissing the Faithful, here adds a special Prayer, which is preceded by these words of admonition:

LET US PRAY.

Bow down your heads to God.

OREMUS.

Humiliate capita vestra Deo.

PRAYER.

Mercifully look down upon us, O Lord, bowing down before thy divine Majesty, that they who have been refreshed with thy divine mysteries, may always be supported by thy heavenly aid. Through, &c.

Inclinantes se, Domine, majestati tuæ, propitius intende: ut qui divino munere sunt refecti, cœlestibus semper nutriantur auxiliis. Per Dominum.

THURSDAY

AFTER ASH WEDNESDAY.

ALTHOUGH the law of the Fasting began yesterday, yet, *Lent*, properly so called, does not begin till the Vespers of Saturday next. In order to distinguish the rest of Lent from these four days which have been added to it, the Church continues to chant Vespers at the usual hour, and allows her Ministers to break their fast before having said that Office. But, beginning with Saturday, the Vespers will be anticipated; every day, (Sundays excepted, which always exclude Fasting,) they will be said at such an early hour, that when the Faithful take their full meal, the Evening Office will be over. It is a remnant of the discipline of the primitive Church, which forbade the Faithful to break their Fast before sun-set, in other words, before Vespers or Even-Song.

The Church has given to these three days after Ash-Wednesday a resemblance to the other Ferias of her Lenten Season, by assigning to each of them a Lesson from the Old Testament, and a Gospel, for Mass. We, of course, insert them, adding a few reflections to each. We also give the Collect of these three days.

The Station, in Rome, for the Thursday after Ash Wednesday, is in the Church of *Saint George in Velabro*, (the Veil of Gold.)

THURSDAY AFTER ASH WEDNESDAY. 237

COLLECT.

O God, who by sin art offended, and by penance pacified, mercifully regard the prayers of thy suppliant people: and turn away the scourges of thy wrath, which we deserve for our sins. Through Christ our Lord. Amen.

Deus, qui culpa offenderis, pœnitentia placaris : preces populi tui supplicantis propitius respice : et flagella tuæ iracundiæ, quæ pro peccatis nostris meremur, averte. Per Christum Dominum nostrum. Amen.

EPISTLE.

Lesson from Isaias the Prophet.

Lectio Isaiæ Prophetæ.

Ch. XXXVIII.

Cap. XXXVIII.

In those days, Ezechias was sick even to death, and Isaias the son of Amos the Prophet came unto him, and said to him : Thus saith the Lord : Take order with thy house, for thou shalt die, and not live. And Ezechias turned his face towards the wall, and prayed to the Lord, and said : I beseech thee, O Lord, remember how I have walked before thee in truth, and with a perfect heart, and have done that which is good in thy sight. And Ezechias wept with great weeping. And the word of the Lord came to Isaias, saying : Go and say to Ezechias : Thus saith the Lord the God of David thy father : I have heard thy prayer, and I have seen thy tears : behold I will add to thy days fifteen years : and I will deliver thee and this city out of the hands of the king of the Assyrians, and I will protect it, saith the Lord Almighty.

In diebus illis, ægrotavit Ezechias usque ad mortem : et introivit ad eum Isaias filius Amos Propheta, et dixit ei : Hæc dicit Dominus : Dispone domui tuæ, quia morieris tu, et non vives. Et convertit Ezechias faciem suam ad parietem, et oravit ad Dominum, et dixit : Obsecro, Domine, memento, quæso, quomodo ambulaverim coram te in veritate, et in corde perfecto, et quod bonum est in oculis tuis fecerim. Et flevit Ezechias fletu magno. Et factum est verbum Domini ad Isaiam dicens : Vade, et dic Ezechiæ : Hæc dicit Dominus Deus David patris tui : Audivi orationem tuam, et vidi lacrymas tuas : ecce ego adjiciam super dies tuos quindecim annos : et de manu regis Assyriorum eruam te, et civitatem istam, et protegam eam, ait Dominus omnipotens.

Yesterday, the Church spoke to us upon the certainty of death. Die we must: we have not only God's infallible word for it, but no reasonable man could ever entertain the thought that he was to be an exception to the rule. But if the fact of our death be certain, the day on which we are to die is also fixed. God, in his wisdom, has concealed the day from us; it becomes our duty not to be taken by surprise. This very night, it might be said to us, as it was to Ezechias: *Take order with thy house, for thou shalt die.* We ought to spend each day, as though it were to be our last. Were God even to grant us, as he did to the holy King of Juda, a prolongation of life, we must come, sooner or later, to that last hour, beyond which there is no time, and eternity begins. The Church's intention in thus reminding us of our mortality, is to put us on our guard against the allurements of this short life, and urge us to earnestness in the great work of regeneration, for which she has been preparing us during these last three weeks. How many there are of those, who, yesterday, received the ashes, and who will never see the joys of Easter, at least in this world! To them, the ceremony has been a prediction of what is to happen to them, perhaps before the month is out. And yet the very same words that were pronounced over *them*, were said to *us*. May not we ourselves be of the number of those, who are thus soon to be victims of death? In this uncertainty, let us gratefully accept the warning, which our Jesus came down from heaven to give us: *Do penance; for the Kingdom of God is at hand.*[1]

[1] St. Matth. iv. 17.

GOSPEL.

Sequel of the holy Gospel according to Matthew.

Ch. VIII.

At that time : When Jesus had entered into Capharnaum, there came to him a centurion, beseeching him, and saying : Lord, my servant lieth at home sick of the palsy, and is grievously tormented. And Jesus saith to him : I will come and heal him. And the centurion making answer, said : Lord, I am not worthy that thou shouldst enter under my roof ; but only say the word, and my servant shall be healed. For I also am a man under authority, having under me soldiers ; and I say to this, Go, and he goeth; and to another: Come, and he cometh ; and to my servant : Do this, and he doeth it. And when Jesus heard this, he marvelled, and said to them that followed him : Amen, I say to you, I have not found so great faith in Israel. And I say unto you, that many shall come from the east and the west, and shall sit down with Abraham, and Isaac, and Jacob, in the kingdom of heaven ; but the children of the kingdom shall be cast out into the exterior darkness : there shall be weeping and gnashing of teeth. And Jesus said to the centurion : Go, and as thou hast believed, so be it done to thee. And the servant was healed at the same hour.

Sequentia sancti Evangelii secundum Matthæum.

Cap. VIII.

In illo tempore : Cum introisset Jesus Capharnaum, accessit ad eum centurio, rogans eum et dicens : Domine, puer meus jacet in domo paralyticus, et male torquetur. Et ait illi Jesus : Ego veniam, et curabo eum. Et respondens centurio, ait: Domine, non sum dignus ut intres sub tectum meum ; sed tantum dic verbo, et sanabitur puer meus. Nam et ego homo sum sub potestate constitutus, habens sub me milites, et dico huic : Vade, et vadit ; et alii : Veni, et venit ; et servo meo : Fac hoc, et facit. Audiens autem Jesus miratus est, et sequentibus se dixit : Amen dico vobis, non inveni tantam fidem in Israël. Dico autem vobis, quod multi ab Oriente et Occidente venient, et recumbent cum Abraham, et Isaac, et Jacob in regno cœlorum ; filii autem regni ejicientur in tenebras exteriores : ibi erit fletus et stridor dentium. Et dixit Jesus centurioni : Vade, et sicut credidisti, fiat tibi. Et sanatus est puer in illa hora.

The Sacred Scriptures, the Fathers, and Theologians, tell us that there are three eminent good works, which are, at the same time, works of penance: Prayer, Fasting, and Almsdeeds. In the Lessons she gives us on these three days, which form as it were the threshold of Lent, the Church instructs us upon these *works*. To-day, it is *Prayer* she recommends to us. Look at this Centurion, who comes to our Saviour, beseeching him to heal his servant. His prayer is humble; in all the sincerity of his heart, he deems himself unworthy to receive Jesus under his roof. His prayer is full of faith; he doubts not, for an instant, that Jesus is able to grant him what he asks. And with what ardour he prays! The faith of this Gentile is greater than that of the Children of Israel, and elicits praise from the Son of God. Such ought to be *our* prayer, when we solicit the cure of our souls. Let us acknowledge that we are not worthy to speak to God, and yet, let us have an unshaken confidence in the power and goodness of Him, who only commands us to pray that he may pour out his mercies upon us. The Season we are now in is one of Prayer; the Church redoubles her supplications; it is for us that she makes them; we must take our share in them. Let us, during this Season of grace, cast off that languor which fastens on the soul at other times; let us remember, that it is Prayer which repairs the faults we have already committed, and preserves us from sin for the future.

Humiliate capita vestra Deo.	Bow down your heads to God.
Parce, Domine, parce populo tuo, ut dignis flagellationibus castigatus, in tua miseratione respiret. Per Christum Dominum nostrum. Amen.	Spare, O Lord, spare thy people; that having been justly chastised, they may find comfort in thy mercy. Through Christ our Lord. Amen.

FRIDAY

AFTER ASH WEDNESDAY.

THE Station for to-day is in the Church of the holy Martyrs, Saints John and Paul.

COLLECT.

Graciously favour us, O Lord, we beseech thee, in the fast we have undertaken : that what we observe outwardly, we may perform with sincere minds. Through Christ our Lord. Amen.

Inchoata jejunia, quæsumus Domine, benigno favore prosequere : ut observantiam, quam corporaliter exhibemus, mentibus etiam sinceris exercere valeamus. Per Christum Dominum nostrum. Amen.

EPISTLE.

Lesson from Isaias the Prophet.

Lectio Isaiæ Prophetæ.

Ch. LVIII.

Cap. LVIII.

Thus saith the Lord God : Cry, cease not, lift up thy voice like a trumpet, and show my people their wicked doings, and the house of Jacob their sins. For they seek me from day to day, and desire to know my ways, as a nation that hath done justice, and hath not forsaken the judgment of

Hæc dicit Dominus Deus: Clama, ne cesses ; quasi tuba, exalta vocem tuam, et annuntia populo meo scelera eorum, et domui Jacob peccata eorum. Me etenim de die in diem quærunt, et scire vias meas volunt : quasi gens quæ justitiam fecerit, et judicium

Dei sui non dereliquerit: rogant me judicia justitiæ: appropinquare Deo volunt. Quare jejunavimus et non aspexisti: humiliavimus animas nostras et nescisti? Ecce in die jejunii vestri invenitur voluntas vestra, et omnes debitores vestros repetitis. Ecce ad lites et contentiones jejunatis, et percutitis pugno impie. Nolite jejunare sicut usque ad hanc diem, ut audiatur in excelso clamor vester. Numquid tale est jejunium, quod elegi, per diem affligere hominem animam suam: numquid contorquere quasi circulum caput suum, et saccum et cinerem sternere: numquid istud vocabis jejunium, et diem acceptabilem Domino? Nonne hoc est magis jejunium, quod elegi? dissolve colligationes impietatis, solve fasciculos deprimentes, dimitte eos qui confracti sunt liberos, et omne onus disrumpe. Frange esurienti panem tuum, et egenos vagosque induc in domum tuam: cum videris nudum, operi eum, et carnem tuam ne despexeris. Tunc erumpet quasi mane lumen tuum, et sanitas tua citius orietur, et anteibit faciem tuam justitia tua, et gloria Domini colliget te. Tunc invocabis, et Dominus exaudiet: clamabis, et dicet: Ecce adsum. Quia misericors sum, Dominus Deus tuus.

their God; they ask of me the judgments of justice: they are willing to approach to God. Why have we fasted, and thou hast not regarded: why have we humbled our souls, and thou hast not taken notice? Behold, in the day of your fast, your own will is found, and you exact of all your debtors. Behold you fast for debates and strife, and strike with the fist wickedly. Do not fast as you have done until this day, to make your cry to be heard on high. Is this such a fast as I have chosen: for a man to afflict his soul for a day? is this it, to wind his head about like a circle, and to spread sackcloth and ashes? wilt thou call this a fast, and a day acceptable to the Lord? Is not this rather the fast that I have chosen? loose the bands of wickedness, undo the bundles that oppress, let them that are broken go free, and break asunder every burden. Deal thy bread to the hungry, and bring the needy and the harbourless into thy house; when thou shalt see one naked, cover him, and despise not thy own flesh. Then shall thy light break forth as the morning, and thy health shall speedily arise, and thy justice shall go before thy face, and the glory of the Lord shall gather thee up. Then shalt thou call, and the Lord shall hear: thou shalt cry, and he shall say: Here I am, for I the Lord thy God am merciful.

We are told, in this Lesson from the Prophet Isaias, what are the dispositions which should accompany our Fast. It is God himself who here speaks to us,—that God who had himself commanded his people to Fast. He tells us, that the fasting from material food is a mere nothing in his eyes, unless they who practise it abstain also from sin. He demands the sacrifice of the body; but it is not acceptable to him, unless that of the soul goes along with it. The living God can never consent to be treated as were the senseless gods of wood and stone, which the Gentiles adored, and which were incapable of receiving any other than a mere external homage. Let, then, the heretic cease to find fault with the Church for her observance of practices, which he pretends to scorn as being *material;* it is *he* that grows material by his system of letting the body have every indulgence. The Children of the Church fast, because fasting is recommended in almost every page of both the Old and New Testament, and because Jesus Christ himself fasted for forty days; but they are fully aware that this practice, which is thus recommended and urged, is then alone meritorious, when it is ennobled and completed by the homage of a heart that is resolved to reform its vicious inclinations. And after all, it would be an injustice, if the body, which has been led into guilt solely through the malice of the soul, were to be made to suffer, and the soul herself be allowed to continue in her sinful course. Hence it is, that they whose ill-health prevents them from observing the bodily austerities of Lent, are equally bound to impose on their soul that spiritual fast, which consists in the amendment of their life, in the avoiding everything that is sinful, and in the zealous performance of every good work in their power.

GOSPEL.

Sequentia sancti Evangelii secundum Matthæum.	Sequel of the holy Gospel according to Matthew.

Cap. V. & VI. — *Ch. V. & VI.*

In illo tempore: Dixit Jesus discipulis suis: Audistis quia dictum est: Diliges proximum tuum, et odio habebis inimicum tuum. Ego autem dico vobis: Diligite inimicos vestros, benefacite his qui oderunt vos: et orate pro persequentibus et calumniantibus vos: ut sitis filii Patris vestri, qui in cœlis est, qui solem suum oriri facit super bonos et malos, et pluit super justos et injustos. Si enim diligitis eos qui vos diligunt, quam mercedem habebitis? Nonne et publicani hoc faciunt? Et si salutaveritis fratres vestros tantum: quid amplius facitis? Nonne et ethnici hoc faciunt? Estote ergo vos perfecti, sicut et Pater vester cœlestis perfectus est. Attendite ne justitiam vestram faciatis coram hominibus, ut videamini ab eis: alioquin mercedem non habebitis apud Patrem vestrum qui in cœlis est. Cum ergo facis eleemosynam, noli tuba canere ante te, sicut hypocritæ faciunt in synagogis, et in vicis, ut honorificentur ab hominibus. Amen dico vobis, receperunt mercedem suam. Te autem faciente eleemosynam, uesciat sinis-

At that time: Jesus said to his disciples: You have heard that it hath been said: Thou shalt love thy neighbour, and hate thy enemy. But I say to you: love your enemies, do good to them that hate you, and pray for them that persecute and calumniate you; that you may be the children of your Father who is in heaven, who maketh his sun to rise upon the good and bad, and raineth upon the just and the unjust. For if you love them that love you, what reward shall you have? do not even the publicans the same? And if you salute your brethren only, what do you do more? do not also the heathens the same? Be you therefore perfect, as also your heavenly Father is perfect. Take heed that you do not your justice before men to be seen by them: otherwise you shall not have a reward of your Father who is in heaven. Therefore, when thou dost an almsdeed, sound not a trumpet before thee, as the hypocrites do in the synagogues and in the streets, that they may be honoured by men. Amen, I say to you, they have received their reward. But when thou dost alms, let not thy left hand know what thy right hand doth; that thy

alms may be in secret, and thy Father who seeth in secret, will repay thee.	tra tua quid faciat dextera tua: ut sit eleemosyna tua in abscondito, et pater tuus qui videt in abscondito, reddet tibi.

Almsdeeds is the third of the great penitential works: it is the sister-virtue of Prayer and Fasting. For this reason, the Church puts before us, to-day, the instructions given by our Saviour on the manner in which we ought to do works of mercy. He puts upon us the duty of loving our fellow-men, without distinction of friends or enemies. God, who has created them all, loves them himself; this is motive enough to make us show mercy to all. If he bears with them, even when they are his enemies by sin, and patiently waits for their conversion even to the end of their lives, so that they who are lost, are lost through their own fault,—what ought not *we* to do, we who are sinners as they are, and their brethren, and created, like them, out of nothing? When, therefore, we do an act of kindness or mercy towards those who have God for their Father, we offer him a most acceptable homage. Charity, the queen of virtues, absolutely requires of us the love of our neighbour, as being part of our love of God; and this Charity, at the same time that it is a sacred obligation incumbent upon each member of the family of mankind, is, in the acts it inspires us to do towards each other, a work of *penance*, because it imposes upon us certain privations, and requires us to overcome every repugnance which nature stirs up within us, when we have to show this Charity to certain individuals. And finally, we must, in our Almsdeeds, follow the counsel our Blessed Saviour gives us; it is the one he recommended to us, when he bade us fast: we must do it in secret, and shun ostentation. Penance loves humility and silence; it has a dread of being noticed by men; the only one whose applause it seeks, is His who *seeth in secret.*

Humiliate capita vestra Deo.	Bow down your heads to God.
Tuere, Domine, populum tuum, et ab omnibus peccatis clementer emunda : quia nulla ei nocebit adversitas, si nulla ei dominetur iniquitas. Per Christum Dominum nostrum. Amen.	Defend, O Lord, thy people, and mercifully cleanse them from all their sins ; for no misfortune can hurt them, if no wickedness rule over them. Through Christ our Lord. Amen.

SATURDAY

AFTER ASH WEDNESDAY.

THE Station for to-day is, as noted in the Missal, in the Church of Saint Trypho, Martyr; but this Church having been destroyed, many centuries ago, the Station is now in that of Saint Augustine, which is built on the same site.

COLLECT.

Give ear, O Lord, to our prayers, and grant that we may, with true devotion, observe this solemn fast, which was wholesomely instituted for giving health to both our souls and bodies. Through Christ our Lord. Amen.

Adesto, Domine, supplicationibus nostris, et concede ut hoc solemne jejunium, quod animabus corporibusque curandis salubriter institutum est, devoto servitio celebremus. Per Christum Dominum nostrum. Amen.

EPISTLE.

Lesson from Isaias the Prophet.

Ch. LVIII.

Thus saith the Lord God: If thou wilt take away the chain out of the midst of thee, and cease to stretch out the finger, and to speak that which is good for nothing. When thou shalt pour out thy

Lectio Isaiæ Prophetæ.

Cap. LVIII.

Hæc dicit Dominus Deus: Si abstuleris de medio tui catenam, et desieris extendere digitum et loqui quod non prodest. Cum effuderis esurienti animam tuam, et animam afflictam repleveris, orietur in tenebris lux tua, et tenebræ tuæ erunt sicut meridies. Et requiem tibi dabit Dominus semper, et implebit splendoribus animam tuam, et ossa tua liberabit, et eris quasi hortus irriguus et sicut fons aquarum, cujus non deficient aquæ. Et ædificabuntur in te deserta sæculorum : fundamenta generationis et generationis suscitabis: et vocaberis ædificator sepium, avertens semitas in quietem. Si averteris a Sabbato pedem tuum, facere voluntatem tuam in die sancto meo, et vocaveris Sabbatum delicatum, et sanctum Domini gloriosum, et glorificaveris eum dum non facis vias tuas, et non invenitur voluntas tua, ut loquaris sermonem : tunc delectaberis super Domino et sustollam te super altitudines terræ, et cibabo te hereditate Jacob patris tui ; os enim Domini locutum est.

soul to the hungry, and shalt satisfy the afflicted soul, then shall thy light rise up in darkness, and thy darkness shall be as the noon-day. And the Lord will give thee rest continually, and will fill thy soul with brightness, and deliver thy bones, and thou shalt be like a watered garden, and like a fountain of water, whose waters shall not fail. And the places that have been desolate for ages, shalt be built in thee : thou shalt raise up the foundations of generation and generation : and thou shalt be called the repairer of the fences, turning the paths into rest. If thou turn away thy foot from the Sabbath, from doing thy own will in my holy day, and call the Sabbath delightful, and the holy of the Lord glorious, and glorify him, while thou dost not thy own ways, and thy own will is not found, to speak a word: then shalt thou be delighted in the Lord, and I will lift thee up above the high places of the earth, and will feed thee with the inheritance of Jacob thy Father. For the mouth of the Lord hath spoken it.

Saturday is a day replete with mystery. It is the day of God's rest ; it is a figure of the eternal peace, which awaits us in heaven after the toils of this life are over. The object of the Church in giving us, today, this Lesson from Isaias, is to teach us how we are to merit our eternal *Sabbath*. We have scarcely entered on our campaign of penance, when this affectionate Mother of ours comes to console us. If we abound in good works during this holy Season, in which we have taken leave of the distracting vanities of the world, the *light* of grace *shall rise up* even in the *darkness* which now clouds our soul. This soul, which has been so long obscured by sin and by the love of the world and self, shall become bright as *the noon-day;* the glory of Jesus' Resurrection shall be ours too; and, if we are faithful to grace, the Easter of time will lead us to the Easter of eternity. Let us, therefore, *build up the places that have been* so long *desolate;* let us *raise up the foundations, repair the fences, turn away our feet* from the violation of holy observances, *do not our own ways and our own will* in opposition to those of our Divine Master; and then, he will give us everlasting *rest,* and *fill* our *soul with* his own *brightness.*

GOSPEL.

Sequel of the holy Gospel according to Mark.
Ch. VI.

At that time: When it was late, the ship was in the midst of the sea, and himself alone on the land. And seeing them labouring in rowing, (for the wind was against them,) and about the fourth watch of the night, he cometh to them, walking upon the sea, and he would have passed by them. But they seeing him walking upon the sea, thought it was an apparition, and they cried out. For they all saw him and were troubled. And immediately he spoke with them, and said to them: Have a good heart, it is I, fear ye not. And he went up to them into

Sequentia sancti Evangelii secundum Marcum.
Cap. VI.

In illo tempore: Cum sero esset, erat navis in medio mari, et Jesus solus in terra. Et videns discipulos suos laborantes in remigando, (erat enim ventus contrarius eis,) et circa quartam vigiliam noctis, venit ad eos ambulans supra mare: et volebat præterire eos. At illi, ut viderunt eum ambulantem supra mare, putaverunt phantasma esse, et exclamaverunt. Omnes enim viderunt eum, et conturbati sunt. Et statim locutus est cum eis, et dixit eis: Confidite, ego sum, nolite timere. Et ascendit ad illos in navim, et cessavit ventus. Et plus magis intra se stupebant: non enim intellexerunt de panibus: erat enim cor eorum obcæcatum. Et cum transfretassent, venerunt in terram Genesareth, et applicuerunt. Cumque egressi essent de navi, continuo cognoverunt eum: et percurrentes universam regionem illam, cœperunt in grabatis eos qui se male habebant circumferre ubi audiebant eum esse. Et quocumque introibat, in vicos, vel in villas, aut civitates, in plateis ponebant infirmos, et deprecabantur eum, ut vel fimbriam vestimenti ejus tangerent: et quotquot tangebant eum, salvi fiebant.

the ship, and the wind ceased. And they were far more astonished within themselves: for they understood not concerning the loaves: for their heart was blinded. And when they had passed over, they came into the land of Genesareth, and set to the shore. And when they were gone out of the ship, immediately they knew him; and running through that whole country, they began to carry about in beds those that were sick, where they heard he was. And whithersoever he entered, into towns, or into villages, or cities, they laid the sick in the streets, and besought him that they might touch but the hem of his garment: and as many as touched him were made whole.

The Ship, the Church, has set sail; the voyage is to last Forty Days. The disciples *labour in rowing, for the wind is against them;* they begin to fear lest they may not be able to gain the port. But Jesus comes to them *on the sea; he goes up to them in the ship;* the rest of the voyage is most prosperous. The ancient Liturgists thus explain the Church's intention in her choice of to-day's Gospel. Forty Days of penance are, it is true, little enough for a long life that has been spent in everything save in God's service; and yet, our cowardice would sink under these Forty Days, unless we had Jesus with us. Let us not fear; it is He; He prays with us, fasts with us, and does all our works of mercy with us. Was it not He that first began these Forty Days of expiation? Let us keep our eyes fixed on him, and *be of good heart.* If we grow tired, let us go to him, as did the poor sick ones, of whom our Gospel speaks. The very touch of his garments sufficed to restore health to such as had lost it; let us go to him in his adorable Sacrament; and the divine life, whose germ is already within us, will develop itself, and the energy, which was beginning to droop in our hearts, will regain all its vigour.

Bow down your heads to God.

May thy faithful, O God, be strengthened by thy gifts; that, by receiving them, they may ever hunger after them, and hungering after them, they may have their desires satisfied in the everlasting possession of them. Through Christ our Lord. Amen.

Humiliate capita vestra Deo.

Fideles tui, Deus, per tua dona firmentur : ut eadem et percipiendo requirant, et quærendo sine fine percipiant. Per Christum Dominum nostrum. Amen.

Let us close our Saturday with a prayer to Mary, the Refuge of Sinners. Let us express the confidence we have in her, by the following devout Sequence. It is taken from the German Missals of the 14th century.

SEQUENCE.

It behoves us, O most holy Virgin, to offer thee, on the altar of our hearts, the offering of our prayers.

For whereas the sacrifice of our prayers has no merit of its own, it may be made acceptable, through thee, to thy Son.

Present to Him, who was sacrificed for sin, the sacrifice of sinners' prayers.

Tibi cordis in altari
Decet preces immolari,
Virgo sacratissima.

Nam cum in se sit inepta,
Tuo Nato sit accepta
Per te precum victima.

Pro peccatis immolato
Peccatorum præsentato
Precum sacrificia.

Per te Deum adit reus,
Ad quem per te venit Deus:
　Amborum tu media.

Nec abhorre peccatores
Sine quibus numquam fores
　Tanto digna Filio.

Si non essent redimendi,
Nulla tibi pariendi
　Redemptorem ratio.

Sed nec Patris ad consessum
Habuisses huc accessum,
　Si non ex te genitum
　Esset ibi positum.

Virgo, Virgo sic promota
Causa nostri, nostra vota
　Promovenda suscipe
　Coram summo Principe.
　　Amen.

It is through thee the sinner comes to God, for this God came to the sinner through thee, O thou the Mediatrix between God and man!

It was for the sake of sinners that thou wast made worthy of such a Son: canst thou, then, despise them?

It was because thére were sinners to be redeemed, that thou wast made Mother of the Redeemer.

Neither wouldst thou be seated nigh the Father's throne, hadst thou not been Mother of Him who shares his Father's throne.

Take then, O Holy Virgin, who for our sakes hast been thus exalted, take thou our prayers, and present them to our Sovereign Lord. Amen.

SEPTUAGESIMA.

PROPER OF THE SAINTS.

SAINTS' Feasts are not very numerous during Septuagesima, especially in those years when this Season commences after the tenth of February. Still, we are obliged to introduce a considerable number in this Volume, in order that we may include even those which fall in this period when Easter is kept at its latest.

We begin with the third of February, the Feast of St. Blase, and close with that of St. Gregory, the twelfth of March. The fewness of Feasts, during this long interval, is explained by the spirit of the Liturgy, which, though it does not altogether exclude them in Lent, purposely avoids having as many as at other times of the Year. Our readers are aware that when Septuagesima begins in January, a part of Lent, greater or less according to circumstances, comes in February; so that, Ash Wednesday may sometimes fall on the fourth of that Month.

We shall be obliged, consequently, to repeat, in our Volume for "Lent," almost all the Feasts we give in this, just as we were necessitated to insert in our " Christmas " the three Sundays of Septuagesima, Sexagesima, and Quinquagesima.

With these few words of preface, we begin our explanation of the Saints' Feasts which occur between the day after the Purification and the furthest limit of the Saturday after Quinquagesima, or the vigil of the first Sunday of Lent.

FEBRUARY 3.

SAINT BLASE,

BISHOP AND MARTYR.

Now that the Church has closed the joyous period of her Forty Days of Christmas, and is putting us through a course of meditations on subjects which are to excite a spirit of penance within us,—each of the Saints' Feasts must produce an impression, which shall be in accordance with that spirit. From this day till Easter, we will study the Saints, as they come to us, in this special light,—how much they laboured and suffered during their pilgrimage of life, and what was the plan they took for conquering the world and the flesh. *They went, says the Psalmist, and wept, casting their seeds: but coming they shall come with joyfulness, carrying their sheaves.*[1] It shall be the same with us; and, at the end of our Lenten labours, our Risen Jesus shall hail us as his living, regenerated, Children.

The Calendar of this portion of the year abounds with *Martyrs;* and, at the very onset, we meet with one of the most celebrated of these glorious champions of Christ. The scene of his pastoral virtues and his martyrdom, was Sebaste, a city of Armenia, the same that will give us forty martyred soldiers on a single day. The devotion to St. Blase is, even to this day, most fervently kept up in the East, especially

Ps. cxxv. 6, 7.

in Armenia. The Western Churches soon began to love and honour his memory, and so universally, that we might call him one of the most *popular* of our Saints. His Feast, however, with us, is only *a simple*, and the Church of Rome has given a mere Lesson on his Life.

Blasius, Sebaste in Armenia cum virtutum laude floreret, ejusdem civitatis episcopus eligitur. Qui quo tempore Diocletianus insatiabilem crudelitatem in Christianos exercebat, se in speluncam abdidit montis Argæi, ubi tamdiu latuit, dum ab Agricolai præsidis militibus venantibus deprehensus, et ad præsidem ductus, ejus jussu conjectus est in vincula. Quo in loco multos ægrotos sanavit, qui ad Blasium, ejus fama sanctitatis adducti, deferebantur. In illis puer fuit, qui, desperata a medicis salute, transversa spina faucibus inhærente, animam agebat. Productus autem ad præsidem Blasius semel et iterum, cum nec blanditiis, nec minis adduci posset ut diis sacrificaret, primum virgis cæsus, deinde in equuleo ferreis pectinibus dilaniatus est: postremo, dempto capite, illustre fidei testimonium Christo Domino dedit, tertio Nonas februarii.

Blase, whose signal virtues made him dear to the people of Sebaste in Armenia, was chosen Bishop of that City. When the Emperor Dioclesian waged his cruel persecution against the Christians, the Saint hid himself in a cave on mount Argeus, and there he remained sometime concealed, but was at length discovered by some soldiers of the governor Agricolaus, whilst they were hunting. They led him to the governor, who gave orders that he should be put into prison. During his imprisonment, many sick people, attracted by the reputation of his sanctity, came to him, and he healed them. Among these was a boy, whose life was despaired of by the physicians, on account of his having swallowed a bone, which could not be extracted from his throat. The Saint was twice brought before the governor, but neither fair promises nor threats could induce him to offer sacrifice to the gods. Whereupon, he was first beaten with rods, and then his flesh was torn with iron hooks whilst he lay stretched on the rack. At length, he was beheaded, and nobly gave testimony to the faith of Christ our Lord, on the third of the Nones of February (February 3rd).

Accept, O glorious Martyr, the praise which we, too, offer thee in union with that given thee by the whole Church. In return for this homage of our veneration, look down upon the Christian people, who are now preparing to enter on the Season of penance, and be converted to the Lord their God by holy compunction and tears. We ask it of thee by thine own combat,—assist us in the one for which *we* are preparing. When duty required thee to undergo tortures and death, it found thee ready and brave; *our* duty is expiation by penance, and thy prayers must get us courage. *Our* enemies are not more cruel than thine, but they are more treacherous, and if we spare them, we are lost. Obtain for us that heavenly assistance, which enabled thee to conquer. We are children of the Martyrs; God forbid we should be degenerate! Pray, too, O holy Pontiff, for the country thou didst water with thy blood. Armenia lost the faith for which thou didst lay down thy life. Intercede for her, that she may be restored to the Church, and let her conversion bring consolation to the few that have remained orthodox and faithful.

February 4.

SAINT ANDREW CORSINI,

BISHOP AND CONFESSOR.

The saintly Bishop, whose Feast we keep to-day, pressingly invites us, by his austere life and his burning zeal for the salvation of souls, to procure, at all costs, our own reconciliation with the Divine Justice. We are indebted for this Feast to a member of the illustrious family of the *Corsini*,—Pope Clement the Twelfth, who, however, was but the instrument used by Divine Providence. The holy Bishop of the little town of Fiesole ever sought to be unknown during his life, and God, who willed that he should be glorified by the whole Church, inspired the Sovereign Pontiff to inscribe his name among the Saints of the universal Calendar. Andrew the Saint, was once a sinner; his example will encourage us in the work of our conversion.

Let us read the account of his virtues as given us by the Church.

Andream Florentiæ ex nobili Corsinorum familia natum parentes precibus a Deo impetrarunt, et beatæ Virgini spoponderunt. Qualis autem futurus esset, divino præsagio, antequam nasceretur, ostensum est: nam mater gravida sibi visa est	Andrew was born at Florence, of the noble Corsini family. He was the fruit of his parents' prayers, and was consecrated by them to the Blessed Virgin. His future was thus shown by God to the mother. She dreamt that she had given birth to a wolf,

which went to the church of the Carmelites, and, as it entered the threshold, was suddenly changed into a lamb. Though his early education was one which was calculated to form him to piety, and to everything that suited his high birth, he, by degrees, fell into a vicious manner of life, notwithstanding the frequent reproaches made him by his mother. But as soon as he was told that he had been consecrated by his parents to the Virgin-Mother of God, and heard of his mother's vision, he entered the Order of Carmelites. The devil ceased not to molest him, even then, with manifold temptations; but nothing could make him change his resolution of entering the religious life. Shortly after his profession, he was sent to Paris for a course of study; having completed it, and taken his degrees, he returned to Italy, and was made superior of his Order in the province of Tuscany.

It happened about that time, that the Church of Fiesole lost its Bishop, and Andrew was chosen as his successor. But looking on himself as unworthy of such a dignity, he hid himself so that no one knew where he was. But a child, who had not yet received the use of speech, miraculously revealed the place, outside the town, where he was; upon which the Saint, fearing that further refusal would be a resistance to the divine will, was consecrated Bishop. Thus

per quietem lupum edidisse, qui, ad Carmelitarum ædem pergens, in ipso templi vestibulo statim in agnum conversus est. Adolescens pie et ingenue educatus, cum sensim ad vitia declinaret, sæpe a matre increpatus fuit. Ubi autem cognovit, se parentum voto Deiparæ Virgini dicatum fuisse, Dei amore succensus, deque visu matris admonitus, Carmelitarum institutum amplexus est, in quo variis tentationibus a dæmone vexatus, numquam tamen potuit a religionis proposito dimoveri. Mox Lutetiam missus, emenso studiorum curriculo, et laurea donatus in patriam revocatur, suique Ordinis regimini in Hetruria præficitur.

Interea Fesulana Ecclesia suo viduata pastore eum sibi Episcopum elegit: quo munere se indignum æstimans, diu latuit ignotus, donec pueri voce mirabiliter loquentis proditus, et extra urbem inventus, ne divinæ contradiceret voluntati episcopatum suscepit. Ea dignitate auctus, humilitati, quam semper coluerat, impensius incubuit, et pastorali solicitudini, misericordiam in pauperes, liberalitatem, orationis assiduitatem, vigilias, aliasque virtutes adjunxit, et spiritu etiam prophetico clarus fuit, adeo ut ejus sanctitas ab omnibus celebraretur.

His permotus Urbanus Quintus ad sedandas Bononiæ turbas Andream legatum misit: quo in munere multa perpessus, civium odia, quæ ad internecionem exarserant, summa prudentia restinxit; tum restituta tranquillitate ad propria reversus est. Nec multo post assiduis laboribus, et voluntaria carnis maceratione confectus, obitus die a beata Virgine sibi prædicto, ad cælestia regna migravit, anno Domini millesimo trecentesimo septuagesimo tertio, ætatis suæ septuagesimo primo. Quem Urbanus Octavus multis magnisque miraculis clarum, sanctorum numero adscripsit. Ejus corpus Florentiæ in Ecclesia sui Ordinis quiescit, et maxima civium veneratione colitur: quibus non semel in præsenti discrimine præsidio fuit.

exalted to so great a dignity, he applied himself more than ever to the practice of humility, which had always been his favourite virtue. To the zeal of a good pastor, he united tender compassion for the poor, abundant almsgiving, a life of prayer, long watchings, and other virtues; all which, together with the gift of prophecy he had received, gained for him a great reputation for sanctity.

Pope Urban the Fifth, hearing of his great merits, sent him, as his Legate, to Bologna, that he might quell a sedition that had arisen in that city. The fulfilment of this charge cost him much suffering; but such was his prudence, that he succeeded in restoring peace among the citizens, and so preventing further bloodshed: he then returned to Fiesole. Not long after this, being worn out by ceaseless labours and bodily mortifications, and having been told by the Blessed Virgin of the precise day of his death, he passed from this life to the kingdom of heaven, in the year of our Lord thirteen hundred and seventy-three, and in the seventieth year of his age. Great was the reputation of his name on account of the many and wonderful miracles wrought through his intercession, and at length he was canonised by Urban the Eighth. His body reposes in the Church of his Order, at Florence. The citizens of that city, having often experienced that his Relics have drawn down the divine protection upon them in times of public calamity, their devotion to the Saint is very great.

Hear, O holy Pontiff, our prayer: we are sinners, and would learn from thee how we are to return to the God we have offended. His mercy was poured out upon thee; obtain the same for us. Have pity on Christians throughout the world, for the grace of repentance is now being offered to all; pray for us, that we may be filled with the spirit of compunction. We have sinned; we sue for pardon; intercession like thine can win it for us. From wolves, change us into lambs. Strengthen us against our enemies; get us an increase of the virtue of humility, which thou hadst in such perfection; and intercede for us with our Lord, that he crown our efforts with perseverance, as he did thine; that thus we may be enabled to unite with thee in singing, for ever, the praises of our Redeemer.

February 5.

SAINT AGATHA,

VIRGIN AND MARTYR.

Since the commencement of the Ecclesiastical Year, we have kept the Feasts of two out of the four illustrious Virgins, whose names are daily honoured in the Holy Sacrifice of the Lamb: the third comes to-day, lighting up the heaven of the Church with her bright soft rays. Lucy, first; then, Agnes; and now, the gracious visit of Agatha. The fourth, Cecily, the immortal Cecily, is to be one of that magnificent constellation, which gives such splendour to the closing of the year. To-day, then, let us keep a Feast in honour of Agatha, the Virgin Daughter of that same fair Sicily, which can boast of her Lucy. We must not allow the holy sadness of our present Season to take aught from the devotion we owe to our Saint. The joy wherewith we celebrate her merits, will lead us to study her virtues. She will repay us by her prayers; she will encourage us to persevere in the path which is to bring us to the God she so nobly loved and served, and with whom she is now for ever united.

Let us begin by reading what the Church tells us of the virtues and combats of this glorious Spouse of Christ.

The holy virgin Agatha was born in Sicily, of noble parents. The cities of Palermo and Catania both claim the honour of having been the place of her birth. She received the crown of a glorious martyrdom at Catania, under the persecution of the Emperor Decius. Her beauty, which was as great as her chaste and innocent life was praiseworthy, attracted the notice of Quintianus, the governor of Sicily. He spared no means whereby to compass his lustful designs upon the innocent virgin ; but seeing that she scorned his offers, he had her apprehended as being guilty of the Christian superstition, and gave her in charge of a woman, named Aphrodisia, who was noted for her power of alluring to evil. But finding that her words and company had no effect on the holy maiden, and that she was immoveable in her resolution to maintain both her faith and her virginity, Aphrodisia told Quintianus that she was but losing her time with Agatha. Whereupon, he ordered the virgin to be brought before him, and he said to her : " Art "not thou, that art so noble "by birth, ashamed to lead "the life of a base and slavish "Christian?" She replied : "Better by far is the baseness "and slavery of a Christian, "than the wealth and pride "of kings."

Angered by her words, the governor bids her choose one of these two : adoration to

Agatha virgo, in Sicilia nobilibus parentibus nata, quam Panormitani et Catanenses civem suam esse dicunt, in persecutione Decii imperatoris Catanæ gloriosi martyrii coronam consecuta est. Nam cum pari pulchritudinis et castitatis laude commendaretur, Quintianus, Siciliæ Prætor, ejus amore captus est. Sed cum, tentata modis omnibus ejus pudicitia, Agatham in suam sententiam perducere non posset, Christianæ superstitionis nomine comprehensam, Aphrodisiæ cuidam mulieri depravandam tradit. Quæ Aphrodisiæ consuetudine cum de constantia colendæ Christianæ fidei, et servandæ virginitatis, removeri non posset, nuntiat illa Quintiano, se in Agatha operam perdere. Quare ille ad se virginem adduci jubet : et, nonne, inquit, te pudet nobili genere natam humilem et servilem Christianorum vitam agere ? Cui Agatha : Multo præstantior est Christiana humilitas et servitus, regum opibus, ac superbia.

Quamobrem iratus Prætor hanc ei optionem dat, velitne potius venerari deos, an vim tormentorum subire. At illa constans in fide, primum colaphis cæsa mittitur in carcerem : unde postridie educta, cum in sententia permaneret, admotis candentibus laminis in equuleo torquetur : tum ei mamilla abscinditur. Quo in vulnere Quintianum appellans Virgo : Crudelis, inquit, tyranne, non te pudet, amputare in femina, quod ipse in matre suxisti ? Mox conjecta in vincula, sequenti nocte a sene quodam, qui se Christi Apostolum esse dicebat, sanata est. Rursum evocata a Prætore, et in Christi confessione perseverans, in acutis testulis, et candentibus carbonibus ei subjectis volutatur.

the gods, or sharp tortures. On her refusal to deny her faith, he ordered her to be buffeted with blows, and cast into prison. On the following day, she was again led to trial. Finding that she was still firm in her purpose, they hoisted her on the rack, and laid hot iron plates on her flesh, and cut off her breasts. Whilst suffering this last torture, she thus spoke to Quintianus : "Cruel tyrant, "art thou not ashamed to cut "a woman's breast, that was "thyself fed at the breast of "thy mother ?" She was then sent back to prison, where, during the night, a venerable old man, who told her that he was the Apostle of Christ, healed her. A third time she was summoned by the governor, and being still firm in confessing Christ, she was rolled upon sharp potsherds, and burning coals.

Quo tempore ingenti terræ motu urbs tota contremuit, ac duo parietes corruentes, Silvinum et Falconium intimos Prætoris familiares oppresserunt. Quare vehementer commota civitate, veritus populi tumultum Quintianus, Agatham semimortuam clam reduci imperat in carcerem. Quæ sic Deum precata : Domine, qui me custodisti ab infantia, qui abstulisti a me amorem seculi, qui me carnificum tormentis superiorem præstitisti, accipe animam meam.

Suddenly, the whole city was shaken by a violent earthquake, and two of the governor's intimate friends were killed by the falling of two walls. The people were in such a state of excitement, that the governor began to fear a sedition, and therefore ordered the almost lifeless Agatha to be secretly conveyed back to her prison. She thus prayed to our Lord : " O "God ! that hast watched "over me from my infancy, "that hast separated me from "the love of this world, that

FEB. 5. ST. AGATHA.

"hast given me strength to
"bear the tortures of my exe-
"cutioners,—receive my soul!"
Her prayer being ended,
her soul took its flight to
heaven, on the Nones of February (February 5th), and the
Christians buried her body.

Ea in oratione migravit in
cœlum Nonis Februarii :
cujus corpus a Christianis
sepelitur.

The ancient Books of the Liturgy abound with verses in honour of St. Agatha; but most of them are so poor in sentiment, that we pass them over. The following beautiful Hymn is the composition of Pope St. Damasus.

HYMN.

Lo! is come the bright festal day of the glorious Martyr and Virgin Agatha, when Christ took her to himself, and a double crown wreathed her brow.

Though noble by birth and blessed with beauty, her grandest riches were her deeds and her faith. Earthly prosperity was nothing in her eyes, but her whole heart was on the precepts of her God.

Her bravery tired out the men that tortured her; she flinched not as they lashed her limbs ; and her wounded breast reveals a. dauntless heart.

Her prison was her paradise, where the Pastor Peter heals his bleeding lamb ; and thence once more she runs to suffer, gladder and braver at every wound.

A Pagan city, once in flames, was saved by Agatha's prayer.

Martyris ecce dies Agathæ
Virginis emicat eximiæ :
Christus eam sibi qua sociat,
Et diadema duplex decorat.

Stirpe decens, elegans specie,
Sed magis actibus atque fide,
Terrea prospera nil reputans,
Jussa Dei sibi corde ligans.

Fortior hæc trucibusque viris,
Exposuit sua membra flagris,
Pectore quam fuerit valido
Torta mamilla docet patulo.

Deliciæ cui carcer erat,
Pastor ovem Petrus hanc recreat :
Inde gavisa magisque flagrans,
Cuncta flagella cucurrit ovans.

Ethnica turba rogum fugiens

Hujus et ipsa meretur opem; Quos fidei titulus decorat, His Venerem magis ipsa premat. Jam renitens quasi sponsa polo, Pro miseris supplica Domino, Sic tua festa coli faciat, Te celebrantibus ut faveat. Gloria cum Patre sit Genito, Spirituique proinde Sacro, Qui Deus unus et omnipotens Hanc nostri faciat memorem. Amen.	The same can check, in Christian hearts, the threatening fire of lust. Now that thou art in heaven, clad as a bride of Christ, intercede with him for us miserable sinners, that he grant us so to spend thy Feast, that our celebration may draw down his grace. Glory be to the Son, together with the Father and the Holy Ghost. May the One Almighty God grant that this his Saint be mindful of us. Amen.

How lovely are thy Palms, O Agatha! But how long and cruel was thy combat for them! The day was thine; thy faith and thy virginity triumphed but the battle-field was streamed with thy blood, and thy glorious wounds bear testimony to the Angels how stern was the courage of thy fidelity to Jesus, thy Spouse. When thine enemies left thee, it was to Him thou didst look up; and then thy soul flew to its rest, in the Bosom of thy King and God. The whole Church keeps feast to-day, praising her Lord in thee, great Martyr and Virgin! She knows the love thou bearest her, and how, amidst the joys of heaven, her interests and her wants are the object of thy prayers. Thou art our Sister; be, too, our Mother, by interceding for us. Centuries have passed away since that day, whereon thy soul quitted the body thou hadst sanctified by purity and suffering; but the great battle between the spirit and the flesh is still waging here on earth, and will so to the end of time. Assist us in the struggle; keep up within our hearts the holy fire, which the world and our passions are ever seeking to quench.

It is now the season, when every Christian should renew his whole being by repentance and compunction. We know the power of thy prayer; let it procure us these gifts:—the fear of God, which keeps down the workings of corrupt nature; the spirit of penance, which repairs the injuries caused by our sins; and a solid love for our dear Lord, which sweetens the yoke, and ensures perseverance. More than once, a whole people has witnessed how a relic of thine, thy Veil, has checked the stream of lava which rolled down the sides of Etna; *we* are threatened with a torrent of vice, which will drive the world back to pagan corruption, unless Divine Mercy stay its wild fury; and prayers such as thine can obtain it for us. Delay not, O Agatha!—each day gives strength to the danger. Not a nation but what is now infected with the poison of a literature that is infidel and immoral; by thy prayers keep the poisonous cup from them that have not tasted, neutralise its power in them that have drunk its venom of death. Oh! spare us the shame of seeing our Europe the slave of sensuality, and the dupe of hell.

February 6.

SAINT DOROTHY,

VIRGIN AND MARTYR.

To-day again, it is one of the most amiable of Christ's spouses that comes to console us by her presence; it is Dorothy, the simple and intrepid virgin, who strews the path of her martyrdom with prodigies of sweetest charity. The religion of Christ alone can produce in timid women, like the Saint of to-day, an energy which, at times, surpasses that of the most valiant Martyrs among men. Thus does our Lord glorify his infinite power, by *crushing* Satan's head with what is by nature so weak. The *enmity put*, by God, between the Woman and the Serpent,[1] is for ever showing itself in those sublime *Acts of the Martyrs*, where the rebel Angel is defeated by an enemy, whom he knew to be weak, and therefore scorned to fear; but that very weakness, which made *her* victory the grander, made *his* humiliation the bitterer. Surely, such History must have taught him how powerful an enemy he has in a Christian woman; and we, who can boast of having so many heroines among the ancestors of our Holy Faith, should cherish their memory, and confide in their protection, for their intercession is powerful with Him they died for. One of the noblest of these comes to us to day; let us celebrate her victory, and merit her patronage.

[1] Gen. iii. 15.

The Lessons given in the Dominican Breviary are so much fuller than the Legend of the Roman Liturgy, that we have not hesitated to insert them here.

The holy virgin Dorothy, of Cesarea in Cappadocia, was apprehended by Apricius, the governor of that province, on account of her professing the faith of Christ. She was put under the care of her two sisters, Chrysta and Callista, who had apostatised from the faith, and would be able to shake the resolute constancy of Dorothy. But she brought them back to the faith, for which they were burnt to death in a cauldron. The governor ordered Dorothy to be hoisted on the rack, and she said to him, as she lay upon it: "Never in my whole "life have I felt such joy, as "I do to-day." Then the governor ordered the executioners to burn her sides with lighted lamps, and beat her for a very long time on the face, and finally behead her with the sword.

Whilst she was being led to the place of execution, she said: "I give thee thanks, O "thou the lover of our souls, "that thou callest me to thy "Paradise!" Theophilus, one of the governor's officers, hearing her words, laughed, and said to her: "Hear me, Bride "of Christ! I'll ask thee to "send me some apples and "roses from this Paradise of "thy Spouse." Dorothy replied: "Well, and so I will." Before she was beheaded, she was allowed a moment for

Dorothea virgo, in Cæsarea Cappadociæ, propter Christi confessionem, ab Apricio illius provinciæ præfecto comprehensa, Crystæ et Callistæ sororibus, quæ a fide defecerant, tradita est, ut eam a proposito removerent. Sed ipsa reduxit eas ad fidem, propter quam in cupam missæ et incensæ sunt. Dorotheam vero jussit præses in catasta levari; quæ dixit ad illum: Numquam in tota vita mea sic lætata sum sicut hodie. Tum ad cjus latera lampades ardentes apponi, dein faciem diutissime cædi, tamdem caput gladio percuti præses imperat.

Ea porro dum duceretur ad supplicium dicente: Gratias tibi, amator animarum, qui me ad Paradisum tuum vocasti, Theophilus quidam præsidis advocatus irridens: Eia tu, inquit, sponsa Christi, mitte mihi de Paradiso sponsi tui mala, aut rosas. Et Dorothea respondit: Et plane ita faciam. Cum ante ictum breviter precari permissa esset, pulchra specie puer ante eam apparuit, ferens in orario tria mala, et tres rosas. Cui illa ait: Obsecro ut feras ea Theophilo. Et mox gladio percussa perrexit ad Christum.

prayer; when lo! a beautiful child came to her, bringing with him in a napkin three apples and three roses. She said to him: "Take them, I "pray thee, to Theophilus." Then, the executioner struck her head off with his sword, and her soul fled to Christ.

Igitur cum Theophilus irridens, promissionem sanctæ Dorotheæ sodalibus narraret, ecce puer ante eum cum orario, in quo ferens tria mala magnifica, et tres rosas elegantissimas, dixit ei: En sicut petenti promisit virgo sacratissima Dorothea, transmisit hæc tibi de paradiso sponsi sui. Tum Theophilus stupens, quod esset Februarius, et gelu cuncta rigerent, ea accepit, atque exclamavit: Vere Deus Christus est. Sicque palam fidem Christi professus, gravissimum quoque pro ea martyrium strenue pertulit.

Whilst Theophilus was jocosely telling his fellows the promise made him by Dorothy, he sees a boy bringing him in a napkin three fine apples, and three most lovely roses, who, as he gave them, said: "Lo! "the most holy virgin Dorothy "sends thee, as she promised, "these gifts from the Paradise "of her spouse." Theophilus was beside himself with surprise, for it was February, and the frost most sharp; but taking the gifts, he exclaimed: "Christ is truly God!" He openly professed the Christian faith, and courageously suffered for the same a most painful martyrdom.

The Missals and Breviaries of the Middle Ages contain several pieces in honour of St. Dorothy. The following is one that was used in Germany, and is most appropriate for the Season of Septuagesima.

SEQUENCE.

Psallat concors symphonia,
Laudes pangat harmonia,
Cum sonora melodia
Cordisque tripudio.

Let tuneful instruments breathe forth concordant strains, and harmony sound forth her praise, and we, with joyous heart, sing sweet melodious hymns.

In hoc festo lætabundo
Dorotheæ corde mundo,

'Tis the pure-hearted Dorothy's happy Feast; let our

glad voices, led on by the organ's peal, proclaim her praise.

O noble and sinless handmaid of Christ! O bright Lamp for us to look at! O cup-bearer, that profferest us rich mystic wines!

Child of Paradise, that payest evil with good, and givest to thine enemy roses and fragrant apples of heaven.

Thou leadest the life of an angel, and whilst in the flesh, livest not according to the flesh; scorning to be spouse of man, because betrothed to Christ.

Thou art his Martyr too, trampling on the pagan gods; and, giving faith to infidels, convertest them from madness to wisdom.

Red fragrant rose! nothing could impair thy beauty. Fabricius may threaten what he lists,—thou hast a heart brave enough for all.

Chains and prisons, racks and buffets, thou sufferest all, yet innocent, deserving none.

Wicked men, whose hopes were bent on evil, beat thy beaming face, for that thou darest to teach them the word of God.

But they could increase their tortures, keen and deadly as they were;—furiously, then, they burn thy innocent breast.

O holy Martyr! we beseech thee,—protect us, get us a fear of sin, and pray that time be given us for true repentance.

Sono plaudat vox jucundo
Neumatum præludio.

Generosa Christi verna
Labe carens et lucerna,
 Mundo lucens ac pincerna,
Vina donans mystica.

Paradisi tu colona,
Quæ pro malo reddis bona,
 Scribæ mittis cœli dona
Rosas, mala pistica.

Vitam ducens Angelorum,
Dum in carne præter forum
 Carnis vivis, spernis torum
Viri propter Dominum.

Martyr Christi quæ profanos
Deos sternis, ac paganos
 Fide vestis, et sic sanos
Mores facis hominum.

Tota manens speciosa,
Velut rubens fragrans rosa,
 Ad conflictum roborosa,
Minante Fabricio.

Vinculata carceraris,
In catasta cruciaris,
 Vultu cæsa flagellaris,
Omni carens vitio.

Gens perversa malæ spei
Quam dum doces verbum Dei,
 Lumen tuæ faciei,
Conterit cum baculis.

Furens auget tormentales
Pœnas sævas et lethales,
 Dum mamillas virginales
Tuas cremat faculis.

Supplicamus: nos tuere
Et peccata fac timere,
 Martyr sancta, confer veræ
Tempus pœnitentiæ.

Virgo bona, crimen terge, Victum dona, mores rege, Ne damnemur gravi lege Causa negligentiæ.	Kind virgin! pray for us, that our sins be cleansed, our souls be nourished with grace, our lives well regulated, that so we be not condemned for negligence by God's dread law of justice.
Sponsa Christi Dorothea, Tua nos virtute bea, Ut purgata mente rea, Digni simus præmio.	O Dorothy, thou spouse of Christ! may thy merits draw down his blessing upon us; and we be found worthy of the reward that he gives to those, whose souls are free from sin.

Deum nobis fac placatum,
Ut post hujus incolatum,
  Sed et locum det optatum
In cœlesti gremio.
    Amen.
	Render our Lord propitious to us, and beseech him to give us, after our sojourn here, the longed-for place of rest in the bosom of his heaven. Amen.

Thy promises, O Dorothy, are faithful as thyself. In the garden of thy heavenly Spouse, thou forgettest not the exiles on earth. How fortunate was Theophilus to have had one of thy promises! He asked for fruits and flowers; he got them; and with them, the richer gifts of faith and perseverance, which we also would now ask thee to send us. Thou knowest our wants. We want courage to conquer the world and our passions; we want the grace of conversion; we want the spirit of penance, without which, we can never reach that heaven of our vocation, where we are to be thy companions in bliss. Promise us thy prayers, and we shall not fail. And on the grand Day of the Easter we are preparing for, our souls, having been purified in the Blood of the Lamb, will be as fragrant as the fruits, and as fair as the flowers, which thou didst send to a pagan, whose prayer was less confident than ours.

February 7.

SAINT ROMUALD,

ABBOT.

The Calendar's list of Martyrs is interrupted for two days; the first of these is the Feast of Romuald, the hero of penance, the Saint of the forests of Camaldoli. He is a son of the great Patriarch St. Benedict, and, like him, is the father of many children. The Benedictine family has a direct line from the commencement, even to this present time; but, from the trunk of this venerable tree there have issued four vigorous branches, to each of which the Holy Spirit has imparted the life and fruitfulness of the parent stem. These collateral branches of the Benedict Order are: Camaldoli, by Romuald; Cluny, by Odo; Vallombrosa, by John Gualbert; and Citeaux, by Robert of Molesmes.

The Saint of this seventh day of February is Romuald. The Martyrs whom we meet with on our way to Lent, give us an important lesson by the contempt they had for this short life. But the teaching offered us by such holy penitents as the great Abbot of Camaldoli, is even more practical than that of the Martyrs. *They that are of Christ,* says the Apostle, *have crucified their flesh, with its vices and concupiscences;*[1] and in these words he tells us what is the

[1] Gal. v. 24.

distinguishing character of every true Christian. We repeat it—what a powerful encouragement we have in these models of mortification, who have sanctified the deserts by their lives of heroic penance! How they make us ashamed of our own cowardice, which can scarcely bring itself to do the little that must be done to satisfy God's justice and merit his grace! Let us take the lesson to heart, cheerfully offer our offended Lord the tribute of our repentance, and purify our souls by works of mortification.

The Office for St. Romuald's Feast gives us the following sketch of his life.

Romualdus Ravennæ, Sergio patre nobili genere natus, adolescens in propinquum monasterium Classense, pœnitentiæ causa secessit : ubi religiosi hominis sermone ad pietatis studium vehementius incensus, viso etiam semel et iterum per noctem in Ecclesia beato Apollinari, quod Dei servus illi futurum promiserat, monachus efficitur. Mox ad Marinum, vitæ sanctitate ac severiore disciplina in finibus Venetorum eo tempore celebrem, se contulit, ut ad arctam et sublimem perfectionis viam eo magistro ac duce uteretur.

Multis Satanæ insidiis, et hominum invidia oppugnatus, tanto humilior se assidue jejuniis et orationibus exercebat, et rerum

Romuald was the son of a nobleman, named Sergius. He was born at Ravenna, and whilst yet a boy, withdrew to the monastery of Classis, there to lead a life of penance. The conversation of one of the Religious increased in his soul his already ardent love of piety ; and after being twice favoured with a visit of Saint Apollanaris, who appeared to him, during the night, in the church which was dedicated to him, he entered the monastic state, agreeably to the promise made him by the holy Martyr. A few years later on, he betook himself to a hermit named Marinus, who lived in the neighbourhood of Venice, and was famed for his holy and austere life, that, under such a master and guide, he might follow the narrow path of high perfection.

Many were the snares laid for him by Satan, and envious men molested him with their persecutions ; but these things only excited him to be more humble, and assiduous in fasting and prayer. In the heavenly contemplation wherewith he was favoured, he shed abundant tears. Yet such was the joy which ever beamed in his face, that it made all who looked at him cheerful. Princes and Kings held him in great veneration, and his advice induced many to leave the world and its allurements, and live in holy solitude. An ardent desire for martyrdom induced him to set out for Pannonia; but a malady, which tormented him as often as he went forward, and left him when he turned back, obliged him to abandon his design.

He wrought many miracles during his life, as also after his death, and was endowed with the gift of prophecy. Like the Patriarch Jacob, he saw a ladder that reached from earth to heaven, on which men, clad in white robes, ascended and descended. He interpreted this miraculous vision as signifying the Camaldolese Monks, whose founder he was. At length, having reached the age of a hundred and twenty, after having served his God by a life of most austere penance for a hundred years, he went to his reward, in the year of our Lord one thousand and twenty-seven. His body was found incorrupt five years after it had been in the grave; and was then buried, with due honour, in the church of his Order at Fabriano.

cœlestium meditatione, vim lacrymarum profundens fruebatur: vultu tamen adeo læto semper erat, ut intuentes exhilararet. Magno apud principes et reges in honore fuit, multique ejus consilio, mundi illecebris abjectis, solitudinem petierunt. Martyrii quoque cupiditate flagravit, cujus causa dum in Pannoniam proficiscitur, morbo quo afflictabatur cum progrederetur, levabatur cum recederet, reverti cogitur.

In vita et post mortem miraculis clarus, spiritu etiam prophetiæ non caruit. Scalam a terra cœlum pertingentem in similitudinem Jacob Patriarchæ, per quam homines in veste candida ascendebant et descendebant, per visum conspexit, eoque Camaldulenses monachos, quorum instituti auctor fuit, designari mirabiliter agnovit. Denique cum annos centum et viginti ageret, et centum ipsos in summa vitæ asperitate Deo servisset, ad eum migravit anno salutis millesimo vigesimo septimo. Ejus corpus quinquennio postquam sepultum fuerat, integrum repertum, Fabriani in Ecclesia sui ordinis honorifice conditum est.

Faithful servant and friend of God! how different was thy life from ours! *We* love the world and its distractions. We think we do wonders if we give, each day, a passing thought to our Creator, and make him, at long intervals, the sole end of some one of our occupations. Yet we know, how each hour is bringing us nearer to that moment, when we must stand before the divine tribunal, with our good and our evil works, to receive the irrevocable sentence we shall have merited. *Thou*, Romuald, didst not thus waste life away. It seemed to thee as though there were but one thought and one interest worth living for,—how best to serve thy God. Lest anything should distract thee from this infinitely dear object, thou didst flee into the desert. There, under the Rule of the great Patriarch, St. Benedict, thou wagedst war against the flesh and the devil; thy tears washed away thy sins, though so light if compared with what *we* have committed; thy soul, invigorated by penance, was inflamed with the love of Jesus, for whose sake thou wouldst fain have shed thy blood. We love to recount these thy merits, for they belong to us in virtue of that Communion which our Lord has so mercifully established between Saints and Sinners. Assist us, therefore, during the penitential Season, which is soon to be upon us; Divine Justice will not despise our feeble efforts, for he will see them beautified by the union he allows them to have with such glorious works as thine. When thou wast living in the Eden of Camaldoli, thy amiable and sweet charity for men was such, that all who came near thee, were filled with joy and consolation: what may we not expect from thee, now that thou art face to face with the God of Love? Remember, too, the Order thou hast founded; protect it, give it increase, and ever make it, to those who become its children, a Ladder to lead them up to heaven.

February 8.

SAINT JOHN OF MATHA,

CONFESSOR.

WE were celebrating, not many days ago, the memory of Peter Nolasco, who was inspired, by the Holy Mother of God, to found an Order for the ransoming of Christian captives from the infidels: to-day, we have to honour the generous Saint, to whom this sublime work was first revealed. He established, under the name of the Most Holy *Trinity*, a body of religious men, who bound themselves by vow to devote their energies, their privations, their liberty, nay, their very life, to the service of the poor slaves who were groaning under the Saracen yoke. The Order of the Trinitarians, and the Order of Mercy, though distinct, have the same end in view, and the result of their labours, during the six hundred years of their existence, has been the restoring to liberty and preserving from apostacy upwards of a million slaves. John of Matha, assisted by his faithful cooperator, Felix of Valois, (whose feast we shall keep at the close of the Year,) established the centre of his grand work at Meaux, in France. We are preparing for Lent, when one of our great duties will have to be that of charity towards our suffering brethren: what finer model could we have than John of Matha, and his whole Order, which was called into existence for no other object than that of delivering from the horrors of slavery brethren who were utter strangers to their deliverers, but were in suffering and in bondage. Can we imagine any almsgiving, let it be ever so generous, which can bear comparison with this devotedness of men, who bind themselves by their Rule, not only to traverse every Christian land begging alms for the ransom of slaves, but to change places with the poor captives, if their liberty cannot be otherwise obtained? Is it not, as far as human weakness permits, following to the very letter, the example of the Son of God himself, who came down from heaven that he might be our ransom and Redeemer? We repeat it,—with such models as these before us, we shall feel ourselves urged to follow the injunction we are shortly to receive from the Church, of exercising works of mercy towards our fellow-creatures, as being one of the essential elements of our Lenten penance.

But it is time we should listen to the account given us by the Liturgy of the virtues of this apostolic man, who has endeared himself, both to the Church and mankind, by his heroism of charity.

| Joannes de Matha, Ordinis sanctissimæ Trinitatis Redemptionis captivorum institutor, Falcone in Provincia natus est, parentibus pietate et nobilitate conspicuis. Studiorum causa Aquas Sextias, mox Parisios profectus, confectoque theologiæ curriculo, magisterii lauream adeptus, doctrinæ, et virtutum splendore enituit: quibus motus Parisiensis Antistes, ad sacrum presbyteratus ordinem, præ humilitate reluctantem promovit, eo consilio, ut in ea | John of Matha, the Institutor of the Order of the Most Holy Trinity for the Ransom of captives, was born at Faucon, in Provence, of parents conspicuous for their nobility and virtue. He went through his studies first at Aix, and afterwards at Paris, where, after having completed his theological course, he received the degree of Doctor. His eminent learning and virtues induced the Bishop of Paris to promote him, in spite of his humble resistance, to the holy order of priesthood, that, |

FEB. 8. ST. JOHN OF MATHA.

during his sojourn in that city, he might be a bright example to young students by his talents and piety. Whilst celebrating his first mass in the Bishop's chapel, in the presence of the Prelate and several assistants, he was honoured by a signal favour from heaven. There appeared to him an Angel clad in a white and brilliant robe; he had on his breast a red and blue cross, and his arms were stretched out, crossed one above the other, over two captives, one a Christian, the other a Moor. Falling into an ecstacy at this sight, the man of God at once understood that he was called to ransom captives from the infidels.

But, that he might the more prudently carry out so important an undertaking, he withdrew into a solitude. There, by divine appointment, he met with Felix of Valois, who had been living many years in that same desert. They agreed to live together, and for three years did John devote himself to prayer, and contemplation, and the practice of every virtue. It happened, that as they were one day seated near a fountain, conferring with each other on holy things, a stag came towards them, bearing a red and blue cross between his antlers. John, perceiving that Felix was surprised by so strange an occurrence, told him of the vision he had had in his first mass. They gave themselves more fervently

civitate commorans, sapientia et moribus, studiosæ juventuti præluceret. Cum autem in sacello ejusdem episcopi, ipso cum aliis adstante, primum Deo sacrum offerret, cœlesti favore meruit recreari. Nam Angelus candida et fulgenti veste indutus, cui in pectore crux rubei et cærulei coloris assuta erat, brachiis cancellatis, et super duos captivos ad latera positos, christianum unum, alterum maurum, extensis apparuit. Qua visione in exstasim raptus, intellexit protinus vir Dei, se ad redimendos ab infidelibus captivos destinari.

Quo vero maturius in re tanti momenti procederet, in solitudinem secessit; ibique divino nutu factum est, ut Felicem Valesium in ipsa eremo jam multis annis degentem repererit. Cum quo inita societate, se per triennium in oratione et contemplatione, omniumque virtutum studio exercuit. Contigit autem, ut dum secum de rebus divinis prope fontem colloquerentur, cervus ad eos accesserit, crucem inter cornua gerens, rubei et cærulei coloris. Cumque Felix ob rei novitatem miraretur, narravit ei Joannes visionem in prima missa habitam: et exinde ferventius orationi incumbentes, ter in somnis admoniti, Romam proficisci decreverunt, ut a summo Pontifice novi Ordinis pro redimendis captivis institutionem impetrarent. Electus fuerat eo tempore Innocentius Tertius; qui, illis benigne acceptis, dum secum de re proposita deliberaret, in festo sanctæ Agnetis secundo, Laterani intra missarum solemnia, ad sacræ Hostiæ elevationem, Angelus ei candida veste, cruce bicolori, specie redimentis captivos apparuit. Quo viso, Pontifex institutum approbavit, et novum Ordinem sanctissimæ Trinitatis Redemptionis captivorum vocari jussit, ejusque professoribus albas vestes, cum cruce rubei et cærulei coloris præbuit.

Sic stabilito Ordine, sancti Fundatores in Galliam redierunt; primoque Cœnobio Cervi Frigidi in diœcesi Meldensi constructo, ad ejus regimen Felix remansit, et Joannes Romam cum aliquot sociis reversus est, ubi Innocentius domum, ecclesiam, et hospitale sancti Thomæ de Formis in monte Cœlio eis donavit, cum multis redditibus, et possessionibus. Datis quoque litteris ad Miramolinum regem Marochii, opus redemptionis felici auspicio incho-

than ever to prayer, and having been thrice admonished in sleep, they resolved to set out for Rome, there to obtain permission from the Sovereign Pontiff to found an Order for the ransom of captives. Innocent the Third, who had shortly before been elected Pope, received them kindly, and whilst deliberating upon what they proposed, it happened, that as he was celebrating mass in the Lateran Church, on the second feast of St. Agnes, there appeared to him, during the elevation of the sacred Host, an Angel robed in white, bearing a two-coloured cross, and in the attitude of one that was rescuing captives. Whereupon, the Pontiff gave his approbation to the new institute, and would have it called the Order of the Most Holy Trinity for the Ransom of captives, bidding its members wear a white habit, with a red and blue cross.

The Order being thus established, its holy Founders returned to France, and erected their first Monastery at Cerfroid, in the diocese of Meaux. Felix was left to govern it, and John returned, accompanied by a few of his brethren, to Rome. Innocent the Third gave them the house, church, and hospital of Saint Thomas *de Formis*, together with various revenues and possessions. He also gave them letters to Miramolin, king of Morocco, and thus was prosperously begun the work of

FEB. 8. ST. JOHN OF MATHA. 281

Ransom. John afterwards went into Spain, a great portion of which country was then under the Saracen yoke. He stirred up kings, princes, and others of the Faithful, to compassion for the captives and the poor. He built monasteries, founded hospitals, and saved the souls of many captives by purchasing their freedom. Having, at length, returned to Rome, he spent his days in doing good. Worn out by incessant labour and sickness, and burning with a most ardent love of God and his neighbour, it was evident that his death was at hand. Wherefore, calling his brethren round him, he eloquently besought them to labour in the work of Ransom, which heaven had intrusted to them, and then slept in the Lord, on the sixteenth of the Calends of January (December 17th), in the year of grace 1213. His body was buried with the honour that was due to him in the same Church of Saint Thomas *de Formis*.

atum fuit. Tum ad hispanias, sub jugo Saracenorum, magna ex parte oppressas, Joannes profectus est, regumque, principum, atque aliorum fidelium animos ad captivorum et pauperum commiserationem commovit. Monasteria ædificavit, hospitalia erexit, magnoque lucro animarum, plures captivos redemit. Romam tandem reversus, sanctisque operibus incumbens, assiduis laboribus attritus, et morbo confectus, ardentissimo Dei, et proximi amore exæstuans, ad extremum devenit. Quare fratribus convocatis, eisque ad opus Redemptionis cœlitus præmonstratum efficaciter cohortatis, obdormivit in Domino, sextodecimo kalendas Januarii, anno salutis millesimo ducentesimo decimo tertio, ejusque corpus in ipsa ecclesia Sancti Thomæ de Formis condigno honore tumulatum fuit.

And now, generous hearted Saint, enjoy the fruits of thy devoted charity. Our Blessed Redeemer recognises thee as one of his most faithful imitators, and the whole court of heaven is witness of the recompense wherewith he loves to honour thy likeness to himself. We must imitate thee; we must walk in thy footsteps; for we, too, hope to reach the same eternal resting-place. Fraternal Charity will lead us to Heaven, for the works it inspires us to do, have the power of freeing the soul from sin, as our Lord assures us.[1] *Thy* charity was formed on the model of that which is in the heart of God, who loves our soul, yet disdains not to provide for the wants of our body. Seeing so many souls in danger of apostacy, thou didst run to their aid, and men were taught to love a religion which can produce heroes of charity like thee. Thy heart bled at hearing of the bodily sufferings of these captives, and thy hand broke the chains of their galling slavery. Teach us the secret of ardent charity. Is it possible that we can see a soul in danger of being lost, and remain indifferent? Have we forgotten the divine promise, told us by the Apostle: *He that causeth a sinner to be converted from the error of his way, shall save his soul from death, and shall cover a multitude of* his own *sins?*[1] Get us, also, a tender compassion for such as are in bodily suffering and poverty, that so we may be generous in comforting them under these trials, which are but too often an occasion of their blaspheming Providence. Dear friend and Liberator of slaves! pray, during this holy Season, for those who groan under the captivity of sin and Satan, for those, especially, who, taken with the phrensy of earthly pleasures, feel not the weight of their chains, but sleep on peacefully through their slavery. Ransom them by thy prayers, convert them to the Lord their God, lead them back to the land of freedom. Pray for France which was thy country, and save her from infidelity. Protect the venerable remnants of thy Order, that so it may labour for the present wants of the Christian world, since the object, for which thou didst institute it, has ceased to require its devotedness.

---

[1] Ecclus. iii. 33.   [2] St. James, v. 20.

FEBRUARY 9.

SAINT APOLLONIA,

VIRGIN AND MARTYR.

THE holy Virgin who this day claims the homage of our devotion and praise, is offered to us by the Church of Alexandria. Apollonia is a Martyr of Christ; her name is celebrated and honoured throughout the whole world; and she comes to us on this ninth day of February, to add her own example to that which we have so recently had from her Sister Saints, Agathy and Dorothy; like them, she bids us fight courageously for heaven. To her, this present life was a thing of little value, and no sooner does she receive God's inspiration to sacrifice it, than she does what her would-be executioners intended doing, —she throws herself into the flames prepared for her. It is no unusual thing, now-a-days, for men that are wearied of the trials, or afraid of the humiliations, of this world, to take away their own lives, and prefer suicide to the courageous performance of duty: but Apollonia's motive for hastening her death by a moment's anticipation was, to testify her horror of the apostacy that was proposed to her. This is not the only instance we meet with, during times of Persecution, of the Holy Spirit's inspiring this lavish sacrifice, to saintly Virgins, who trembled for their faith or their virtue. It is true, such examples are rare; but they teach us, among other things, that our lives belong to God alone, and that we should be in a readiness of mind to give them to him, when and as he pleases to demand them of us.

There is one very striking circumstance in the martyrdom of St. Apollonia. Her executioners, to punish the boldness wherewith she confessed our Lord Jesus Christ, beat out her teeth. This has suggested to the Faithful, when suffering the cruel pain of tooth-ache, to have recourse to St. Apollonia; and their confidence is often rewarded, for God would have us seek the protection of his Saints, not only in our spiritual, but even in our bodily, sufferings and necessities.

The Liturgy thus speaks the praises of our Saint.

Apollonia, virgo Alexandrina, sub Decio imperatore, cum ingravescente jam ætate, ad idola sisteretur, ut eis venerationem adhiberet, illis contemptis, Jesum Christum verum Deum colendum esse prædicabat. Quamobrem omnes ei contusi sunt et evulsi dentes: ac, nisi Christum detestata deos coleret, accenso rogo combusturos vivam minati sunt impii carnifices. Quibus illa, se quamvis mortem pro Jesu Christi fide subituram, respondit. Itaque comprehensa ut combureretur, cum paulisper, quasi deliberans quid agendum esset, stetisset, ex illorum manibus elapsa, alacris in ignem sibi paratum, majori Spiritus Sancti flamma intus accensa, se injecit. Unde brevi consumpto corpore, purissimus spiritus in

Apollonia was a Virgin of Alexandria. In the persecution under the Emperor Decius, when she was far advanced in years, she was brought up to trial, and ordered to pay adoration to idols. She turned from them with contempt, and declared that worship ought to be given to Jesus Christ, the true God. Whereupon, the impious executioners broke and pulled out her teeth; then lighting a pile of wood, they threatened to burn her alive, unless she would hate Christ, and adore their gods. She replied, that she was ready to suffer every kind of death for the faith of Jesus Christ. Upon this, they seized her, intending to do as they said. She stood for a moment, as though hesitating what she should do; then, snatching herself from their hold, she suddenly threw herself into the fire, for there was within her the intenser flame of the Holy Ghost. Her body was soon consumed, and her most pure soul took its flight, and was graced with the everlasting crown of martyrdom.

cœlum ad sempiternam martyrii coronam evolavit.

What energy was thine, Apollonia! Thy persecutors threaten thee with fire; but far from fearing it, thou art impatient for it, as though it were a throne, and thou ambitious to be queen. Thy dread of sin took away the fear of death, nor didst thou wait for man to be thy executioner. This thy courage surprises our cowardice; and yet, the burning pile,—into which thou didst throw thyself when asked to apostatise, and which was a momentary pain leading thy soul to eternal bliss,—was nothing when we compare it with that everlasting fire, to which the sinner condemns himself, almost every day of his life. He heeds not the flames of hell, and deems it no madness to purchase them at the price of some vile passing pleasure. And with all this, worldlings can be scandalised at the Saints, and call them exaggerated, extravagant, imprudent,—because they believed that there is but one thing necessary! Awaken in our hearts, Apollonia, the fear of sin, which gnaws for eternity the souls of them who die with its guilt upon them. If the fire, which had a charm for thee, seems to us the most frightful of tortures, let us turn our fear of suffering and death into a preservative against sin, which plunges men into that abyss, whence *the smoke of their torments shall ascend for ever and ever*,[1] as St. John tells us in his Revelations. Have pity on us, most brave and prudent Martyr. Pray for sinners. Open their eyes to see the evils that threaten them. Get us the fear of God, that so we may merit his mercies, and begin in good earnest to love him.

[1] Apoc. xiv. 11.

February 10.

SAINT SCHOLASTICA,

VIRGIN.

The Sister of the Patriarch Saint Benedict comes to us to-day, sweetly inviting us to follow her to heaven. Apollonia the Martyr is succeeded by Scholastica the fervent daughter of the Cloister. Both of them are the Spouses of Jesus, both of them wear a crown, for both of them fought hard, and won the palm. Apollonia's battle was with cruel persecutors, and in those hard times when one had to die to conquer; Scholastica's combat was the life-long struggle, whose only truce is the soldier's dying breath. The Martyr and the Nun are sisters now in the Heart of Him they both so bravely loved.

God, in his infinite wisdom, gave to St. Benedict a faithful co-operatrix,—a Sister of such angelic gentleness of character, that she would be a sort of counterpoise to the Brother, whose vocation, as the Legislator of monastic life, needed a certain dignity of grave and stern resolve. We continually meet with these contrasts in the lives of the Saints; and they show us that there is a link, of which flesh and blood know nothing; a link which binds two souls together, gives them power, harmonises their differences of character, and renders each complete. Thus it is in heaven with the several hierarchies of the Angels; a mutual love, which is founded on God himself, unites them together, and makes them live in the eternal happiness of the tenderest brotherly affection.

Scholastica's earthly pilgrimage was not a short one; and yet it has left us but the history of the Dove, which told the Brother, by its flight to heaven, that his Sister had reached the eternal home before him. We have to thank St. Gregory the Great for even this much, which he tells us as a sequel to the holy dispute she had with Benedict, three days previous to her death. But how admirable is the portrait thus drawn in St. Gregory's best style! We seem to understand the whole character of Scholastica:—an earnest simplicity, and a child-like eagerness, for what was worth her desiring it; an affectionate and unshaken confidence in God; a winning persuasiveness, where there was opposition to God's will, which, when it met such an opponent as Benedict, called on God to interpose, and gained its cause. The old poets tell us strange things about the swan, how sweetly it can sing when dying; how lovely must not have been the last notes of the Dove of the Benedictine Cloister, as she was soaring from earth to heaven!

But how came Scholastica, the humble retiring Nun, by that energy, which could make her resist the will of her Brother, whom she revered as her master and guide? What was it told her that her prayer was not a rash one, and that what she asked for was a higher good than Benedict's unflinching fidelity to the Rule he had written, and which it was his duty to teach by his own keeping it? Let us hear St. Gregory's answer: "It is not to be wondered " at, that the Sister, who wished to prolong her " Brother's stay, should have prevailed over him; for, " whereas St. John tells us, that *God is Charity*, it " happened by a most just judgment, that she that " had the stronger love, had the stronger power."

Our Season is appropriate for the beautiful lesson taught us by St. Scholastica,—fraternal charity. Her example should excite us to the love of our neighbour, that love which God bids us labour for, now that we are intent on giving Him our undivided service, and our complete conversion. The Easter Solemnity we are preparing for, is to unite us all in the grand Banquet, where we are all to feast on the one Divine Victim of Love. Let us have our nuptial garment ready; for He that invites us, insists on our having *union* of heart when *we dwell in his House.*[1]

The Church has inserted in her Office of this Feast the account given by St. Gregory of the last interview between St. Scholastica and St Benedict. It is as follows:

Ex libro secundo dialogorum sancti Gregorii Papæ.	From the second book of the Dialogues of Saint Gregory, Pope.
Scholastica venerabilis patris Benedicti soror, omnipotenti Domino ab ipso infantiæ tempore dedicata, ad eum semel per annum venire consueverat. Ad quam vir Dei non longe extra januam in possessione monasterii descendebat. Quadam vero die venit ex more, atque ad eam cum discipulis venerabilis ejus descendit frater; qui totum diem in Dei laudibus, sacrisque colloquiis ducentes, incumbentibus jam noctis tenebris, simul acceperunt cibum. Cumque adhuc ad mensam sederent, et inter sacra colloquia tardior se hora protraheret, eadem	Scholastica was the Sister of the venerable father Benedict. She had been consecrated to Almighty God from her very infancy, and was accustomed to visit her Brother once a year. The man of God came down to meet her at a house belonging to the monastery, not far from the gate. It was the day for the usual visit, and her venerable Brother came down to her accompanied by some of his brethren. The whole day was spent in the praises of God and holy conversation; and at night-fall, they took their repast together. Whilst they were at table, and it grew late as they conferred with each other on sacred

---

[1] Ps. lxvii. 7.

things, the holy Nun thus spoke to her Brother: "I be-"seech thee, stay the night "with me, and let us talk till "morning on the joys of "heaven." He replied: "What "is this thou sayest, Sister? "On no account may I remain "out of the monastery." The evening was so fair, that not a cloud could be seen in the sky. When, therefore, the holy Nun heard her Brother's refusal, she clasped her hands together, and, resting them on the table, she hid her face in them, and made a prayer to the God of all power. As soon as she raised her head from the table, there came down so great a storm of thunder and lightning, and rain, that neither the venerable Benedict, nor the brethren who were with him, could set foot outside the place where they were sitting.

The holy virgin had shed a flood of tears as she leaned her head upon the table, and the cloudless sky poured down the wished-for rain. The prayer was said, the rain fell in torrents; there was no interval; but so closely on each other were prayer and rain, that the storm came as she raised her head. Then the man of God, seeing that it was impossible to reach his monastery amidst all this lightning, thunder, and rain, was sad, and said complainingly: "God forgive "thee, Sister! What hast "thou done?" But she replied: "I asked thee a favour, "and thou wouldst not hear

sanctimonialis femina soror ejus eum rogavit dicens: Quæso te, ut ista nocte me non deseras, ut usque mane de cœlestis vitæ gaudiis loquamur. Cui ille respondit: Quid est quod loqueris, soror? manere extra cellam nullatenus possum. Tanta vero erat cœli serenitas, ut nulla in aere nubes appareret. Sanctimonialis autem femina, cum verba fratris negantis audivisset, insertas digitis manus super mensam posuit, et caput in manibus omnipotentem Dominum rogatura declinavit. Cumque levaret de mensa caput, tanta coruscationis et tonitrui virtus, tantaque inundatio pluviæ erupit, ut neque venerabilis Benedictus, neque fratres, qui cum eo aderant, extra loci limen, quo consederant, pedem movere potuerint.

Sanctimonialis quippe femina caput in manibus declinans, lacrymarum fluvium in mensam fuderat, per quas serenitatem aeris ad pluviam traxit. Nec paulo tardius post orationem inundatio illa secuta est: sed tanta fuit convenientia orationis et inundationis, ut de mensa caput jam cum tonitruo levaret: quatenus unum, idemque esset momentum, et levare caput, et pluviam deponere. Tunc vir Dei inter coruscos, et tonitruos, atque ingentis pluviæ inundationem, videns se ad monasterium non posse remeare, cœpit conqueri contristatus, dicens: Parcat tibi omnipotens Deus, soror, quid est quod fecisti? Cui illa respondit: Ecce rogavi te, et audire me noluisti; rogavi Deum meum, et audivit me; modo ergo, si potes, egredere, et, me dimissa, ad monasterium recede. Ipse autem exire extra tectum non valens, qui remanere sponte noluit, in loco mansit invitus. Sicque factum est, ut totam noctem pervigilem ducerent, atque per sacra spiritalis vitæ colloquia, sese vicaria relatione satiarent.

Cumque die altero eadem venerabilis femina ad cellam propriam recessisset, vir Dei ad monasterium rediit. Cum ecce post triduum in cella consistens, elevatis in aera oculis, vidit ejusdem sororis suæ animam de corpore egressam, in columbæ specie cœli secreta penetrare. Qui tantæ ejus gloriæ congaudens, omnipotenti Deo in hymnis et laudibus gratias reddidit, ejusque obitum fratribus denuntiavit. Quos etiam protinus misit, ut ejus corpus ad monasterium deferrent, atque in sepulchro, quod sibi ipsi paraverat, ponerent. Quo facto, contigit ut quorum mens una semper in Deo fuerat, eorum quoque corpora nec sepultura separaret.

"me; I asked it of my God, "and he granted it. Go, now, "if thou canst, to the monas"tery, and leave me here!" But it was not in his power to stir from the place; so that, he who would not stay willingly, had to stay unwillingly, and spend the whole night with his Sister, delighting each other with their questions and answers about the secrets of spiritual life.

On the morrow, the holy woman returned to her monastery, and the man of God to his. When lo! three days after, he was in his cell; and raising his eyes, he saw the soul of his Sister going up to heaven, in the shape of a dove. Full of joy at her being thus glorified, he thanked his God in hymns of praise, and told the brethren of her death. He straightways bade them go and bring her body to the monastery; which having done, he had it buried in the tomb he had prepared for himself. Thus it was, that, as they had ever been one soul in God, their bodies were united in the same grave.

We select the following from the *Monastic Office* for the Feast of our Saint.

RESPONSORIES AND ANTIPHONS.

℟. The venerable Scholastica, the Sister of the most holy Father Benedict, * Being from her very infancy consecrated to Almighty God, never left the path of righteousness.
℣. O ye children! praise the Lord; praise ye the Name of the Lord. * Being.

℟. Anxious to be trained by the saintly life and the words of his holy teaching, she used to visit him once a year: * And the man of God instructed her in heavenly doctrine.
℣. Blessed is he that heareth Benedict's words, and keepeth those things which he hath written. * And.

℟. The holy virgin Scholastica, like a watered garden, * was enriched with the ceaseless dew of heaven's graces.
℣. Like a fountain of water whose stream shall not fail. * Was enriched.

℟. The Lord granted her the desire of her heart: * And from Him she obtained what her Brother refused.
℣. The Lord is good to all them that trust in him, to the soul that seeketh him. * And.

℟. Alma Scholastica, sanctissimi Patris Benedicti soror, * ab ipso infantiæ tempore omnipotenti Domino dedicata, viam justitiæ non deseruit.
℣. Laudate pueri Dominum, laudate Nomen Domini. * Ab ipso infantiæ.

℟. Exemplo vitæ venerabilis, et verbo sanctæ prædicationis informari cupiens, ad eum semel in anno venire consueverat ; * Et eam vir Dei doctrinis cœlestibus instruebat.
℣. Beatus qui audit verba ipsius, et servat ea quæ scripta sunt. * Et eam.

℟. Sancta virgo Scholastica, quasi hortus irriguus,* Gratiarum cœlestium jugi rore perfundebatur.
℣. Sicut fons aquarum, cujus non deficient aquæ.* Gratiarum.

℟. Desiderium cordis ejus tribuit ei Dominus : * A quo obtinuit quod a fratre obtinere non potuit.
℣. Bonus est Dominus omnibus sperantibus in eum, animæ quærenti illum. * A quo obtinuit.

℞. Moram faciente Sponso, ingemiscebat Scholastica dicens : * Quis dabit mihi pennas sicut columbæ, et volabo et requiescam ?
℣. En dilectus meus loquitur mihi : Surge, amica mea, et veni. * Quis dabit.

℞. The Bridegroom tarrying, Scholastica moaned, saying : * Who will give me the wings of a dove, and I will fly and take my rest?
℣. Lo ! my beloved speaketh unto me : Arise, my love, and come. * Who will.

℞. In columbæ specie Scholastica visa est, fraterna mens lætata est hymnis et immensis laudibus : * Benedictus sit talis exitus, multo magis talis introitus !
℣. Totus cœlesti gaudio perfusus remansit Pater Benedictus. * Benedictus.

℞. Scholastica was seen in the form of a dove, and the Brother's glad soul sang hymns and praises beyond measure : * Blessed be such a departure, and still more blessed such an entrance !
℣. Father Benedict was filled with heavenly joy. * Blessed.

R. Anima Scholasticæ ex arca corporis instar columbæ egressa, portans ramum olivæ, signum pacis et gratiæ. * In cœlos evolavit.
℣. Quæ cum non inveniret ubi requiesceret pes ejus. * In cœlos evolavit.

℞. Scholastica's soul went forth, like a dove, from the ark of her body, bearing an olive branch, the sign of peace and grace. * She took her flight to heaven.
℣. She found not whereon to rest her feet. * She took.

ANT. Exsultet omnium turba fidelium pro gloria virginis almæ Scholasticæ ; lætentur præcipue catervæ virginum, celebrantes ejus solemnitatem, quæ fundens lacrymas, Dominum rogavit, et ab eo plus potuit, quia plus amavit.

ANT. Let all the assembly of the Faithful rejoice at the glory of the venerable virgin Scholastica ; but, above the rest, let the choirs of virgins be glad, as they celebrate the feast of her who besought her Lord with many tears, and had more power with him, because she had more love.

ANT. Hodie sacra virgo Scholastica in specie columbæ, ad æthera tota festiva perrexit : hodie cœles-

ANT. On this day, the holy virgin Scholastica took her flight, in the shape of a dove, all joyfully to heaven:

The same *Benedictine Breviary* gives us these two Hymns for this Feast.

HYMN.

O Scholastica, blessed spouse of Christ! O Dove of the cloister! the citizens of heaven proclaim thy merits, and we, too, sing thy praises with joyful hymns and loving hearts.

Thou didst scorn the honours and glory of the world; thou didst follow the teaching of thy Brother and his Holy Rule; and, rich in the fragrance of every grace, thou caredst for heaven alone.

Oh! what power was in thy love, and how glorious thy victory, when thy tears drew rain from the skies, and forced the Patriarch of Nursia, to tell thee what he knew of the land above!

And now thou shinest in heaven's longed-for light; thou art as a seraph in thy burning love, beautiful in thy bright grace; and united with thy divine Spouse, thou art reposing in the splendour of glory.

Have pity on us the Faithful of Christ, and drive from us the miseries which cloud our hearts; that thus, the Sun of light eternal may sweetly shine upon us, and fill us with the joys of his everlasting beams.

Te beata sponsa Christi,
Te, columba virginum,
Siderum tollunt coloni
Laudibus, Scholastica:
Nostra te lætis salutant
Vocibus præcordia.

Sceptra mundi cum coronis
Docta quondam spernere,
Dogma fratris insecuta
Atque sanctæ Regulæ,
Ex odore gratiarum,
Astra nosti quærere.

O potens virtus amoris!
O decus victoriæ!
Dum fluentis lacrymarum
Cogis imbres currere,
Ore Nursini parentis
Verba cœli suscipis.

Luce fulges expetita
In polorum vertice,
Clara flammis charitatis
Cum nitore gratiæ:
Juncta Sponso conquiescis
In decore gloriæ.

Nunc benigna pelle nubes
Cordibus fidelium,
Ut serena fronte splendens
Sol perennis luminis,
Sempiternæ claritatis
Impleat nos gaudiis.

Gloriam Patri canamus
Unicoque Filio;
Par tributum proferamus
Inclyto Paraclito,
Nutibus cujus creantur,
Et reguntur sæcula.
  Amen.

Let us sing a hymn of glory to the Father, and to his only Son; let us give an equal homage of our praise to the Blessed Paraclete: yea, to God, the Creator and Ruler of all, be glory without end. Amen.

HYMN.

Jam noctis umbræ concidunt,
Dies cupita nascitur,
Qua virgini Scholasticæ
Sponsus perennis jungitur.
  Brumæ recedit tædium,
Fugantur imbres nubibus,
Vernantque campi siderum
Æternitatis floribus.

  Amoris auctor evocat,
Dilecta pennas induit;
Ardens ad oris oscula
Columba velox evolat.

  Quam pulchra gressum promoves,
O chara proles Principis!
Nursinus Abbas aspicit,
Grates rependit Numini.
  Amplexa Sponsi dextera,
Metit coronas debitas,
Immersa rivis gloriæ,
Deique pota gaudiis.

  Te, Christe, flos convallium,
Patremque cum Paraclito,
Cunctos per orbis cardines
Adoret omne sæculum.
  Amen.

The shades of night are passing away: the longed-for day is come, when the virgin Scholastica is united to her God, her Spouse.
Winter's tedious gloom is over; the rainy clouds are gone; and the Spring of the starry land yields its eternal flowers.
The God of love bids his beloved come; and she, taking the wings of a dove, flies swiftly to the embrace so ardently desired.
How beautiful is thy soaring, dear daughter of the King! Thy Brother, the Abbot, sees thee, and fervently thanks his God.
Scholastica receives the embrace of her Spouse, and the crown her works have won; inebriated with the torrent of glory, she drinks of the joys of her Lord.
May the world-wide creation of every age, adore thee, O Jesus, sweet Flower of the vale, together with the Father and the Holy Ghost. Amen.

Dear Spouse of the Lamb! Innocent and simple Dove! How rapid was thy flight to thy Jesus, when called home from thine exile! Thy Brother's eye followed thee for an instant, and then heaven received thee, with a joyous welcome from the choirs of the Angels and Saints. Thou art now at the very source of that love which here filled thy soul, and gained thee everything thou asked of thy Divine Master. Drink of this fount of life to thy heart's eternal content. Satiate the ambition taught thee by thy Brother in his Rule, when he says that we must "desire Heaven with all the might of our spirit."[1] Feed on that sovereign Beauty, who himself feeds, as he tells us, *among the lilies*.[2]

But forget not this lower world, which was to thee, what it is to us,—a place of trial, for winning heavenly honours. During thy sojourn here, thou wast *the Dove in the clifts of the rock*,[3] as the Canticle describes a soul like thine own; there was nothing on this earth which tempted thee to spread thy wings in its pursuit, there was nothing worthy of thy giving it the treasure of the love, which God had put in thy heart. Timid before men, and simple as innocence ever is, thou knewest not that thou hadst *wounded the Heart of the Spouse*.[4] Thy prayers were made to him with all the humility and confidence of a soul that had never been disloyal; and he granted thee thy petitions with the promptness of tender love: so that thy Brother,—the venerable Saint,—he who was accustomed to see nature obedient to his command,—yes, even Benedict was overcome by thee in that contest, wherein thy simplicity was more penetrating than his profound wisdom.

And who was it, O Scholastica, that gave thee this sublime knowledge, and made thee, on that day of thy last visit, wiser than the great Patriarch, who was raised up in the Church to be the living rule of

---

[1] Ch. iv. Instrument 46.
[2] Cant. ii. 16.
[3] *Ibid*. ii. 14.
[4] *Ibid*. iv. 9.

them that are called to Perfection? It was the same God who chose Benedict to be one of the pillars of the Religious State; but who wished to show, that a holy and pure and tender charity is dearer to him, than the most scrupulous fidelity to rules, which are only made for leading men to what *thou* hadst already attained. Benedict, himself such a lover of God, knew all this; the subject so dear to thy heart was renewed, and Brother and Sister were soon lost in the contemplation of that Infinite Beauty, who had just given such a proof that he would have you neglect all else. Thou wast ripe for heaven, O Scholastica! Creatures could teach thee no more love of thy Creator; he would take thee to himself. A few short hours more, and the Divine Spouse would speak to thee those words of the ineffable Canticle, which the Holy Spirit seems to have dictated for a soul like thine: *Arise, make haste, my Love, my Dove, my beautiful one, and come! Show me thy face; let thy voice sound in mine ears; for thy voice is sweet, and comely is thy face.*[1]

Thou hast left us, O Scholastica! but do not forget us. Our souls have not the same beauty in the eyes of our God as thine, and yet they are called to the same heaven. It may be that years are still needed to fit them for the celestial abode, where we shall see thy grand glory. Thy prayer drew down a torrent of rain upon the earth; let it now be offered for us, and obtain for us tears of repentance. Thou couldst endure no conversation which had not eternity for its subject; give us a disgust for useless and dangerous talk, and a relish for hearing such as are on God and Heaven. Thy heart had mastered the secret of fraternal charity, yea of that affectionate charity, which is so well-pleasing to our Lord; soften our hearts to the love of our neighbour, banish

---

[1] Cant. ii. 10, 14.

from them all coldness and indifference, and make us love one another as God would have us love.

Dear Dove of holy solitude! remember the Tree, whose branches gave thee shelter here on earth. The Benedictine cloister venerates thee, not only as the Sister, but also as the Daughter of its sainted Patriarch. Cast thine eye upon the remnants of that Tree, which was once so vigorous in its beauty and its fruits, and under whose shadow the nations of the West found shelter for so many long ages. Alas! the hack and hew of impious persecutions have struck its root and branches. Every land of Europe, as well as our own, sits weeping over the ruins. And yet, root and branches, both must needs revive, for we know that it is the will of thy Divine Spouse, O Scholastica, that the destinies of this venerable Tree keep pace with those of the Church herself. Pray that its primitive vigour be soon restored; protect, with thy maternal care, the tender buds it is now giving forth; cover them from the storm; bless them; make them worthy of the confidence wherewith the Church deigns to honour them!

February 14.

SAINT VALENTINE,

PRIEST AND MARTYR.

The Church honours, on this fourteenth day of February, the memory of the holy Priest, Valentine, who suffered martyrdom towards the middle of the third century. The ravages of time have deprived us of the details of his life and sufferings; so that extremely little is known of our Saint. This is the reason of there being no Lessons of his Life in the Roman Liturgy. His name, however, has always been honoured throughout the whole Church, and it is our duty to revere him as one of our protectors during the Season of Septuagesima. He is one of those many holy Martyrs, who meet us at this period of our Year, and encourage us to spare no sacrifice which can restore us to, or increase within us, the grace of God.

Pray, then, O holy Martyr, for the Faithful, who are so persevering in celebrating thy memory. The day of Judgment will reveal to us all thy glorious merits: oh! intercede for us, that we may then be made thy companions at the right hand of the Great Judge, and be united with thee eternally in heaven.

ANTIPHON.

Ant. Iste sanctus pro lege Dei sui certavit usque ad	Ant. This Saint fought, even unto death, for the law

of his God, and feared not the words of the wicked; for he was set upon a firm rock.

mortem, et a verbis impiorum non timuit; fundatus enim erat supra firmam petram.

LET US PRAY.

Grant, we beseech thee, O Almighty God, that we who solemnise the festival of blessed Valentine, thy Martyr, may, by his intercession, be delivered from all the evils that threaten us. Through Christ our Lord. Amen.

OREMUS.

Præsta, quæsumus, omnipotens Deus, ut qui beati Valentini Martyris tui natalitia colimus, a cunctis malis imminentibus ejus intercessione liberemur. Per Christum Dominum nostrum. Amen.

February 15.

SAINTS FAUSTINUS AND JOVITA,

MARTYRS.

The two Brothers, whom we are to honour to-day, suffered martyrdom in the beginning of the second century, and their memory has ever been celebrated in the Church. The glory of the great ones of this world passes away, and men soon forget even their very names. Historians have oftentimes a difficulty in proving that such heroes ever existed, or, if they did exist, that they flourished at such a period, or achieved anything worth notice. Brescia, the capital of one of the Italian Provinces, can scarcely mention the names of those who were its governors or leading men, in the second century; and yet here are two of her citizens, whose names will be handed down, with veneration and love, to the end of the world, and the whole of Christendom is filled with the praise of their glorious martyrdom. Glory, then, to these sainted Brothers, whose example so eloquently preaches to us the great lesson of our Season,—fidelity in God's service.

The sufferings which merited for them the crown of immortality, are thus recorded in the Liturgy.

| Faustinus et Jovita fratres nobiles Brixiani, in multis Italiæ urbibus quo vincti, | The two brothers, Faustinus and Jovita were born of a noble family in Brescia. Dur- |

ing the persecution under Trajan, they were led captives through various cities of Italy, in each of which they were made to endure most cruel sufferings, by reason of their brave confession of the Christian faith, which nothing could induce them to deny. At Brescia, they were for a long time confined in chains; then were exposed to wild beasts, and cast into fire, from neither of which tortures did they receive hurt or harm. From Brescia they were sent to Milan, still fettered with the same chains: and there their faith was put to the test of every torment that cruelty could devise; but, like gold that is tried by fire, their faith shone the brighter by these sufferings. After this, they were sent to Rome, where they received encouragement from Pope Evaristus; but there, also, were made to endure most cruel pains. At length, they were taken to Naples, and there, again, put to sundry tortures; after which, they were bound hand and foot, and cast into the sea; but were miraculously delivered by Angels. Many persons were converted to the true faith, by seeing their courage in suffering, and the miracles they wrought. Finally, they were led back to Brescia, at the commencement of the reign of the Emperor Adrian; there they were beheaded, and received the crown of a glorious martyrdom.

sæviente Trajani persecutione, ducebantur, acerbissima supplicia perpessi, fortes in christianæ fidei confessione perstiterunt. Nam Brixiæ diu vinculis constricti, feris etiam objecti in ignemque conjecti, et a bestiis et flamma integri et incolumes servati sunt; inde vero iisdem catenis colligati Mediolanum venerunt, ubi eorum fides tentata exquisitissimis tormentis, tanquam igne aurum, in cruciatibus magis enituit. Postea Romam missi, ab Evaristo Pontifice confirmati, ibi quoque crudelissime torquentur. Denique perducti Neapolim, in ea etiam urbe varie cruciati, vinctis manibus pedibusque in mare demerguntur: unde per Angelos mirabiliter erepti sunt. Quare multos et constantia in tormentis, et miraculorum virtute ad Christi fidem converterunt. Postremo reducti Brixiam, initio suscepti ab Adriano imperii, securi percussi, illustrem martyrii coronam acceperunt.

When we compare our trials with yours, noble Martyrs of Christ, and our combats with those that you had to fight,—how grateful ought we not to be to our Lord for his having so mercifully taken our weakness into account! Should we have been able to endure the tortures, wherewith you had to purchase heaven, we that are so easily led to break the law of God, so tardy in our conversion, so weak in faith and charity? And yet, we are made for that same heaven, which you now possess. God holds out a crown to us also, and we are not at liberty to refuse it. Rouse up our courage, brave Martyrs! Get us a spirit of resistance against the world and our evil inclinations; that thus, we may confess our Lord Jesus Christ, not only with our lips, but with our works too, and testify, by our conduct, that we are Christians.

FEBRUARY 18.

SAINT SIMEON,

BISHOP AND MARTYR.

How venerable our Saint of to-day, with his hundred and twenty years, and his episcopal dignity, and his Martyr-crown! He succeeded the Apostle St. James in the See of Jerusalem; he had known Jesus, and had been his disciple; he was related to Jesus, for he was of the House of David; his father was Cleophas, and his Mother that Mary, whom the tie of kindred united so closely to the Blessed Mother of God, that she has been called her Sister. What grand titles these of Simeon who comes with all our other Martyrs of Septuagesima, to inspirit us to penance! Such a veteran, who had been a cotemporary of the Saviour of the world, and was a Pastor who could repeat to his flock the very lessons this Jesus had given him, —such a Saint, we say, could never rejoin his Divine Master save by the path of martyrdom, and that martyrdom must be the Cross. Like Jesus, then, he dies on a Cross, and his death, which happened in the year 106, closes the first period of the Christian Era, or, as it is called, *The Apostolic Age.* Let us honour this venerable Pontiff, whose name awakens within us the recollection of all that is dear to our Faith. Let us ask him to extend to us that fatherly love, which nursed the Church of Jerusalem for so many long years. He will bless us from that throne which he won by the Cross, and will obtain for us the grace we so much need,—the grace of conversion.

The following is the Lesson given on St. Simeon:

Simeon, filius Cleophæ, post Jacobum proximus Hierosolymis ordinatus episcopus, Trajano imperatore, apud Atticum consularem est accusatus, quod christianus esset, et Christi propinquus. Comprehendebantur enim omnes eo tempore, quicumque ex genere David orti essent. Quare multis cruciatus tormentis, eodem passionis genere, quod Salvator noster subierat, afficitur, mirantibus omnibus, quod homo ætate confectus (erat enim centum et viginti annorum) acerbissimos crucis dolores fortiter constanterque pateretur.

Simeon, the son of Cleophas, was ordained Bishop of Jerusalem, and was St. James' immediate successor in that See. In the reign of the Emperor Trajan, he was accused to the Consul Atticus of being a Christian and a relation of Christ, for, at this time, all they, that were of the House of David, were seized. After having endured various tortures, Simeon was put to death by the same punishment which our Saviour suffered, and all the beholders were filled with astonishment to find how, at his age, (for he was a hundred and twenty years old,) he could go through the intense pains of crucifixion, without showing a sign of fear or irresolution.

Receive, most venerable Saint! the humble homage of our devotion. What is all human glory compared with thine! Thou wast of the family of Christ; thy teaching was that which His divine lips had given thee; thy charity for men was formed on the model of his Sacred Heart; and thy death was the closest representation of His. We may not claim the honour *thou* hadst, of calling ourselves *Brothers of the Lord Jesus*; but pray for us, that we may be of those, of whom he thus speaks: *Whosoever shall do the will of my Father that is in heaven, he is my brother, and sister, and mother.*[1] We have not, like

---

[1] St. Matth. xii. 50.

thee, received the doctrine of salvation from the very lips of Jesus; but we have it in all its purity, by means of holy Tradition, of which thou art one of the earliest links; oh! obtain for us a docility to this word of God, and pardon for our past disobedience. We have not to be nailed to a cross, as thou wast; but the world is thickly set with trials, to which our Lord himself gives the name of the *Cross*. These we must bear with patience, if we would have part with Jesus in his glory. Pray for us, O Simeon, that henceforth we may be more faithful; that we never more become rebels to our duty; and that we may repair the faults we have so often committed by infringing the law of our God.

February 22.

Saint Peter's Chair at Antioch.

We are called upon, a second time, to honour St. Peter's Chair: first, it was his Pontificate in Rome; to-day, it is his Episcopate at Antioch. The seven years spent by the Prince of the Apostles in the second of these cities, were the grandest glory she ever had; and they are too important a portion of the life of St. Peter to be passed by without being noticed in the Christian Cycle.

Three years had elapsed since our Lord's Ascension. The Church had already been made fruitful by martyrdom, and from Jerusalem she had spread into distant countries. Antioch, the first of the cities of Asia, had received the Gospel; and it was there, that they who professed the faith of Jesus were first called "Christians." Jerusalem was doomed to destruction for her having not only refused to acknowledge, but also for her having crucified, the Messias: it was time for Peter, in whom resided the supreme power, to deprive the faithless City of the honour she had heretofore enjoyed, of possessing within her walls the Chair of the Apostolate. It was towards the Gentiles that the Holy Spirit drove those *Clouds*, which were shown to Isaias as the symbol of the holy Apostles.[1] Accordingly, it was in Antioch, the

---

[1] Is. lx. 8.

third Capital of the Roman Empire, that Peter first places the august Throne, on which, as Vice-gerent of Christ, he presides over the Church,—that new family, of which all Nations are invited to become members.

But the progress of the Apostles was so rapid; the conquests they made, in spite of every opposition, were so extensive,—that the Vicar of Christ was inspired to leave Antioch, after he had honoured it with the Chair during the space of seven years. Alexandria, the second City of the Empire, is also to be made a See of Peter; and Rome, the Capital of the world, awaits the grand privilege, for which God had long been preparing her. Onwards, then, does the Prince advance, bearing with him the destinies of the Church; where he fixes his last abode, and where he dies, there will he have his Successor in his sublime dignity of Vicar of Christ. He leaves Antioch, making one of his disciples, Evodius, its Bishop. Evodius succeeds Peter as Bishop of Antioch; but that See is not to inherit the Headship of the Church, which goes whithersoever Peter goes. He sends Mark, another of his disciples, to take possession, in his name, of Alexandria; and this Church he would have be the second in the world, and though he has not ruled it in person, he raises it above that of Antioch. This done, he goes to Rome, where he permanently establishes that Chair, on which he will live, and teach, and rule, in his Successors, to the end of time.

And here we have the origin of the three great Patriarchal Sees, which were the object of so much veneration in the early ages:—the first, is Rome, which is invested with all the prerogatives of the Prince of the Apostles, which, when dying, he transmitted to her; the second, is Alexandria, which owes her pre-eminence to Peter's adopting her as his second See; the third, is Antioch, whither he repaired in person, when he left Jerusalem to bring to the Gentiles the grace of adoption. If, therefore, Antioch is below Alexandria in rank, Alexandria never enjoyed the honour granted to Antioch,—of having been governed, in person, by him whom Christ appointed to be the supreme Pastor of his Church. Nothing, then, could be more just, than that Antioch should be honoured, in that she has had the privilege of having been, for seven years, the centre of Christendom; and this is the object of to-day's Feast.

The Children of the Church have a right to feel a special interest in every solemnity that is kept in memory of St. Peter. The Father's Feast is a Feast for the whole family; for to him it owes its very life. If there be but one fold, it is because there is but one Shepherd. Let us, then, honour Peter's divine prerogative, to which Christianity owes its preservation; and let us often reflect upon the obligations we are under to the Apostolic See. On the Feast of the *Chair at Rome*, we saw how *Faith* is taught, and maintained, and propagated by the Mother-Church, which has inherited the promises made to Peter. To-day, let us consider the Apostolic See as the sole source of the legitimate *Power*, whereby mankind is ruled and governed in all that concerns eternal salvation.

Our Saviour said to Peter: *To thee will I give the Keys of the Kingdom of heaven*,[1] that is to say, of the Church. He said to him, on another occasion: *Feed my lambs, feed my sheep.*[2] So that, Peter is Prince; for, in the language of the sacred Scriptures, *Keys* denote princely power: he is also Pastor, and universal Pastor; for the *whole* flock is comprised under the two terms, Lambs and Sheep. And yet, there are *other* Pastors in every portion of the

---

[1] St. Matth. xvi. 19. [2] St. John, xxi. 15, 17.

Christian world. The Bishops, whom *the Holy Ghost hath placed to rule the Church of God*,[1] govern, in his name, their respective Dioceses, and are also Pastors. How comes it, that the *Keys*, which were given to Peter, are found in other hands than his?—The Catholic Church explains the difficulty to us by her Tradition. She says to us, by Tertullian: "Christ "gave the Keys to Peter, and through him to the "Church."[2] By St. Optatus of Milevum: "For the "sake of unity, Peter was made the first among all "the Apostles, and he *alone* received the Keys, that "he might give them to the rest."[3] By St. Gregory of Nyssa: "It was through Peter that Christ gave "to Bishops the Keys of their heavenly prerogative."[4] By St. Leo the Great: "If our Lord willed that "there should be something in common to Peter and "the rest of the Princes of his Church, it was only on "this condition,—that whatsoever he gave to the rest, "he gave it to them through Peter."[5]

Yes, the Episcopate is most sacred, for it comes from the hands of Jesus Christ through Peter and his successors. Such is the unanimous teaching of Catholic Tradition, which is in keeping with the language used by the Roman Pontiffs, from the earliest Ages, who have always spoken of the dignity of Bishops as consisting in their being "called to a share of their own solicitude." Hence St. Cyprian does not hesitate to say, that "our Saviour, wishing "to establish the Episcopal dignity and constitute "his Church, says to Peter: *To thee will I give the* "*Keys of the Kingdom of heaven;* and here we "have, both the institution of Bishops, and the con-"stitution of the Church."[6] This same doctrine is clearly stated in a Letter written to Pope St. Symmachus by St. Cesarius of Arles, (who lived in the

---

[1] Acts, xx. 28.
[2] Scorpiac. *Cap.* x.
[3] Contra Parmenianum, *Lib.* vii.
[4] Opp., *tom.* iii.
[5] In anniv. assumpt. *Serm.* iv.
[6] *Epist.* xxxiii.

5th century) : "The Episcopate flows from the blessed "Apostle Peter; and consequently, it belongs to Your "Holiness to prescribe to the several Churches the "rules which they are to follow."[1] This fundamental principle, which St. Leo the Great has so ably and eloquently developed, (as we have seen on the Feast of the Chair at Rome, January 18th,)—this principle, which is taught us by universal Tradition, is laid down with all possible precision in the magnificent Letters, still extant, of Pope St. Innocent the First, who preceded St. Leo by several years. Thus, he writes to the Council of Carthage, "that the Episco- "pate, with all its authority, emanates from the "Apostolic See;"[2] to the Council of Milevum, "that "Bishops must look upon Peter as the source whence "both their name and their dignity are derived;"[3] to St. Victricius, Bishop of Rouen, "that the Aposto- "late and the Episcopate both owe their origin to "Peter."[4]

Controversy is not our object. All we aim at by giving these quotations from the Fathers on the prerogatives of Peter's Chair, is to excite the Faithful to be devoted to it and venerate it. This we have endeavoured to do, by showing them, that this *Chair* is the source of the spiritual authority, which, in its several degrees, rules and sanctifies them. Yes, all spiritual authority comes from Peter; all comes from the Bishop of Rome, in whom Peter will continue to govern the Church to the end of time. Jesus Christ is the founder of the Episcopate; it is the Holy Ghost who establishes Bishops to rule the Church;— but the mission, the institution, which assigns the Pastor his Flock, and the Flock its Pastor, these are given by Jesus Christ and the Holy Ghost through the ministry of Peter and his Successors..

---

[1] *Epist.* x.
[2] *Idem.* xxix.
[3] *Idem.* xxx.
[4] *Idem.* ii.

How sacred, how divine, is this authority of the *Keys*, which is first given by heaven itself to the Roman Pontiff; then is delegated by him to the Prelates of the Church; and thus guides and blesses the whole Christian world! The Apostolic See has varied its mode of transmitting such an authority according to the circumstances of the several Ages; but the one source of the whole *Power* was always the same,—*the Chair of Peter*. We have already seen how, at the commencement, there were three Chairs: Rome, Alexandria, and Antioch; and all three were sources of the canonical institution of the Bishops of their respective provinces; but they were all three Chairs of Peter, for they were founded by him that they might preside over their Patriarchates, as St. Leo,[1] St. Gelasius,[2] and St. Gregory the Great,[3] expressly teach. But, of these three Chairs, the Pontiff of Rome had his authority and his institution from heaven; whereas, the two other Patriarchs could not exercise their rights, until they were recognised and confirmed by him who was Peter's successor, as Vicar of Christ. Later on, two other Sees were added to these first three: but it was only by the consent of the Roman Pontiff that Constantinople and Jerusalem obtained such an honour. Let us notice, too, the difference there is between the *accidental* honours conferred on four of these Churches, and the *divine* prerogative of the Church of Rome. By God's permission, the Sees of Alexandria, Antioch, Constantinople, and Jerusalem, were defiled by heresy; they became *Chairs of pestilence*;[4] and, having corrupted the faith they received from Rome, they could not transmit to others the mission they themselves had forfeited. Sad indeed was the ruin of such pillars as these! Peter's hand had

---

[1] *Epist.* civ. Ad. Anatolium.
[2] Concil. Romanum. Labb. *tom.* iv.
[3] *Epist.* ad Eulogium.
[4] Ps. i. 1.

placed them in the Church. They had merited the love and veneration of men; but they fell; and their fall gave one more proof of the solidity of that edifice, which Christ himself had built on Peter. The unity of the Church was made more visible. Obliged by the treachery of her own favoured children to deprive them of the privileges they had received from her, Rome was, more evidently than ever, the sole source of pastoral Power.

We, then, both priests and people, have a right to know whence our Pastors have received their Power. From whose hand have they received the *Keys?* If their mission come from the Apostolic See, let us honour and obey them, for they are sent to us by Jesus Christ, who has invested them, through Peter, with his own authority. If they claim our obedience without having been sent by the Bishop of Rome, we must refuse to receive them, for they are not acknowledged by Christ as his Ministers. The holy anointing may have conferred on them the sacred character of the Episcopate;—it matters not; they must be as aliens to us, for they have not been sent,— they are not Pastors.

Thus it is, that the Divine Founder of the Church, who willed that she should be *a City seated on a mountain*,[1] gave her *Visibility;* it was an essential requisite; for since all were called to enter her pale, all must be able to see her. But he was not satisfied with this. He moreover willed, that the spiritual power exercised by her Pastors should come from a visible source; so that the Faithful might have a sure means of verifying the claims of those who were to guide them in His name. Our Lord, we say it reverently, owed this to us; for, on the Last Day, he will not receive us as his Children, unless we shall have been members of his Church, and have lived in

---

[1] St. Matth. v. 15.

union with him by the ministry of Pastors lawfully constituted. Honour, then, and submission to Jesus in his Vicar! honour and submission to the Vicar of Christ in the Pastors he sends!

As a tribute of our devotion to the Prince of the Apostles, let us recite, in his honour, the following Hymn, composed by St. Peter Damian.

HYMN.

O Prince of the Apostolic Senate! Herald of our Lord! First Pastor of the Faithful! watch over the Flock intrusted to thee.	Senatus apostolici Princeps et præco Domini: Pastor prime fidelium, Custodi gregem creditum.
Lead us through verdant pastures, feeding us with the nourishment of the Word; and lead us, thus fed, into the heavenly fold, whither thou hast already gone.	Per pascua virentia, Nos verbi fruge recrea: Refectas oves prævius Caulis infer cœlestibus.
To thee, Peter, have been delivered the Keys of heaven's gate; and all things, both in heaven and on earth, acknowledge thy authority.	Supernæ Claves januæ Tibi, Petre, sunt traditæ: Tuisque patent legibus Terrena cum cœlestibus.
'Tis thou that choosest the city where is to be established the Rock of the true faith, the foundation of the building, on which the Catholic Church stands immoveable.	Tu Petram veræ fidei, Tu basim ædificii Fundas, in qua Catholica Fixa surgit Ecclesia.
Thy shadow, as thou passest by, heals the sick; and Tabitha, that made garments for the poor, was raised to life at thy bidding.	Umbra tua, dum graderis, Fit medicina languidis; Textrinis usa vestium Sprevit Tabitha feretrum.
Bound with two chains, thou wast set free by an	Catena vinctum gemina Virtus solvit angelica;

Veste sumpta cum caligis, Patescunt fores carceris.	Angel's power; he bids thee put on thy garments and thy sandals, and lo! the prison-door is opened.
Sit Patri laus ingenito, Sit decus Unigenito, Sit utriusque parili Majestas summa Flamini. Amen.	To the Father unbegotten, and to the Only-Begotten Son, and to the co-equal Spirit of them both, be praise and kingly highest power. Amen.

Glory be to thee, O Prince of the Apostles, on thy Chair at Antioch, where thou didst for seven years preside over the universal Church! How magnificent are the stations of thy Apostolate!—Jerusalem, Antioch, Alexandria (by thy disciple Mark,) and Rome,—these are the Cities which have been honoured by thy august Chair. After Rome, Antioch was the longest graced by its presence: justly, therefore, do we honour this Church, which was thus made, by thee, the Mother and Mistress of all other Churches. Alas! all her beauty has now left her; her faith is dead; she is in bondage to the Saracen. Save her, take her once more under thy power, bring her into allegiance to Rome, where thou hast thy Chair, not for seven years only, but for all ages. The gates of hell have let loose the fury of every tempest upon thee, firm Rock of the Church! and we ourselves have seen the immortal Chair banished for a time from Rome. The words of St. Ambrose then came to our minds: "Where *Peter* is, there is "the *Church*." How could we despair? Did we not know, that it was God's inspiration which made thee choose Rome for the fixed resting place of thy Throne? No human will can put asunder what God has united; the Bishop of Rome must ever be the Vicar of Christ; and the Vicar of Christ, let sacrilege and persecution banish him as they will, must ever be the Bishop of Rome. Holy Apostle! calm the wildness of the tempest, lest the weak should take scandal. Beseech our Lord that he permit not the residence of thy Successor to be disturbed in that Holy City, which has been chosen for so great an honour. If it be, that her inhabitants deserve punishment for their offences,—spare them for the sake of their brethren of the rest of the world; and pray for them, that their Faith may once more become what it was when St. Paul praised it, and said to them: *Your Faith is spoken of in the whole world.*[1]

---

[1] Rom. i. 8.

February 23.

SAINT PETER DAMIAN,

CARDINAL AND DOCTOR OF THE CHURCH.

It is the Feast of the austere reformer of the 11th century, Peter Damian, the precursor of the holy Pontiff Gregory the Seventh, that we are called upon to celebrate to-day. To him is due a share of that glorious regeneration, which was effected at that troubled period when *judgment* had to *begin at the House of God*.[1] The life he had led under the Monastic Rule had fitted him for the great contest. So zealously did he withstand the disorders and abuses of his times, that we may attribute to him, at least in great measure, the ardent faith of the two centuries which followed the scandals of the 10th. The Church ranks him among her Doctors, on account of his admirable Writings; and his penitential life ought to excite us to be fervent in the work we have in hand,—the work of our Conversion.

The following Lessons, read by the Church, on this Feast, give us a sketch of our Saint's Life.

Petrus, Ravennæ honestis parentibus natus, adhuc lactens a matre numerosæ pro-	Peter was born at Ravenna, of respectable parents. His mother, wearied with the care

[1] I. St. Peter, iv. 17.

of a large family, abandoned him when a babe ; but one of her female servants found him in an almost dying state, and took care of him, until such time as the mother, repenting of her unnatural conduct, consented to treat him as her child. After the death of his parents, one of his brothers, a most harsh man, took him as a servant, or more truly as his slave. It was about this period of his life that he performed an action, which evinced his virtue and his filial piety. He happened to find a large sum of money ; but instead of using it for his own wants, he gave it to a priest, begging him to offer up the Holy Sacrifice for the repose of his father's soul. Another of his brothers, called Damian (after whom, it is said, he was named), had him educated ; and so rapid and so great was the progress he made in his studies, that he was the admiration of his masters. He became such a proficient in the liberal sciences, that he was made to teach them in the public schools, which he did with great success. During all this time, it was his study to bring his body into subjection to the spirit ; and to this end, he wore a hair-shirt under an outwardly comfortable dress, and practised frequent fasting, watching, and prayer. Being in the very ardour of youth, and being cruelly buffeted by the sting of the flesh, he, during the night, would go and plunge himself into a frozen

lis pertæsa abjicitur, sed domesticæ mulieris opera semivivus exceptus ac recreatus, genitrici ad humanitatis sensum revocatæ redditur. Utroque orbatus parente, tamquam vile mancipium sub aspera fratris tutela duram servitutem exercuit. Religionis in Deum ac pietatis erga patrem egregium tunc specimen dedit ; inventum siquidem forte nummum non propriæ inediæ sublevandæ, sed sacerdoti, qui divinum Sacrificium ad illius expiationem offerret, erogavit. A Damiano fratre, a quo, uti fertur, cognomentum accepit, ejus cura litteris eruditur, in quibus brevi tantum profecit, ut magistris admirationi esset. Quum autem liberalibus scientiis floreret et nomine, eas cum laude docuit. Interim ut corpus rationi subderet, sub molibus vestibus cilicium adhibuit, jejuniis, vigiliis, et orationibus solerter insistens. Calente juventa, dum carnis stimulis acriter urgeretur, insultantium libidinum faces rigentibus fluvii mersus aquis noctu exstinguebat : tum venerabilia quæque loca obire, totumque Psalterium recitare consueverat. Ope assidua pauperes levabat, quibus frequenter pastis convivio, propriis ipse manibus ministrabat.

pool of water, that he might quench the impure flame which tormented him; or, he would make pilgrimages to holy sanctuaries, and recite the entire Psaltery. His charities to the poor were unceasing, and when he provided them with a meal, which was frequently, he would wait upon them himself.

Perficiendæ magis vitæ causa, in Avellanensi Eugubinæ Diœcesis Cœnobio, Ordinis Monachorum Sanctæ Crucis Fontis Avellanæ, a beato Ludolpho sancti Romualdi discipulo fundato nomen dedit. Non ita multo post in Monasterium Pomposianum, mox in Cœnobium Sancti Vincentii Petræ Pertusæ ab Abbate suo missus, utrumque Asceterium verbo sacro, præclaris institutionibus et moribus excoluit. Ad suos revocatus, post Præsidis obitum Avellanitarum Familiæ præficitur, quam novis variis in locis exstructis domiciliis, et sanctissimis institutis ita auxit, ut alter ejus Ordinis Parens, ac præcipuum ornamentum jure sit habitus. Salutarem Petri sollicitudinem alia quoque diversi instituti Cœnobia, Canonicorum Conventus, et populi sunt experti. Urbinati Diœcesi non uno nomine profuit: Theuzoni Episcopo in causa gravissima assedit, ipsumque in recte administrando Episcopatu consilio et opera juvit. Divinorum contemplatione, cor-

Out of a desire to lead a still more perfect life, he became a religious in the Monastery of Avellino, in the diocese of Gubbio, of the Order of the Monks of Holy Cross of Fontavellana, which was founded by the blessed Ludolphus, a disciple of St. Romuald. Being sent by his Abbot, not very long after, first to the Monastery of Pomposia, and then to that of Saint Vincent of Pietra-Pertusa, he edified both Houses by his preaching, admirable teaching, and holy life. At the death of the Abbot of Avellino, he was recalled to that Monastery, and was made its superior. The institute was so benefited by his government, not only by the new Monasteries which he founded in several places, but also by the very saintly regulations he drew up, that he was justly looked upon as the second Founder of the Order, and its brightest ornament. Houses of other Orders, Canons, yea entire congregations of the Faithful, were benefited by Peter's enlightened zeal. He was a benefactor, in more ways than one, to the diocese of Urbino: he aided the Bishop Theuzo in a most important suit, and assisted him, both by advice and work, in the right administration of his diocese. His spirit of holy contemplation, his corporal austerities, and the saintly tenor of his whole conduct, gained for him so high a reputation, that Pope Stephen the Ninth, in spite of Peter's extreme reluctance, created him Cardinal of the holy Roman Church and Bishop of Ostia. The saint proved himself worthy of these honours by the exercise of the most eminent virtues, and by the faithful discharge of his Episcopal office.

It would be impossible to describe the services he rendered to the Church and the Sovereign Pontiffs, during those most trying times, by his learning, his prudence as Legate, and his untiring zeal. His life was one continued struggle against simony, and the heresy of the Nicolaites. He purged the Church of Milan of these disorders, and brought her into subjection to the Holy See. He courageously resisted the anti-popes Benedict and Cadolaus. He deterred Henry 4th, king of Germany, from an unjust divorce of his wife. He restored the people of Ravenna to their allegiance to the Roman Pontiff, and absolved them from interdict. He reformed the abuses which had crept in among the Canons of Velletri. There was scarcely a single Cathedral Church in

poris macerationibus, cæterisque spectatæ sanctimoniæ exemplis excelluit. His motus Stephanus Nonus, Pontifex Maximus, eum licet invitum et reluctantem sanctæ Romanæ Ecclesiæ Cardinalem creavit, et Ostiensem Episcopum. Quas Petrus dignitates splendidissimis virtutibus, et consentaneis Episcopali ministerio operibus gessit.

Difficillimo tempore Romanæ Ecclesiæ, Summisque Pontificibus doctrina, Legationibus, aliisque susceptis laboribus mirifice adfuit. Adversus Nicolaitarum et Simoniacam hæreses ad mortem usque strenue decertavit. Hujusmodi depulsis malis, Mediolanensem Ecclesiæ Romanæ conciliavit. Benedicto, et Cadaloo, falsis Pontificibus, fortiter restitit. Henricum Quartum Germaniæ regem ab iniquo uxoris divortio deterruit: Ravennates ad debita Romano Pontifici obsequia revocatos sacris restituit. Canonicos Veliternos ad sanctioris vitæ leges composuit. In Provincia præsertim Urbinate vix ulla fuit Episcopalis Ecclesia, de qua Petrus non sit bene meritus: Eugubinam, quam aliquando creditam habuit, multis levavit incommodis : alias alibi, quando oportuit, perinde curavit, ac si suæ essent tutelæ commissæ. Cardinalatu, et Episcopali dignitate depositis, nihil de pristina juvandi proximos sedulitate remisit. Jejunium Sextæ Feriæ in honorem sanctæ Crucis Jesu Christi, Horarias beatæ Dei Genitricis preces, ejusque die Sabbato cultum propagavit. Inferendæ quoque sibi verberationis morem ad patratorum scelerum expiationem provexit. Demum sanctitate, doctrina, miraculis, et preclare actis illustris, dum e Ravennate Legatione rediret, Faventiæ octavo Kalendas Martii migravit ad Christum. Ejus corpus ibidem apud Cistercienses multis miraculis clarum frequenti populorum veneratione colitur. Ipsum Faventini non semel in præsenti discrimine propitium experti, patronum apud Deum delegerunt : Leo vero Duodecimus, Pontifex Maximus, Officium Missamque in ejus honorem tamquam Confessoris Pontificis, quæ aliquibus in Diœcesibus, atque in Ordine Camaldulensium jam celebrabantur, ex Sacrorum Rituum Congregationis consulto, addita Doctoris qualitate, ad universam extendit Ecclesiam.

the Province of Urbino that had not experienced the beneficial effects of Peter's holy zeal : thus, that of Gubbio, which was for some time under his care, was relieved by him of many evils ; and other Churches, that needed his help, found him as earnest for their welfare as though he were their own Bishop. When he obtained permission to resign his dignity as Cardinal and his Bishopric, he relented nothing of his former charity, but was equally ready in doing good to all. He was instrumental in propagating many devout practices; among these may be mentioned, fasting on Fridays in honour of the Holy Cross ; the reciting the Little Office of our Lady ; the keeping the Saturday as a day especially devoted to Mary ; the taking the discipline in expiation of past sins. At length, after a life which had edified the world by holiness, learning, miracles, and glorious works,—on his return from Ravenna, whither he had been sent as Legate, he slept in Christ, on the eighth of the Calends of March (February 23rd), at Faënza. His relics, which are kept in the Cistercian Church of that town, are devoutly honoured by the Faithful, and many miracles are wrought at the holy shrine. The inhabitants of Faënza have chosen him as the Patron of their City, having several times experienced his protection when threatened by danger. His

Mass and Office, which were kept under the rite of Confessor and Bishop, had been long observed in several Dioceses, and by the Camaldolese Order; but they were extended to the whole Church by a decree of the Congregation of Sacred Rites, which was approved by Pope Leo the Twelfth, who also added to the name of the Saint that of *Doctor*.

Thy soul was inflamed by the zeal of God's House, O Peter! God gave thee to his Church in those sad times when the wickedness of the world had robbed her of well nigh all her beauty. Thou hadst the spirit of an Elias within thee, and it gave thee courage to waken the servants of the Lord: they had slept, and while they were asleep, the enemy came, and the field was oversown with tares.[1] Then did better days dawn for the Spouse of Christ; the promises made her by our Lord were fulfilled; but who was *the Friend of the Bridegroom?*[2] who was the chief instrument used by God to bring back to his House its ancient beauty? A Saint who bore the glorious name of *Peter* Damian!—In those days, the *Sanctuary* was degraded by secular interference. The *Princes* of the earth *said: Let us possess the Sanctuary of God for an inheritance.*[3] The Church, which God intended to be *Free*, was but a slave, in the power of the rulers of this world; and the vices, which are inherent to human weakness, defiled the Temple. But God had pity on the Spouse of Christ, and for her deliverance he would use human agency: he chose thee, Peter, as his principal co-operator in restoring order. Thy example and thy labours pre-

---

[1] St. Matth. xiii. 25.   [2] St. John, iii. 29.   [3] Ps. lxxxii. 13.

pared the way for Gregory, the faithful and dauntless Hildebrand, into whose hands the Keys once placed, and the work of regeneration was completed. Thou hast fought the good fight; thou art now in thy rest; but thy love of the Church, and thy power to help, are greater than ever. Watch, then, over her interests. Obtain for her Pastors that Apostolic energy and courage, which alone can cope with enemies so determined as hers are. Obtain for her Priests the holiness which God demands from them that are the *salt of the earth.*[1] Obtain for the Faithful the respect and obedience they owe to those who direct them in the path of salvation. Thou wast not only the Apostle, thou wast moreover the model, of penance in the midst of a corrupt age; pray for us, that we may be eager to atone for our sins by works of mortification. Excite within our souls the remembrance of the sufferings of our Redeemer, that so his Passion may urge us to repentance and hope. Increase our confidence in Mary, the Refuge of Sinners, and make us, like thyself, full of filial affection towards her, and of zeal that she may be honoured and loved by those who are around us.

[1] St. Matth. v. 13.

February 24.

SAINT MATTHIAS,

APOSTLE.

In Leap-Year, the Feast of St. Matthias is kept on the 25th of February.

An Apostle of Jesus Christ, St. Matthias, is one of the Blessed choir, which the Church would have us honour during the Season of Septuagesima. Matthias was one of the first to follow our Saviour, and he was an eye-witness of all his divine actions up to the very day of the Ascension. He was one of the seventy-two Disciples; but our Lord had not conferred upon him the dignity of an Apostle. And yet, he was to have this great glory, for it was of him that David spoke, when he prophesied that *another should take the Bishopric*[1] left vacant by the apostacy of Judas the Traitor. In the interval between Jesus' Ascension and the Descent of the Holy Ghost, the Apostolic College had to complete the mystic number fixed by our Lord himself, so that there might be "*The Twelve*" on that solemn day, when the

---

[1] Ps. cviii. 8; Acts, i. 16.

Church, filled with the Holy Ghost, was to manifest herself to the Synagogue. *The lot fell on Matthias;*[1] he shared with his Brother-Apostles in the Jerusalem persecution, and, when the time came for the Ambassadors of Christ to separate, he set out for the countries allotted to him. Tradition tells us, that these were Cappadocia and the provinces bordering on the Caspian Sea.

The virtues, labours and sufferings of St. Matthias have not been handed down to us: this explains there being no proper Lessons on his Life, as there are for the Feasts of the rest of the Apostles. Clement of Alexandria records, in his Writings, several sayings of our holy Apostle. One of these is so very appropriate to the spirit of the present Season, that we consider it a duty to quote it. "It behoves us to "combat the flesh, and make use of it, without pam-"pering it by unlawful gratifications. As to the "soul, we must develop her power by Faith and "Knowledge."[2] How profound is the teaching contained in these few words! Sin has deranged the order which the Creator had established. It gave the outward man such a tendency to grovel in things which degrade him, that the only means left us for the restoration of the Likeness and Image of God unto which we were created, is the forcibly subjecting the Body to the Spirit. But the Spirit itself, that is, the Soul, was also impaired by Original Sin, and her inclinations were made prone to evil:— what is to be *her* protection? Faith and Knowledge. *Faith* humbles her, and then exalts and rewards her; and the reward is *Knowledge.* Here we have a summary of what the Church teaches us during the two Seasons of Septuagesima and Lent. Let us thank the holy Apostle, in this his Feast, for leaving us such a lesson of spiritual wisdom and fortitude. The

---

[1] Acts, i.   [2] Stromat., *Lib.* iii. *Cap.* iv.

same traditions, which give us some slight information regarding the holy life of St. Matthias, tell us that his Apostolic labours were crowned with the palm of martyrdom. Let us celebrate his triumph by the following Stanzas, which are taken from the Menæa of the Greeks.

HYMN.

(Die IX. Augusti.)

O Blessed Matthias! thou, a spiritual Eden, didst flow, like a full river, from the divine fountain; thou didst water the earth with thy mystic rivulets, and make it fruitful. Do thou, therefore, beseech the Lord that he grant peace and much mercy to our souls.

O Apostle Matthias! thou didst complete the sacred college, from which Judas had fallen; and, by the power of the Holy Ghost, thou didst put to flight the darkness of idolatry by the admirable lightnings of thy wise words. Do thou now beseech the Lord that he grant peace and much mercy to our souls.

He that is the True Vine sent thee, a fruitful branch, bearing the grapes that give out the wine of salvation. When they drank it that before were slaves to ignorance, they turned from the drunkenness of error.

Being made, O glorious Matthias, the chariot of God's Word, thou didst break for ever the wheels of error, and

Matthia beate, Eden spiritualis, fontibus divinis ut fluvius inundans scaturisti, et mysticis terram irrigasti rivulis, et illam fructiferam reddidisti; ideo deprecare Dominum ut animabus nostris pacem concedat et magnam misericordiam.

Matthia Apostole, divinum replevisti collegium ex quo Judas ceciderat, et divinis sapientum sermonum tuorum fulgoribus tenebras fugasti idololatriæ, virtute Spiritus Sancti; et nunc deprecare Dominum, ut mentibus nostris concedat pacem et magnam misericordiam.

Ut multifrugiferum palmitem te Vitis vera direxit, colentem uvam quæ salutis vinum profundit; illud bibentes qui detinebantur ignorantia, erroris temulentiam rejecerunt.

Erroris axes, iniquitatis currus, Verbi Dei ipse currus factus, gloriose, in perpetuum contrivisti; et idololatras, et columnas et templa radicitus divina virtute destruxisti, Trinitatis vero templa ædificasti clamantia : Populi, superexaltate Christum in sæcula.

Ut spirituale Cœlum apparuisti, enarrans gloriam unigeniti Filii Dei ineffabilem, Matthia venerabilis ; fulgur Spiritus Sancti, piscator errantium, lumen divinæ claritatis, mysteriorum doctor ; ipsum in lætitia unanimi voce celebremus.

Amicum te dixit Salvator, suis obtemperantem mandatis, beate Apostole, et ipsius regni hæredem, et cum ipso sedentem in throno in futura terribili die, sapientissime Matthia, collegii duodenarii Apostolorum complementum.

Crucis velamine instructus, vitæ sæviens mare trajecisti, beate, et ad requiei portum pervenisti ; et nunc lætus cum Apostolorum choro judicum altissimo adstare digneris, Dominum pro nobis exorans misericordem.

Lampas aureo nitore fulgens, Spiritus Sancti ellychnio ardens, lingua tua

the chariots of iniquity. By the divine power, thou didst defeat the idolaters, and destroy the pillars and the temples ; but thou didst build up to the Trinity other temples, which echoed with these words : All ye people, praise Christ above all for ever !

O venerable Matthias ! thou, like a spiritual firmament, didst proclaim the glory of the Only-Begotten Son of God. Let us with one glad voice celebrate the praise of this Apostle, who was effulgent with the Holy Ghost ; he was the fisher of them that had gone astray, the light that reflected the divine brightness, the teacher of the mysteries.

O blessed Apostle ! the Saviour called thee his Friend, because thou didst keep his commandments. Thou art heir to his kingdom, and thou art to sit with him, on a throne, at the last terrible day, O most wise Matthias, who didst complete the twelve of the Apostolic college.

Guided by the sail of the Cross, thou, O blessed one, didst pass over the troubled sea of life, and didst reach the haven of rest. Do thou now vouchsafe to join the glad choir of the Apostles, and beseech the infinite Judge, that he would show himself a merciful Lord unto us.

Thy tongue was a bright lamp of glittering gold, burning with the flame of the Holy

Ghost. Thou didst consume all strange doctrines, thou didst quench all fire that was profane, and to them that sat in the darkness of ignorance, thou, O wise Matthias, didst show a brilliant light.

apparuit, extranea comburens dogmata, extraneum extinguens ignem, o sapiens Matthia, lucem fulgurans sedentibus in tenebris ignorantiæ.

February 26.

Saint Margarite of Cortona,

penitent.

Close to the faithful Virgins, who form the Court of Jesus, there stand those holy women, whose repentance has merited for them a prominent place in the Calendar of the Church. They are the bright trophies of God's Mercy. They expiated their sins by a life of penance; the tears of their compunction wiped away their guilt; He that is Purity itself has found them worthy of his love, and, when Pharisees affect to be shocked at his allowing them to be near him, he warmly defends them. Foremost among these is Mary Magdalene, to whom *much was forgiven, because she loved much;*[1] but there are two on the list of Penitent Saints whose names shine most brightly on the Calendar of this portion of the year, and were, like Mary Magdalene, ardent in their love of the Divine Master, whom they had once offended:—these are, Mary of Egypt, and Margarite of Cortona. It is the second of these who to-day tells us the consoling truth, that if *sin* separate us from God, *penance* has the power of not only disarming his anger, but of forming between God and the sinner that ineffable bond of love, which the Apostle alludes to when he says: *Where sin hath abounded, grace hath more abounded.*[2]

---

[1] St. Luke, vii. 47. [2] Rom. v. 20.

FEB. 26. ST. MARGARITE OF CORTONA.

Let us study the virtues of the illustrious Penitent of the 13th century. They are thus summed up by the Church in the Lessons of to-day's Feast.

Margarite of Cortona, (so called from the town where she died,) was born at Alviano in Tuscany. In her early youth she was a slave to the pleasures of this world, and led a vain and sinful life in the city of Montepulciano. Her attention was, one day, attracted by a dog, which seemed to wish her to follow it. She did so, and it led her to a pile of wood, which covered a large hole. Looking in, she saw the body of her lover, whose enemies had murdered him, and thrown his mangled corpse into that place. She suddenly felt that the hand of God was upon her, and being overwhelmed with intense sorrow for her sins, she went forth, and wept bitterly. She returned to Alviano, cut off her hair, laid aside her trinkets, and, putting on a dark-coloured dress, she abandoned her evil ways and the pleasures of the world. She was to be found in the Churches, with a rope tied round her neck, prostrated on the ground, and imploring pardon of all whom she had scandalised by her past life. She shortly afterwards set out for Cortona, and there, in sackcloth and ashes, she sought how she might appease the divine anger. For three years did she try herself in the practice of every virtue; and

Margarita, a loco dormitionis Cortonensis appellata, Laviani in Tuscia ortum habuit. Primis adolescentiæ suæ annis mundi voluptatibus capta, in Montis Politiani civitate, vanam et lubricam vitam duxit: sed cum amasium ab hostibus fæde transfossum, indicio canis in fovea sub strue lignorum tumulatum fortuito reperisset, illico facta est manus Domini super eam, quæ magno culparum suarum mœrore tacta, exiit foras et flevit amare. Itaque Lavianum reversa, crine detonso, neglecto capite, pullaque veste contecta, erroribus suis mundique illecebris nuntium misit; inque ædibus Deo sacris fune ad collum alligato, humi procumbens, ab omnibus quos antea moribus suis palam offenderat, veniam exoravit. Mox Cortonam profecta, in cinere et cilicio ab se læsam Dei majestatem placare studuit, donec post triennale virtutum experimentum a Fratribus Minoribus spiritualis vitæ ducibus, Tertii Ordinis habitum impetravit. Uberes exinde lacrymæ ei familiares fuerunt, atque ima suspiria tanta animi contritione ducta, ut diu elinguis consisteret. Lectulus nuda humus, cervical lapis aut lignum porrexit; atque ita noctes insomnes in cœlestium meditatione trahere consuevit, nullum amplius pravum desiderium ͥperpessa, dum bonus spiritus promptior infirmam carnem ad subeundos labores erigebat.

A dæmone insidiis, funestisque conatibus lacessita, mulier fortis hostem, ex verbis detectum, semel atque iterum invicta repulit. Ad eludendem vanæ gloriæ lenocinium, quo a malo spiritu petebatur, præteritos mores suos per vicos et plateas alta voce accusare non destitit, omni supplicio se ream inclamans; nec, nisi a confessario deterrita, in speciosam faciem, olim impuri amoris causam, sævire abstinuit, ægre ferens suam formam longa carnis maceratione non aboleri. Quibus aliisque magnæ pœnitentiæ argumentis, suorum criminum labe expiata, atque ita de se triumphatrix, ut sensus plane omnes a mundi illecebris custodiret, digna

at the end of that time, she obtained permission from the Friars Minors, (under whose spiritual guidance she had placed herself,) to receive the habit of the Third Order. From that time forward, her tears were almost incessant; and the sighs which deep contrition wrung from her heart were such as to leave her speechless for hours. Her bed was the naked ground; and her pillow, a stone or piece of wood; so that she frequently passed whole nights in heavenly contemplation. Evil desires no longer tormented her, for her fervent spirit was so prompt, that the weak flesh was made to labour and obey.

The devil spared neither snares nor violent assaults, whereby to lead her from her holy purpose: but she, like a strong woman, detected him by his words, and drove him from her. This wicked spirit having tempted her to vain glory, she went into the streets, and cried out with a loud voice, that she had been a great sinner, and deserved the worst of punishments. It was obedience to her confessor that alone prevented her from disfiguring her features, which had been the cause of much sin: for the long and severe penance she had imposed on herself had not impaired her beauty. By these and such like exercises of a mortified life, she cleansed her soul from the stains of her sins, and gained such a victory over herself, that the allurements of the world had not the slightest effect upon her, and our Lord rewarded her by frequently visiting her. She also received the grace she so ardently desired, of being allowed to have a share in the sufferings of Jesus and Mary: so much so, indeed, that, at times, she lay perfectly unconscious, as though she were really dead. All this made her be looked up to as a guide in the path of perfection, and persons would come to her, even from distant countries, in order to seek her counsel. By the heavenly light granted her, she could read the hearts and consciences of others, and could see the sins committed against our Lord in various parts of the world, for which she would offer up, in atonement, her own sorrow and tears. Great indeed was the good she effected by the ardent charity she bore to God and her neighbour. She healed the sick who came to her, and drove out the devil from such as were possessed. A mother besought her, with many tears, to restore her child to life, which she did. Her prayers more than once averted war, when on the point of being declared. In a word, both the living and the dead experienced the effects of her unbounded charity.

Whilst engaged in these manifold holy works, she relented not in the severity of

facta est quæ sæpe Domini consuetudine frueretur. Ejusdem quoque Christi et Virginis Matris dolorum, quod ipsa ardenter expetierat, particeps facta, cunctis sensibus destituta, et vere mortua interdum visa est. Ad eam proinde veluti ad perfectionis magistram, ex dissitis etiam regionibus plurimi conveniebant: ipsa vero cælesti, quo erat perfusa, lumine, cordium secreta, conscientias hominum, imo et peccata in remotis licet partibus Deum offendentium cum dolore et lacrymis detegens, summaque in Deum et proximum charitate fervens, ingentem animarum fructum operata est. Ægris ad se venientibus salutem, obsessis a dæmone liberationem impetravit. Puerum defunctum, lugente matre, ad vitam reduxit. Imminentes bellorum tumultus assiduis orationibus sedavit. Denique summæ pietatis operibus vivos et mortuos sibi demeruit.

Tot sanctis operibus occupata, de rigore, quo assidue corpus suum exercebat, nihil remisit, neque a studio cœlestia meditandi se avelli passa est, in utroque vitæ genere plane admiranda, utramque sororem, Magdalenam et Martham, referens. Tandem pro se Dominum orans, ut ex hac valle lacrymarum sursum in cœlestem patriam evocaretur, exaudita est oratio ejus, die atque hora dormitionis ei patefactis. Meritis itaque et laboribus plena, ac cœlestibus donis cumulata, cœpit corporis viribus destitui, perque dies decem et septem nullo cibo, sed divinis tantum colloquiis refecta est: tum sanctissimis Ecclesiæ sacramentis rite susceptis, vultu hilari, atque oculis in cælum conversis, octavo Kalendas Martias, anno ætatis quinquagesimo, suæ conversionis vigesimo tertio, humanæ vero salutis millesimo ducentesimo nonagesimo septimo, felix migravit ad Sponsum. Corpus in hanc usque diem vegetum, incorruptum, illæsum et suaviter olens, summa religione colitur in Ecclesia fratrum Minorum, quæ jam ab eadem Margarita appellatur, miraculis continuo floruit: quibus permoti Romani Pontifices, ad augendum ejus cultum plurima liberaliter indulserunt. Benedictus vero Decimus tertius, in festo Pentecostes, die sexta decima Maii anni millesimi septingestimi vigesimi octavi, solemnem ejus Canon-

her bodily mortifications, or in her contemplation of heavenly things. The two lives of Mary and Martha were admirably blended together in her; and rich in the merits of each, she besought our Lord to take her from this vale of tears and give her to enter the heavenly country. Her prayer was heard, and the day and the hour of her death were revealed to her. Laden with meritorious works and divine favours, her bodily strength began to fail. For the last seventeen days of her life her only food was that of conversation with her Creator. At length, after receiving the most holy Sacraments of the Church, with a face beaming with joy, and her eyes raised up to heaven, her happy soul fled to its divine Spouse, on the eighth of the Calends of March (February 22nd), in the fiftieth year of her age, the twenty-third of her conversion, and in the year of our Lord one thousand two hundred and ninety-seven. Her body, —which, even to this day, is fresh, incorrupt, and unaltered, and sheds a sweet fragrance,— is devoutly honoured in the Church, (called, after her, *Saint Margarite's*,) belonging to the Friars Minors. The many miracles which have been wrought at her shrine, have induced the Sovereign Pontiffs to promote devotion to Saint Margarite by the grant of many spiritual favours. She was canonised,

FEB. 26. ST. MARGARITE OF CORTONA. 333

with great solemnity, by Pope Benedict the 13th, on the 16th of May, which was the Feast of Pentecost, in the year 1728.

izationem religiosissime celebravit.

If the Angels of God rejoiced on the day of thy conversion, when Margarite the sinner became the heroic and saintly Penitent,—what a grand Feast must they not have kept when thy soul left this world, and they led thee to the eternal nuptials with the Lamb! Thou art one of the brightest trophies of Divine Mercy, and when we think of the Saint of Cortona, our hearts glow with hope. We are sinners; we have deserved hell; and yet when we hear thy name, Heaven and Mercy seem so near to us, yea, even to *us*. Margarite of Cortona! see how like we are to thee in thy weakness, and thy wanderings from the fold; but thou forcest us to hope that we may, like thee, be converted, do penance, and reach Heaven at last. The instrument of thy conversion was Death; and is not Death busy enough around *us?* The sight of that corpse taught thee, and with an irresistible eloquence, that sin is madness, for it exposes the soul to fall into infinite misery;—how comes it that Death is almost daily telling *us* that life is uncertain, and that our eternal lot may be decided at any hour, and yet the lesson is so lost upon us? We are hard-hearted sinners, and we need thy prayers, O fervent Lover of Jesus! The Church will soon preach to us the great *Memento;* she will tell us that we are but dust, and into dust must speedily return. Oh! that this warning might detach us from the world and ourselves, and man us to the resolution of Penance, that port of salvation for them that have suffered shipwreck; oh! that it might excite within us the desire of returning to that God, who knows not how to resist the poor soul who comes to him, after all her sins, throws herself into the bosom of his mercy, and asks him to forgive! Thy example proves that we may hope for every grace. Pray for us, and exercise in our favour that maternal charity which filled thy heart, even when thou wast living here below.

March 4.

SAINT CASIMIR,

CONFESSOR.

It is from a Court that we are to be taught to-day the most heroic virtues. Casimir is a Prince; he is surrounded by all the allurements of youth and luxury; and yet he passes through the snares of the world with as much safety and prudence, as though he were an Angel in human form. His example shows us what *we* may do. The world has not smiled on us as it did on Casimir; but, how much we have loved it! If we have gone so far as to make it our idol, we must now break what we have adored, and give our service to the Sovereign Lord, who alone has a right to it. When we read the Lives of the Saints, and find that persons, who were in the ordinary walk of life, practised extraordinary virtues, we are inclined to think that they were not exposed to great temptations, or that the misfortunes they met in the world, made them give themselves up unreservedly to God's service. Such interpretations of the actions of the Saints are shallow and false, for they ignore this great fact,—that there is no condition or state, however humble, in which man has not to combat against the evil inclinations of his heart, and that corrupt nature alone is strong enough to lead him to sin. But in such a Saint as Casimir, we have no difficulty in recognising that all his Christian energy was from God, and not from any natural source; and we rightly conclude, that *we,* who have the same good God, may well hope that this Season of spiritual regeneration will change and better us. Casimir preferred death to sin. But is not every Christian bound to be thus minded every' hour of the day? And yet, such is the infatuation produced by the pleasures or advantages of this present life, that we, every day, see men plunging themselves into sin, which is the death of the soul; and this, not for the sake of saving the life of the body, but for a vile and transient gratification, which is oftentimes contrary to their temporal interests. What stronger proof could there be than this, of the sad effects produced in us by Original Sin?—The examples of the Saints are given us as a light to lead us in the right path: let us follow it, and we shall be saved. Besides, we have a powerful aid in their merits and intercession: let us take courage at the thought, that these Friends of God have a most affectionate compassion for us their Brethren, who are surrounded by so many and great dangers.

The Church, in her Liturgy, thus describes to us the virtues of our young Prince.

Casimirus, patre Casimiro, matre Elisabetha Austriaca, Poloniæ regibus ortus, a pueritia sub optimis magistris pietate, et bonis artibus instructus, juveniles artus aspero domabat cilicio, et assiduis extenuabat jejuniis. Regii spreta lecti mollitie, dura cubabat humo, et clam intempesta nocte, præ foribus templorum pronus in terra divinam exorabat clementiam. In Christi contemplanda

Casimir was the son of Casimir, king of Poland, and of Elizabeth of Austria. He was put, when quite a boy, under the care of the best masters, who trained him to piety and learning. He brought his body into subjection by wearing a hairshirt, and by frequent fasting. He could not endure the soft bed which is given to kings, but lay on the hard floor, and during the night, he used privately to steal from his room, and go to the

Church, where, prostrate before the door, he besought God to have mercy on him. The Passion of Christ was his favourite subject of meditation; and when he assisted at Mass, his mind was so fixed on God, that he seemed to be in one long ecstacy.

Great was his zeal for the propagation of the Catholic faith, and the suppression of the Russian schism. He persuaded the king, his father, to pass a law, forbidding the schismatics to build new churches, or to repair those which had fallen to ruin. Such was his charity for the poor and all sufferers, that he went under the name of the Father and Defender of the Poor. During his last illness, he nobly evinced his love of purity, which virtue he had maintained unsullied during his whole life. He was suffering a cruel malady; but he courageously preferred to die, rather than suffer the loss, whereby his physicians advised him to purchase his cure,—the loss of his priceless treasure.

Being made perfect in a short space of time, and rich in virtue and merit, after having foretold the day of his death, he breathed forth his soul into the hands of his God, in the twenty-fifth year of his age, surrounded by Priests and Religious. His body was taken to Vilna, and was honoured by many miracles. A young girl was raised to life at his shrine; the blind recovered their sight,

Passione assiduus, Missarum solemniis adeo erecta in Deum mente solebat adesse, ut extra se rapi videretur.

Catholicam promovere fidem summopere studuit, et Ruthenorum schisma abolere: quapropter Casimirum patrem induxit, ut legem ferret, ne schismatici nova templa construerent, nec vetera collabentia restaurarent. Erga pauperes et calamitatibus oppressos beneficus et misericors, Patris et Defensoris egenorum nomen obtinuit. Virginitatem, quam ab incunabulis servavit illæsam, sub extremo vitæ termino fortiter asseruit, dum gravi pressus infirmitate, mori potius, quam castitatis jacturam ex medicorum consilio subire, constanter decrevit.

Consummatus in brevi, virtutibus et meritis plenus, prænuntiato mortis die, inter sacerdotum, et religiosorum choros spiritum Deo reddidit, anno ætatis vigesimo quinto. Corpus Vilnam delatum multis claret miraculis. Etenim, præterquam quod puella defuncta vitam, cæci visum, claudi gressum, et varii infirmi sanitatem ad ejus sepul-

chrum recuperarunt. Lithuanis exiguo numero ad potentissimi hostis insperatam irruptionem trepidantibus in aere apparens, insignem tribuit victoriam. Quibus permotus Leo Decimus, eumdem Sanctorum catalogo adscripsit.	the lame the use of their limbs, and the sick their health. He appeared to a small army of Lithuanians, who were unexpectedly attacked by a large force, and gave them the victory over the enemy. Leo the Tenth was induced by all these miracles to insert his name among the Saints.

Enjoy thy well-earned rest in heaven, O Casimir! Neither the world with all its riches, nor the court with all its pleasures, could distract thy heart from the eternal joys it alone coveted and loved. Thy life was short, but full of merit. The remembrance of heaven made thee forget the earth. God yielded to the impatience of thy desire to be with him, and took thee speedily from among men. Thy life, though most innocent, was one of penance, for knowing the evil tendencies of corrupt nature, thou hadst a dread of a life of comfort. When shall *we* be made to understand that penance is a debt we owe to God,—a debt of expiation for the sins we have committed against him? Thou didst prefer death to sin; get *us* a fear of sin, that greatest of all the evils that can befal us, because it is an evil which strikes at God himself. Pray for us during this holy Season, which is intended as a preparation for penance; impress our minds with the truths now put before us. The Christian world is honouring thee to-day; repay its homage by thy blessing. Poland, thy fatherland, is in mourning; comfort her. She was once the bulwark of the Church, and kept back the invasion of schism, heresy, and infidelity; and now she is crushed by tyrants, who seek to rob her of her faith;—pray for her that she may be freed from her oppressors, and, by regaining her ancient zeal for the faith, be preserved from the apostacy into which her enemies are seeking to drive her.

March 6.

SAINTS PERPETUA AND FELICITAS,

MARTYRS.

THE real Feast of these two illustrious heroines of the Faith is to-morrow, which is the anniversary of their martyrdom and triumph; but the memory of the Angel of the Schools, St. Thomas of Aquin, shines so brightly on the seventh of March, that it almost eclipses the two glorious stars of Africa. In consequence of this, the Holy See allows certain Churches to anticipate their Feast, and keep it to-day. We take advantage of this permission, and at once offer to the Christian reader the glorious spectacle, of which Carthage was the scene, in the year 203. Nothing could give us a clearer idea of that spirit of the Gospel, according to which we are now studying to conform our whole life. Here are two women, two mothers; God asks great sacrifices from them; he asks them to give him their lives, nay, more than their lives; and they obey with that simplicity and devotedness which made Abraham merit to be the Father of Believers.

Their two names, as St. Augustine observes, are a presage of what awaits them in heaven: a *perpetual felicity*. The example they set of Christian fortitude, is, of itself, a victory, which secures to the true Faith, a triumph in the land of Africa. St. Cyprian will soon follow them, with his bold and eloquent appeal to the African Christians, inspiring them to die for their Faith : but his words, grand as they are, are less touching than the few pages written by the hand of the brave Perpetua, who, though only twenty-two years of age, relates, with all the self-possession of an angel, the trials she had to go through for God ; and when she had to hurry off, to the amphitheatre, she puts her pen into another's hand, bidding him go on where she leaves off, and write the rest of the battle. As we read these charming pages, we seem to be in the company of the Martyrs; the power of divine grace, which could produce such heroism amidst a people demoralised by paganism, appears so great that even *we* grow courageous; and the very fact that the instruments employed by God for the destruction of the pagan world, were frequently women, we cannot help saying with St. John Chrysostom : " I feel an " indescribable pleasure in reading the Acts of the " Martyrs; but when the Martyr is a woman, my " enthusiasm is doubled. For the frailer the instru- " ment, the greater is the grace, the brighter the " trophy, the grander the victory; and this, not " because of her weakness, but because the devil " is conquered by *her*, by whom *he* once con- " quered us. He conquered by a woman, and " now a woman conquers him. She that was once " his weapon, is now his destroyer, brave and " invincible. That first one sinned, and died; this " one died that she might not sin. Eve was flushed " by a lying promise, and broke the law of God ; our " heroine disdained to live, when her living was to " depend on her breaking her faith to Him who was " her dearest Lord. What excuse, after this, for " men, if they be soft and cowards ? Can *they* hope " for pardon, when *women* fought the holy battle " with such brave, and manly, and generous hearts?"[1]

---

[1] *Homil. de diversis novi Testamenti locis.*

MARCH 6.   SS. PERPETUA AND FELICITAS.   341

The Lessons appointed to be read on the Feast of our two Saints, give us the principal incidents of their Martyrdom. The passage from the account written by Perpetua herself, which is quoted in these Lessons, will make some of our readers long to read the whole of what she has left us. They will find it in our first volume of the *Acts of the Martyrs*.

During the reign of the Emperor Severus, several Catechumens were apprehended at Carthage, in Africa. Among these were Revocatus and his fellow servant Felicitas, Saturninus and Secundulus, and Vivia Perpetua, a lady by birth and education, who was married to a man of wealth. Perpetua was about twenty-two years of age, and was suckling an infant. She has left us the following particulars of her martyrdom. "As soon as our persecutors had apprehended us, my father came to me, and, out of his great love for me, he tried to make me change my resolution. I said to him: 'Father, 'I cannot consent to call 'myself other than what I 'am,—a Christian.' At these words he rushed at me, threatening to tear out my eyes. But he only struck me, and then he left me, when he found that the arguments suggested to him by the devil, were of no avail. A few days after this, we were baptised; and the Holy Ghost inspired me to look on this baptism as a preparation for bodily suffering. A few more days elapsed, and we were sent to

Severo imperatore, apprehensi sunt in Africa adolescentes catechumeni, Revocatus et Felicitas conserva ejus, Saturninus et Secundulus: inter quos et Vivia Perpetua, honeste nata, liberaliter instituta, matronaliter nupta, habens filium ad ubera. Erat autem ipsa annorum circiter viginti duorum. Hæc ordinem martyrii sui conscriptum manu sua reliquit. Quum adhuc, inquit, cum persequutoribus essemus, et me pater avertere, pro sua affectione, perseverarat: Pater, inquio, aliud me dicere non possum, nisi quod sum Christiana. Tunc pater, motus in hoc verbo, misit se in me, ut oculos mihi erueret. Sed vexavit tantum; et profectus est victus cum argumentis diaboli. In spatio paucorum dierum baptizati sumus: mihi autem Spiritus dictavit, nihil aliud petendum in aqua, nisi sufferentiam carnis. Post paucos dies, recipimur in carcerem: et expavi, quia numquam experta eram tales tenebras. Mox rumor cucurrit ut audiremur. Supervenit autem et de civitate pater meus, consumptus tædio; et ascendit ad me, ut me dejiceret, dicens: Miserere, filia, canis meis; miserere patri, si dignus sum a te pater vocari. Aspice ad fratres tuos, aspice ad matrem tuam: aspice ad filium tuum, qui post te vivere non poterit. Depone animos, ne universos nos extermines. Hæc dicebat pater pro sua pietate: se ad pedes meos jactans, et lacrymis non filiam, sed dominam me vocabat. Et ego dolebam canos patris mei: quod solus de passione mea gavisurus non esset de toto genere meo. Et confortavi eum, dicens: Hoc fiet quod Deus voluerit. Scito enim nos non in nostra potestate esse constitutos, sed in Dei. Et recessit a me contristatus.

prison. I was terrified, for I was not accustomed to such darkness. The report soon spread that we were to be brought to trial. My father left the city, for he was heartbroken, and he came to me, hoping to shake my purpose. These were his words to me: 'My child, have pity on my 'old age. Have pity on thy 'father, if I deserve to be call-'ed Father. Think of thy 'brothers, think of thy mo-'ther, think of thy son, who 'cannot live when thou art 'gone. Give up this mad 'purpose, or thou wilt bring 'misery upon thy family.' Whilst saying this, which he did out of love for me, he threw himself at my feet, and wept bitterly, and said he besought this of me, not as his child, but as his lady. I was moved to tears to see my aged parent in this grief, for I knew that he was the only one of my family that would not rejoice at my being a martyr. I tried to console him, and said: 'I will do 'whatsoever God shall ordain. 'Thou knowest that we be-'long to God, and not to our-'selves.' He then left me, and was very sad.

Alio die, quum pranderemus, subito rapti sumus ut audiremur: et pervenimus ad forum. Ascendimus in catasta. Interrogati cæteri confessi sunt. Ventum est et ad me. Et apparuit pater illico cum filio meo: et extraxit me de gradu, et dixit supplicans: Miserere

"On the following day, as we were taking our repast, they came upon us suddenly, and summoned us to trial. We reached the forum. We were made to mount a platform. My companions were questioned, and they confessed the faith. My turn came next, and I immediately saw my father approaching towards me, holding my infant son. He drew me from the platform, and besought me, saying: 'Have pity on 'thy babe!' Hilarian, too, the governor, said to me: 'Have pity on thy aged fa-'ther, have pity on thy babe! 'Offer up sacrifice for the 'Emperors.' I answered him: 'I cannot; I am a Christian.' Whereupon, he sentences all of us to be devoured by the wild beasts; and we, full of joy, return to our prison. But as I had hitherto always had my child with me in prison, and fed him at my breast, I immediately send word to my father, beseeching him to let him come to me. He refused; and from that moment, neither the babe asked for the breast, nor did I suffer inconvenience; for God thus willed it." All this is taken from the written account left by the blessed Perpetua, and it brings us to the day before she was put to death. As regards Felicitas, she was in the eighth month of her pregnancy, when she was apprehended. The day of the public shows was near at hand, and the fear that her martyrdom would be deferred on account of her being with child, made her very sad. Her fellow-martyrs, too, felt much for her, for they could not bear the thought of seeing so worthy a companion disappointed in the hope, she had in common with themselves, of so soon reaching heaven.

infanti. Et Hilarianus procurator: Parce, inquit, canis patris tui, parce infantiæ pueri: fac sacrum pro salute imperatorum. Et ego respondi: Non facio: christiana sum. Tunc nos universos pronuntiat et damnat ad bestias: et hilares descendimus ad carcerem. Sed quia consueverat a me infans mammas accipere, et mecum in carcere manere, statim mitto ad patrem, postulans infantem. Sed pater dare noluit: et, quomodo Deus voluit, neque ille amplius mammas desideravit, neque mihi fervorem fecerunt. Atque hoc scripsit beata Perpetua usque in pridie certaminis. Felicitas vero, quæ prægnans octo jam mensium fuerat apprehensa, instante spectaculi die, in magno erat luctu, ne propter ventrem differretur. Sed et commartyres ejus graviter contristabantur, ne tam bonam sociam in via ejusdem spei relinquerent. Conjuncto itaque gemitu, ad Dominum orationem fuderunt ante tertium diem muneris. Statim post orationem dolores eam invaserunt. Et quum in partu laborans doleret, ait illi quidam ex ministris: Quæ sic modo doles, quid facies objecta bestiis, quas contempsisti quum sacrificare noluisti? Et illa respondit: Modo ego patior quod patior: illic autem alius erit in me qui patietur pro me; quia et ego pro illo passura sum.

Ita enixa est puellam, quam sibi quædam soror in filiam educavit.

Illuxit dies victoriæ illorum : et processerunt de carcere in amphitheatrum, quasi in cœlum, hilares, vultu decori : si forte, gaudio paventes, non timore. Sequebatur Perpetua placido vultu, et pedum incessu ut matrona Christi dilecta : vigorem oculorum suorum dejiciens ab omnium conspectu. Item Felicitas, salvam se peperisse gaudens, ut ad bestias pugnaret. Illis ferocissimam vaccam diabolus præparavit. Itaque reticulis indutæ producuntur. Inducitur prior Perpetua. Jactata est et concidit in lumbos : et ut conspexit tunicam a latere discissam,

Uniting, therefore, in prayer, they with tears besought God in her behalf. It was the last day but two before the public shows. No sooner was their prayer ended, than Felicitas was seized with pain. One of the gaolers, who overheard her moaning, cried out : 'If this 'pain seem to thee so great, 'what wilt thou do when thou 'art being devoured by the 'wild beasts, which thou pre-'tendedst to heed not when 'thou wast told to offer sacri-'fice.' She answered : 'What 'I am suffering now, it is in-'deed *I* that suffer ; but there, 'there will be another in me, 'who will suffer for me, be-'cause I shall be suffering for 'Him.' She was delivered of a daughter, and one of our sisters adopted the infant as her own.

The day of their victory dawned. They left their prison for the amphitheatre, cheerful, and with faces beaming with joy, as though they were going to heaven. They were excited, but it was from delight, not from fear. The last in the group was Perpetua. Her placid look, her noble gait, betrayed the Christian matron. She passed through the crowd and saw no one, for her beautiful eyes were fixed upon the ground. By her side was Felicitas, rejoicing that her safe delivery enabled her to encounter the wild beasts. The devil had prepared a savage cow for them. They were put into a net. Felicitas was brought forward the first. She was tossed into the air, and fell upon her back. Observing that one side of her dress was torn, she adjusted it, heedless of her pain, because thoughtful for modesty. Having recovered from the fall, she put up her hair which was disheveled by the shock, for it was not seemly that a martyr should win her palm and have the appearance of one distracted by grief. This done, she stood up. Seeing Felicitas much bruised by her fall, she went to her, and giving her her hand, she raised her from the ground. Both were now ready for a fresh attack; but the people were moved to pity, and the martyrs were led to the gate called Sana-Vivaria. There Perpetua, like one that is roused from sleep, awoke from the deep ecstacy of her spirit. She looked around her, and said to the astonished multitude: 'When will the cow attack us?' They told her that it had already attacked them. She could not believe it, until her wounds and torn dress reminded her of what had happened. Then beckoning to her brother, and to a catechumen named Rusticus, she thus spoke to them. 'Be staunch in the faith, and 'love one another, and be not 'shocked at our sufferings.'

God soon took Secundulus from this world, for he died whilst he was in the prison. Saturninus and Revocatus were

ad velamentum femorum adduxit, pudoris potius memor quam doloris. Dehinc requisita et dispersos capillos infibulavit. Non enim decebat martyrem dispersis capillis pati; ne in sua gloria plangere videretur. Ita surrexit; et elisam Felicitatem quum vidisset accessit et manum ei tradidit, et sublevavit illam. Et ambæ pariter steterunt; et populi duritia devicta, revocatæ sunt in portam Sanavivariam. Illic Perpetua, quasi a somno expergita, adeo in spiritu et extasi fuerat, circumspicere coepit: et stupentibus omnibus, ait: Quando producimur ad vaccam illam, nescio. Et quum audisset quod jam evenerat; non prius credidit, nisi quasdam notas vexationis in corpore et habitu suo recognovisset. Exinde accersitum fratrem suum, et catechumenum Rusticum nomine, adloquuta est eos, dicens: In fide state, et invicem omnes diligite; et passionibus nostris ne scandalizemini.

Secundulum Deus maturiore exitu de sæculo adhuc in carcere evocaverat. Saturninus et Revocatus leopardum experti, etiam ab urso vexati sunt. Saturus apro oblatus est; deinde ad ursum tractus, qui de cavea prodire noluit : itaque bis illæsus revocatur. In fine spectaculi, leopardo objectus, de uno morsu ejus tanto perfusus est sanguine, ut populus reverenti illi secundi baptismatis testimonium reclamaverit: Salvum lotum, salvum lotum. Exinde jam exanimis, prosternitur cum cæteris ad jugulationem solito loco. Et quum populus illos in medium postularet, ut gladio penetrante in eorum corpore, oculos suos comites homicidii adjungeret ; ultro surrexerunt, et se quo volebat populos transtulerunt: ante jam osculati invicem, ut martyrium per solemnia pacis consummarent. Cæteri quidem immobiles et cum silentio ferrum receperunt : multo magis Saturus, qui prior reddidit spiritum. Perpetua autem, ut aliquid doloris gustaret, inter costas puncta exululavit ; et errantem dexteram tirunculi gladiatoris ipsa in jugulum suum posuit. Fortasse tanta femina aliter non potuisset occidi, quia ab immundo spiritu timebatur, nisi ipsa voluisset.

exposed first to a leopard, and then to a bear. Saturus was exposed to a boar, and then to a bear, which would not come out of its den ; thus was he twice left uninjured : but at the close of the games, he was thrown to a leopard, which bit him so severely, that he was all covered with blood, and as he was taken from the amphitheatre, the people jeered at him for this second baptism, and said : 'Saved, washed ! Saved, 'washed !' He was then carried off, dying as he was, to the appointed place, there to be despatched by the sword, with the rest. But the people demanded that they should be led back to the middle of the amphitheatre, that their eyes might feast on the sight, and watch the sword as it pierced them. The Martyrs hearing their request, cheerfully stood up, and marched to the place where the people would have them go ; but first they embraced one another, that the sacrifice of their martyrdom might be consummated with the solemn kiss of peace. All of them, without so much as a movement or a moan, received the swordman's blow, save only Saturus, who died from his previous wounds, and Perpetua, who was permitted to feel more than the rest. Her executioner was a novice in his work, and could not thrust his sword through her ribs : she slightly moaned, then took his right hand, and pointing his sword towards her throat, told him that that was the place to strike. Perhaps it was that such a woman could not be otherwise slain than by her own consent, for the unclean spirit feared her.

The Holy See has approved of the three following Hymns composed in honour of our two Martyrs. We unite them under one conclusion.

HYMN.

Let the Church, the Spouse of Christ, celebrate in holy praise, the two dauntless women; and sing, in joyous hymns, how the weaker sex had here two manly hearts.

Both were born in Afric's sunny land; and now both shine throughout the whole world as the two glorious combatants, wearing bright laurels on their brows.

Perpetua is honoured by her fellow-citizens as being of high birth, and had but recently contracted an honourable marriage. But there was an honour far higher, in her eyes,—the love and service of Christ.

Felicitas, though she served an earthly master, was free in this,—that she was a servant of the great King. Like Perpetua, she thirsts for battle; and like her, she culls a palm.

Perpetua was besieged by her father, who sought, by tears

Christi Sponsa piis laudibus efferat
Binus impavido pectore feminas:
In sexu fragili corda virilia
Hymnis pangat ovantibus.

Ad lucem genitæ sole sub Africo,
Nunc ambæ pugiles actibus inclytis
In toto radiant orbe: micantibus
Fulgent tempora laureis.
Exornat generis Perpetuam decus;
Sponso connubiis juncta recentibus
Clarescit; sed honos hanc trahit altior;
Christi fœdera prætulit.

Se Regis famulam libera profitens,
Dum servile jugum Felicitas subit:
Ad luctam properans gressibus æmulis,
Palmas ad similes volat.
Frustra Perpetuam fletibus et minis

Impugnat genitor : quæ simul angitur,
Errantem miserans. Oscula
  filio
  Lactenti dedit ultima.

Terris Eva parens quæ
  mala contulit,
Horum sentit onus Felicitas
  grave ;
Nunc et passa sibi partu-
  riens gemit,
  Mox passura Deo libens.

Cœli Perpetuæ panditur
  ostium ;
Inspectare datur : jam sibi
  prælia
Exortura videt; sed requiem
  Deus
  Post certamina conferet.
Tangit scala domus aurea
  cœlitum :
Ast utrumque latus cuspi-
  dibus riget ;
Lapsos terribilis faucibus
  excipit
  Hanc infra recubans
  draco.
Ascendas, mulier, nec
  draco terreat ;
Contritumque caput sit tibi
  pro gradu,
Per quem sidereos incipias
  pede
  Orbes scandere concito.
Hortus deliciis jam patet
  affluens,
In quo mulget oves Pastor
  amabilis :
Huc optata venis, filia : sic
  ait,
  Hanc dulci recreans cibo.

In circum rapitur : fœdus
  et horrida

and threats, to make her deny her faith. She, on her side, was full of grief and pity at seeing him a victim of error. Her babe was taken from her; she kissed him and was content.

Felicitas begins her sufferings by those cruel pangs which Eve, our mother, brought upon the earth. Now, in child-birth, she suffers for herself, and she moans; but, in her martyrdom, she suffers for her God, and she rejoices.

The gate of heaven is thrown open to Perpetua, and she is permitted to look within. She there learns that a contest awaits her, but that, after the battle, God will grant her repose.

She sees a golden ladder reaching to the palace of heaven; but both its sides are armed with spikes, and at its foot lies an angry dragon, which devours them that fall.

Ascend, Perpetua! fear not the dragon. Trample on his head, and make it a stepping-stone, whereby thou mayst quickly mount to the starry land above.

There shalt thou find a paradise of delights, where the loving shepherd caresses his sheep. "Thou art welcome here, my daughter!" Thus did he address the Martyr, and then gave her to eat of sweetest food.

In another vision, she thought she was hurried to the

amphitheatre. There she was met by a man, whose face was swarth and terrible to look at. He brandished his sword. She encountered him, threw him on the ground, and trampled on his head. A cry was heard: "Thou hast conquered! Come, take the prize!"

But at length came the glorious day of victory for the soldiers of Christ. On, Martyrs, to the field! Perpetua and Felicitas! the court of heaven is longing to receive you!

The wild beast rushes upon them, tossing, tearing, and wounding their tender limbs. See, Felicitas! thy sister's hand emboldens thee to renew the fight.

God looks down from heaven on the two brave combatants, and calls them to the prize. Their blood streams from the wounds, and their spirits speed their way to the bosom of Christ.

The sword, the welcome sword, is thrust; the Martyrs die, all save Perpetua; bravely she takes the trembling lictor's hand, and offering him her neck, tells him his surest aim is there.

Go, now, brave-hearted ones, to him who is your Spouse, and there eternally enjoy the bliss he has in store for you. He gave us you as models; oh, show your power, and help us your clients.

Eternal glory be to the Father, and to the Son, and

Occurrit specie vir gladium
  vibrans:
Dejectus territur femineo
  pede.
Victrix, suscipe præmia.

Luxit clara dies, vincere
  qua datur
Athletis Domini. Pergite
  Martyres:
Omnis Perpetuam curia
  Cœlitum,
Et te, Felicitas, cupit.
Quassat Perpetuæ membra tenerrima;
Elidit sociam bellua. Te
  soror
Stans, o Felicitas, ad nova
  prælia
Erectam reparat manu.
E cœli pugilum respiciens
  Deus
Certamen, geminas ad bravium vocat.
Effuso properet sanguine
  spiritus,
  In Christi remeans sinum.
Optatus penetrat corpora
  Martyrum
Lictoris gladius: sed trepidam manum
Fortis Perpetuæ dextera dirigit,
Præbens guttura cuspidi.
Nunc, o magnanimæ, gaudia quæ manent
In Sponsi thalamo carpite
  jugiter
Vos exempla dedit: præsidium potens
Vestris ferte clientibus.
Laus æterna Patri, laus
  quoque Filio;

Par individuo gloria Flamini ; In cunctis resonet Christiadum choris Virtus martyribus data. Amen.	to the co-equal Spirit! And let every choir in Christian lands sound forth its praise to the grace bestowed on Martyrs. Amen.

Perpetua! Felicitas! Oh! glorious and prophetic names, which come like two bright stars of March, pouring out upon us your rays of light and life! You are heard in the songs of the Angels; and we poor sinners, as we echo them on earth, are told to love and hope. You remind us of that brave woman, who, as the Scripture says, kept up the battle begun by men: *The valiant men ceased:* who will follow them? *A Mother in Israel.*[1] Glory be to that Almighty power, which loves to *choose the weak things of the world that it may confound the strong!*[2] Glory to the Church of Africa, the daughter of the Church of Rome; and glory to the Church of Carthage, which had not then heard the preachings of her Cyprian, and yet could produce two such noble hearts!

As to thee, Perpetua, thou art held in veneration by the whole Christian world. Thy name is mentioned by God's Priests in the Holy Mass, and thus thy memory is associated with the Sacrifice of the Man-God, for love of whom thou didst lay down thy life. And those pages written by thine own hand, how they reveal to us the generous character of thy soul! how they comment those words of the Canticle: *Love is strong as death!*[3] It was thy *love* of God that made thee suffer, and die, and conquer. Even before the water of Baptism had touched thee, thou wast enrolled among the Martyrs. When the hard trial came of resisting a father, who wished thee to lay down the palm of martyrdom,—how bravely didst

---

[1] Judges, v. 7. [2] I. Cor. i. 27. [3] Cant. viii. 6.

thou not triumph over thy filial affection, in order to save that which is due to our Father who is in heaven! Nay, when the hardest test came,—when the babe that fed at thy breast was taken from thee in thy prison,—even then thy *love* was *strong* enough for the sacrifice, as was Abraham's, when he had to immolate his Isaac.

Thy fellow-martyrs deserve our admiration; they are so grand in their courage; but thou, dear Saint, surpassest them all. Thy love makes thee more than brave in thy sufferings, it makes thee forget them. "Where wast thou," we would ask thee in the words of St. Augustine, "where wast thou, that thou didst "not feel the goading of that furious beast, asking "when it was to be, as though it had not been? "Where wast thou? What didst thou see, that "made thee see not this? On what wast thou "feasting, that made thee dead to sense? What "was the love that absorbed, what was the sight that "distracted, what was the chalice that inebriated "thee? And yet the ties of flesh were still holding "thee, the claims of death were still upon thee, the cor- "ruptible body was still weighing thee down!"[1] But our Lord had prepared thee for the final struggle, by asking sacrifice at thy hands. This made thy life wholly spiritual, and gave thy soul to dwell, by love, with Him, who had asked thee for all and received it; and thus living in union with Jesus, thy spirit was all but a stranger to the body it animated.

It was impatient to be wholly with its Sovereign Good. Thy eager hand directs the sword that is to set thee free; and as the executioner severs the last tie that holds thee, how voluntary was thy sacrifice, how hearty thy welcome of death! Truly, thou wast the Valiant, the *Strong Woman*,[2] that conqueredst the wicked serpent! Thy greatness of soul has

---

[1] Sermon for the Feast of SS. Perpetua and Felicitas.
[2] Prov. xxxi. 10.

merited for thee a high place among the heroines of our holy Faith, and for sixteen hundred years thou hast been honoured by the enthusiastic devotion and love of the servants of God.

And thou, too, Felicitas! receive the homage of our veneration, for thou wast found worthy to be a fellow-martyr with Perpetua. Though she was a rich matron of Carthage, and thou a servant, yet Baptism and Martyrdom made you companions and sisters. The Lady and the Slave embraced, for Martyrdom made you equal; and as the spectators saw you hand in hand together, they must have felt, that there was a power in the Religion they persecuted, which would put an end to Slavery. The power and grace of Jesus triumphed in thee, as it did in Perpetua; and thus was fulfilled thy sublime answer to the pagan, who dared to jeer thee,—that when the hour of trial came, it would not be *thou* that wouldst suffer, but Christ, who would suffer in thee. Heaven is now the reward of thy sacrifice; well didst thou merit it. And that babe, that was born in thy prison, what a happy child to have for its mother a Martyr in heaven! How wouldst thou not bless both it and the mother who adopted it! Oh! what *fitness*, in such a soul as thine, for the *Kingdom of God*![1] Not once *looking back*, but ever bravely speeding onwards to him that called thee. Thy felicity is perpetual in heaven; thy glory on earth shall never cease.

And now, dear Saints, Perpetua and Felicitas, intercede for us during this season of grace. Go, with your palms in your hands, to the throne of God, and beseech him to pour down his mercy upon us. It is true, the days of paganism are gone by; and there are no persecutors clamouring for our blood. You, and countless other Martyrs, have won victory

---

[1] St. Luke, ix. 62.

for Faith; and that Faith is now ours; we are Christians. But there is a second paganism, which has taken deep root among us. It is the source of that corruption which now pervades every rank of society, and its own two sources are indifference, which chills the heart, and sensuality, which induces cowardice. Holy Martyrs! pray for us that we may profit by the example of your virtues, and that the thought of your heroic devotedness may urge us to be courageous in the sacrifices which God claims at our hands. Pray, too, for the Churches which are now being established on that very spot of Africa, which was the scene of your glorious martyrdom: bless them, and obtain for them, by your powerful intercession, firmness of faith and purity of morals.

March 7.

SAINT THOMAS OF AQUIN,

Doctor of the Church.

The Saint we are to honour to-day, is one of the sublimest and most lucid interpreters of Divine Truth. He rose up in the Church many centuries after the Apostolic Age, nay, long after the four great Latin Doctors, Ambrose, Augustine, Jerome, and Gregory. The Church, the ever young and joyful Mother, is justly proud of her Thomas, and has honoured him with the splendid title of *The Angelical Doctor*, on account of the extraordinary gift of understanding wherewith God had blessed him; just as his co-temporary and friend, St. Bonaventure, has been called *the Seraphic Doctor*, on account of the wonderful unction which abounds in the writings of this worthy disciple of St. Francis. Thomas of Aquin is an honour to mankind, for perhaps there never existed a man whose intellect surpassed his. He is one of the brightest ornaments of the Church, for not one of her Doctors has equalled him in the clearness and precision wherewith he has explained her doctrines. He received the thanks of Christ himself, for having *well written* of him and his mysteries. How welcome ought not this Feast of such a Saint to be to us during this Season of the Year, when our main study is our return and conversion to God? What greater blessing could we have than the coming to know this God ? Has not our ignorance of God, and his claims, and his perfections, been the greatest misery of our past lives ? Here we have a Saint whose prayers are most efficacious in procuring for us that knowledge, which is *unspotted, and converteth souls, and giveth wisdom to little ones, and gladdeneth the heart, and enlighteneth the eyes.*[1] Happy we if this spiritual wisdom be granted us ! We shall then see the vanity of everything that is not eternal, the righteousness of the divine commandments, the malice of sin, and the infinite goodness wherewith God treats us when we repent.

Let us learn from the Church the claims of the Angelical Doctor to our admiration and confidence.

Thomas was born of noble parents, his father being Landulph, Count of Aquino, and his mother a rich Neapolitan lady, by name Theodora. When he was five years old, he was sent to Monte Cassino, that he might receive from the Benedictine Monks his first training. Thence he was sent to Naples, where he went through a course of studies, and, young as he was, joined the Order of Friars Preachers. This step caused great displeasure to his mother and brothers, and it was therefore deemed advisable to send him to Paris. He was waylaid by his brothers, who seized him, and imprisoned him in the castle of Saint John. After having made several unsuccessful attempts to induce him to abandon the

Thomas, Landulpho comite Aquinate, et Theodora Neapolitana, nobilibus parentibus natus, quintum annum agens, Monachis sancti Benedicti Casinatibus custodiendus traditur. Inde Neapolim studiorum causa missus, jam adolescens Fratrum Prædicatorum Ordinem suscepit. Sed matre ac fratribus id indigne ferentibus, Lutetiam Parisiorum mittitur. Quem fratres in itinere per vim raptum in arcem castri Sancti Joannis perducunt, ubi varie exagitatus, ut sanctum propositum mutaret, mulierem etiam, quæ ad labefactandam ejus constantiam introducta fuerat, titione fugavit. Mox beatus juvenis flexis genibus ante signum crucis orans, ibique somno

---

[1] Ps. xviii. 8, 9.

correptus, per quietem sentire visus est, sibi ab Angelis constringi lumbos ; quo ex tempore omni postea libidinis sensu caruit. Sororibus, quæ ut eum a pio consilio removerent, in castrum venerant, persuasit, ut contemptis curis sæcularibus, ad exercitationem cœlestis vitæ se conferrent.

Emissus e castro per fenestram, Neapolim reducitur. Unde Romam, postea Parisium a fratre Joanne Teutonico, Ordinis Prædicatorum generali Magistro, ductus, Alberto Magno doctore philosophiæ ac theologiæ operam dedit : viginti quinque annos natus, Magister est appellatus, publiceque philosophos ac theologos summa cum laude est interpretatus. Nunquam se lectioni aut scriptioni dedit, nisi post orationem. In difficultatibus locorum sacræ Scripturæ, ad orationem jejunium adhibebat. Quin etiam sodali suo fratri Reginaldo dicere solebat, quidquid sciret, non tam studio aut labore suo peperisse, quam divinitus traditum accepisse. Neapoli, cum ad

holy life he had chosen, they assailed his purity, by sending to him a wicked woman : but he drove her from his chamber with a fire-brand. The young saint then threw himself on his knees before a crucifix. Having prayed some time, he fell asleep, and it seemed to him that two Angels approached to him, and tightly girded his loins. From that time forward, he never suffered the slightest feeling against purity. His sisters, also, had come to the castle, and tried to make him change his mind ; but he, on the contrary, persuaded them to despise the world, and devote themselves to the exercise of a holy life.

It was contrived that he should escape through a window of the castle, and return to Naples. He was thence taken by John the Teutonic, the general of the Dominican Order, first to Rome, and then to Paris, in which latter city he was taught philosophy and theology by Albert the Great. At the age of twenty-five, he received the title of Doctor, and explained in the public schools, and in a manner that made him the object of universal admiration, the writings of philosophers and theologians. He always applied himself to prayer, before reading or writing anything. When he met with any difficult passage in the Sacred Scriptures, he both fasted and prayed. He used often to say to his companion, Brother

MARCH 7. ST. THOMAS OF AQUIN.

Reginald, that if he knew anything, it was more a gift from God, than the fruit of his own study and labour. One day, when at Naples, as he was praying, with more than his usual fervour, before a crucifix, he heard these words: "Well hast thou written of "me, Thomas! What reward "wouldst thou have me give "thee?" He answered: "None "other, Lord, but thyself."

There was not a book which he had not most carefully read. His favourite spiritual book was the *Conferences of the Fathers*. He was most zealous in preaching the Word of God. On one occasion, during Easter Week, as he was preaching in the Church of St. Peter, a woman touched the hem of his habit, and was cured of an issue of blood. His writings are so extraordinary, not only for their number and their variety, but also for their clearness in the explaining difficult points of doctrine, that he has received the title of *Angelical Doctor*. He was invited to Rome by Pope Urban the Fourth, but nothing could induce him to accept the honours which were offered him. He refused the Archbishopric of Naples, which Pope Clement the Fourth begged him to accept. He was sent by Gregory the Tenth to the Council of Lyons; but having got as far as Fossa Nova, he fell sick, and was received as a guest in the Monastery of that place, and wrote a commentary on the

imaginem crucifixi vehementius oraret, hanc vocem audivit : Bene scripsisti de me, Thoma; quam ergo mercedem accipies? Cui ille: Non aliam, Domine nisi teipsum.

Nullum fuit scriptorum genus in quibus non esset diligentissime versatus. Collationes Patrum assidue pervolutabat, nec tamen a prædicatione divini verbi desistebat. Quod cum faceret per Octavam Paschæ in Basilica Sancti Petri, mulierem quæ ejus fimbriam tetigerat, a fluxu sanguinis liberavit. Scripta ejus et multitudine, et varietate, et facilitate explicandi res difficiles, adeo excellunt, ut ob eam causam etiam nomen Doctoris Angelici jure sit adeptus. Ab Urbano Quarto Romam vocatus, adduci non potuit ut honores acciperet. Archiepiscopatum Neapolitanum, etiam deferente Clemente Quarto Pontifice, recusavit. Missus a Gregorio Decimo ad Concilium Lugdunense, in monasterio Fossæ Novæ in morbum incidit, ubi, ægrotus, Cantica canticorum explanavit. Ibidem obiit quinquagenarius, anno salutis millesimo ducentesimo septuagesimo quarto, Nonis Martii. Miraculis et vivus et mortuus floruit. A Joanne Vigesimo secundo in Sanctorum numerum relatus est, anno millesimo trecentesimo vigesimo tertio: cujus corpus postea, Urbano Quinto summo Pontifice, Tolosam translatum est.

Canticle of Canticles. There he died, in the fiftieth year of his age, in the year of our Lord 1274, on the Nones of March (March 7th). His sanctity was made manifest by miracles, both before and after his death. He was canonised by John the Twenty-second, in the year 1323. His body was translated to Toulouse, during the Pontificate of Urban the Fifth.

The Dominican Order, of which St. Thomas is one of the grandest ornaments, has inserted the three following Hymns in its Liturgy of his Feast.

HYMN.

Exsultet mentis jubilo
Laudans turba fidelium,
Errorum pulso nubilo
Per novi solis radium.

Thomas in mundi vespere,
Fudit thesauros gratiæ:
Donis plenus ex æthere
Morum, et sapientiæ.

De cujus fonte luminis,
Verbi coruscant faculæ,
Scripturæ sacræ Numinis,
Et veritatis Regulæ.

Fulgens doctrinæ radiis,
Clarus vitæ munditia,
Splendens miris prodigiis.
Dat toto mundo gaudia.

Laus Patri sit, ac Genito,
Simulque Sancto Flamini,

Let the assembly of the Faithful exult in spiritual joy, and give praise to God, who has made a new sun to shine in our world, and disperse the clouds of error.

It was in the evening of the world that Thomas shed his treasures of heavenly light. Heaven had enriched him with gifts of virtue and wisdom:

From this fountain of light we have derived a brighter knowledge of the Word, the understanding of the Divine Scriptures, and the rules of truth.

The effulgent rays of his wisdom, the light of his spotless life, and the splendour of his miracles, have filled the universe with joy.

Praise, then, be to the Father, and to the Son, and to

the Holy Ghost. And may our God, by the intercession and merits of his Saint, admit us into the choir of the blessed in heaven. Amen.

Qui sancti Thomæ merito
Nos cœli jungat agmini.
Amen.

HYMN.

Noble by birth and parentage, Thomas, whilst in the bloom of youth, embraced the Order of Preachers.

Like to the star of morn, brightly does he shine amidst the luminaries of earth, and, more than any Doctor of the Church, refutes the doctrines of the Gentiles.

He explores the depth of mysteries, and brings to light the hidden gems of truth, for he teaches us what the mind of man had else never understood.

God gives him to the Church as a Fountain of wisdom, like to that four-branched river of Paradise. He made him to be her Gedeon's sword, her Trumpet, her Vase, her Torch.

Praise, then, be to the Father, and to the Son, and to the Holy Ghost. And may our God, by the intercession and merits of his Saint, admit us into the choir of the blessed in heaven. Amen.

Thomas insignis genere,
Claram Ducens originem,
Subit ætatis teneræ
Prædicatorum Ordinem.

Typum gessit Luciferi,
Splendens in cœtu nubium,
Plusquam doctores cæteri
Purgans dogma Gentilium.

Profunda scrutans fluminum,
In lucem pandit abdita,
Dum supra sensus hominum
Obscura facit cognita.

Fit paradisi fluvius,
Quadripartite pervius :
Fit Gedeonis gladius,
Tuba, lagena, radius.

Laus Patri sit, ac Genito
Simulque Sancto Flamini,
Qui sancti Thomæ merito,
Nos cœli jungat agmini.
Amen.

HYMN.

Lauda, Mater Ecclesia,
Thomæ felicem exitum,
Qui pervenit ad gaudia
Per Verbi vitæ meritum.

Dear Church, our Mother! the happy death of thy Thomas deserves a hymn of praise. By the merits of Him that is

Fossa Nova tunc suscipit
Thecam thesauri gratiæ,
Cum Christo Thomam efficit,
Hæredem regni gloriæ.

Manens doctrinæ veritas,
Et funeris integritas,
Mira fragrans suavitas,
Ægris collata sanitas.

Monstrat hunc dignum laudibus
Terræ, ponto, et superis;
Nos juvet suis precibus,
Deo commendet meritis.

Laus Patri sit, ac Genito,
Simulque Sancto Flamini,
Qui sancti Thomæ merito
Nos cœli jungat agmini.
Amen.

the Word of Life, he is now in endless joy.

It was at Fossa Nova that the rich treasury of grace was welcomed as a guest. It was there that he received from Christ the inheritance of eternal glory.

He has left us the fruits of truth; he has left us his glorious relics, which breathe forth a heavenly fragrance, and work cures for the suffering sick.

Right well, then, is honour his due; earth, and sea, and heaven, all may give him praise. May his prayers and merits intercede for us with God.

Praise, then, be to the Father, and to the Son, and to the Holy Ghost. And may our God, by the intercession and merits of his Saint, admit us into the choir of the blessed in heaven. Amen.

How shall we worthily praise thee, most holy Doctor! How shall we thank thee for what thou hast taught us? The rays of the Divine Sun of Justice beamed strongly upon thee, and thou hast reflected them upon us. When we picture thee contemplating Truth, we think of those words of our Lord: *Blessed are the clean of heart, for they shall see God.*[1] Thy victory over the concupiscence of the flesh merited for thee the highest spiritual delights; and our Redeemer chose thee, because of the purity of thy angelic soul, to compose for his Church the Office whereby she should celebrate the Divine Sacrament of his Love. Learning did not impair thy

---

[1] St. Matth. v. 8.

humility. Prayer was ever thy guide in thy search after Truth; and there was but one reward, for which, after all thy labours, thou wast ambitious,—the possession of God.

Thy life, alas! was short. The very master-piece of thy angelical writings was left unfinished. But thou hast not lost thy power of working for the Church. Aid her in her combats against error. She holds thy teachings in the highest estimation, because she feels that none of her Saints has ever known so well as thou, the secrets and Mysteries of her Divine Spouse. Now, perhaps more than in any other age, *Truths are decayed*—*they are diminished among the children of men;*[1] strengthen us in our Faith, get us Light. Check the conceit of those shallow self-constituted philosophers, who dare to sit in judgment over the actions and decisions of the Church, and force their contemptible theories upon a generation that is too ill-instructed to detect their fallacies. The atmosphere around us is gloomy with ignorance; loose principles, and truths spoilt by cowardly compromise, are the fashion of our times; pray for us, bring us back to that bold and simple acceptance of truth, which gives life to the intellect and joy to the heart.

Pray, too, for the grand Order, which loves thee so devoutly, and honours thee as one of the most illustrious of its many glorious children. Draw down upon the family of thy Patriarch Saint Dominic the choicest blessings, for it is one of the most powerful auxiliaries of God's Church.

We are on the eve of the holy season of Lent; we are preparing for the great work of earnest conversion of our lives. Thy prayers must gain for us the knowledge both of the God we have offended by our sins, and of the wretched state of a soul that is

---

[1] Ps. xi. 2.

at enmity with its Maker. Knowing this, we shall hate our sins; we shall desire to purify our souls in the Blood of the spotless Lamb; we shall generously atone for our faults by works of penance.

March 8.

SAINT JOHN OF GOD,

CONFESSOR.

This day month we were keeping the feast of St. John of Matha, whose characteristic virtue was charity; our Saint of to-day was like him: love for his neighbour led him to devote himself to the service of them that most needed help. Both are examples to us of what is a principal duty of this present Season: they are models of Fraternal Charity. They teach us this great lesson,—that our love of God is false, if our hearts are not disposed to show mercy to our neighbour, and help him in his necessities and troubles. It is the same lesson as that which the Beloved Disciple gives us, when he says: *He that hath the substance of this world, and shall see his brother in need, and shall put up his mercy from him,—how doth the Charity of God abide in him?*[1] But, if there can be no love of God, where there is none for our neighbour,—the love of our neighbour itself is not genuine, unless it be accompanied by a love of our Creator and Redeemer. The charity which the world has set up, which it calls *Philanthropy*, and which it exercises not in the name of God, but solely for the sake of man,—this pretended virtue is a mere delusion, is incapable of producing love

---

[1] I. St. John, iii. 17.

between those who give and those who receive, and its results must, necessarily, be unsatisfactory. There is but one tie, which can make men love one another:—that tie is God, who created them all, and commands them all to be one in him. To serve mankind for its own sake, is to make a god of it; and even viewing the workings of the two systems in this single point of view,—the relief they afford to temporal suffering,—what comparison is there between mere Philanthropy, and that supernatural Charity of the humble disciples of Christ, who make *Him* the very motive and end of all they do for their afflicted brethren? The Saint, we honour to-day, was called *John of God*, because the Name of God was ever on his lips. His heroic acts of charity had no other motive than that of pleasing God; God alone was the inspirer of the tender love he had for his suffering fellow-creatures. Let us imitate his example, for our Lord assures us, that he considers as done to himself, whatsoever we do even for the least of his disciples.

The Liturgy thus portrays the virtues of our Saint.

Joannes de Deo, ex catholicis piisque parentibus in oppido Montis-Majoris, junioris regni Lusitaniæ natus, quam sublimiter in sortem Domini fuerit electus, insuetus splendor super ejus domo refulgens, sonitusque æris campani sua sponte emissus, ab ipso ejus nativitatis tempore non obscure prænuntiarunt. A laxioris vivendi ratione, divina operante virtute, revocatus, magnæ sanctitatis exhibere specimen cœpit, et ob auditam prædicationem verbi Dei sic ad me-	John of God was born of Catholic and virtuous parents, in Portugal, in the town of Montemor. At his birth, a bright light shone upon the house, and the church bell was heard to ring of itself; God thus evincing to what great things he destined this his servant. For some time he fell into a lax way of living; but was reclaimed by God's grace, and led a very holy life. His conversion was effected by his hearing a sermon, and so fervently did he practise the exercises of a devout life, that, from the very first, he seemed to have at-

tained the height of perfection. He gave whatsoever he possessed to the poor who were in prison. Extraordinary were the penances he inflicted on himself; and the contempt he had for himself induced him to do certain things, which led some people to accuse him of madness, so that he was for some time confined in a madhouse. His charity only increased by such treatment. He collected alms sufficient to build two large hospitals in the city of Granada, where also he began the new Order, wherewith he enriched the Church. This Order was called the Institute of Friars Hospitallers. Its object was to assist the sick, both in their spiritual and corporal wants. Its success was very great, and it had Houses in almost all parts of the world.

The Saint often carried the sick poor on his own shoulders to the hospital, and there he provided them with everything they could want, whether in soul or body. His charity was not confined within the limits of his hospitals. He secretly provided food for indigent widows, and girls whose virtue was exposed to danger. Nothing could exceed the zeal wherewith he laboured to reclaim such as had fallen into sins of impurity. On occasion of an immense fire breaking out in the royal Hospital of Granada, John fearlessly threw himself into the midst of the flames.

liora se excitatum sensit, ut jam ab ipso sanctioris vitæ rudimento consummatum aliquid, perfectumque visus sit attigisse. Bonis omnibus in pauperes carceribus inclusos erogatis, admirabilis pœnitentiæ, suique ipsius contemptus cuncto populo spectaculum factus a plerisque ceu demens graviter afflictus, in carcerem amentibus destinatum conjicitur. At Joannes cœlesti charitate magis incensus, gemino atque amplo valetudinario ex piorum eleemosynis in civitate Granatensi exstructo, jactoque novi Ordinis fundamento, Ecclesiam nova prole fœcundavit, Fratrum hospitalitatis, infirmis præclaro animarum corporumque profectu inservientium, et longe lateque per orbem diffusorum.

Pauperibus ægrotis, quos propriis quandoque humeris domum deferebat, nulla re ad animæ corporisque salutem proficua deerat. Effusa quoque extra nosocomium charitate, indigentibus mulieribus viduis, et præcipue virginibus periclitantibus, clam alimenta subministrabat, curamque indefessam adhibebat, ut carnis concupiscentiam a proximis hujusmodi vitio inquinatis exterminaret. Cum autem maximum in regio Granatensi valetudinario excitatum fuisset incendium, Joannes impavidus prosiliit in ignem, huc illuc discurrens, quousque tum infirmos humeris exportatos, tum lectulos e fenestris projectos ab igne vindicavit, ac per dimidiam horam inter flammas jam in immensum succrescentes versatus, exinde divinitus incolumis, universis civibus admirantibus, exivit, in schola charitatis edocens, segniorem in eum fuisse ignem qui foris usserat, quam qui intus accenderat.

Multiplici asperitatum genere, demississima obedientia, extrema paupertate, orandi studio, rerum divinarum contemplatione, ac in beatam Virginem pietate mirifice excelluit, et lacrymarum dono enituit. Denique gravi morbo correptus, omnibus Ecclesiæ sacramentis rite sancteque refectus, viribus licet destitutus, propriis indutus vestibus e lectulo surgens, ac provolutus in genua, manu et corde Christum Dominum e cruce pendentem perstringens: octavo Idus Martii, anno millesimo quingentesimo quinquagesimo, obiit in osculo Domini : quem etiam mortuus tenuit, nec dimisit, et in eadem corporis constitutione sex circiter horas, quousque inde dimotus fuisset, tota civitate inspectante, mirabiliter per-

He went through the several wards, taking the sick upon his shoulders, and throwing the beds through the windows, so that all were saved. He remained half an hour amidst the flames, which raged with wildest fury in every part of the building. He was miraculously preserved from the slightest injury, and came forth to the astonishment of the whole city, teaching the people, who had witnessed what had happened, that, in the disciples of charity, there is a fire within their hearts more active than any which could burn the body.

Among the virtues wherein he wonderfully excelled, may be mentioned his many practices of bodily mortification, profound obedience, extreme poverty, love of prayer, contemplation, and devotion to the Blessed Virgin. He also possessed, in an extraordinary degree, the gift of tears. At length, falling seriously ill, he fervently received the last Sacraments. Though reduced to a state of utter weakness, he dressed himself, rose from his bed, fell on his knees, devoutly took the Crucifix into his hands, pressed it to his heart, and kissing it, died on the eighth of the Ides of March (March 8th), in the year 1550. He remained in this same attitude, with the Crucifix still in his hands, for about six hours after his death. The entire city came to see the holy corpse, which gave forth a heavenly fragrance. The body was then removed, in order that it might be buried. God honoured his servant by many miracles, both before and after his death, and he was canonised by Pope Alexander the Eighth.

mansit, odorem mire fragrantem diffundens. Quem ante et post obitum plurimis miraculis clarum Alexander Octavus, Pontifex Maximus, in Sanctorum numerum retulit.

What a glorious life was thine, O John of God! It was one of charity, and of miracles wrought by charity. Like Vincent of Paul, thou wast poor, and, in thy early life, a shepherd-boy like him; but the charity, which filled thy heart, gave thee a power to do what worldly influence and riches never can. Thy name and memory are dear to the Church; they deserve to be held in benediction by all mankind, for thou didst spend thy life in serving thy fellow-creatures, for God's sake. That motive gave thee a devotedness to the poor, which is an impossibility for those who befriend them from mere natural sympathy. Philanthropy may be generous, and its workings may be admirable for ingenuity and order; but it never can look upon the poor man as a sacred object, because it refuses to see God in him. Pray for the men of this generation, that they may at length desist from perverting charity into a mere mechanism of relief. The poor are the representatives of Christ, for he himself has willed that they be such: and if the world refuse to accept them in this their exalted character,—if it deny their resemblance to our Redeemer,—it may succeed in degrading the poor, but this very degradation will make them enemies of its insulter. Thy predilection, O John of God, was for the sick; have pity, therefore, on our times, which are ambitious to eliminate the supernatural, and exclude God from the world by what is called *secularisation* of society. Pray for us, that we may see how evil a thing it is to have changed the Christian for the worldly spirit. Enkindle holy charity within our hearts, that during these days, when we are striving to draw down the mercy of God upon ourselves, we also may show mercy. May we, as thou didst, imitate the example of our Blessed Redeemer, who gave himself to us who were his enemies, and deigned to adopt us as his Brethren. Protect also the Order thou didst institute, and which has inherited thy spirit; that it may prosper, and spread in every place the sweet odour of that Charity, which is its very name.

March 9.

SAINT FRANCES OF ROME,

widow.

The period intervening between the Purification of our Blessed Lady and Ash-Wednesday (when it occurs at its latest date), gives us thirty-six days; and these offer us a Feast of every order of Saint. The Apostles have given us St. Matthias, and St. Peter's Chair at Antioch; the Martyrs have sent us, from their countless choir, Simeon, Blase, Valentine, Faustinus and Jovita, Perpetua and Felicitas, and the Forty Soldiers of Sebaste, whose Feast is kept to-morrow; the holy Pontiffs have been represented by Andrew Corsini, and Peter Damian, who, together with Thomas of Aquin, is one of the Doctors of the Church; the Confessors have produced Romuald of Camaldoli, John of Matha, John of God, and the angelic prince Casimir; the Virgins have gladdened us with the presence of Agatha, Dorothy, Apollonia, and Scholastica, three wreathed with the red roses of martyrdom, and the fourth with her fair lilies of the *enclosed garden*[1] of her Spouse; and lastly, we have had a Penitent-Saint, Margarite of Cortona. The state of Christian marriage is the only one that has not yet deputed a Saint during this season which is the least rich in Feasts of the whole year. The

---

[1] Cant. iv. 12.

deficiency is supplied to-day, by the admirable Frances of Rome.

Having, for forty years, led a most saintly life in the married state, upon which she entered when but twelve years of age, Frances retired from the world, where she had endured every sort of tribulation. But she had given her heart to her God long before she withdrew to the Cloister. Her whole life had been spent in the exercise of the highest Christian perfection, and she had ever received from our Lord the sublimest spiritual favours. Her amiable disposition had won for her the love and admiration of her husband and children: the rich venerated her as their model, the poor respected her as their devoted benefactress and mother.

God recompensed her angelic virtues, by these two special graces: the almost uninterrupted sight of her Guardian Angel, and the receiving most sublime revelations. But there is one trait of her life, which is particularly striking, and reminds us forcibly of St. Elizabeth of Hungary, and of St. Jane Frances Chantal:—her austere practices of penance. Such an innocent, and yet such a mortified life, is full of instruction for us. How can *we* think of murmuring against the obligation of mortification, when we find a saint like this practising it during her whole life? True, we are not bound to imitate her in the *manner* of her penance; but penance we must do, if we would confidently approach that God, who readily pardons the sinner when he repents, but whose justice requires atonement and satisfaction.

The Church thus describes the life, virtues, and miracles of St. Frances.

Francisca, nobilis matrona romana, ab ineunte ætate, illustria dedit virtutum exempla: etenim pueriles ludos, et illecebras mundi	Frances, a noble lady of Rome, led a most virtuous life, even in her earliest years. She despised all childish amusements, and

worldly pleasures, her only delight being solitude and prayer. When eleven years old, she resolved on consecrating her virginity to God, and seeking admission into a Monastery. But she humbly yielded to the wishes of her parents, and married a young and rich nobleman, by name Lorenzo Ponziani. As far as it was possible, she observed, in the married state, the austerities of the most perfect life to which she had aspired. She carefully shunned theatrical entertainments, banquets, and other such amusements. Her dress was of serge, and extremely plain. Whatever time remained after she had fulfilled her domestic duties was spent in prayer and works of charity. But her zeal was mainly exercised in endeavouring to persuade the ladies of Rome, to shun the world, and vanity in dress. It was with a view to this that she founded, during her husband's life, the House of Oblates of the Congregation of Monte-Oliveto, under the Rule of St. Benedict. She bore her husband's banishment, the loss of all her goods, and the trouble which befel her whole family, not only with heroic patience, but was frequently heard to give thanks, saying with holy Job: "The Lord hath given, and "the Lord hath taken away: "blessed be the name of the "Lord!"

At the death of her husband, she fled to the aforesaid

respuens, solitudine, et oratione magnopere delectabatur. Undecim annos nata, virginitatem suam Deo consecrare, et monasterium ingredi proposuit. Parentum tamen voluntati humiliter obtemperans, Laurentio de Pontianis, juveni æque diviti ac nobili nupsit. In matrimonio arctioris vitæ propositum, quantum licuit, semper retinuit: a spectaculis, conviviis, aliisque hujusmodi oblectamentis abhorrens, lanea ac vulgari veste utens, et quidquid a domesticis curis supererat temporis, orationi, aut proximorum utilitati tribuens, in id vero maxima solicitudine incumbens, ut matronas romanas a pompis sæculi, et ornatis vanitate revocaret. Quapropter domum Oblatarum, sub Regula sancti Benedicti, Congregationis Montis Oliveti, adhuc viro alligata, in Urbe instituit. Viri exilium, bonorum jacturam, ac universæ domus moerorem non modo constantissime toleravit, sed gratias agens cum beato Job, illud frequenter usurpabat: Dominus dedit, Dominus abstulit: sit nomen Domini benedictum.

Viro defuncto, ad prædictam Oblatarum domum convolans, nudis pedibus, fune ad collum alligato, humi prostrata, multis cum lacrymis earum numero adscribi suppliciter postulavit. Voti compos facta, licet esset omnium mater, non alio tamen quam ancillæ, vilissimæque feminæ, et immunditiæ vasculi titulo gloriabatur. Quam vilem sui existimationem, et verbo declaravit, et exemplo. Sæpe enim e suburbana vinea revertens, et lignorum fascem proprio capiti impositum deferens, vel eisdem onustum agens per Urbem asellum, pauperibus subveniebat, in quos etiam largas eleemosynas erogabat, ægrotantesque in xenodochiis visitans, non corporali tantum cibo, sed salutaribus monitis recreabat. Corpus suum vigiliis, jejuniis, cilicio, ferreo cingulo, crebrisque flagellis, in servitutem redigere jugiter satagebat. Cibum illi semel in die, herbæ et legumina: aqua potum præbuit. Hos tamen corporis cruciatus aliquando confessarii mandato, a cujus ore nutuque pendebat, modice temperavit.

Divina mysteria, præsertim vero Christi Domini Passionem, tanto mentis ardore, tantaque lacrymarum vi contemplabatur, ut præ

House of Oblates, and there, barefooted, with a rope tied round her neck, and prostrate on the ground, she humbly, and with many tears, begged admission. Her petition being granted, she, though mother of the whole community, gloried in calling herself every-one's servant, and a worthless woman, and a vessel of dishonour. She evinced the contempt she had for herself by her conduct, as well as by her expressions. Thus, when returning from a vineyard in the suburbs, she would go through the city, sometimes carrying faggots on her head, sometimes driving an ass laden with them. She looked after, and bestowed abundant alms upon the poor. She visited the sick in the hospitals, and consoled them, not only with corporal food, but with spiritual advice. She was untiring in her endeavours to bring her body into subjection, by watchings, fasting, wearing a hair shirt and an iron girdle, and by frequent disciplines. Her food, which she took but once in the day, consisted of herbs and pulse, and her only drink was water. But she would somewhat relent in these corporal austerities, as often as she was requested to do so by her confessor, whom she obeyed with the utmost exactitude.

Her contemplation of the divine mysteries, and especially of the Passion, was made with such intense fervour and abundance of tears, that she

MARCH 9. ST. FRANCES OF ROME. 373

seemed as though she would die with grief. Frequently, too, when she was praying, and above all after Holy Communion, she would remain motionless, with her soul fixed on God, and rapt in heavenly contemplation. The enemy of mankind seeing this, endeavoured to frighten her out of so holy a life, by insults and blows; but she feared him not, invariably baffled his attempts, and, by the assistance of her Angel Guardian, whose visible presence was granted to her, she gained a glorious victory. God favoured her with the gift of healing the sick, as also with that of prophecy, whereby she foretold future events, and could read the secrets of hearts. More than once, when she was intent on prayer, either in the bed of a torrent, or during a storm of rain, she was not touched by the water. On one occasion, when all the bread they had was scarcely enough to provide a meal for three of the sisters, she besought our Lord, and he multiplied the bread; so that after fifteen persons had eaten as much as they needed, there was sufficient left to fill a basket. At another time, when the sisters were gathering wood outside the City walls, in the month of January, she amply quenched their thirst by offering them bunches of fresh grapes, which she plucked from a vine, and which she had miraculously obtained. Her virtues and miracles procured for

doloris magnitudine pene confici videretur. Sæpe etiam cum oraret, maxime sumpto sanctissimæ Eucharistiæ sacramento, spiritu in Deum elevata, ac cœlestium contemplatione rapta, immobilis permanebat. Quapropter humani generis hostis variis eam contumeliis ac verberibus a proposito dimovere conabatur: quem tamen illa imperterrita semper elusit, Angeli præsertim præsidio, cujus familiari consuetudine gloriosum de eo triumphum reportavit. Gratia curationum, et prophetiæ dono enituit, quo et futura prædixit, et cordium secreta penetravit. Non semel aquæ, vel per rivum decurrentes, vel e cœlo labentes, intactam prorsus, cum Deo vacaret, reliquerunt. Modica panis fragmenta, quæ vix tribus sororibus reficiendis fuissent satis, sic ejus precibus Dominus multiplicavit, ut quindecim inde exsaturatis, tantum superfuerit, ut canistrum impleverit: et aliquando, earumdem Sororum extra Urbem mense Januario ligna parantium, sitim recentis uvæ racemis ex vite in arbore pendentibus mirabiliter obtentis, abunde expleverit. Denique meritis, et miraculis clara, migravit ad Dominum, anno ætatis suæ quinquagesimo sexto, quam Paulus Quintus, Pontifex Maximus, in Sanctarum numerum retulit.

her the greatest veneration from all. Our Lord called her to himself in the fifty-sixth year of her age, and she was canonised by Pope Paul the Fifth.

O Frances! sublime model of every virtue! thou wast the glory of Christian Rome, and the ornament of thy sex. How insignificant are the pagan heroines of old compared with thee! Thy fidelity to the duties of thy state, and all thy saintly actions, had God for their one single end and motive. The world looked on thee with amazement, as though heaven had lent one of its Angels to this earth. Humility and penance put such energy into thy soul, that every trial was met and mastered. Thy love for those whom God himself had given thee, thy calm resignation and interior joy under tribulation, thy simple and generous charity, to every neighbour,—all was evidence of God's dwelling within thy soul. Thy seeing and conversing with thy Angel Guardian, and the wonderful revelations granted thee of the secrets of the other world,—how much these favours tell us of thy merits? Nature suspended her laws at thy bidding; she was subservient to thee, as to one that was already face to face with the Sovereign Master, and had the power to command. We admire these privileges and gifts granted thee by our Lord; and now beseech thee to have pity on us, who are so far from being in that path, in which thou didst so perseveringly walk. Pray for us, that we may be Christians, practically and earnestly; that we may cease to love the world and its vanities; that we may courageously take up the yoke of our Lord, and do penance; that we may give up our pride; that we may be patient and firm under temptation. Such was thy influence with our Heavenly Father, that thou hadst but to pray, and a vine produced the richest clusters of fruit, even in the midst of winter.

Our Jesus calls himself the *True Vine;* ask him to give us of the wine of his divine love, which his Cross has so richly prepared for us. When we remember how frequently thou didst ask him to let thee suffer, and accept thy sufferings for poor sinners, we feel encouraged to ask thee to offer thy merits to him for us. Pray, too, for Rome, thy native city, that her people may be staunch to the faith, edifying by holiness of life, and loyal to the Church. May thy powerful intercession bring blessings on the Faithful throughout the world, add to their number, and make them fervent as were our fathers of old.

March 10.

THE FORTY MARTYRS.

We know the mystery of the number *Forty*. This tenth of March brings it before us. Forty new advocates! Forty encouraging us to enter bravely on our career of Penance! On the frozen pool, which was their field of battle, these Martyrs reminded one another that Jesus had fasted for Forty Days, and that they themselves were Forty in number! Let us, in our turn, compare *their* sufferings with the Lenten exercises which the Church imposes upon us; and humble ourselves in seeing our cowardice; or, if we begin with fervour, let us remember, that the grand thing is to be faithful to the end, and bring to the Easter Solemnity the crown of our perseverance. Our Forty Martyrs patiently endured the cruelest tortures; the fear of God, and their deep-rooted conviction that he had an infinite claim to their fidelity, gave them the victory. How many times *we* have sinned, and had not such severe temptations as theirs to palliate our fall? How can we sufficiently bless that Divine mercy, which spared us, instead of abandoning us as he did that poor apostate, who turned coward and was lost! But, on what condition did God spare us? That we should not spare ourselves, but do penance. He put into our hands the rights of his own Justice; Justice, then, must be satisfied, and *we* must exercise it

MARCH 10. THE FORTY MARTYRS. 377

against ourselves. The Lives of the Saints will be of great help to us in this, for they will teach us how we are to look upon sin, how to avoid it, and how strictly we are bound to do penance for it, after having committed it.

The Church in her Liturgy, thus relates to us the martyrdom of the Soldiers of Sebaste.

During the reign of the Emperor Licinius, and under the presidency of Agricolaus, the city of Sebaste, in Armenia, was honoured by being made the scene of the martyrdom of forty soldiers, whose faith in the Lord Jesus Christ, and patience in bearing tortures, were so glorious. After having been frequently confined in a horrid dungeon, shackled with chains, and having had their faces beaten with stones, they were condemned to pass a most bitter winter night in the open air, and on a frozen pool, that they might be frozen to death. When there, they united in this prayer: "Forty have we entered on "the battle; let us, O Lord, "receive Forty Crowns, and "suffer not our number to be "broken. The number is an "honoured one, for thou didst "fast for forty days, and the "divine law was given to the "world after the same number "of days was observed. Elias, "too, sought God by a forty "days' fast, and was permitted "to see him." Thus did they pray.

All the guards, except one, were asleep. He overheard their prayer, and saw them

Licinio Imperatore, et Agricolao præside, ad Sebasten Armeniæ urbem, quadraginta militum fides in Jesum Christum, et fortitudo in cruciatibus perferendis enituit. Qui sæpius in horribilem carcerem detrusi, vinculisque constricti, cum ora ipsorum lapidibus contusa fuissent, hiemis tempore frigidissimo, nudi sub aperto aere supra stagnum rigens pernoctare jussi sunt, ut frigore congelati necarentur. Una autem erat omnium oratio : Quadraginta in stadium ingressi sumus, quadraginta item, Domine, corona donemur ; ne una quidem huic numero desit. Est in honore hic numerus, quem tu quadraginta dierum jejunio decorasti, per quem divina lex ingressa est in orbem terrarum. Elias quadraginta dierum jejunio Deum quærens, ejus visionem consecutus est. Et hæc quidem illorum erat oratio.

Cæteris autem custodibus somno deditis, solus vigilabat janitor, qui et illos orantes, et luce circumfusos, et quosdam e cœlo descendentes Angelos tanquam a Rege missos, qui coronas triginta novem militibus distribuerent, intuens, ita secum loquebatur: Quadraginta hi sunt; quadragesimi corona ubi est? Quæ dum cogitaret, unus ex illo numero, cui animus ad frigus ferendum defecerat, in proximum tepefactum balneum desiliens, sanctos illos summo dolore affecit. Verum Deus illorum preces irritas esse non est passus: nam rei eventum admiratus janitor, mox custodibus e somno excitatis, detractisque sibi vestibus, ac se christianum esse clara voce professus, martyribus se adjunxit. Cum vero præsidis satellites janitorem quoque christianum esse cognovissent, baccilis comminuta omnium eorum crura fregerunt.

encircled with light, and Angels coming down from heaven, like messengers sent by a King, who distributed crowns to thirty-nine of the soldiers. Whereupon, he thus said to himself: "There are "forty men; where is the "fortieth crown?" Whilst thus pondering, one of the number lost his courage; he could bear the cold no longer, and threw himself into a warm bath, which had been put near at hand. His saintly companions were exceedingly grieved at this. But God would not suffer their prayer to be void. The sentinel, astonished at what he had witnessed, went immediately and awoke the guards; then, taking off his garments, he cried out, with a loud voice, that he was a Christian, and associated himself with the Martyrs. No sooner did the governor's guards perceive that the sentinel had also declared himself to be a Christian, than they approached the Martyrs, and, with clubs, broke their legs.

In eo supplicio mortui sunt omnes præter Melithonem, natu minimum. Quem cum præsens mater ejus fractis cruribus adhuc viventem vidisset, sic cohortata est: Fili, paulisper sustine, ecce Christus ad januam stat adjuvans te. Cum vero reliquorum corpora plaustris imponi cerneret, ut in rogum inferrentur, ac filium suum relinqui, quod speraret impia turba,

All died under this torture except Melitho, who was the youngest of the forty. His mother, who was present, seeing that he was still living after his legs were broken, thus encouraged him: "My son, "be patient yet awhile. Lo! "Christ is at the door, helping "thee." But, as soon as she saw the other bodies being placed on carts, that they might be thrown on the pile, and her son left behind (for the impious men hoped, that, if the boy survived, he might be induced to worship the idols,) she lifted him up into her arms, and, summing up all her strength, ran after the waggons, on which the Martyrs' bodies were being carried. Melithon died in his mother's arms, and the holy woman threw his body on the pile, where the other martyrs were, that as he had been so united with them in faith and courage, he might be one with them in burial, and go to heaven in their company. As soon as the bodies were burnt, the pagans threw what remained into a river. The relics miraculously flowed to one and the same place, just as they were when they were taken from the pile. The Christians took them, and respectfully buried them.

puerum, si vixisset, ad idolorum cultum revocari posse; ipso in humeros sublato, sancta mater vehicula martyrum corporibus onusta strenue persequebatur; in cujus amplexu Melithon spiritum Deo reddidit, ejusque corpus in eumdem illum cæterorum martyrum rogum pia mater injecit: ut qui fide et virtute conjunctissimi fuerant, funeris etiam societate copulati, una in cœlum pervenirent. Combustis illis, eorum reliquiæ projectæ in profluentem, cum mirabiliter in unum confluxissent locum, salvæ ct integræ repertæ, honorifico sepulchro conditæ sunt.

That we may the more worthily celebrate the memory of the Forty Martyrs, we borrow a few stanzas from the Hymn in which the Greek Liturgy so enthusiastically sings their praises.

HYMN.

(*Die IX. Martii.*)

The holy Martyrs, generously suffering present evils, and rejoicing in the hope of reward, said to each other: "It is not our raiment, but "the old man that we have put "off. The winter is cold; but "Paradise is sweet. The ice is "a torture; but the repose is "pleasant. Fellow-soldiers! "let us not retreat. Let us

Generose præsentia sufferentes, in præmiis quæ sperabant gaudentes, sancti Martyres ad invicem dicebant: Non vestimentum exuimus, sed veterem hominem deponimus; rigida est hiems, sed dulcis Paradisus; molesta est glacies, sed jucunda requies. Non ergo recedamus, o commilitones; paulum sustineamus, ut victoriæ coronas obtineamus a Christo Domino et Salvatore animarum nostrarum.

Fortissima mente martyrium sustinentes, athletæ admirandi, per ignem et aquam transivistis, et inde ad salutis latitudinem pervenistis, in hæreditatem accipientes regnum cœlorum, in quo divinas pro nobis preces facite, sapientes quadraginta Martyres.

Attonitus stetit quadraginta Martyrum custos coronas aspiciens, et amore hujus vitæ contempto, desiderio gloriæ tuæ, Domine, quæ illi apparuerat, sublevatus est, et cum Martyribus cecinit: Benedictus es, Deus patrum nostrorum.

Vitæ amator miles ad lavacrum currens pestiferum mortuus est; Christi autem amicus egregius raptor coronarum quæ apparuerant, velut in lavacro immortalitatis, cum Martyribus canebat: Benedictus es, Deus patrum nostrorum.

Virili prædita pectore, mater Deo amica, super humeros tollens quem genuerat fructum pietatis, Martyrem cum Martyribus victimam adducit, patris Abrahæ imitatrix. O fili, ad perenniter manentem vitam velocius currens carpe viam, Christi amica mater ad puerum clamabat. Non fero te secundum ad Deum

"suffer for awhile, that we
"may obtain our crowns of
"victory from Christ our Lord,
"the Saviour of our souls."

O admirable combatants! you suffered martyrdom with most brave hearts. You passed through fire and water, and thence you came to the spacious land of salvation, receiving the kingdom of heaven as your inheritance. There, O prudent Forty Martyrs, offer up your holy prayers for us.

The gaoler of the Forty Martyrs stood in astonishment as he beheld the Crowns. Despising this present life, and ambitious to enjoy thy glory, O Lord, which had been shown him in vision, he joined the Martyrs in this hymn: "Blessed art thou, O God of "our fathers!"

The soldier that loved this life, ran to the cursed bath, and there he met with death: but the friend of Christ, he that nobly seized the crown which was offered him, as it were laved in immortality, sang with the Martyrs: "Blessed art thou, the God "of our fathers!"

The mother, whose manly spirit made her dear to God, taking on her shoulders the beloved fruit of her womb, brings him to the Martyrs that he might be a Martyred victim with them. Thus does she imitate our father Abraham. This mother, dear to Christ, cried out to her child: "O my son; quickly run the "path that leads to life eter-

"nal. I cannot brook thy be-
"ing second to any in coming
"to the God, who rewards
"us."

Come, Brethren, let us sing the praises of the troop of Martyrs, who were burnt with frost, and whose ardent zeal set fire to the frosty cold of error. Most heroic army—most holy legion, that fought with shields close knit together—unbroken and unconquered troop—defenders and guardians of the faith—the Forty Martyrs—the sacred choir—the legates of the Church:—their powerful prayers to Christ draw down upon our souls his peace and rich mercy.

præmia largientem pervenire.

Venite, fratres, Martyrum laudibus celebremus phalangem, frigore incensam, et erroris frigus ardenti zelo incendentem; generosissimum exercitum, sacratissimum agmen, concertis pugnans clypeis, infractum et invictum, defensores fidei et custodes, Martyres quadraginta, divinam choream legatos Ecclesiæ, potenter Christum deprecantes ut pacem animis nostris concedat et magnam misericordiam.

Valiant Soldiers of Christ! who meet us, with your mysterious number, at this commencement of our Forty Days' Fast,—receive the homage of our devotion. Your memory is venerated throughout the whole Church, and your glory is great in heaven. Though engaged in the service of an earthly Prince, you were the Soldiers of the Eternal King: to Him were you faithful, and from Him did you receive your crown of eternal glory. We, also, are his Soldiers; we are fighting for the kingdom of heaven. Our enemies are many and powerful; but, like you, we can conquer them, if, like you, we use the arms which God has put in our hands. Faith in God's word, hope in his assistance, humility, and prudence,—with these, we are sure of victory. Pray for us, O Holy Martyrs, that we may keep from all compromise with our enemies; for our defeat is certain, if we try to serve two masters. During these Forty Days, we must put our arms in order, repair our lost strength, and renew our engagements; come to our assistance, and get us a share in your brave spirit. A crown is also prepared for us: it is to be won on easier terms than yours, and yet we shall lose it, unless we keep up within us an esteem for our vocation. How many times, in our past lives, have we not forfeited that glorious crown? But God, in his mercy, has offered it to us again, and we are resolved on winning it. Oh! for the glory of our common Lord and Master, make intercession for us.

March 12.

SAINT GREGORY THE GREAT,

POPE AND DOCTOR OF THE CHURCH.

AMONG all the Pastors, whom our Lord Jesus Christ has placed, as his Vicegerents, over the universal Church, there is not one whose merits and renown have surpassed those of the holy Pope, whose feast we keep to-day. His name is *Gregory,* which signifies *watchfulness;* his surname is *the Great,* and he was in possession of that title when God sent the Seventh Gregory, the glorious Hildebrand, to govern his Church.

In recounting the glories of this illustrious Pontiff, it is but natural we should begin with his zeal for the Services of the Church. The Roman Liturgy, which owes to him some of its finest Hymns, may be considered as his work, at least in this sense, that it was he who collected together and classified the prayers and rites drawn up by his predecessors, and reduced them to the form, in which we now have them. He collected also the ancient chants of the Church, and arranged them in accordance with the rules and requirements of the Divine Service. Hence it is, that our sacred music is called the *Gregorian Chant,* which gives such solemnity to the Liturgy, and inspires the soul with respect and devotion during the celebration of the great Mysteries of our Faith.

He is, then, the Apostle of the Liturgy, and this alone would have immortalised his name; but we must look for far greater things from such a Pontiff as Gregory. His name was added to the three, who had hitherto been honoured as the great Doctors of the Latin Church. These three were Ambrose, Augustine, and Jerome; who else could be the fourth but Gregory? The Church found in his Writings such evidence of his having been guided by the Holy Ghost,—such a knowledge of the Sacred Scriptures, such a clear appreciation of the Mysteries of Faith, and such unction and authority in his teachings, that she gladly welcomed him as a new guide for her children.

Such was the respect, wherewith everything he wrote was treated, that his very Letters were preserved as so many precious treasures. This immense *Correspondence* shows us, that there was not a country, scarcely even a city, of the Christian world, on which the Pontiff had not his watchful eye steadily fixed; that there was not a question, however local or personal, which, if it interested religion, did not excite his zeal and arbitration, as the Bishop of the universal Church. If certain writers of modern times had but taken the pains to glance at these Letters, written by a Pope of the 6th century, they would never have asserted, as they have done, that the prerogatives of the Roman Pontiff are based on documents, fabricated, as they say, two hundred years after the death of Gregory.

Throned on the Apostolic See, our Saint proved himself to be a rightful heir of the Apostles, not only as the representative and depository of their authority, but as a fellow-sharer in their mission of calling nations to the true faith. To whom does England owe her having been, for so many ages, *the Island of Saints?* To Gregory, who, touched with compassion for those *Angli*,—of whom, as he playfully said, he would fain make *Angeli*,—sent to their island the Monk Augustine, with forty companions, all of them, as was Gregory himself, children of St. Benedict. The faith had been sown in this land as early as the second century, but it had been trodden down by the invasion of an infidel race. This time the seed fructified, and so rapidly, that Gregory lived to see a plentiful harvest. It is beautiful to hear the aged Pontiff speaking with enthusiasm about the results of his English mission. He thus speaks in the twenty-seventh Book of his *Morals:* " Lo ! the language of " Britain, which could once mutter naught save bar- " barous sounds, has long since begun to sing, in the " divine praises, the Hebrew *Alleluia!* Lo ! that " swelling sea is now calm, and Saints walk on its " waves. The tide of barbarians, which the sword of " earthly princes could not keep back, is now hemmed " in at the simple bidding of God's Priests."[1]

During the fourteen years that this holy Pope held the place of Peter, he was the object of the admiration of the Christian world, both in the East and West. His profound learning, his talent for administration, his position,—all tended to make him beloved and respected. But who could describe the virtues of his great soul ?—that contempt for the world and its riches, which led him to seek obscurity in the cloister ; that humility, which made him flee the honours of the Papacy, and hide himself in a cave, where, at length, he was miraculously discovered, and God himself put into his hands the Keys of Heaven, which he was evidently worthy to hold, because he feared the responsibility ; that zeal for the whole flock, of which he considered himself not the master, but the servant, so much so indeed that he assumed the title, which the Popes have ever since retained, of *Servant of the Servants of God;*

---

[1] *Moral in Job.* Lib. xxvii. Cap. xi.

that charity which took care of the poor throughout the whole world; that ceaseless solicitude, which provided for every calamity, whether public or private; that unruffled sweetness of manner, which he showed to all around him, in spite of the bodily sufferings which never left him during the whole period of his laborious pontificate; that firmness in defending the deposit of the Faith, and crushing error wheresoever it showed itself; in a word, that vigilance with regard to discipline, which made itself felt for long ages after in the whole Church? All these services, and glorious examples of virtue have endeared our Saint to the whole world, and will make his name be blessed by all future generations, even to the end of time.

Let us now read the abridged Life of our Saint, as given us in the Liturgy.

Gregorius magnus, Romanus, Gordiani Senatoris filius, adolescens philosophiæ operam dedit, et prætorio officio functus, patre mortuo, sex monasteria in Sicilia ædificavit; Romæ septimum sancti Andreæ nomine in suis ædibus, prope Basilicam sanctorum Joannis et Pauli ad clivum Scauri: ubi Hilarione ac Maximiano magistris monachi vitam professus, postea Abbas fuit. Mox Diaconus Cardinalis creatus, Constantinopolim a Pelagio Pontifice ad Tiberium Constantinum Imperatorem legatus mittitur, apud quem memorabile etiam illud effecit, quod Eutychium Patriarcham, qui scripserat contra veram ac tractabilem corporum resurrectio-

Gregory the Great, a Roman by birth, was son of the Senator Gordian. He applied early to the study of philosophy, and was intrusted with the office of Pretor. After his father's death he built six monasteries in Sicily, and a seventh, under the title of Saint Andrew, in his own house in Rome, near the Basilica of Saints John and Paul, on the hill Scaurus. In this last named monastery, he embraced the monastic life, under the guidance of Hilarion and Maximian, and was, later on, elected Abbot. Shortly afterwards, he was created Cardinal-Deacon, and was by Pope Pelagius sent to Constantinople, as Legate, to confer with the Emperor Constantine. Whilst there he achieved that celebrated victory over the

Patriarch Eutychius, who had written against the resurrection of the flesh, maintaining that it would not be a real one. Gregory so convinced him of his error, that the Emperor threw his book into the fire. Eutychius himself fell ill not long after, and when he perceived his last hour had come, he took between his fingers the skin of his hand, and said before the many who were there: "I "believe that we shall all rise "in this flesh."

On his return to Rome, he was chosen Pope, by unanimous consent, for Pelagius had been carried off by the plague. He refused, as long as it was possible, the honour thus offered him. He disguised himself, and hid himself in a cave; but he was discovered by a pillar of fire shining over the place, and was consecrated at Saint Peter's. As Pontiff, he was an example to his successors by his learning and holiness of life. He every day admitted pilgrims to his table, among whom he received, on one occasion, an Angel, and, on another, the Lord of Angels, who wore the garb of a pilgrim. He charitably provided for the poor, both in and out of Rome, and kept a list of them. He re-established the Catholic faith in several places where it had fallen into decay. Thus, he put down the Donatists in Africa, and the Arians in Spain; and drove the Agnoites out of Alexandria.

nem, ita convicit, ut ejus librum imperator in ignem injiceret. Quare Eutychius paulo post cum in morbum incidisset, instante morte, pellem manus suæ tenebat multis præsentibus, dicens: Confiteor quia omnes in hac carne resurgemus.

Romam rediens, Pelagio pestilentia sublato, summo omnium consensu Pontifex eligitur: quem honorem ne acciperet, quamdiu potuit, recusavit. Nam alieno vestitu in spelunca delituit: ubi deprehensus indicio igneæ columnæ, ad Sanctum Petrum consecratur. In pontificatu multa successoribus doctrinæ ac sanctitatis exempla reliquit. Peregrinos quotidie ad mensam adhibebat: in quibus et Angelum, et Dominum Angelorum peregrini facie accepit. Pauperes et urbano et externos, quorum numerum descriptum habebat, benigne sustentabat. Catholicam fidem multis locis labefactatam restituit. Nam Donatistas in Africa, Arianos in Hispania repressit: Agnoitas Alexandria ejecit. Pallium Syagrio Augustodunensi Episcopo dare noluit, nisi Neophytos hæreticos expelleret ex Gallia. Gothos hæresim Arianam relinquere coegit. Missis in Britanniam doctis et sanctis viris Augustino et aliis monachis, insulam ad Jesu Christi fidem convertit, vere a Beda presbytero Angliæ vocatus Apostolus. Joannis patriarchæ Constantinopolitani audaciam fregit, qui sibi universalis Ecclesiæ Episcopi nomen arrogabat. Mauritium imperatorem, eos qui milites fuissent, monachos fieri prohibentem, a sententia deterruit.

Ecclesiam ornavit sanctissimis institutis et legibus. Apud Sanctum Petrum coacta Synodo, multa constituit. In iis, ut in Missa Kyrie eleison novies repeteretur; ut extra id tempus, quod continetur Septuagesima et Pascha, Alleluia diceretur: ut adderetur in Canone: Diesque nostros in tua pace disponsas. Litainas, Stationes, et Ecclesiasticum officium auxit. Quatuor Conciliis, Nicæno, Constantinopolitano, Ephesino et Chalcedonensi, tamquam quatuor Evangeliis honorem haberi voluit. Episcopis Siciliæ, qui ex antiqua Ecclesiarum consuetudine Romam singulis trienniis conveniebant, quinto quoque anno semel venire indulsit.

He refused to give the pallium to Syagrius, Bishop of Autun, until he should have expelled the Neophyte heretics from Gaul. He induced the Goths to abandon the Arian heresy. He sent Augustine and other Monks into Britain, and, by these learned and saintly men, converted that island to the faith of Christ Jesus; so that Bede truly calls him the "Apostle of England." He checked the haughty pretensions of John, the Patriarch of Constantinople, who had arrogated to himself the title of "Bishop " of the Universal Church." He obliged the Emperor Mauritius to revoke the decree, whereby he had forbidden any soldier to become a monk.

He enriched the Church with many most holy practices and laws. In a Council held at St. Peter's, he passed several decrees. Among these, the following may be mentioned: That in the Mass, the *Kyrie eleison* should be said nine times; that the *Alleluia* should always be said, except during the interval between Septuagesima and Easter. That these words should be inserted in the Canon: *Diesque nostros in tua pace disponsas (And mayst thou dispose our days in thy peace).* He increased the number of Processions (Litanies) and stations, and completed the Office of the Church. He would have the four Councils, of Nicea, Constantinople, Ephesus, and Chalcedon, to be received with the same honour as the four Gospels. He allowed the Bishops of Sicily, who, according to the ancient custom of their Churches, used to visit Rome every three years, to make that visit once every fifth year. He wrote several books; and Peter the Deacon assures us, that he frequently saw the Holy Ghost resting on the head of the Pontiff, whilst he was dictating. It is a matter of wonder, that with his incessant sickness and ill health he could have said, done, written, and decreed, as he did. At length, after performing many miracles, he was called to his reward in heaven, after a pontificate of thirteen years, six months, and ten days; it was on the fourth of the Ides of March (March 12th), which the Greeks also observe as a great Feast, on account of this Pontiff's extraordinary learning and virtue. His body was buried in the Basilica of Saint Peter, near the Secretarium.

Multo libros confecit: quos cum dictaret, testatus est Petrus Diaconus se Spiritum Sanctum columbæ specie in ejus capite sæpe vidisse. Admirabilia sunt quæ dixit, fecit, scripsit, decrevit, præsertim infirma semper et ægra valetudine. Qui denique multis editis miraculis, Pontificatus anno decimo tertio, mense sexto, die decimo, quarto Idus Martii, qui dies festus a Græcis etiam propter insignem hujus Pontificis sapientiam ac sanctitatem, præcipue honore celebratur ad cœlestem beatitudinem evocatus est. Cujus corpus sepultum est in Basilica Sancti Petri, prope Secretarium.

To these admirable Lessons we subjoin a selection of Antiphons and Responsories, which are taken from an Office approved of by the Holy See, for this Feast of so great a Saint.

ANTIPHONS AND RESPONSORIES.[*]

The blessed Gregory, being raised to the Chair of Peter,

Beatus Gregorius in cathedra Petri sublimatus, Vi-

---

[*] We may be permitted to express a hope, that the day is not far distant, when the Proper Offices, approved of by the Holy See, will be adopted in England, for those Saints in which England has a special interest. Proper Hymns, &c., have been composed and approved for St. Augustine of Canterbury and St. Anselm.

[TRANSLATOR.]

gilantis nomen factis implevit.

Pastor eximius pastoralis vitæ specimen tradidit et regulam.

Dum paginæ sacræ mysteria panderet, columba nive candidior apparuit.

Gregorius, monachorum speculum, pater Urbis, orbis deliciæ.

Gregorius, respiciens Anglorum juvenes, ait: Angelicam habent faciem; et tales Angelorum in cœlis decet esse consortes.

fulfilled, by his actions, the meaning of his name,—*the Watchman*.

This glorious Pastor was the model, and wrote the rule, of the Pastoral Life.

Whilst he was interpreting the Mysteries of the Sacred Volume, there was seen upon him a dove whiter than snow.

Gregory was the mirror of monks, the father of the City, and the favourite of mankind.

Gregory looks upon some youths from Anglia, and says: They have the faces of Angels, and such children must needs be companions of Angels in heaven.

℟. Gregorius, ab annis adolescentiæ suæ, Deo cœpit devotus existere.* Et ad supernæ vitæ patriam totis desideriis anhelavit.

℣. Pauperibus opes distribuens, Christum pro nobis egenum, egenus ipse sequutus est.

* Et ad supernæ vitæ patriam totis desideriis anhelavit.

℟. From his early youth, Gregory was devout in God's service,* And with all his heart sighed after the land of heavenly life.

℣. He distributed his wealth to the poor, and became poor himself, after the example of Christ, who made himself poor for us.

* And with all his heart sighed after the land of heavenly life.

℟. Sex in Sicilia monasteria constituens, fratres illic Christo servituros aggregavit; septimum vero intra Romanæ urbis muros instituit:* In quo et ipse mi-

℟. Six Monasteries did he found in Sicily, and put in them communities of Brethren, who should serve Christ; a seventh also he founded within the walls of Rome's

city,* Wherein he, too, enrolled himself in the heavenly warfare.

℣. He despised the world with its flowers, and sought out a place of solitude most dear to his soul.

* Wherein he, too, enrolled himself in the heavenly warfare.

℟. When they were in search of him to set him on the throne of the Papal dignity, he fled to the woods and caves and hid himself ;* But a bright pillar of light was seen to shine upon him, in a straight line from the high heavens.

℣. The people, in their eager desire to have so excellent a Pastor, besieged heaven with their fastings and prayers.

* But a bright pillar was seen to shine upon him, in a straight line from the highest heavens.

℟. Lo! now I am tossed by the waves of the great sea, and am buffeted by the storms of pastoral care :* And when I remember my former life, I sigh like one that looks back on the shore he has left behind.

℣. I am carried to and fro on huge waves, which scarcely permit me to see the port I sailed from.

* And when I remember my former life, I sigh like one that

litiam cœlestem agressus est.

℣. Mundum cum flore despiciens, dilectæ solitudinis locum quæsivit.

* In quo et ipse militiam cœlestem aggressus est.

℟. Ad summi Pontificatus apicem quæsitus, quum ad sylvarum et cavernarum latebras confugisset,* Visa est columna lucis a summo cœli usque ad eum linea recta refulgens.

℣. Tam eximium pastorem sitiens populus, jejuniis et orationibus ad cœlum insistebat.

* Visa est columna lucis a summo cœli usque ad eum linea recta refulgens.

℟. Ecce nunc magni maris fluctibus quatior, pastoralis curæ procellis illisus :* Et quum priorem vitam recolo, quasi post tergum reductis oculis viso littore suspiro.

℣. Immensis fluctibus turbatus feror, vix jam portum valeo videre quem reliqui.

* Et quum priorem vitam recolo, quasi post tergum

reductis oculis, viso littore suspiro.

looks back on the shore he has left behind.

℟. E fonte Scripturarum moralia et mystica proferens, fluenta Evangelii populos derivavit :* Et defunctus adhuc loquitur.

℣. Velut aquila perlustrans mundum amplitudine charitatis majoribus et minimis providet.

* Et defunctus adhuc loquitur.

℟. He drew moral and mystical interpretations from the Scripture fountain, and made the streams of the Gospel flow upon the people :* And being dead, he yet speaketh.

℣. Like an eagle flying from one end of the world to the other, he provided for all, both little and great, by his large-hearted charity.

* And being dead, he yet speaketh.

℟. Cernens Gregorius Anglorum adolescentulos, dolebat tam lucidi vultus homines a tenebrarum principe possideri:* Tantamque frontis speciem, mentem ab internis gaudiis vacuam gestare.

℣. Ex intimo corde longa trahens suspiria, lugebat imaginem Dei ab antiquo serpente deturpatam.

* Tantamque frontis speciem, mentem ab internis gaudiis vacuam gestare.

℟. As he gazed on the boys of Anglia, it grieved him to think that such bright faced youths should be in the power of the prince of darkness : *And that they who had such comely faces, should have souls devoid of interior joy.

℣. Deeply did he sigh, and, from his inmost soul, grieve that the image of God should be disfigured by the old serpent.

* And that they, who had such comely faces, should have souls devoid of interior joy.

℟. Quum Joannes episcopus arroganter primæ Sedis jura dissolvere tentaret, surrexit Gregorius fortis et

℟. When John, the Bishop, arrogantly strove to interfere with the rights of the first See, bravely and meekly did

MARCH 12. ST. GREGORY THE GREAT.

Gregory rise up,* Radiant with Apostolic authority, and humble exceedingly.

℣. Unflinchingly did he defend the Keys of Peter, and guard from insult the principal Chair.

* Radiant with Apostolic authority, and humble exceedingly.

mansuetus : * Apostolica fulgens auctoritate, humilitate præclarus.

℣. Petri claves invictus asseruit, et cathedram principalem illæsam custodivit.

* Apostolica fulgens auctoritate, humilitate præclarus.

℟. Gregory, a Pontiff great in merit and name, restored the ancient melodies used in the Divine praise, * And united the songs of the Church Militant with those of the Spouse Triumphant.

℣. His mystic pen transcribed the book of the Sacraments, and handed down to posterity the institutions of the ancient Fathers.

* And united the songs of the Church Militant with those of the Spouse Triumphant.

℟. Gregorius, præsul meritis et nomine dignus, antiquas divinæ laudis modulationes renovans, * Militantis Ecclesiæ vocem triumphantis Sponsæ concentibus sociavit.

℣. Sacramentorum codicem mystico calamo rescribens, veterum Patrum instituta posteris transmisit.

* Militantis Ecclesiæ vocem triumphantis Sponsæ concentibus sociavit.

℟. He regulated the Stations to be made at the Basilicas and Cemeteries of the Martyrs : * And the army of Christ went in procession, with Gregory at their head.

℣. He was the leader of the heavenly warfare, and gave to all their spiritual armour.

* And the army of Christ went in procession, with Gregory at their head.

℟. Stationes per Basilicas et Martyrum Cœmeteria ordinavit : * Et sequebatur exercitus Domini Gregorium præeuntem.

℣. Ductor cœlestis militiæ arma spiritualia proferebat.

* Et sequebatur exercitus Domini Gregorium præeuntem.

St. Peter Damian, whose Feast we kept a few days back, composed the following Hymn in honour of our Apostle.

HYMN.

Anglorum jam Apostolus,
Nunc Angelorum socius,
Ut tunc, Gregori, gentibus
Succurre jam credentibus.

Tu largas opum copias,
Omnemque mundi gloriam
Spernis, ut inops inopem
Jesum sequaris principem.

Videtur egens naufragus,
Dum stipem petit Angelus;
Tu munus jam post geminum,
Præbes et vas argenteum.

Ex hoc te Christus tempore
Suæ præfert Ecclesiæ:
Sic Petri gradum percipis,
Cujus et normam sequeris.

O Pontifex egregie,
Lux et decus Ecclesiæ,
Non sinas in periculis,
Quos tot mandatis instruis.

Mella cor obdulcantia
Tua distillant labia,
Fragrantum vim aromatum
Tuum vincit eloquium.

Scripturæ sacræ mystica
Mire solvis ænigmata,
Theorica mysteria
Te docet ipsa Veritas.

Tu nactus apostolicam
Vicem simul et gloriam,
Nos solve culpæ nexibus,
Redde polorum sedibus.

O Gregory, that once wast the Apostle of the Angli, and now art a companion of the Angels! protect now, as of old, the nations that believe in Christ.

Thou spurnest wealth and riches, and all the glory of the world, that so thou, being poor, mayst follow the Lord Jesus, who was poor.

An Angel presents himself to thee, in the garb of one that was shipwrecked, and asks an alms; thou first makest him a double gift, and then thou givest him a silver vase.

After this, Christ puts thee over his Church, for thou didst imitate the virtues, and now thou hast the honours, of Peter.

O excellent Pontiff! Light and ornament of the Church! Thou hast so richly instructed us,—assist us in our dangers.

From thy lips there flows honey that brings sweetness to the heart. Thy words are more fragrant than the richest perfume.

Admirably dost thou solve the obscure figures of Sacred Writ. The divine mysteries are taught thee by Him that is the very Truth.

O thou that hast the office and the glory of the Apostles, pray for us, that we may be loosened from the bonds of sin, and obtain the thrones prepared for us above.

To the unbegotten Father, and to his Only Begotten Son, and to the Spirit of them both, be praise and highest kingship. Amen.	Sit Patri laus ingenito, Sit decus Unigenito, Sit utriusque parili Majestas summa Flamini. Amen.

Father of the Christian people! Vicar of the charity, as well as of the authority, of Christ! O Gregory, *vigilant* Pastor! the Church, which thou hast so faithfully loved and served, turns to thee with confidence. Thou canst not forget the flock, which keeps up such an affectionate remembrance of thee; hear the prayer she offers thee on this thy solemnity. Protect and guide the Pontiff, who now holds the place of Peter, as thou didst; enlighten and encourage him in the difficulties wherewith he is beset. Bless the Hierarchy of the Pastors, which has received from thee such magnificent teachings and such admirable examples. Assist it to maintain inviolate the sacred trust of Faith; bless the efforts it is now making for the restoration of ecclesiastical Discipline, without which, all is disorder and confusion. God chose thee as the regulator of the Divine Service, the Holy Liturgy; foster, by thy blessing, the zeal which is now rising up among us for those holy traditions of Prayer, which have been so neglected; teach us the long-forgotten secret, that the best way of praying, is to use the Prayers of the Church. Unite all Churches in obedience to the Apostolic See, which is the ground and pillar of Faith, and the fountain of Spiritual Authority.

The terrible schism, which has separated the East from Catholic unity, began to show itself during thy Pontificate. Byzantium has now consummated her crime, which has degraded and enslaved her; and yet she seems blind to the real cause of all her miseries. In these latter days she has been abetted in her sin and her haughtiness;—Russia, the despotic power that has her hands steeped in the blood of

Martyrs, has made common cause with her in rebellion against the Church, and we have heard the proud threat, that she will rest not till she have put "one foot on the Tomb of our Lord in Jerusalem, "and the other on the Confession of Saint Peter in "Rome," so that mankind shall make a god of the Czar!—Rouse up the zeal of the Christian world, O Gregory! and inflame them with holy resistance to this false christ. May his fall become a lasting monument of the vengeance of our true Christ, Jesus our Saviour, and a fulfilment of the promise he made to his Church: That the Gates of hell shall never prevail against the Rock. We know, O holy Pontiff, that this promise is to be fulfilled; but we dare to pray, that we may see its accomplishment verified even in *our* times.

But there is one country, which was most dear to thee,—our own native land. O Apostle of England! look down with affection on this island, which has now rebelled from Rome, and has become the resort of countless false religions. But now, after three centuries of apostacy from the true Faith, the hand of God's mercy is pressing her to conversion. She is thine own child in Christ Jesus: wilt thou not aid her return to Him? Wilt thou not guide her, by thy prayers, to come forth out of the darkness, which still so thickly clouds her, and follow the Light which heaven holds out to her? Oh! if England were once more Catholic, who can tell the good she would do? for what country is there that can do grander things for the Propagation of the Faith? Pray for her, then; she may regain her glorious title of *Isle of Saints*, for she has thee for her Apostle!

These are the days of salvation; Lent is upon us;—pray for the Faithful, who are now entering on their career of penance. Obtain for them compunction of heart, love of Prayer, and an appreciation of the Liturgy and its Mysteries. The solemn and devout Homilies, which thou didst address, at this Season, to the people of Rome, are still read to us; may they sink into our hearts, and fill them with fear of God's Justice, and hope in his Mercy, for his Justice and Mercy change not to suit the time. We are weak and timid, and this makes us count as harsh the laws of the Church, which oblige us to fasting and abstinence; get us brave hearts, brave with the spirit of mortification. Thy holy Life is an example to us, and thy Writings are our instruction; what we still want, is to be made true Penitents, and this thy Intercession must do for us: that so, we may return, with the joy of a purified conscience, to the divine *Alleluia*, which thou hast taught us to sing on earth, and which we hope to chant together with thee, in Heaven.

OUR work of preparation is over: we are ready to obey our Mother's call to Lent. During the three past weeks, we have studied the Fall of our First Parents, and the miseries it brought upon man; the necessity of a Saviour; the Justice of God, against which the human race dared to rebel; the terrible chastisement of the Deluge, wherewith that revolt was punished; and finally, the Covenant made by God, through Abraham, with those who are faithful to him, and shun the maxims of a perverse and guilty world.

Now we are to see the accomplishment of the great Mysteries, whereby the wounds of our Fall were healed, the Divine Justice was disarmed, and God's grace was poured out upon us, and delivered us from the yoke of Satan and the World.

The Man-God, whose sweet presence has been less sensible during this Septuagesima Season, is now about to show himself to us again, but, this time it is on his way to Calvary, where he is to be immolated for our Redemption. The dolorous Passion, which our sins have imposed upon him, is about to be brought before us: the greatest of Anniversaries will soon be upon us.

Let us be all attention to the Mysteries: let us be

fervent in the great work of our own purification. Let us walk on courageously in the path of Penance, so that each day the burden of our sins may be lightened, and, after we have partaken, by heartfelt compassion, of the cup of our Redeemer's Passion, our lips will be once more permitted to sing the songs of joy, and our hearts will thrill at Easter with the loud burst of the Church's *Alleluia!*

THE
SEVEN PENITENTIAL PSALMS.

I.

DAVID, struck down by sickness, asks pardon of God, and beseeches him to heal the wounds of his soul.

PSALM 6.

O Lord, rebuke me not in thy indignation, nor chastise me in thy wrath.

Have mercy on me, O Lord, for I am weak; heal me, O Lord, for my bones are troubled.

And my soul is troubled exceedingly: but thou, O Lord, how long?

Turn to me, O Lord, and deliver my soul: O save me, for thy mercy's sake.

For there is no one in death that is mindful of thee: and who shall confess to thee in hell?

I have laboured in my groanings, every night I will wash my bed: I will water my couch with my tears.

My eye is troubled through indignation: I have grown old among all mine enemies.

Domine, ne in furore tuo arguas me: * neque in ira tua corripias me.

Miserere mei, Domine, quoniam infirmus sum: * sana me Domine, quoniam conturbata sunt ossa mea.

Et anima mea turbata est valde: * sed tu Domine usquequo?

Convertere, Domine, et eripe animam meam: * salvum me fac propter misericordiam tuam.

Quoniam non est in morte qui memor sit tui: * in inferno autem quis confitebitur tibi?

Laboravi in gemitu meo, lavabo per singulas noctes lectum meum: * lacrymis meis stratum meum rigabo.

Turbatus est a furore oculus meus: * inveteravi inter omnes inimicos meos.

Discedite a me, omnes qui operamini iniquitatem : * quoniam exaudivit Dominus vocem fletus mei.

Exaudivit Dominus deprecationem meam : * Dominus orationem meam suscepit.

Erubescant et conturbentur vehementer omnes inimici mei : * convertantur et erubescant valde velociter.

Depart from me, all ye workers of iniquity : for the Lord hath heard the voice of my weeping.

The Lord hath heard my supplication : the Lord hath received my prayer.

Let all mine enemies be ashamed and be very much troubled : let them be turned back, and be ashamed very speedily.

II.

David experiences the happiness felt by a soul whose sins have been forgiven her by God; he expresses his feelings, by comparing himself to a sick man, who was at the point of death, and is restored to health.

PSALM 31.

Beati, quorum remissæ sunt iniquitates : * et quorum tecta sunt peccata.

Beatus vir, cui non imputavit Dominus peccatum : * nec est in spiritu ejus dolus.

Quoniam tacui, inveteraverunt ossa mea : * dum clamarem tota die.

Quoniam die ac nocte gravata est super me manus tua : * conversus sum in ærumna mea, dum configitur spina.

Delictum meum cognitum tibi feci : * et injustitiam meam non abscondi.

Dixi : Confitebor adversum me injustitiam meam

Blessed are they whose iniquities are forgiven : and whose sins are covered.

Blessed is the man, to whom the Lord hath not imputed sin : and in whose spirit there is no guile.

Because I was silent, my bones grew old : whilst I cried out all the day long.

For day and night thy hand was heavy upon me : I am turned in my anguish, whilst the thorn is fastened.

I have acknowledged my sin to thee : and my injustice I have not concealed.

I said, I will confess against myself my injustice to the

Lord: and thou hast forgiven the wickedness of my sin.	Domino : * et tu remisisti impietatem peccati mei.
For this shall every one that is holy pray to thee, in a seasonable time.	Pro hac orabit ad te omnis sanctus : * in tempore opportuno.
And yet, in a flood of many waters they shall not come nigh unto him.	Veruntamen in diluvio aquarum multarum : * ad eum non approximabunt.
Thou art my refuge from the trouble which hath encompassed me : my joy! deliver me from them that surround me.	Tu es refugium meum a tribulatione, quæ circumdedit me : * exsultatio mea, erue me a circumdantibus me.
Thou hast said to me: "I "will give thee understanding, "and I will instruct thee in "this way in which thou shalt "go : I will fix mine eyes "upon thee."	Intellectum tibi dabo, et instruam te in via hac qua gradieris : * firmabo super te oculos meos.
"Do not become like the "horse and the mule, who "have no understanding.	Nolite fieri sicut equus et mulus : * quibus non est intellectus.
"With bit and bridle bind "fast their jaws, who come "not near unto thee."	In camo et fræno maxillas eorum constringe : * qui non approximant ad te.
Many are the scourges of the sinner : but mercy shall encompass him that hopeth in the Lord.	Multa flagella peccatoris : * sperantem autem in Domino misericordia circumdabit.
Be glad in the Lord, and rejoice ye just : and glory, all ye right of heart.	Lætamini in Domino, et exsultate justi : * et gloriamini omnes recti corde.

III.

The Royal Prophet feels the consequences left in him by his past sins, and he begs God to have pity on him.

PSALM 37.

Rebuke me not, O Lord, in thy indignation : nor chastise me in thy wrath.	Domine, ne in furore tuo arguas me : * neque in ira tua corripias me.
For thine arrows are	Quoniam sagittæ tuæ in-

fixæ sunt mihi : * et confirmasti super me manum tuam.

Non est sanitas in carne mea a facie iræ tuæ : * non est pax ossibus meis a facie peccatorum meorum.

Quoniam iniquitates meæ supergressæ sunt caput meum : * et sicut onus grave gravatæ sunt super me.

Putruerunt, et corruptæ sunt cicatrices meæ, * a facie insipientiæ meæ.

Miser factus sum, et curvatus sum usque in finem : * tota die contristatus ingrediebar.

Quoniam lumbi mei impleti sunt illusionibus : * et non est sanitas in carne mea.

Afflictus sum et humiliatus sum nimis : * rugiebam a gemitu cordis mei.

Domine, ante te omne desiderium meum : * et gemitus meus a te non est absconditus.

Cor meum conturbatum est, dereliquit me virtus mea : * et lumen oculorum meorum, et ipsum non est mecum.

Amici mei et proximi mei : * adversum me appropinquaverunt et steterunt.

Et qui juxta me erant, de longe steterunt : * et vim faciebant qui quærebant animam meam.

Et qui inquirebant mala mihi, locuti sunt vanitates: * et dolos tota die meditabantur.

Ego autem tanquam sur-

fastened in me : and thy hand hath been strong upon me.

There is no health in my flesh, because of thy wrath : there is no peace for my bones, because of my sins.

For my iniquities are gone over my head : and as a heavy burden, are become heavy upon me.

My sores are putrefied and corrupted, because of my foolishness.

I am become miserable and am bowed down even to the end : I walked sorrowful all the day long.

For my loins are filled with illusions : and there is no health in my flesh.

I am afflicted and humbled exceedingly : I roared with the groaning of my heart.

O Lord, all my desire is before thee : and my groaning is not hidden from thee.

My heart is troubled, my strength hath left me : and the light of mine eyes itself is not with me.

My friends and my neighbours have drawn near, and stood against me.

And they that were near me, stood afar off : and they that sought my soul, used violence.

And they that sought evils to me, spoke vain things : and studied deceits all the day long.

But, I as a deaf man, heard

not : and as a dumb man not opening his mouth.

And I became as a man that heareth not : and that hath no reproofs in his mouth.

For in thee, O Lord, have I hoped : thou wilt hear me, O Lord my God.

For I said : Lest at any time mine enemies rejoice over me : and whilst my feet are moved, they speak great things against me.

For I am ready for scourges : and my sorrow is continually before me.

For I will declare my iniquity : and I will think for my sin.

But mine enemies live, and are stronger than I : and they that hate me wrongfully, are multiplied.

They that render evil for good, have detracted me : because I followed goodness.

Forsake me not, O Lord my God : do not thou depart from me.

Attend unto my help, O Lord, the God of my salvation.

dus non audiebam : * et sicut mutus non aperiens os suum.

Et factus sum sicut homo non audiens : * et non habens in ore suo redargutiones.

Quoniam in te, Domine, speravi : * tu exaudies me, Domine Deus meus.

Quia dixi : Nequando supergaudeant mihi inimici mei : * et dum commoventur pedes mei, super me magna locuti sunt.

Quoniam ego in flagella paratus sum : * et dolor meus in conspectu meo semper.

Quoniam iniquitatem meam annuntiabo : * et cogitabo pro peccato meo.

Inimici autem mei vivunt, et confirmati sunt super me : * et multiplicati sunt qui oderunt me inique.

Qui retribuunt mala pro bonis, detrahebant mihi : * quoniam sequebar bonitatem.

Ne derelinquas me, Domine Deus meus : * ne discesseris a me.

Intende in adjutorium meum : * Domine, Deus salutis meæ.

IV.

The grief and prayer of David, when the Prophet Nathan was sent, by God, to reproach him for the twofold crime he had committed by his sin with Bethsabee, are the subject of this Psalm.

PSALM 50.

Miserere mei Deus : * secundum magnam misericordiam tuam.

Et secundum multitudinem miserationum tuarum: * dele iniquitatem meam.

Amplius lava me ab iniquitate mea : * et a peccato meo munda me.

Quoniam iniquitatem meam ego cognosco : * et peccatum meum contra me est semper.

Tibi soli peccavi, et malum coram te feci : * ut justificeris in sermonibus tuis, et vincas cum judicaris.

Ecce enim in iniquitatibus conceptus sum : * et in peccatis concepit me mater mea.

Ecce enim veritatem dilexisti : * incerta et occulta sapientiæ tuæ manifestasti mihi.

Asperges me hyssopo, et mundabor : * lavabis me, et super nivem dealbabor.

Auditui meo dabis gaudium et lætitiam : * et exsultabunt ossa humiliata.

Averte faciem tuam a peccatis meis : * et omnes iniquitates meas dele.

Cor mundum crea in me Deus : * et spiritum rectum innova in visceribus meis.

Ne projicias me a facie tua : * et Spiritum Sanctum tuum ne auferas a me.

Have mercy on me, O God, according to thy great mercy.

And according to the multitude of thy tender mercies, blot out my iniquity.

Wash me yet more from my iniquity, and cleanse me from my sin.

For I know my iniquity, and my sin is always before me.

To thee only have I sinned, and have done evil before thee: that thou mayst be justified in thy words, and mayst overcome when thou art judged.

For behold! I was conceived in iniquities, and in sins did my mother conceive me.

For behold! thou hast loved truth : the uncertain and hidden things of thy wisdom thou hast made manifest to me.

Thou shalt sprinkle me with hyssop, and I shall be cleansed: thou shalt wash me, and I shall be made whiter than snow.

To my hearing thou shalt give joy and gladness : and the bones that have been humbled, shall rejoice.

Turn away thy face from my sins : and blot out all my iniquities.

Create a clean heart in me, O God : and renew a right spirit within my bowels.

Cast me not away from thy face : and take not thy Holy Spirit from me.

Restore unto me the joy of thy salvation : and strengthen me with a perfect spirit.

I will teach the unjust thy ways : and the wicked shall be converted to thee.

Deliver me from blood, O God, thou God of my salvation ! and my tongue shall extol thy justice.

O Lord, thou wilt open my lips : and my mouth shall declare thy praise.

For if thou hadst desired sacrifice, I would indeed have given it : with burnt-offerings thou wilt not be delighted.

A sacrifice to God is an afflicted spirit : a contrite and humbled heart, O God, thou wilt not despise.

Deal favourably, O Lord, in thy good-will with Sion : that the walls of Jerusalem may be built up.

Then shalt thou accept the sacrifice of justice, oblations, and whole burnt-offerings : then shall they lay calves upon thine altar.

Redde mihi lætitiam salutaris tui : * et Spiritu principali confirma me.

Docebo iniquos vias tuas : * et impii ad te convertentur.

Libera me de sanguinibus, Deus, Deus salutis meæ : * et exsultabit lingua mea justitiam tuam.

Domine, labia mea aperies : * et os meum annuntiabit laudem tuam.

Quoniam si voluisses sacrificium, dedissem utique : * holocaustis non delectaberis.

Sacrificium Deo spiritus contribulatus: * cor contritum et humiliatum, Deus, non despicies.

Benigne fac, Domine, in bona voluntate tua Sion : * ut ædificentur muri Jerusalem.

Tunc acceptabis sacrificium justitiæ, oblationes, et holocausta : * tunc imponent super altare tuum vitulos.

V.

David laments over the captivity of God's people in Babylon, and prays for the restoration of Sion. His words are appropriate for the soul, who grieves over her sins, and implores to be regenerated by grace.

PSALM 101.

Hear, O Lord, my prayer : and let my cry come unto thee.

Domine, exaudi orationem meam : * et clamor meus ad te veniat.

Non avertas faciem tuam a me : * in quacumque die tribulor, inclina ad me aurem tuam.

In quacumque die invocavero te : * velociter exaudi me.

Quia defecerunt sicut fumus dies mei : * et ossa mea sicut cremium aruerunt.

Percussus sum ut fœnum, et aruit cor meum : * quia oblitus sum comedere panem meum.

A voce gemitus mei : * adhæsit os meum carni meæ.

Similis factus sum pelicano solitudinis : * factus sum sicut nycticorax in domicilio.

Vigilavi : * et factus sum sicut passer solitarius in tecto.

Tota die exprobrabant mihi inimici mei : * et qui laudabant me adversum me jurabant.

Quia cinerem tanquam panem manducabam : * et potum meum cum fletu miscebam.

A facie iræ et indignationis tuæ : * quia elevans allisisti me.

Dies mei sicut umbra declinaverunt : * et ego sicut fœnum arui.

Tus autem, Domine, in æternum permanes : * et memoriale tuum in generationem et generationem.

Tu exsurgens misereberis Sion : * quia tempus mise-

Turn not away thy face from me : in the day when I am in trouble, incline thine ear to me.

In what day soever I shall call upon thee, hear me speedily.

For my days are vanished like smoke : and my bones are grown dry like fuel for the fire.

I am smitten as grass, and my heart is withered : because I forgot to eat my bread.

Through the voice of my groaning, my bone hath cleaved to my flesh.

I am become like to a pelican of the wilderness : I am like a night-raven in the house.

I have watched, and am become as a sparrow all alone on the house top.

All the day long mine enemies reproached me : and they that praised me, did swear against me.

For I did eat ashes like bread : and mingled my drink with weeping.

Because of thy anger and indignation : for having lifted me up, thou hast thrown me down.

My days have declined like a shadow : and I am withered like grass.

But thou, O Lord, endurest for ever : and thy memorial to all generations.

Thou shalt arise and have mercy on Sion : for it is time

to have mercy on it, for the time is come.

For the stones thereof have pleased thy servants: and they shall have pity on the earth thereof.

And the Gentiles shall fear thy name, O Lord: and all the kings of the earth thy glory.

For the Lord hath built up Sion: and he shall be seen in his glory.

He hath had regard to the prayer of the humble: and he hath not despised their petition.

Let these things be written unto another generation: and the people that shall be created, shall praise the Lord.

Because he hath looked forth from his high Sanctuary: from heaven, the Lord hath looked upon the earth.

That he might hear the groans of them that are in fetters: that he might release the children of the slain.

That they may declare the Name of the Lord in Sion, and his praise in Jerusalem.

When the people assembled together, and kings to serve the Lord.

He, (*the Royal Prophet,*) *longing to see these glorious things,* answered him, *though still* in the way of his strength: Declare unto me the fewness of my days;

Call me not away in the midst of my days: thy years are unto generation and generation.

In the beginning, O Lord,

rendi ejus, quia venit tempus.

Quoniam placuerunt servis tuis lapides ejus: * et terræ ejus miserebuntur.

Et timebunt gentes nomen tuum, Domine: * et omnes reges terræ gloriam tuam.

Quia ædificavit Dominus Sion: * et videbitur in gloria sua.

Respexit in orationem humilium: * et non sprevit precem eorum.

Scribantur hæc in generatione altera: * et populus qui creabitur laudabit Dominum.

Quia prospexit de excelso Sancto suo: * Dominus de cœlo in terram aspexit.

Ut audiret gemitus compeditorum: * ut solveret filios interemptorum.

Ut annuntient in Sion Nomen Domini: * et laudem ejus in Jerusalem.

In conveniendo populos in unum: * et reges, ut serviant Domino.

Respondit ei in via virtutis suæ: * paucitatem dierum meorum nuntia mihi.

Ne revoces me in dimidio dierum meorum: * in generatione et generationem anni tui.

Initio tu, Domine, terram

fundasti : * et opera manuum tuarum sunt cœli.

Ipsi peribunt, tu autem permanes : * et omnes sicut vestimentum veterascent.

Et sicut opertorium mutabis eos, et mutabuntur : * tu autem idem ipse es, et anni tui non deficient.

Filii servorum tuorum habitabunt : * et semen eorum in sæculum dirigetur.

thou foundedst the earth : and the heavens are the works of thy hands.

They shall perish, but thou remainest : and all of them shall grow old, like a garment.

And as a vesture thou shalt change them, and they shall be changed : but thou art always the self-same, and thy years shall not fail.

The children of thy servants shall continue : and their seed shall be directed for ever.

VI.

The sinner seeing the *depths* of the abyss, into which sin has led him, can hope for help from none but his God, whose mercy is infinite.

PSALM 129.

De profundis clamavi ad te, Domine : * Domine, exaudi vocem meam.

Fiant aures tuæ intendentes : * in vocem deprecationis meæ.

Si iniquitates observaveris Domine : * Domine, quis sustinebit?

Quia apud te propitiatio est : et propter legem tuam sustinui te, Domine.

Sustinuit anima mea in verbo ejus : * speravit anima mea in Domino.

A custodia matutina usque ad noctem : * speret Israël in Domino.

Quia apud Dominum misericordia : * et copiosa apud eum redemptio.

Out of the depths I have cried to thee, O Lord : Lord, hear my voice.

Let thine ears be attentive to the voice of my supplication.

If thou, O Lord, wilt mark iniquities : Lord, who shall stand it?

For with thee there is merciful forgiveness : and by reason of thy law, I have waited for thee, O Lord.

My soul hath relied on his word : my soul hath hoped in the Lord.

From the morning-watch even until night, let Israel hope in the Lord.

Because with the Lord there is mercy : and with him, plentiful redemption.

And he shall redeem Israel from all his iniquities.

Et ipse redimet Israël : * ex omnibus iniquitatibus ejus.

VII.

David, who had taken refuge in a cave, sees himself surrounded by the army of Saul; he beseeches God not to deal with him according to the rigour of his just judgments, but to show him a way, whereby to escape the danger that threatens him. The sinner implores God to deliver him from the sins and temptations which beset him.

PSALM 142.

Hear, O Lord, my prayer; give ear to my supplication in thy truth : hear me in thy justice.

Domine, exaudi orationem meam, auribus percipe obsecrationem meam in veritate tua : * exaudi me in tua justitia.

And enter not into judgment with thy servant : for in thy sight no man living shall be justified.

Et non intres in judicium cum servo tuo : * quia non justificabitur in conspectu tuo omnis vivens.

For the enemy hath persecuted my soul : he hath brought down my life to the earth.

Quia persecutus est inimicus animam meam : * humiliavit in terra vitam meam.

He hath made me to dwell in darkness, as those that have been dead of old; and my spirit is in anguish within me : my heart within me is troubled.

Collocavit me in obscuris sicut mortuos seculi : et anxiatus est super me spiritus meus : * in me turbatum est cor meum.

I remembered the days of old, I meditated on all thy works : I meditated upon the works of thy hands.

Memor fui dierum antiquorum, meditatus sum in omnibus operibus tuis : * in factis manuum tuarum meditabar.

I stretched forth my hands to thee : my soul is as earth without water, unto thee.

Expandi manus meas ad te : * anima mea sicut terra sine aqua tibi.

Velociter exaudi me, Domine : * defecit spiritus meus.

Non avertas faciem tuam a me : * et similis ero descendentibus in lacum.

Auditam fac mihi mane misericordiam tuam : * quia in te speravi.

Notam fac mihi viam in qua ambulem : * quia ad te levavi animam meam.

Eripe me de inimicis meis, Domine, ad te confugi * doce me facere voluntatem tuam, quia Deus meus es tu.

Spiritus tuus bonus deducet me in terram rectam : * propter Nomen tuum, Domine, vivificabis me in æquitate tua.

Educes de tribulatione animam meam : * et in misericordia tua disperdes inimicos meos.

Et perdes omnes qui tribulant animam meam : * quoniam ego servus tuus sum.

Ant. Ne reminiscaris, Domine, delicta nostra, vel parentum, nostrorum, neque vindictam sumas de peccatis nostris.

Hear me speedily, O Lord : my spirit hath fainted away.

Turn not away thy face from me : lest I be like unto them that go down into the pit.

Cause me to hear thy mercy in the morning : for in thee have I hoped.

Make the way known to me, wherein I should walk : for I have lifted up my soul to thee.

Deliver me from mine enemies, O Lord ; to thee have I fled : teach me to do thy will, for thou art my God.

Thy good Spirit shall lead me into the right land : for thy Name's sake, O Lord, thou wilt quicken me in thy justice.

Thou wilt bring my soul out of trouble : and in thy mercy, thou wilt destroy mine enemies.

And thou wilt cut off all them that afflict my soul : for I am thy servant.

Ant. Remember not, O Lord, our offences, nor those of our parents, and take not revenge on our sins.

THE LITANIES

FOR THE DEVOTION OF THE

FORTY HOURS.

Lord, have mercy on us.	Kyrie, eleison.
Christ, have mercy on us.	Christe, eleison.
Lord have mercy on us.	Kyrie, eleison.
Christ, hear us.	Christe, audi nos.
Christ, graciously hear us.	Christe, exaudi nos.
God the Father of heaven, Have mercy on us.	Pater de cœlis, Deus, Miserere nobis.
God the Son, Redeemer of the world, Have mercy on us.	Fili, Redemptor mundi, Deus, Miserere nobis.
God the Holy Ghost, Have mercy on us.	Spiritus Sancte, Deus, Miserere nobis.
Holy Trinity, one God, Have mercy on us.	Sancta Trinitas, unus Deus, Miserere nobis.
Holy Mary, Pray for us.	Sancta Maria, Ora pro nobis.
Holy Mother of God, Pray for us.	Sancta Dei Genitrix, Ora.
Holy Virgin of Virgins, Pray for us.	Sancta Virgo Virginum, Ora.
Saint Michael, Pray for us.	Sancte Michael, Ora.
Saint Gabriel,	Sancte Gabriel, Ora.
Saint Raphael,	Sancte Raphael, Ora.
All ye holy Angels and Archangels,	Omnes sancti Angeli et Archangeli, Orate.
All ye holy orders of blessed Spirits,	Omnes sancti, beatorum Spirituum ordines, Orate.
Saint John Baptist,	Sancte Joannes Baptista, Ora.
Saint Joseph,	Sancte Joseph, Ora.
All ye holy Patriarchs and Prophets,	Omnes sancti Patriarchæ et Prophetæ, Orate.

Sancte Petre,	Ora.	Saint Peter,
Sancte Paule,	Ora.	Saint Paul,
Sancte Andrea,	Ora.	Saint Andrew,
Sancte Jacobe,	Ora.	Saint James,
Sancte Joannes,	Ora.	Saint John,
Sancte Thoma,	Ora.	Saint Thomas,
Sancte Jacobe,	Ora.	Saint James,
Sancte Philippe,	Ora.	Saint Philip,
Sancte Bartholomæe,	Ora.	Saint Bartholomew,
Sancte Matthæe,	Ora.	Saint Matthew,
Sancte Simon,	Ora.	Saint Simon,
Sancte Thaddæe,	Ora.	Saint Thaddeus,
Sancte Matthia,	Ora.	Saint Matthias,
Sancte Barnaba,	Ora.	Saint Barnaby,
Sancte Luca,	Ora.	Saint Luke,
Sancte Marce,	Ora.	Saint Mark,
Omnes sancti Apostoli et Evangelistæ,	Orate.	All ye holy Apostles and Evangelists,
Omnes sancti Discipuli Domini,	Orate.	All ye holy Disciples of our Lord,
Omnes sancti Innocentes,	Orate.	All ye holy Innocents,
Sancte Stephane,	Ora.	Saint Stephen,
Sancte Laurenti,	Ora.	Saint Laurence,
Sancte Vincenti,	Ora.	Saint Vincent,
Sancti Fabiane et Sebastiane,	Orate.	Saints Fabian and Sebastian,
Sancti Joannes et Paule,	Orate.	Saints John and Paul,
Sancti Cosma et Damiane,	Orate.	Saints Cosmas and Damian,
Sancti Gervasi et Protasi,	Orate.	Saints Gervasius and Protasius,
Omnes sancti Martyres,	Orate.	All ye holy Martyrs,
Sancte Sylvester,	Ora.	Saint Sylvester,
Sancte Gregori,	Ora.	Saint Gregory,
Sancte Ambrosi,	Ora.	Saint Ambrose,
Sancte Augustine,	Ora.	Saint Augustine,
Sancte Hieronyme,	Ora.	Saint Jerome,
Sancte Martine,	Ora.	Saint Martin,
Sancte Nicolae,	Ora.	Saint Nicholas,
Omnes sancti Pontifices et Confessores,	Orate.	All ye holy Bishops and Confessors,
Omnes sancti Doctores,	Orate.	All ye holy Doctors,
Sancte Antoni,	Ora.	Saint Antony,

Saint Benedict,	Sancte Benedicte,	Ora.
Saint Bernard,	Sancte Bernarde,	Ora.
Saint Dominic,	Sancte Dominice,	Ora.
Saint Francis,	Sancte Francisce,	Ora.
All ye holy Priests and Levites,	Omnes sancti Sacerdotes et Levitæ,	Orate.
All ye holy Monks and Hermits,	Omnes sancti Monachi et Eremitæ,	Orate.
Saint Mary Magdalene,	Sancta Maria Magdalena,	Ora.
Saint Agatha,	Sancta Agatha,	Ora.
Saint Lucy,	Sancta Lucia,	Ora.
Saint Agnes,	Sancta Agnes,	Ora.
Saint Cecily,	Sancta Cæcilia,	Ora.
Saint Catharine,	Sancta Catharina,	Ora.
Saint Anastasia,	Sancta Anastasia,	Ora.
All ye holy Virgins and Widows,	Omnes sanctæ Virgines et Viduæ,	Orate.
All ye men and women, Saints of God, Make intercession for us.	Omnes Sancti et Sanctæ Dei, Intercedite pro nobis.	
Be merciful to us, Spare us, O Lord.	Propitius esto, Parce nobis, Domine.	
Be merciful to us, Graciously hear us, O Lord.	Propitius esto, Exaudi nos, Domine.	
From all evil, Deliver us, O Lord.	Ab omni malo, Libera nos, Domine.	
From all sin, Deliver us, O Lord.	Ab omni peccato, Libera nos, Domine.	
From thy wrath,	Ab ira tua,	Libera.
From all dangers that threaten us,	Ab imminentibus periculis,	Libera.
From plague, famine, and war,	A peste, fame, et bello,	Libera.
From sudden and unprovided death,	A subitanea et improvisa morte,	Libera.
From the snares of the devil,	Ab insidiis diaboli,	Libera.
From anger, hatred, and all ill-will,	Ab ira, et odio, et omni mala voluntate,	Libera.
From the spirit of fornication,	A spiritu fornicationis,	Libera,
From lightning and tempest,	A fulgure et tempestate,	Libera.
From everlasting death,	A morte perpetua,	Libera.
Through the mystery of thy holy Incarnation.	Per mysterium sanctæ Incarnationis tuæ,	Libera.
Through thy Coming,	Per Adventum tuum,	Libera.

Per Nativitatem tuam, Libera,	Through thy Nativity,
Per Baptismum et sanctum Jejunium tuum, Libera.	Through thy Baptism and holy Fasting,
Per Crucem et Passionem tuam, Libera.	Through thy Cross and Passion,
Per Mortem et Sepulturam tuam, Libera.	Through thy Death and Burial,
Per sanctam Resurrectionem tuam, Libera.	Through thy holy Resurrection,
Per admirabilem Ascensionem tuam, Libera.	Through thy admirable Ascension,
Per adventum Spiritus Sancti Paracliti, Libera.	Through the coming of the Holy Ghost the Comforter,
In die Judicii, Libera.	In the day of Judgment,
Peccatores, Te rogamus, audi nos.	We sinners, We beseech thee, hear us.
Ut nobis parcas, Te rogamus, audi nos.	That thou spare us, We beseech thee, hear us.
Ut nobis indulgeas, Te rogamus.	That thou pardon us,
Ut ad veram pœnitentiam nos perducere digneris, Te rogamus.	That thou vouchsafe to bring us to true penance,
Ut Ecclesiam tuam sanctam regere et conservare digneris, Te rogamus.	That thou vouchsafe to govern and preserve thy holy Church,
Ut Domnum Apostolicum, et omnes ecclesiasticos ordines, in sancta religione conservare digneris, Te rogamus.	That thou vouchsafe to preserve our Apostolic Prelate, and all ecclesiastical orders, in holy religion,
Ut inimicos sanctæ Ecclesiæ humiliare digneris, Te rogamus.	That thou vouchsafe to humble the enemies of thy holy Church,
Ut Turcarum et Hæreticorum conatus reprimere, et ad nihilum redigere digneris, Te rogamus.	That thou vouchsafe to defeat the attempts of Turks and Heretics, and bring them to nought,
Ut Regibus et Principibus Christianis pacem et veram concordiam donare digneris, Te rogamus.	That thou vouchsafe to give peace and true concord to Christian Kings and Princes.
Ut cuncto populo Christiano pacem et unitatem largire digneris, Te rogamus.	That thou vouchsafe to grant peace and unity to all Christian people,

That thou vouchsafe to strengthen and preserve us in thy holy service,

That thou lift up our minds to heavenly desires,

That thou render eternal good things to all our benefactors,

That thou deliver our souls, and those of our brethren, kinsfolk and benefactors, from eternal damnation,

That thou vouchsafe to give and preserve the fruits of the earth,

That thou vouchsafe to give eternal rest to all the Faithful departed,

That thou vouchsafe graciously to hear us.

O Son of God, We beseech thee, hear us.

O Lamb of God, who takest away the sins of the world, Spare us, O Lord,

O Lamb of God, who takest away the sins of the world, Graciously hear us, O Lord.

O Lamb of God, who takest away the sins of the world, Have mercy on us.

Christ, hear us.
Christ, graciously hear us.
Lord, have mercy on us.
Christ, have mercy on us.
Lord, have mercy on us.
Our Father. *(In secret.)*
℣. And lead us not into temptation.
℟. But deliver us from evil.

Ut nosmetipsos in tuo sancto servitio confortare et conservare digneris,
  Te rogamus.
Ut mentes nostras ad cœlestia desideria erigas,
  Te rogamus.
Ut omnibus benefactoribus nostris sempiterna bona retribuas, Te rogamus.
Ut animas nostras, fratrum, propinquorum, et benefactorum nostrorum ab æterna damnatione eripias, Te rogamus.
Ut fructus terræ dare et conservare digneris,
  Te rogamus.
Ut omnibus fidelibus defunctis requiem æternam donare digneris,
  Te rogamus.
Ut nos exaudire digneris,
  Te rogamus.
Fili Dei, Te rogamus.

Agnus Dei, qui tollis peccata mundi,
  Parce nobis, Domine.
Agnus Dei, qui tollis peccata mundi,
  Exaudi nos, Domine.
Agnus Dei, qui tollis peccata mundi, Miserere nobis.

Christe, audi nos.
Christe, exaudi nos.
Kyrie, eleison.
Christe, eleison.
Kyrie, eleison.
Pater noster. *(In secret.)*
℣. Et ne nos inducas in tentationem.
℟. Sed libera nos a malo.

PSALM 69.

Deus, in adjutorium meum intende :* Domine, ad adjuvandum me festina.

Confundantur et revereantur: * qui quærunt animam meam.

Avertantur retrorsum et erubescant: * qui volunt mihi mala.

Avertantur statim erubescentes : * qui dicunt mihi Euge, Euge.

Exsultent et lætentur in te omnes qui quærunt te :* et dicant semper, magnificetur Dominus qui diligunt salutare tuum.

Ego vero egenus et pauper sum :* Deus adjuva me.

Adjutor meus et liberator meus es tu : * Domine, ne moreris.

Gloria Patri, et Filio, * et Spiritui Sancto.

Sicut erat in principio, et nunc, et semper : * et in sæcula sæculorum, Amen.

℣. Salvos fac servos tuos.
℟. Deus meus sperantes in te.
℣. Esto nobis, Domine, turris fortitudinis.
℟. A facie inimici.

℣. Nihil proficiat inimicus in nobis.
℟. Et filius iniquitatis non apponat nocere nobis.
℣. Domine, non secundum peccata nostra facias nobis.

O God, come to my assistance : O Lord, make haste to help me.

Let them be confounded and ashamed that seek my soul.

Let them be turned backward, and blush for shame, that desire evils to me.

Let them be presently turned away, blushing for shame, that say to me : 'Tis well, 'Tis well.

Let all that seek thee, rejoice and be glad in thee: and let such as love thy salvation, say always, the Lord be magnified.

But I am needy and poor : O God help me.

Thou art my helper and my deliverer: O Lord, make no delay.

Glory be to the Father, and to the Son, and to the Holy Ghost.

As it was in the beginning, is now, and ever shall be, world without end, Amen.

℣. Save thy servants.
℟. Trusting in thee, O my God.
℣. Be unto us, O Lord, a tower of strength.
℟. From the face of the enemy.
℣. Let not the enemy prevail against us.
℟. Nor the son of iniquity have any power to hurt us.
℣. O Lord, deal not with us according to our sins.

℞. Nor reward us according to our iniquities.

℣. Let us pray for our chief Bishop N.

℞. May our Lord preserve him, and give him life, and make him blessed upon earth, and deliver him not to the will of his enemies.

℣. Let us pray for our benefactors.

℞. Vouchsafe, O Lord, for thy name's sake, to reward, with eternal life, all them that have done us good.

℣. Let us pray for the Faithful departed.

℞. Eternal rest give to them, O Lord, and let perpetual light shine upon them.

℣. May they rest in peace.

℞. Amen.

℣. For our absent brethren.

℞. O my God, save thy servants trusting in thee.

℣. Send them help, O Lord, from thy holy place.

℞. And from Sion protect them.

℣. O Lord, hear my prayer.

℞. And let my cry come unto thee.

℣. The Lord be with you.

℞. And with thy spirit.

℞. Neque secundum iniquitates nostras retribuas nobis.

℣. Oremus pro Pontifice nostro N.

℞. Dominus conservet eum, et vivificet eum, et beatum faciat eum in terra, et non tradat eum in animam inimicorum ejus.

℣. Oremus pro benefactoribus nostris.

℞. Retribuere dignare, Domine, omnibus nobis bona facientibus, propter nomen tuum, vitam æternam.

℣. Oremus pro fidelibus defunctis.

℞. Requiem æternam dona eis, Domine, et lux perpetua luceat eis.

℣. Requiescant in pace.

℞. Amen.

℣. Pro fratribus nostris absentibus.

℞. Salvos fac servos tuos, Deus meus, sperantes in te.

℣. Mitte eis, Domine, auxilium de sancto.

℞. Et de Sion tuere eos.

℣. Domine, exaudi orationem meam.

℞. Et clamor meus ad te veniat.

℣. Dominus vobiscum.

℞. Et cum spiritu tuo.

LET US PRAY.

O God, who, in this wonderful Sacrament, hast left us a perpetual memorial of thy Passion: grant us, we

OREMUS.

Deus, qui nobis, sub Sacramento mirabili, Passionis tuæ memoriam reliquisti: tribue, quæsumus, ita nos Corporis et Sanguinis tui sacra Mysteria venerari, ut Redemptionis tuæ fructum in nobis jugiter sentiamus.

beseech thee, so to reverence the sacred Mysteries of thy Body and Blood, that in our souls we may always be sensible of the fruit of the Redemption thou hast purchased for us.

[1] Concede nos famulos tuos, quæsumus, Domine Deus, perpetua mentis et corporis sanitate gaudere: et gloriosa beatæ Mariæ semper Virginis intercessione, a præsenti liberari tristitia, et æterna perfrui lætitia.

[1] Grant, O Lord, we beseech thee, that we thy servants may enjoy constant health of body and mind: and by the glorious intercession of Blessed Mary, ever a Virgin, be delivered from all present affliction, and come to that joy, which is eternal.

Omnipotens sempiterne Deus, miserere famulo tuo Pontifici nostro N., et dirige eum, secundum tuam clementiam, in viam salutis æternæ; ut, te donante, tibi placita cupiat, et tota virtute perficiat.

O Almighty and Eternal God, have mercy on thy servant N., our chief Bishop, and direct him, according to thy clemency, in the way of everlasting salvation; that, by thy grace, he may desire those things that are agreeable to thee, and perform them with all his strength.

Deus refugium nostrum et virtus, adesto piis Ecclesiæ tuæ precibus, auctor ipse pietatis, et præsta; ut quod fideliter petimus, efficaciter consequamur.

O God, our refuge and strength, fountain of all goodness, mercifully give ear to the fervent prayers of thy Church, and grant, that what we ask with faith, we may effectually obtain.

Omnipotens sempiterne Deus, in cujus manu sunt omnium potestates, et omnia jura regnorum, respice in auxilium Christianorum; ut gentes paganorum et hæreticorum, quæ in sua feritate et fraude confidunt, dexteræ tuæ potentia conterantur.

O Almighty and Eternal God, in whose hand are all the powers and all the rights of kingdoms, come to the assistance of thy Christian people; that all pagan and heretical nations, who trust in their own violence and craft, may be broken by the might of thy right hand.

---

[1] This Collect varies in Advent, and at Christmas. See the Collects for these times in *page* 421.

O Almighty and Eternal God, who hast dominion over the living and the dead, and art merciful to all, whom thou foreknowest shall be thine by faith and good works; we humbly beseech thee, that they, for whom we have determined to offer up our prayers, whether this present world still detain them in the flesh, or the world to come hath already received them out of their bodies, may, by the clemency of thy goodness, all thy Saints interceding for them, obtain pardon and full remission of all their sins. Through our Lord Jesus Christ, thy Son, who liveth and reigneth, one God with thee and the Holy Ghost, world without end.
℟. Amen.
℣. O Lord, hear my prayer.

℟. And let my cry come unto thee.
℣. May the Almighty and most merciful Lord graciously hear us.
℟. And may he ever graciously hear us, Amen.
℣. May the souls of the Faithful, through the mercy of God, rest in peace.
℟. Amen.

Omnipotens sempiterne Deus, qui vivorum dominaris simul et mortuorum, omniumque misereris, quos tuos fide et opere futuros esse prænoscis; te supplices exoramus; ut pro quibus effundere preces decrevimus, quosque vel præsens sæculum adhuc in carne retinet, vel futurum jam exutos corpore suscepit, intercedentibus omnibus Sanctis tuis, pietatis tuæ clementia, omnium delictorum suorum veniam consequantur. Per Dominum nostrum Jesum Christum Filium tuum, qui tecum vivit et regnat, in unitate Spiritus Sancti, Deus, per omnia sæcula sæculorum.
℟. Amen.
℣. Domine exaudi orationem meam.
℟. Et clamor meus ad te veniat.
℣. Exaudiat nos omnipotens et misericors Dominus.
℟. Et exaudiat nos semper, Amen.
℣. Fidelium animæ, per misericordiam Dei, requiescant in pace.
℟. Amen.

The *second* of these six Collects is thus varied:

From Advent to Christmas Day.

O God, who wast pleased that thy Word, at the message of an Angel, should take flesh

Deus, qui de beatæ Mariæ Virginis utero, Verbum tuum, Angelo nuntiante, carnem suscipere voluisti: præsta supplicibus tuis, ut qui vere eam Genitricem Dei credimus, ejus apud te intercessionibus adjuvemur.

in the womb of the Blessed Virgin Mary: grant to us thy humble servants, that we, who believe her to be truly the Mother of God, may be assisted by her intercessions with thee.

From Christmas Day to the Purification.

Deus, qui salutis æternæ, Beatæ Mariæ virginitate fœcunda, humano generi præmia præstitisti: tribue quæsumus, ut ipsam pro nobis intercedere sentiamus, per quam meruimus auctorem vitæ suscipere, Dominum nostrum Jesum Christum Filium tuum.

O God, who by the fruitful Virginity of Blessed Mary, hast given to mankind the rewards of eternal salvation: grant, we beseech thee, that we may experience Her intercession, by whom we received the Author of Life, our Lord Jesus Christ thy Son.

END OF SEPTUAGESIMA.

Made in the USA
Monee, IL
24 February 2026